Programming Language Foundations

Aaron Stump
Department of Computer Science
University of Iowa

To my beloved wife Madeliene, whose care and
support made this book possible

Publisher:	Don Fowley
Executive Editor:	Beth Lang Golub
Editorial Assistant:	Joseph Romano
Cover Designer:	Kenji Ngieng
Associate Production Manager:	Joyce Poh

This book was set in LaTex by the author and printed and bound by Edward Brothers Malloy. This book is printed on acid free paper.

Founded in 1807, John Wiley & Sons, Inc. has been a valued source of knowledge and understanding for more than 200 years, helping people around the world meet their needs and fulfill their aspirations. Our company is built on a foundation of principles that include responsibility to the communities we serve and where we live and work. In 2008, we launched a Corporate Citizenship Initiative, a global effort to address the environmental, social, economic, and ethical challenges we face in our business. Among the issues we are addressing are carbon impact, paper specifications and procurement, ethical conduct within our business and among our vendors, and community and charitable support. For more information, please visit our website: www.wiley.com/go/citizenship.

Library of Congress Cataloging-in-Publication Data

Stump, Aaron.
  Programming language foundations / Aaron Stump, Department of Computer Science, University of Iowa. -- First edition.
      pages cm
  Includes index.
  ISBN 978-1-118-00747-1 (hardback)
  1. Programming languages (Electronic computers) 2. Programming languages (Electronic computers)--Semantics. I. Title.
  QA76.7.S84 2013
  005.1--dc23

                          2013020038

Printed in the United States of America
10 9 8 7 6 5 4 3 2 1

Contents

Preface

Programming languages are arguably the most important artifacts in all of Computer Science. For programming languages provide the basic means for defining abstractions, and ensuring that those abstractions are correctly and efficiently realized on a computer system (consisting of the hardware as abstracted by the operating system or other layers of infrastructure like a virtual machine). Just as all the riches of world literature depend on the expressive power of natural language, so too all the glories of modern software systems depend on the programming languages used to create them. The remarkable expansion of computing into all aspects of modern society – in healthcare, finance, defense, energy, business operations, news and media, entertainment, and social interactions – would be impossible without programming languages.

Indeed, if machine language were the only language for programming, the incredible power of modern microprocessors (CPUs) could not be effectively harnessed in well-organized and abstracted programs. In a world with only machine-language programming (or even assembly-language), the rate of progress for computing, and even for society more generally, would have been greatly slowed. In fact, the pressures to organize code into more reusable and comprehensible units than is possible in machine language are so great, and the operations we are implementing in software are so complex, that I cannot really imagine an alternative history of computing that lacks programming languages (except possibly a failed history where computing did not develop). Indeed, part of what makes the study of programming languages so interesting and important is that those same pressures continue to drive the creation and evolution of programming languages to this day. Far from leading to consolidation around one or two well-designed and well-implemented languages, the continuing development of computing has driven the invention of many new programming languages, in both academia and industry.

With programming languages playing such a critical role in Computer Science, it is of great importance that serious students of computing understand them deeply. The deepest understanding we know how to achieve in this area comes through the mathematical study of programming language *semantics*. We wish to define mathematically what programs mean. It turns out that there are several different ways to do this, which we will consider in this book. A mathematical definition of the semantics of programs is a powerful theoretical tool. Probably the most important use of this tool is to justify various schemes of *program verifica-*

tion. Program verification is concerned with proving that programs satisfy some desired properties. Sometimes these properties are implicit, such as the property that all attempts to access an array do so using an index within the bounds of the array. In other cases, the properties are explicitly formulated in a specification language; for example, one might write a specification stating that the list returned by a call to a function `mergesort` is, in fact, sorted. In either case, the field of program verification seeks to ascertain whether or not a given piece of code meets its specification. To give a precise definition of what it means for code to satisfy a specified property requires a precise definition of the semantics of the program. The central concern of this book is to study such semantics, using several different mathematical tools developed in the past century or so.

The centrality of theoretical study of programming languages to Computer Science as a discipline is further demonstrated by the number of Turing award winners whose work is in this area.[1] Of the 58 winners as of 2012, we will have occasion in this book to touch on ideas due to 6: Cook, Dijkstra, Floyd, Hoare, Milner, and Scott. Certainly a number of other Turing award winners have worked on problems closely related to the topics in this book as well (Backus, Liskov, and Clarke, Emerson, and Sifakis, for example).

So to summarize: the primary reason to study programming language foundations is to gain a deeper understanding for programming languages themselves, and through them, of computing in general. There are several secondary benefits. Since the modern study of programming languages is quite mathematical, and depends on a firm grasp of numerous careful distinctions, it provides excellent training in rigor and precision – certainly valuable qualities for any computer scientist. Also, while the majority of students taking a graduate course in programming language foundations will not invent their own full-fledged programming languages, some certainly will. Furthermore, many will have occasion to implement domain-specific languages of various kinds, such as for configuration files for complex applications, or in defining interfaces to tools or libraries (where the interface can easily become a kind of restricted language). Familiarity with the foundations of programming languages can help provide guidance for such endeavors. Finally, study of the material in this book will help strengthen programmers' intuitions for reasoning about their programs, through a sharper view of program semantics.

Courses which could use this book

This book could be used in several different kinds of courses on programming languages:

Graduate-level programming language foundations. A graduate-level class on programming language semantics could cover Chapters 1 through 5, to get a broad overview of topics in different areas of programming languages theory. Chapters 2 through 4 provide examples of all three forms of semantics traditionally

---

[1]The Turing award is Computer Science's highest honor, like a Nobel prize.

considered – denotational, operational, and axiomatic – for a single language in the familiar paradigm of imperative programming. This gives a nice overview of different semantic methods.

Graduate-level theory of functional programming. For a graduate-level class that is focused more exclusively on theory of functional programming languages, the course outline will be quite different from the previous one. The course can begin with Chapters 5 and 6 on untyped lambda calculus, thus skipping all the material on the WHILE imperative programming language. Such a course could then proceed with Chapters 7 and 10 on simple and polymorphic types, respectively, and Chapter 11 on functional programming.

Graduate-level survey of programming language semantics. Some graduate-level courses may prefer to provide a somewhat less technical survey of programming language semantics. For such a course, start with 2.1 for the syntax and informal semantics of WHILE, and then proceed to Chapter 4 on WHILE's operational semantics, Sections 4.1 and 4.2. Cover Section 8.3 on operational semantics of a concurrent version of WHILE, and then Chapter 5 on untyped lambda calculus, Chapter 7 on simply typed lambda calculus, and then Chapter 11 on practical functional programming based on lambda calculus. This will give a more programming-oriented course, with less emphasis on mathematical semantics.

Advanced undergraduate-level programming languages concepts While this book is primarily aimed for graduate-level courses, it could be used in an advanced undergraduate course on programming languages concepts, as a supplement to books more focused on issues like parsing, names and scoping, data and control abstractions, resource management, and further practical matters. Such a course could start similarly to the graduate-level survey course, with 2.1 for the syntax and informal semantics of WHILE, and then Chapter 4 for WHILE's operational semantics. It may then be interesting to cover Chapters 5 and 6, on programming in untyped lambda calculus. Section 9.2 on combinators may also be an interesting source of material for such a class, as students may find it stimulating to try programming in the very low-level functional language of combinators.

Other resources

This book is not intended as a research reference, but as a textbook. As such, I have not sought to provide a comprehensive bibliography of original or secondary sources for most of the concepts introduced. The following textbooks, as well as quite a few others, also cover semantics of programming languages, and I heartily recommend them to the readers of this book. I have learned much of what I know about this topic from them:

- "The Formal Semantics of Programming Languages", Glynn Winskel, MIT Press, 1993.

- "Types and Programming Languages", Benjamin C. Pierce, MIT Press, 2002.

- "Foundations for Programming Languages", John C. Mitchell, MIT Press, 1996.

- "Theories of Programming Languages", John C. Reynolds, Cambridge University Press, 1998.

"Practical Foundations for Programming Languages", Robert Harper, Cambridge University Press, 2012 appeared while I was completing this book, and is another excellent source.

My goal in writing this book is to provide coverage, in a single volume, of the topics considered in many contemporary courses on semantics of programming languages, and which I believe are foundational for deep knowledge of programming languages. I have also sought to provide as accessible and lightweight a treatment of that material as I can. In addition to those books covering semantics of programming languages, there are several other sources I highly recommend for students of the theory of programming languages:

- "Term Rewriting and All That", Franz Baader and Tobias Nipkow, Cambridge University Press, 1999.

- "Proofs and Types", Jean-Yves Girard, Yves Lafont, and Paul Taylor, Cambridge University Press, 1989; also available for free online.

- "Lambda Calculi with Types", Henk Barendregt, in The Handbook of Logic in Computer Science, 1993; also available for free online.

This list by no means exhausts the important and rewarding sources on semantics, lambda calculus, type theory, and related topics available, but is intended just as a selection of next sources for further study, closely related to this book. Background in term rewriting is important for anyone studying operational semantics and advanced type systems for programming languages, and "Term Rewriting and All That" is a great introduction to the topic. It provides a thorough introduction to term-rewriting systems, particularly first-order term rewriting systems, and presents material on abstract reduction systems, positions and syntactic operations on terms, and confluence, which is very relevant for studying reduction relations for programming-language semantics, as done in Chapter 5 of this book. For more advanced topics, readers can also consult [38].

"Proofs and Types" provides deep coverage of important type systems like the simply typed lambda calculus, System F, and System T, with good discussions also of the Curry-Howard isomorphism. The material there is relevant for Chapters 7 and 10. Furthermore, the book, while dense, is very clearly written, with as light a notation as one can really imagine for these complex topics.

Finally, a goldmine of knowledge on lambda calculus and type systems is to be found in "Lambda Calculi with Types", a beloved reference for many aspiring type theorists. This covers more advanced type systems, and emphasizes the differences when one studies type assignment systems for pure lambda calculus (as we will do in Section 7.3 of this book) as opposed to syntax-directed type systems for lambda calculus with annotated terms (see Section 7.8 of this book). While I have consulted it less than the above books, another very important reference on lambda calculus is Barendregt's great work "The Lambda Calculus, Its Syntax and Semantics" [5], which covers many topics related to untyped lambda calculus, including its denotational semantics.

From mathematics to practice

Giving formal mathematical definitions for the semantics of programming languages requires quite a bit of technical machinery. I have chosen to introduce the necessary formal concepts and notations as needed, in "Interludes" throughout the text. A few other basics from discrete mathematics are in the "Mathematical Background" section at the end of the book.

Technical material of the kind covered in this book is very concise, and can be rather abstract. You may find you have to read through definitions or statements of theorems several times and think about them, in order to get a firm grasp of what is being said. Of course, I am trying to provide as much support for you as I can, by including examples and trying to provide informal motivations for the technical definitions. But even so, the material is dense and needs serious focused attention to comprehend.

To try to keep the book from remaining solely at the most airy and abstract levels, I have included several sections on "connections to practice", which touch on ways in which the ideas we are studying in the main sections of the book connect to more applied or practical topics in Computer Science. While it is not feasible to be comprehensive in describing all the different ways programming-language semantics and related ideas impact the more practical aspects of programming language design and implementation, or other application areas, I hope these sections will help ground some of this material for readers.

Acknowledgments

I am grateful to the research communities in Programming Languages, Computational Logic, and related fields for developing the beautiful results which I have sought to convey in textbook form in this book. I would like to express my appreciation for my colleagues at The University of Iowa, particularly Cesare Tinelli, with whom I have organized a Computational Logic group since 2008. I have also been very lucky to have enthusiastic and talented students in my Programming Language Foundations and related classes here at Iowa and previously at Washington University in St. Louis, particularly my own doctoral students Edwin Westbrook, Duckki Oe, Harley Eades III, Peng Fu, and Ryan McCleeary. Thanks to them and to all my previous students, for feedback on the notes and manuscript from which this book arose, and for stimulating interest in the subject. I am also grateful to my editor Beth Golub and the others at Wiley who helped bring this book to press.

On the personal side, I also wish to express appreciation to the faith communities of St. Wenceslaus Catholic Church and St. Mary's Catholic Church in Iowa City, particularly their pastors Fr. Michael Phillips and Fr. John Spiegel, which have provided great environments for the spiritual side of intellectual life in my time at Iowa. Written works and biographies of St. Josemaria Escriva, St. Jean Vianney, St. Damian of Molokai, St. Faustina Kowalska, Gabrielle Bossis, Bl. Teresa of Calcutta, and Bl. John Paul II nourished the humanistic and religious side of my mind in the time I was writing this book.

Finally, I would like to wish you, the reader, great success in your study of the foundations of programming language, and ask for your patience with the shortcomings of this book.

Aaron Stump
Iowa City, May 2013

Part I
Central Topics

Chapter 1
Semantics of First-Order Arithmetic

In this chapter, we will begin our study of semantics by considering a *denotational semantics* for a logical language called $FO(\mathbb{Z})$ ("First-Order Arithmetic"). You can pronounce $FO(\mathbb{Z})$ as "foz". A denotational semantics is a way of explaining the meaning of a formal language by describing what objects are denoted by the expressions of the language. Since those descriptions are given by means of (a different) language, denotational semantics can be seen as defining the meaning of one language by translation into another. So a denotational approach to French would explain the meaning of French expressions by stating in another language (English, say) which things are meant or which objects denoted by various French phrases. This could just as well be viewed as showing how to translate those French phrases into English. The difference between saying that *chat* denotes a cat and saying that *chat* is translated "cat" may be one for philosophers to analyze, but for us is rather slim.

This way of explaining the meaning of a language seems so natural that one might doubt there could be any other. But there are alternatives. For example, another form of semantics we will see in later chapters explains the meaning of a language by explaining how the language's expressions are used. If I wish to let someone walk ahead of me, I might say "after you". If you are not a native English speaker and do not know this usage of that phrase, you could very well pick it up just by seeing what happens when I say it as another person and I approach a doorway at the same time. Or if you do not speak Bulgarian, you could just as well learn that внимавай ("vnee**ma**vai") means "watch out" by seeing one Bulgarian speaker warn another of an impending accident with that phrase.

The $FO(\mathbb{Z})$ language we will use for our first foray into denotational semantics is a logical language for making statements about the mathematical integers. Some examples of natural-language statements that we can express in $FO(\mathbb{Z})$ are:

- "For any number n, there is a prime number greater than n."

- "The sum of two odd numbers is even."

- "If x is greater than y, and y is greater than z, then x is greater than z" (transitivity of the arithmetic greater-than relation).

In addition to serving as a warm-up for defining the syntax and semantics of the WHILE imperative programming language in Chapter 2, $FO(\mathbb{Z})$ will also be valuable later in the book (in particular, for the axiomatic semantics in Chapter 3).

1.1   Syntax of $FO(\mathbb{Z})$ terms

The syntax of $FO(\mathbb{Z})$ is defined in two parts. First, we define **terms**, which are expressions intended to denote an integer. Then we define **formulas**, which are intended to denote either truth or falsity. We start with the syntax of terms. The definition is made using some basic conventions which we will use throughout this book (see also the Mathematical Background section):

$$
\begin{array}{lll}
\textit{variables } x & & \\
\textit{numerals } n & ::= & 0 \mid 1 \mid 2 \mid \cdots \\
\textit{operators } op & ::= & + \mid * \mid - \\
\textit{terms } t & ::= & x \mid n \mid t \; op \; t' \mid -t
\end{array}
$$

Here, we are defining the syntax of kinds of expressions using a formalism based on context free grammars. In this book, we will refer to all different syntactic entities as **expressions**. Each kind of expression is defined by a phrase of the form:

$$\textit{name } v ::= \cdots$$

The name (like *terms* in this grammar for $FO(\mathbb{Z})$) will be used for the set of all expressions accepted by this phrase of the grammar. Next, we list a particular meta-variable (in the case of *terms*, the meta-variable is t) which we will use to refer to elements of that set. Then we list the different productions that generate the elements of the set (for example, we list out the different ways we can form an element of the set of *terms*, for example by having two terms with an *op* between them). We use different meta-variables for possibly different expressions of the same kind; for example, we are writing $t \; op \; t'$ in the definition of terms t to mean that the two terms given as arguments to *op* may be different terms. If we omit productions, as for *variables* above, then there is some countably infinite but otherwise unspecified set of expressions, distinct from all others, which constitute that kind of expression. Note that we will sometimes use the terminology **syntactic category** for a kind of expression like *terms*.

Everywhere we use a meta-variable (like t), the value of that meta-variable is an element of the corresponding set (here, *terms*). So if in a proof we say "consider an arbitrary t and F," then we are performing some generic reasoning that is true for any element t of *terms* and any element F of *formulas*. An element of *terms* we will call a *term*, and similarly for other kinds of expressions. We generally work with ambiguous grammars in this book, leaving the important details of crafting deterministically parseable syntax to the domain of compilers. We will consider all our grammars to allow the implicit use of parentheses for disambiguation.

1.2   Informal semantics of $FO(\mathbb{Z})$ terms

A term like $3 + 4 + 5$ is intended to denote the number 12. Here we already see some of the potential for confusion when describing a denotational semantics. We are trying to explain (informally) the meaning of a particular expression in the syntactic category of *terms*. The meaning we have in mind is a number. How do we indicate which number is meant? If I were trying to explain the meaning of the French phrase "la Tour Eiffel", I could translate that into English as "the Eiffel Tower". Even better, if we were in Paris, I could just point to the famous monument, thus explaining the meaning by ostension. With an abstract object like a number, it's much less clear whether or not that is possible (though one could certainly imagine pointing to twelve chess pieces to give the idea). So we have to use our meta-language of English to state the meaning of the phrase $3 + 4 + 5$ in this particular object language of terms. This can be confusing, if we forget that the phrase "$3 + 4 + 5$" is in a formal language we are studying, while the phrase "12" is in our informal meta-language of English.

To continue: in order to assign a meaning to a term with variables in it, like the term $3 + (x * 5)$, we will assume we have some mapping σ from variables to integers. We will write Σ for the set of all such mappings. For example, if $\sigma(x) = 4$, then the term $3 + (x * 5)$ has the same meaning (with respect to that mapping σ) as $3 + (4 * 5)$, namely 23. If we use a different mapping σ', with $\sigma'(x) = 2$, say, then of course we will get a different meaning (13 in this case).

1.3   Syntax of $FO(\mathbb{Z})$ formulas

For formulas of $FO(\mathbb{Z})$, the syntax is:

built-in predicate symbols pred	::=	$= \mid \neq \mid < \mid > \mid \leq \mid \geq$
user-specified predicate symbols P		
connectives conn	::=	$\wedge \mid \vee \mid \Rightarrow \mid \Leftrightarrow$
formulas F	::=	$True \mid False \mid t \; pred \; t' \mid P \; t_1 \cdots t_n \mid F \; conn \; F'$
		$\mid \neg F \mid \forall x. F \mid \exists x. F$

We are including some familiar built-in predicate symbols *pred* for making basic statements about the integers, as well as allowing for the possibility of user-specified predicate symbols P. We could just as well do something similar for terms: allow user-defined as well as built-in operators on terms. It will be sufficient for our purposes just to take built-in operators on terms for our language.

We will adopt some standard conventions for parsing $FO(\mathbb{Z})$ formulas, to allow us to drop some parentheses. Predicates P and *pred* bind more tightly than connectives (like $\wedge$). Also, conjunction ($\wedge$) and disjunction ($\vee$) bind more tightly than implication ($\Rightarrow$), which in turn binds more tightly than $\Leftrightarrow$. Finally, the quantifiers ($\forall$ and $\exists$) bind least tightly of all. We will demonstrate these conventions in Section 1.5 below.

It is generally assumed for first-order logic that predicate symbols have a fixed **arity**, which is the number of arguments they must be given. For example, all our built-in predicate symbols have arity 2, and must be used with exactly two arguments in a formula. As a terminological aside: arity-2 predicates are called **binary** predicates, while arity-1 predicates are called **unary** (sometimes also **monadic**).

Also, note that it is standard terminology in logic to call formulas which are not built from other formulas **atomic**. In $FO(\mathbb{Z})$, the atomic formulas are the ones of the form $P\,t_1\cdots t_n$ or $t\,pred\,t'$. Most presentations of first-order logic use the syntax $P(t_1,\ldots,t_n)$, where we are using $P\,t_1\cdots t_n$. The latter is notationally a little lighter, and will help get us ready for the applicative notation we will use for functional programming and lambda calculus in later chapters. One more aside: when we say **"of the form"**, then there exists values for the new meta-variables which appear in the meta-expression. So if we say that formula F is of the form $P\,t_1\cdots t_n$, we are saying that there exist terms t_1 through t_n such that $F \equiv P\,t_1\cdots t_n$, where $\equiv$ means syntactic identity of the given two expressions.

1.4   Some alternative logical languages for arithmetic

The language $FO(\mathbb{Z})$ formalizes first-order arithmetic using standard ideas from logic. It has the pragmatic limitation, however, that all quantifiers (implicitly) range over the integers. If we wished to express also propositions about the rationals or reals, $FO(\mathbb{Z})$ would not be very convenient for doing so. It is possible to encode rationals, or even a countable subset of the reals, as integers. For example, one could encode a rational as an ordered pair of the numerator and denominator (perhaps as relative primes), and then use a standard pairing function to map such pairs to integers. A simple pairing function maps (x, y) to $2^x 3^y$, for example. Other such functions exist with some nicer properties, like surjectivity. With such an encoding, we could use $FO(\mathbb{Z})$ for expressing statements about the rationals or a countable subset of the reals. A more convenient approach, however, would use a different logic, one which includes different sorts (types) for variables natively. So we would be able to write $\forall x : \mathbb{Q}.\cdots$, for example, to quantify over the rationals. A logic that supports this kind of sorted (typed) quantification is called a **multi-sorted** logic.

In $FO(\mathbb{Z})$, we also cannot quantify directly over functions or predicates on the integers. Again, since we can give an integer encoding of a subset of the set of all functions operating on the integers (think of writing out the code for a computable function in binary, and then take the integer representation of that binary number as the code for the function), we could use $FO(\mathbb{Z})$ to quantify over functions, but it is again more convenient to use a logic that builds in quantification over functions and predicates.

A logical language that allows quantifications over functions and predicates is called a **higher-order** logic. All such logics I know (at least the consistent ones!) are also multi-sorted logics, as the sort system is used to express what sort of function some entity is. For example, we might write $int \rightarrow int$ as the sort for some quantified variable, to indicate that it is a unary operations on integers. A logic that only allows quantification over entities which are not directly recognized as functions by the logic itself is called **first-order**. Notice that we could have a first-order multi-sorted logic where one of the sorts is intended to name a set of functions. So we might have a sort $int \rightarrow int$, and quantify over that sort. The difference between this situation and a true higher-order logic is that with the first-order multi-sorted logic, the logic itself will not recognize x of sort $int \to int$ as a function. We would not be able to use it in the syntax of terms directly as if it were another built-in operator op. In contrast, with a higher-order logic, we are able to do this.

1.5   Informal semantics of $FO(\mathbb{Z})$ formulas

Informally, the meanings of the logical symbols in the grammar for $FO(\mathbb{Z})$ are:

$\land$ And (conjunction).

$\lor$ Or (disjunction).

$\Rightarrow$ Implies (implication, "if-then").

$\Leftrightarrow$ Iff (equivalence, "if-and-only-if").

$\forall$ For all (universal quantification).

$\exists$ There is (existential quantification).

We can translate the English sentences from the start of this chapter into $FO(\mathbb{Z})$ formulas as follows:

- "For any number n, there is a prime number greater than n." To translate this sentence, we will use the universal quantifier $\forall$ for "for any number n". We will also need to use the existential quantifier $\exists$ for "there is a prime number". The existential quantifier requires us to give a name to the entity we are stating exists, so we will call that prime number y. Finally, we are going to use a user-specified predicate symbol $Prime$ (not built-in) for the property of being prime. The formula is then:

$$\forall n.\exists y.((Prime\ y) \land (y > n))$$

Here, the formula is written with enough parentheses to allow unambiguous parsing without the conventions mentioned in the previous section. As stated there, those conventions allow us to drop some parentheses from formulas like this one. Since predicates (like $Prime$ and $>$) bind more tightly than connectives (like $\land$), we can drop the two innermost pairs of parentheses. Also, since connectives bind more tightly than quantifiers ($\forall$ and $\exists$), we can drop the outer pair of parentheses. So the formula can be unambiguously written as just

$$\forall n.\exists y.Prime\ y \land y > n$$

Note that if we wanted to define $Prime$, we could do so with the following formula:

$$\forall x.\ ((Prime\ x)\ \Leftrightarrow\ \forall y.\forall z.((y * z = x)\ \Rightarrow\ ((y = 1)\ \lor\ (z = 1))))$$

This formula is equivalent to the usual definition, where x is prime iff its only divisors are 1 and x. The definition here has the advantage that it does not require a definition of the "divides" relation. Here, the formula includes sufficient parentheses for unambiguous parsing without our $FO(\mathbb{Z})$ parsing conventions. Using those conventions, we can actually drop all the parentheses:

$$\forall x.\ Prime\ x \ \Leftrightarrow\ \forall y.\forall z.y * z = x \ \Rightarrow\ y = 1 \ \lor\ z = 1$$

Arguably it might be preferable to include some extra parentheses which are not strictly required, just to aid readability:

$$\forall x.\ Prime\ x \ \Leftrightarrow\ (\forall y.\forall z.y * z = x \ \Rightarrow\ (y = 1 \ \lor\ z = 1))$$

- "The sum of two odd numbers is even."

$$(Odd\ x \ \land\ Odd\ y) \ \Rightarrow\ Even\ (x + y)$$

Our parsing conventions would allow us to drop the parentheses around the conjunction, but they are retained here for readability. As usual when translating from a natural language, there is some flexibility in interpretation. Here, we are using variables x and y without a universal quantification ($\forall$). These variables occur **free** in the formula: there is no quantification to introduce them. We could reasonably have used such quantification, however, which would give the formula:

$$\forall x.\forall y.\ (Odd\ x \ \land\ Odd\ y) \ \Rightarrow\ Even\ (x + y)$$

In this latter translation, all **occurrences** of x and y are **bound** in the formula: wherever an x is used, for example (and the place where it is used is called an occurrence), there is an enclosing quantification of x (in this case, the outer $\forall x$). Whichever translation we use, of course, we are availing ourselves of user-specified predicate symbols for "odd" and "even", each of arity 1 (so the symbols are unary).

- "If x is greater than y, and y is greater than z, then x is greater than z" (transitivity of the arithmetic greater-than relation).

$$(x > y \ \land\ y > z) \ \Rightarrow\ x > z$$

As in the previous case, we could also translate this formula using quantifiers:

$$\forall x.\forall y.\forall z.(x > y \ \land\ y > z) \ \Rightarrow\ x > z$$

1.6   Formal semantics of $FO(\mathbb{Z})$ terms

As mentioned in Section 1.2, we will give the formal semantics of $FO(\mathbb{Z})$ terms using functions σ which assign integer values to the variables which appear (free) in the term. In this book, we will make use of some standard notation for **finite functions** (which are functions that have a finite domain; that is, they accept just a finite number of inputs). A function that maps input i_1 to output o_1 (whatever kinds of things the inputs and outputs are) and so on up to mapping i_n to o_n will be written as

$$\{i_1 \mapsto o_1, \cdots, i_n \mapsto o_n\}$$

If we have a function σ, it is often useful to have notation for **overriding**: we construct another function σ' which behaves just the way σ does, except that given input i, it returns output o. Standard notation for this is:

$$\sigma[i \mapsto o]$$

So for example, the function described as follows maps x_1 to 5 and x_2 to 4, since it overrides the finite function $\{x_1 \mapsto 3, x_2 \mapsto 4\}$ to map x_1 to 5 instead of 3:

$$\{x_1 \mapsto 3, x_2 \mapsto 4\}[x_1 \mapsto 5]$$

Multiple uses of overriding can be collapsed, as long as we know the variables involved are distinct:

$$\sigma[x \mapsto 2][y \mapsto 3] = \sigma[x \mapsto 2, y \mapsto 3]$$

Using this notation for finite functions and overriding, we can define the semantics of $FO(\mathbb{Z})$ terms formally as follows. Suppose σ is any function from (at least) the set of all variables in the term to the set of integers. We will call such functions **assignments**, as they assign a value to variables in the term. The meaning of a term t with respect to assignment σ is an integer $term[\![t]\!]\sigma$. This function $term[\![\cdot]\!]\cdot$ is defined as follows:

$$
\begin{aligned}
term[\![x]\!]\sigma &= \sigma(x) \\
term[\![n]\!]\sigma &= n \\
term[\![t + t']\!]\sigma &= \text{the sum of } term[\![t]\!]\sigma, \ term[\![t']\!]\sigma \\
term[\![t * t']\!]\sigma &= \text{the product of } term[\![t]\!]\sigma, \ term[\![t']\!]\sigma \\
term[\![t - t']\!]\sigma &= \text{the difference of } term[\![t]\!]\sigma, \ term[\![t']\!]\sigma \\
term[\![-t]\!]\sigma &= \text{the arithmetic negation of } term[\![t]\!]\sigma
\end{aligned}
$$

This is a **well-founded recursive definition**: the right hand sides of the equations make use of the function being defined, but they do so only in such a way that the recursion eventually must stop. In this case, the recursive calls on the right hand side are all made on **strict** (or **proper**) subexpressions of the term appearing on the left hand side. A strict subexpression of an expression e is one that appears inside e but is not e itself, since unless otherwise specified, every expression is considered a trivial subexpression of itself. Our terms are finite expressions, and hence we cannot make recursive calls forever on smaller and smaller strict subexpressions.

In each case of the above definition, we are defining the meaning of a $FO(\mathbb{Z})$ operator by the standard mathematical function we associate with that symbol. With the operator "+", for example, we associate the actual mathematical function which adds integers. I have deliberately avoided partial function like $\div$, as these require more machinery in the semantics for terms. If when we write a symbol like "$+$" in our meta-linguistic discussion of the WHILE language, we keep straight whether we mean the symbol $+$ or the mathematical function $+$, we can write the above definition more concisely (if a bit cryptically) as:

$$
\begin{aligned}
term[\![x]\!]\sigma &= \sigma(x) \\
term[\![n]\!]\sigma &= n \\
term[\![t + t']\!]\sigma &= term[\![t]\!]\sigma + term[\![t']\!]\sigma \\
term[\![t * t']\!]\sigma &= term[\![t]\!]\sigma * term[\![t']\!]\sigma \\
term[\![t - t']\!]\sigma &= term[\![t]\!]\sigma - term[\![t']\!]\sigma \\
term[\![-t]\!]\sigma &= -term[\![t]\!]\sigma
\end{aligned}
$$

So we are giving the meaning of arithmetic symbols in terms of arithmetic functions which we denote (at the meta-level) with the exact same symbols. A definition like this is absurd from a foundational point of view: if the reader does not know what the $+$ function is, then s/he will get almost no information out of the defining equation for the semantics of $t + t'$ (by **defining equation**, I mean the single equation which states what the value of the interpretation $term[\![\cdot]\!]\sigma$ is for expressions of that form).

Our definition of the semantics of $FO(\mathbb{Z})$ terms is an instance of the general approach to denotational semantics described at the start of this chapter. We are trying to state that the symbol "$+$" denotes addition, but we are using the meta-language symbol $+$ to refer to the mathematical operation of addition. This would be like saying that the meaning of "le tour Eiffel" is le tour Eiffel. This is hardly very informative, unless we already know what our meta-language phrase "le tour Eiffel" means. In the case of the semantics of $FO(\mathbb{Z})$, since we do know what those meta-language expressions involving "$+$", "$*$", and the rest mean, the above definition makes clear that the semantics we have in mind for our object language of $FO(\mathbb{Z})$ terms is the one suggested by the symbols we are using in the object language. We could just as well have had some less standard interpretation of these symbols in mind. For example, perhaps we intend "$+$" to denote addition modulo 37. In that case, we would have a defining equation for the semantics of "$+$" like the following one, which would precisely express what we intend:

$$
term[\![t + t']\!]\sigma = (term[\![t]\!]\sigma + term[\![t']\!]\sigma) \bmod 37
$$

Or we might have wished to define the semantics of a new operator $\oplus$ in terms of operations we already understand; for example, writing gcd for the function returning the greatest common divisor of two integers, we might define:

$$
term[\![t \oplus t']\!]\sigma = gcd(term[\![t]\!]\sigma, term[\![t']\!]\sigma)
$$

In such situations, we go beyond just saying that $+$ in the object language means $+$ in the meta-language, and are thus arguably more informative. Nevertheless, saying that object-language $+$ means meta-language $+$ carries important non-trivial information, since after all, the interpretation of object-language $+$ could easily have been some other operation. We will see below, especially in the next chapter, a number of important examples where we give more illuminating semantics for an operator than just that it means what it usually means in the meta-language.

Finally, note that the defining equation for the semantics of variables x is the one place in the definition where the assignment σ is used. The defining equation tells us that the meaning of x with respect to σ is just $\sigma(x)$. So if σ tells us that x is mapped to 5, then $term[\![x]\!]\sigma$ is 5. If it weren't for this clause, we could define the semantics of a term without reference to this σ. This would greatly simplify the other clauses of the definition. We would be able to write, for example, just the following for the defining equation for the semantics of +-terms:

$$term[\![t - t']\!] = term[\![t]\!] - term[\![t']\!]$$

The interpretation of a term t would be just $term[\![t]\!]$, with no dependence on an assignment σ. Unfortunately, since one defining equation of our above definition requires this assignment (namely, the defining equation for the semantics of variables), the interpretation must take this assignment as an extra argument, and must propagate it through the other defining equations. We will find in many other situations in this book that the need for a parameter like σ in one part of the formal definition of some concept leads to the propagation of that parameter throughout other parts of the definition.

1.6.1 Examples

Here is an example of computing the interpretation of a term step by step, using the above definition. Here, and elsewhere, we will often write interpretations like $term[\![t]\!]\sigma$ as just $[\![t]\!]\sigma$.

$$
\begin{aligned}
[\![(x * y) + 1]\!]\{x \mapsto 4, y \mapsto 5\} &= [\![x * y]\!]\{x \mapsto 4, y \mapsto 5\} + [\![1]\!]\{x \mapsto 4, y \mapsto 5\} \\
&= [\![x * y]\!]\{x \mapsto 4, y \mapsto 5\} + 1 \\
&= ([\![x]\!]\{x \mapsto 4, y \mapsto 5\} * [\![y]\!]\{x \mapsto 4, y \mapsto 5\}) + 1 \\
&= (4 * [\![y]\!]\{x \mapsto 4, y \mapsto 5\}) + 1 \\
&= (4 * 5) + 1 \\
&= 21
\end{aligned}
$$

Here is another example, showing that it is fine for the assignment's domain to include more variables than just the ones in the term:

$$
\begin{aligned}
[\![3 + (x * 5)]\!]\{x \mapsto 4, y \mapsto 5\} &= [\![3]\!]\{x \mapsto 4, y \mapsto 5\} + [\![x * 5]\!]\{x \mapsto 4, y \mapsto 5\} \\
&= 3 + [\![x * 5]\!]\{x \mapsto 4, y \mapsto 5\} \\
&= 3 + ([\![x]\!]\{x \mapsto 4, y \mapsto 5\} * [\![5]\!]\{x \mapsto 4, y \mapsto 5\}) \\
&= 3 + (4 * [\![5]\!]\{x \mapsto 4, y \mapsto 5\}) \\
&= 3 + (4 * 5) \\
&= 23
\end{aligned}
$$

Finally, consider the term $x + (y * z)$ and the assignment $\{w \mapsto 2, x \mapsto 3\}$. As this assignment does not map all the variables in the term, the interpretation of the term with respect to this assignment is undefined.

1.7   Formal semantics of $FO(\mathbb{Z})$ formulas

The formal semantics of $FO(\mathbb{Z})$ formulas is defined as follows. We interpret formulas as boolean values (which we define to be either *True* or *False*). Also, we will suppose that some interpretation has been specified for the predicate symbols P that occur in the formula, as relations on integers (since otherwise, their meaning is not specified by the semantics). With each boolean connective *conn*, we associate the usual boolean operation: for example, with $\wedge$, we associate the boolean operation which takes two arguments, and returns *True* iff both arguments are *True*. We abbreviate our official notation $formula[\![F]\!]\sigma$ as just $[\![F]\!]\sigma$, in the following definition:

$$
\begin{array}{rcl}
[\![True]\!]\sigma & = & True \\
[\![False]\!]\sigma & = & False \\
[\![t\ pred\ t']\!]\sigma & = & \text{The relation for } pred \text{ holds for } term[\![t]\!]\sigma, term[\![t']\!]\sigma \\
[\![P\ t_1 \cdots t_n]\!]\sigma & = & \text{The relation for } P \text{ holds for } term[\![t_1]\!]\sigma, \cdots, term[\![t_n]\!]\sigma \\
[\![F\ conn\ F']\!]\sigma & = & \text{The boolean function for } conn \text{ returns } True \text{ for } [\![F]\!]\sigma, [\![F']\!]\sigma \\
[\![\neg F]\!]\sigma & = & \text{Boolean negation returns } False \text{ for } [\![F]\!]\sigma \\
[\![\forall x.\,F]\!]\sigma & = & \text{For all integers } v,\ [\![F]\!]\sigma[x \mapsto v] \text{ is } True \\
[\![\exists x.\,F]\!]\sigma & = & \text{For some integer } v,\ [\![F]\!]\sigma[x \mapsto v] \text{ is } True
\end{array}
$$

In the last two defining clauses, for $\forall$ and $\exists$, we override the assignment σ to map variable x to integer v. If the **body** F of a universally quantified formula is true with respect to all such overridings of σ, then the universal formula is true with respect to σ: F truly holds for all values that the quantified variable x can assume. Similarly, for existential quantification, the definition just requires that the body F is true with respect to an overriding with some assignment of value v to variable x. When $[\![F]\!]\sigma = True$, we say that σ satisfies F, and sometimes write $\sigma \models F$.

The interpretation of predicate symbols P could be given by means of formulas which do not contain P. For example, using the formula we mentioned in Section 1.5 above, we could write

$$[\![Prime\ t]\!]\sigma = [\![(\forall y.\forall z.y * z = t \implies (y = 1 \vee z = 1))]\!]\sigma$$

One could also specify recursive predicates, although a proper consideration of recursion must wait until Chapter 2.

1.7.1   Examples

Here are the step-by-step interpretations of several example formulas. First, suppose we have some state σ where $\sigma(x) = 2$ and $\sigma(y) = 3$:

$$
\begin{array}{rcl}
[\![x + y > y]\!] & = & [\![x + y]\!]\sigma > [\![y]\!]\sigma \\
& = & ([\![x]\!]\sigma + [\![y]\!]\sigma) > [\![y]\!]\sigma \\
& = & (2 + 3) > 3 \\
& = & 5 > 3 \\
& = & True
\end{array}
$$

If we interpret the same formula in a state σ' where $\sigma'(x) = -2$ and $\sigma'(y) = -3$, then we get a different value for the meaning of the formula:

$$
\begin{aligned}
[\![x + y > y]\!] &= [\![x + y]\!]\sigma > [\![y]\!]\sigma \\
&= [\![x]\!]\sigma + [\![y]\!]\sigma > [\![y]\!]\sigma \\
&= -2 + -3 > -3 \\
&= -5 > -3 \\
&= \textit{False}
\end{aligned}
$$

For a somewhat more complicated example, let σ be some arbitrary state:

$$
\begin{aligned}
& [\![\forall x. \forall y.\ x < y \ \Rightarrow x < 2 * y]\!]\sigma \\
=\ & \forall v_1 \in \mathbb{Z}.\ [\![\forall y.\ x < y \ \Rightarrow x < 2 * y]\!]\sigma[x \mapsto v_1] \text{ is } \textit{True} \\
=\ & \forall v_1 \in \mathbb{Z}.\ (\forall v_2 \in \mathbb{Z}.\ [\![x < y \ \Rightarrow x < 2 * y]\!]\sigma[x \mapsto v_1,\ y \mapsto v_2] \text{ is } \textit{True}) \text{ is } \textit{True} \\
=\ & \forall v_1 \in \mathbb{Z}.\ (\forall v_2 \in \mathbb{Z}.\ [\![x < y]\!]\sigma[x \mapsto v_1,\ y \mapsto v_2] \text{ is } \textit{True} \text{ implies} \\
& \qquad\qquad\qquad [\![x < 2 * y]\!]\sigma[x \mapsto v_1,\ y \mapsto v_2] \text{ is } \textit{True}) \text{ is } \textit{True} \\
=\ & \forall v_1 \in \mathbb{Z}.\ (\forall v_2 \in \mathbb{Z}.\ v_1 < v_2 \text{ implies } v_1 < 2 * v_2) \text{ is } \textit{True} \\
=\ & \textit{False}
\end{aligned}
$$

To justify the last step, we must show that the stated property fails to hold for some integers v_1 and v_2. An example pair of such integers is -3 for v_1 and -2 for v_2. We do have $-3 < -2$, but not $-3 < 2 * -2$, since this is equivalent to $-3 < -4$.

1.8   Compositionality

A hallmark of denotational semantics is that it is **compositional**: the meaning of a bigger expression is defined in terms of the meanings of its strict subexpressions. We can see this clearly in a case like the defining clause for $t + t'$:

$$
term[\![t + t']\!]\sigma = term[\![t]\!]\sigma + term[\![t']\!]\sigma
$$

Let us write this in a crudely simplified form:

Meaning of $t + t' =$ Something computed from meaning of t and meaning of t'

This crude form helps emphasize that the meaning of the **compound** expression (i.e., the expression built from strictly smaller subexpressions) is computed, in some way, from the meanings of the strict subexpressions (that is, from the meanings of t and t'). We will see later that for some other kinds of semantics, particularly operational semantics (Chapter 4), the meaning of an expression is not defined in a compositional way.

1.9   Validity and satisfiability

Two important basic definitions from logic are the following. Recall that we are writing Σ for the set of functions mapping some set of variables to the integers, and we are implicitly assuming that any time we write $[\![\phi]\!]\sigma$, we are considering only assignments σ which give a value to all the free variables of ϕ.

Definition 1.9.1 (Validity of a Formula). *A formula ϕ is **valid** iff for all assignments $\sigma \in \Sigma$, $[\![\phi]\!]\sigma = True$. The notation $\models \phi$ is often used to express that ϕ is valid.*

Definition 1.9.2 (Satisfiability of a Formula). *A formula ϕ is **satisfiable** iff for some assignment $\sigma \in \Sigma$, $[\![\phi]\!]\sigma = True$.*

For our purposes, we will assume that the interpretations of the user-specified predicate symbols P are given in advance, and we will consider a formula valid or satisfiable relative to given such interpretations. The alternative is not to consider these symbols as coming with a single fixed interpretation. Rather, the notion of validity is defined so that it requires the interpretation of ϕ to be true for all possible interpretations of the user-specified predicate symbols, as well as all possible assignments. Similarly, the notion of satisfiability requires the interpretation of ϕ to be true for some possible interpretation of the user-specified predicate symbols, and some possible assignment. This alternative is standard in logic and universal algebra, but the one we pursue here will be sufficient for our purposes.

Theorem 1.9.3. *A formula ϕ is valid iff $\neg\phi$ is not satisfiable.*

Proof. Suppose ϕ is valid. From the definition of validity above, this is equivalent to stating that for all assignments $\sigma \in \Sigma$, we have $[\![\phi]\!]\sigma = True$. By the semantics of negation, this is equivalent to $[\![\neg\phi]\!]\sigma = False$. Since this is true for every assignment σ, that is equivalent to stating that there is no assignment σ where $[\![\neg\phi]\!]\sigma = True$. So, by the definition of satisfiability above, this is equivalent to stating that $\neg\phi$ is not satisfiable. $\qquad\square$

For example, the formula $x = y$ is satisfiable, since its interpretation with respect to the assignment $\{x \mapsto 1,\ y \mapsto 1\}$ is *True*. That same formula is not valid, since there exists an assignment which makes its interpretation false; an example is $\{x \mapsto 1,\ y \mapsto 2\}$. For an example of a valid formula, we can take $x * y = y * x$. No matter what integer values we assign to the variables x and y, the two sides of this equation will have the same interpretation, since multiplication is commutative. So the interpretation of the equation will always be *True*, no matter what the assignment, and the formula is valid.

1.10   Interlude: proof by natural-number induction

So far, we have relied on basic properties of arithmetic, like commutativity at the end of the previous section, when considering the interpretations of terms and formulas. But how does one prove properties of arithmetic operators in the first place? The answer is that we must begin with some assumed properties, or some definitions, of the arithmetic operators, and then prove based on those that the operators have certain properties, like commutativity. Or for another example, suppose we wish to prove a formula like the following, where we take the variables x and y to be quantifying over the set of natural numbers:

$$\forall x.\forall y.2^{x+y} = 2^x * 2^y$$

How is this done? Suppose we know some basic facts about exponentiation, addition, and multiplication. We will consider in later chapters how to define arithmetic operations in such a way that basic facts about them can be easily proved, but for now, let us assume we know some basic properties, but not other slightly more complex properties, such as the one above. Then we can use **proof by natural-number induction**, together with basic rules of logic, to prove these properties. With natural-number induction, we have some property of a single natural number which we must prove. Let us write $P(n)$ for this property, to show that we are focusing on the number referred to by the variable n. Our goal is to prove $\forall n.P(n)$. If there are multiple universally quantified variables, we would have to pick just one (or possibly introduce a new variable), to focus on. For the above formula, the property might be

$$\forall y.2^{n+y} = 2^n * 2^y$$

There are other possibilities, of course. We have chosen here to focus on x, and we could just have well focused on y. In general, identifying which variable to focus on, or more generally, what property P to try to prove, can require significant ingenuity.

We are required first to prove $P(0)$; that is, the property except with 0 instead of n. $P(0)$ is called the **base case** of the induction proof. Then we are required to prove $P(n+1)$, assuming $P(n)$. This assumption that the property holds for n while we are trying to prove it for the successor of n is called the **induction hypothesis**, or IH. This case, where we must prove $P(n+1)$ assuming $P(n)$, is called the **inductive case** (or alternatively, the **step case**) of the induction proof.

For our example concerning exponentiation, we must prove the following for our base case:

$$\forall y.2^{0+y} = 2^0 * 2^y$$

To prove a universally quantified formula $\forall y. F$, it suffices to consider some arbitrary y, about which we make no assumptions, and then prove F. So let y be an arbitrary natural number (since we are taking all our quantifiers in this example as ranging over natural numbers), and prove

$$2^{0+y} = 2^0 * 2^y$$

Now we will make use of a couple very basic facts about these arithmetic operations:

$$
\begin{aligned}
0 + y &= y \\
2^0 &= 1 \\
1 * x &= x
\end{aligned}
$$

So we prove the desired conclusion using this chain of equations:

$$2^{0+y} = 2^y = 1 * 2^y = 2^0 * 2^y$$

Now we turn to the inductive case of this natural-number induction. We are required to prove this formula, which is just $P(n + 1)$ for the property P we have chosen to prove holds of all natural numbers:

$$\forall y.2^{(n+1)+y} = 2^{n+1} * 2^y$$

To do this, we are allowed to make use of this induction hypothesis, which is just $P(n)$:

$$\forall y.2^{n+y} = 2^n * 2^y$$

To begin, assume an arbitrary natural number y, and prove

$$2^{(n+1)+y} = 2^{n+1} * 2^y$$

We will now make use of these very basic facts about our operators:

$$
\begin{aligned}
(n+1)+y &= (n+y)+1 \\
2^{x+1} &= 2 * 2^x
\end{aligned}
$$

We can now reason as follows:

$$2^{(n+1)+y} = 2^{(n+y)+1} = 2 * 2^{n+y}$$

At this point, there are no obvious basic facts that apply to help us transform the rightmost term in this chain of equalities into the desired $2^{n+1} * 2^y$. So we appear to be stuck. But we have not yet used our induction hypothesis (IH), and it does apply at this point. We can instantiate the quantified y in the induction hypothesis with this arbitrary y we are currently considering. That will give us this equation:

$$2^{n+y} = 2^n * 2^y$$

Observe carefully that the IH tells us

$$\forall y.2^{n+y} = 2^n * 2^y$$

Only y is quantified here, not n. So we can instantiate the quantified y with something else (the y we are currently considering), but we cannot instantiate n: it has to remain fixed.

Now we can extend our chain of equational reasoning:

$$2^{(n+1)+y} = 2^{(n+y)+1} = 2 * 2^{n+y} = 2 * 2^n * 2^y$$

We are almost done. We just have to use the basic fact $2 * 2^n = 2^{n+1}$:

$$2^{(n+1)+y} = 2^{(n+y)+1} = 2 * 2^{n+y} = 2 * 2^n * 2^y = 2^{n+1} * 2^y$$

This shows exactly what we were supposed to prove, and so the inductive step of this proof is complete now. That also completes the proof by natural-number induction of our original formula.

1.10.1   Choosing the induction hypothesis

The proof in the previous section demonstrates several phenomena which appear commonly in proofs by induction. First, we have a choice of which variable to use for the induction. In the case of the above example, our goal formula has both x and y universally quantified, and it would be legal to attempt a proof by induction on either of them. A common heuristic to choose which variable to use for induction is to pick a variable that is used in a position in the statement of the theorem, where partial knowledge of the value of that variable will enable the application of some algebraic fact to simplify the formula to be proved. We used basic facts like $2^{x+1} = 2 * 2^x$ in our proof, and these were enabled by knowing that the argument to the exponentiation function was a successor number (and similarly in the base case, we used $2^0 = 1$). Since we allowed ourselves to use basic facts about arithmetic, we could just as well have done induction on either x or y to enable these simplifications of the goal formula. If we were working directly from recursive definitions of the arithmetic operators, then one choice will usually be preferable. For example, suppose we give this recursive definition of addition (which is commonly used), based on a view of natural numbers as generated by 0 and a successor operation S (where $S(2) = 3$, for example):

$$\begin{aligned} 0 + y &= y \\ (S(x)) + y &= S(x + y) \end{aligned}$$

In this case, the first argument to plus is the one which will enable algebraic simplifications, if we know it is 0 or else know that it is a successor number. So in that case, it would be more convenient in our example to do induction on x than on y, since x is used as the first argument to plus in the statement of the theorem:

$$\forall x. \forall y. 2^{x+y} = 2^x * 2^y$$

A second phenomenon we can observe here is that once one chooses which variable to use for induction, the other quantified variables (in this case just y) must be taken into account. In general, suppose we are trying to prove a formula of this form:

$$\forall x_1. \ \cdots \ \forall x_n. \ F$$

Suppose we decide to do induction on x_i. Then we will first have to assume arbitrary x_1 through x_{i-1}. This is because the proper form for standard mathematical induction is to prove a formula of the form $\forall x. \ P(x)$, by proving $P(0)$ and then $P(n) \Rightarrow P(n+1)$. So if we want to do induction on a variable in the middle of a list of universally quantified variables, like this x_i, we must first get the variables to the left of x_i in the quantifier prefix out of the way. We have to assume arbitrary x_1 through x_{i-1} before we begin the induction on x_i. Once we do begin our induction, we will be proving $\forall x_i. P(x_i)$, where P is the formula:

$$\forall x_{i+1}. \ \cdots \ \forall x_n. \ F$$

So we have retained x_{i+1} through x_n as quantified variables in our goal, and more importantly in our induction hypothesis. Having these variables quantified in the induction hypothesis gives us more power when we are trying to complete the inductive case of the proof by induction, because we can instantiate them with arbitrary other terms. In our example proof above, this power was actually not used: in the inductive case we just instantiated the quantified y with the arbitrary y we were considering in that case. So the extra flexibility was not needed, and in fact was just distracting, as we technically had to instantiate the quantified y before we could make use of our induction hypothesis as we wished. In this case, it would have been simpler to reorder the quantified variables in our goal formula like this:

$$\forall y. \forall x. 2^{x+y} = 2^x * 2^y$$

Then our proof could first consider an arbitrary y, and then do induction on x. The step case would then just be to prove

$$2^{(n+1)+y} = 2^{n+1} * 2^y$$

assuming (as IH)

$$2^{n+y} = 2^n * 2^y$$

Notice that now we do not have any quantification of y in the formulas involved (either the goal formula or the induction hypothesis). For this particular proof, that would be a little simpler than what we considered above. In some proofs, of course, we need the extra flexibility of keeping variables universally quantified in the induction hypothesis. One quickly finds out which variables require more flexibility and which do not, so making the wrong choice about which variables to retain quantified in the IH and which to dispatch before beginning the induction is easily corrected.

1.10.2   Strong natural-number induction

Natural-number induction as just considered is sometimes called **weak induction**. This is to contrast it with **strong induction**, sometimes also called complete induction or course-of-values induction. For strong induction, we are again trying to prove $\forall n. P(n)$. But now we are just required to prove $P(n)$, for an arbitrary natural number n, under the following strong induction hypothesis:

$$\forall x. \, x < n \Rightarrow P(x)$$

That is, we are allowed to assume that the property P holds for every natural number x which is strictly smaller than n. This is useful when some function mentioned in the theorem we are trying to prove makes recursive calls on a number smaller than the predecessor of n. For example, suppose we define the natural-number logarithm function as follows, where we leave $log(0)$ undefined, and where we write $/2$ for natural-number division by 2:

$$log(1) \quad = \quad 0$$
$$log(S(S(x))) \quad = \quad S(log(S(S(x))/2))$$

Suppose we want to prove

$$\forall n.n > 0 \Rightarrow 2^{log(n)} \leq n$$

We proceed by strong induction on n. We must prove

$$n > 0 \Rightarrow 2^{log(n)} \leq n$$

under the strong induction hypothesis

$$\forall x.\, x < n \Rightarrow x > 0 \Rightarrow 2^{log(x)} \leq x$$

Let us first case split on whether $n = 1$ or $n > 1$. In the first case, we prove the goal formula as follows:

$$2^{log(n)} = 2^{log(1)} = 2^0 = 1 \leq 1 = n$$

In the second case, n must be equal to $S(S(n'))$ for some n'. So we have

$$2^{log(n)} = 2^{log(S(S(n')))} = 2^{S(log(S(S(n'))/2))} = 2 * 2^{log(S(S(n'))/2)}$$

Now we know that $S(S(n'))/2 < n$, using the following reasoning, where we use without proof the basic property on natural-number division that $n'/2 \leq n'$:

$$S(S(n'))/2 = S(n'/2) \leq S(n') < S(S(n')) = n$$

Since $S(S(n'))/2 < n$, we may instantiate our strong induction hypothesis with $S(S(n'))$ to extend the chain of reasoning we started just above:

$$2^{log(n)} = 2^{log(S(S(n')))} = 2^{S(log(S(S(n'))/2))} = 2 * 2^{log(S(S(n'))/2)} \leq 2 * (S(n'/2))$$

Now we will use the further basic property of natural-number division that $2 * (n/2) \leq n$, to finish the chain of reasoning:

$$
\begin{aligned}
& 2^{log(n)} \\
=\ & 2^{log(S(S(n')))} \\
=\ & 2^{S(log(S(S(n'))/2))} \\
=\ & 2 * 2^{log(S(S(n'))/2)} \\
\leq\ & 2 * (S(n'/2)) \\
=\ & S(S(2 * (n'/2))) \\
\leq\ & S(S(n')) \\
=\ & n
\end{aligned}
$$

This completes the proof by strong induction. We made use of our induction hypothesis not for the predecessor $S(n')$ of n, but for $S(n'/2)$. Proof by weak natural-number induction would not have allowed us to do this.

1.10.3   Aside: deriving strong induction from weak induction

The principle of strong natural-number induction can be derived using weak natural-number induction. Assume that we have some property $P(n)$. Then we can formulate strong induction like this:

$$(\forall n.(\forall n'.n' < n \Rightarrow P(n')) \Rightarrow P(n)) \Rightarrow \forall n.P(n)$$

We wish to use weak induction to prove this formula. First, let us assume the antecedent of this implication:

$$\forall n.(\forall n'.n' < n \Rightarrow P(n')) \Rightarrow P(n) \tag{1.1}$$

Now the crucial insight is in crafting a suitable induction hypothesis. Let $P'(n)$ be the property

$$\forall n'.n' \leq n \Rightarrow P(n')$$

We will prove $\forall n.P'(n)$ by weak induction on n. Notice that $\forall n.P'(n)$ is just

$$\forall n.\forall n'.n' \leq n \Rightarrow P(n')$$

This implies $\forall n.P(n)$, since if we assume an arbitrary n, we can instantiate the two universal quantifiers just above with n, to obtain:

$$n \leq n \Rightarrow P(n)$$

And of course, the antecedent $n \leq n$ of this implication is valid, so we can indeed conclude $P(n)$. This argument shows that in order to prove $\forall n.P(n)$ as we wish to do, it is sufficient to prove $\forall n.P'(n)$, for the property P' we identified above.

So now we will prove $\forall n.P'(n)$ by weak induction on n. For the base case, we must prove

$$\forall n'.n' \leq 0 \Rightarrow P(n')$$

This is equivalent to having to prove just $P(0)$, since if $n' \leq 0$, then we have (for natural number n') $n' = 0$. By Hypothesis 1.1 above, we can obtain a proof of $P(0)$ if we can prove

$$\forall n'.n' < 0 \Rightarrow P(n')$$

But this formula is easily proved, since if we assume an arbitrary n' strictly less than 0, we can derive a contradiction: no natural number is strictly smaller than 0.

So let us consider now the step case of our proof by weak natural-number induction. We must show

$$\forall n'.n' \leq S(n) \Rightarrow P(n')$$

under the induction hypothesis

$$\forall n'.n' \leq n \Rightarrow P(n')$$

So assume an arbitrary $n' \leq S(n)$. Let us case split on whether we have $n' = S(n)$ or else $n' < S(n)$. Suppose the former. So we must prove $P(S(n))$. Hypothesis 1.1 above would let us conclude this if we could only prove

$$\forall n'.n' < S(n) \Rightarrow P(n')$$

But this formula is equivalent to

$$\forall n'.n' \leq n \Rightarrow P(n')$$

and that formula is exactly our induction hypothesis. So this first case of our case split on whether $n' = S(n)$ or else $n' < S(n)$, is proved, and we consider now the second. So assume $n' < S(n)$. This is equivalent to $n' \leq n$. We must show $P(n')$. This follows directly from our induction hypothesis, since $n' \leq n$. That completes the step case of our proof by weak natural-number induction that the principle of strong induction is valid.

1.11   Proof by structural induction

In the section we have an example of an important variation on proof by induction, which we just considered in the last section. This is proof by structural induction. The theorem we are proving, while technically useful, is not profoundly important in its own right. But structural induction is used often in the study of programming language semantics, and will appear frequently later in this book.

Theorem 1.11.1. *Suppose $[\![t]\!]\sigma$ is defined, and suppose that $\sigma \subseteq \sigma'$. Then $[\![t]\!]\sigma'$ is also defined, and equals $[\![t]\!]\sigma$.*

Proof. We first need to make sure the meaning of the assumption $\sigma \subseteq \sigma'$ is clear. Since assignments σ are just functions from a finite set of variables to integers, and since functions are relations, which in turn are just sets, it makes sense to state that two assignments σ and σ' are in the subset relationship ($\subseteq$). See the Mathematical Background for a review of these ideas.

Now our proof proceeds by induction on the structure of t. We must consider all the possible cases for the form of t. In each case, we are allowed to use as an assumption the formula which we are trying to prove, but we can only do so with an immediate subterm of t in place of t. That assumption is our induction hypothesis, and is similar to the induction hypothesis in proof by natural-number induction. In both forms of proof, we are allowed to use what we are trying to prove, but only on smaller data: either the predecessor number or the immediate subterms of a term.

Using the IH only for immediate terms of t ensures that we cannot appeal to our induction hypothesis forever: one cannot find smaller and smaller subterms of finite terms t forever, just as in natural-number induction, one cannot find forever smaller and smaller natural-number predecessors of a number. At some point these decreasing sequences must stop. Those stopping points are the base cases of the induction, and the other cases are the inductive cases. For natural numbers, the sole base case is for when the number n in question equals 0, and the step case is for when $n = n' + 1$ for some $n' \in \mathbb{N}$. For $FO(\mathbb{Z})$ terms, there is one base case for when the term t in question is equal to some variable x, and another for when it is equal to some $n \in \mathbb{N}$. There is one step case for when $t = t_1$ op t_2 for some operator op, and some terms t_1, t_2; there is another step case for when $t = -t_1$, for some term t_1. Let us now consider these cases for t.

Case: $t = x$, for some variable x. In this case, $[\![t]\!]\sigma = \sigma(x)$, by the defining equation for the interpretation of variables. Since $[\![t]\!]\sigma$ is defined, we know that $\sigma(x)$ is defined. We are assuming that $\sigma \subseteq \sigma'$, so we know that $\sigma'(x) = \sigma(x)$. And since $[\![t]\!]\sigma' = \sigma'(x)$, again by the defining equation for the interpretation of variables, we can conlude with the desired result: $[\![t]\!]\sigma'$ is defined and equal to $[\![t]\!]\sigma'$. To summarize:

$$[\![t]\!]\sigma = [\![x]\!]\sigma = \sigma(x) = \sigma'(x) = [\![x]\!]\sigma' = [\![t]\!]\sigma'$$

Case: $t = n$, for some $n \in \mathbb{N}$. In this case, $[\![t]\!]\sigma = n = [\![t]\!]\sigma'$, which is certainly defined.

Case: $t = t_1 op t_2$, for some terms t_1 and t_2 and some operator op. The induction hypothesis can be applied to conclude what we are trying to prove for the immediate subterms t_1 and t_2 of t. So by the induction hypothesis, we have that $\sigma t_1 \sigma'$ and $\sigma t_2 \sigma'$ are both defined and equal to $\sigma t_1 \sigma'$ and $\sigma t_2 \sigma'$, respectively. So we have:

$$[\![t]\!]\sigma = [\![t_1]\!]\sigma \ op \ [\![t_2]\!]\sigma = [\![t_1]\!]\sigma' \ op \ [\![t_2]\!]\sigma' = [\![t]\!]\sigma'$$

Case: $t = -t_1$, for some term t_1. The reasoning is similar to that of the previous case, using the induction hypothesis for t_1:

$$[\![t]\!]\sigma = -[\![t_1]\!]\sigma = -[\![t_1]\!]\sigma' = [\![t]\!]\sigma'$$

$\square$

1.12   Conclusion

We have seen the syntax, informal semantics, and formal semantics of the $FO(\mathbb{Z})$ language for first-order arithmetic. The semantics considered is denotational. The formal semantics of a $FO(\mathbb{Z})$ term like $x + (3 * y)$ is defined with respect to an assigment σ mapping $FO(\mathbb{Z})$ variables like x and y to integer values. The formal semantics of a $FO(\mathbb{Z})$ formula F is defined similarly. The definitions of both semantics are given as well-founded recursive equations. As such, they are **compositional** semantics: the meaning of a compound expression is given in terms of the meanings of its immediate subexpressions. We considered the basic logical concepts of validity and satisfiability. We will use $FO(\mathbb{Z})$ again, when we consider Hoare Logic in Chapter 3 below. We also reviewed proof by natural-number induction, and saw an example of how to prove a property of our semantics (Theorem 1.11.1) by induction on the structure of terms t. In the next chapter, we will devise a similar semantics for a simple imperative programming language called WHILE. There, we have some new challenges to overcome, in order to give a compositional semantics for while-loops.

1.13 Basic exercises

1.13.1 For Sections 1.1 and 1.3 on $FO(\mathbb{Z})$ syntax

1. For each of the following expressions, state the syntactic category to which the expression belongs, or state that the expression does not belong to any of the syntactic categories defined in the sections listed above:

   (a) 3

   (b) $1 - 2$

   (c) $*$

   (d) $\wedge$

   (e) $x + y \Rightarrow z$

   (f) $x + y = z \Rightarrow False$

   (g) $P\, x\, 1$, assuming that P is a user-specified binary predicate symbol.

2. Add parentheses according to the parsing conventions of Section 1.3, to make explicit the structure of the following formulas (assume that P, Q, and R are user-specified predicate symbols of arity 0):

   (a) $P \wedge Q \Rightarrow R \Leftrightarrow P \vee R$

   (b) $x + y > z \Rightarrow \exists w.\, x > w \wedge w > y$

   (c) $\forall x.\, (\forall y.\, y > x) \Rightarrow x < 0 \wedge x > 0$

3. Which of the following formulas accurately translates the (invalid) statement "if x plus y is greater than 0 then x is greater than 0":

   (a) $x + y > 0 \Leftrightarrow x > 0$

   (b) $x + y > 0 \Rightarrow x > 0$

   (c) $\forall x.\, \forall y.\, x > 0 \Rightarrow y > 0$

1.13.2 For Sections 1.6 and 1.7 on $FO(\mathbb{Z})$ semantics

1. Write out, step by step (as done in Section 1.6.1 above), the computation of the (integer) value of $[\![3 * x * y]\!]\{x \mapsto 3, y \mapsto 4\}$.

2. What is the value of $[\![x + (x * x)]\!]\{x \mapsto 3, y \mapsto 4\}$ (you do not need to write out the computation step by step)?

3. What is the interpretation (using $formula[\![\cdot]\!]$) of the following $FO(\mathbb{Z})$ formulas, with respect to assignment $\varnothing$ (that is, the assignment that does not associate a value with any variable):

   (a) $\forall x . x \neq x$.

   (b) $\forall x . \forall y . x + y > y \Rightarrow x > 0$.

   (c) $2 > 3 \Rightarrow 0 = 1$.

1.14   Intermediate exercises

1.14.1   For Sections 1.1 through 1.5 on $FO(\mathbb{Z})$ syntax and informal semantics

1. Translate the statement "Every two numbers have a common divisor" into a $FO(\mathbb{Z})$ formula, using the divides predicate symbol $|$ (for expressing the concept of one number's dividing another without remainder).

2. Translate the statement "Every two numbers have a least common multiple" into a $FO(\mathbb{Z})$ formula.

3. Translate the statement "For every prime number, there exists a greater prime number", using a unary (1-argument) predicate symbol *Prime*.

4. Translate the statement "There are infinitely many twin primes", using a unary (1-argument) predicate symbol *Prime*. Two numbers are twin primes if they are both prime and their difference is 2. Hint: the previous problem can help express the idea that there are infinitely many of something.

1.14.2   For Sections 1.6 and 1.7 on $FO(\mathbb{Z})$ semantics

1. For each of the following meta-language statements about the semantics of $FO(\mathbb{Z})$ terms and formulas: either prove the statement using the formal definition of the semantics; or else give a counterexample, in the form of specific values for the meta-language variables like ϕ and σ used in the statement.

   (a) $[\![\phi \wedge \phi]\!]\sigma = [\![\phi]\!]\sigma$

   (b) $[\![x + 0]\!]\sigma = [\![x]\!]\sigma$

   (c) $[\![x + y]\!]\sigma > [\![y]\!]\sigma$

2. Let us temporarily define $\sigma \leq \sigma'$ for assignments σ and σ' to mean that for all variables x, if $\sigma(x)$ is defined then so is $\sigma'(x)$ and we have $\sigma(x) \leq \sigma'(x)$. Suppose that t is a term which does not contain the negation or subtraction symbols. Prove by induction on the structure of t that if $\sigma \leq \sigma'$, then $[\![t]\!]\sigma \leq [\![t]\!]\sigma'$. (You can use the proof of Theorem 1.11.1 as a guide.)

1.14.3 For Sections 1.8 and 1.9 on compositionality, validity and satisfiability

1. Which of the following defining equations could we add to the semantics of $FO(\mathbb{Z})$ formulas (Section 1.7) and still have a compositional semantics?

   (a) $term[\![t \oplus t']\!]\sigma \;=\; term[\![t]\!]\sigma^{term[\![t']\!]\sigma}$

   (b) $term[\![t \oplus t']\!]\sigma \;=\; term[\![t]\!](\sigma[x \mapsto term[\![t']\!]\sigma])$

   (c) $term[\![t \oplus t']\!]\sigma \;=\; 42$

2. Argue informally, using basic properties of the standard arithmetic operators and built-in predicates, that the following formula is valid. The basic properties you need are transitivity of the greater-than predicate ($>$) and left- and right-monotonicity of addition.

$$\forall w.\forall x.\forall y.\forall z. w > x \wedge y > z \Rightarrow w + y > x + z$$

3. Give an example of a formula which is invalid but not unsatisfiable.

4. Write the shortest valid $FO(\mathbb{Z})$ formula you can, counting the number of characters needed to write out any symbols (like variables, operators, and predicate symbols), and counting one space between symbols. Do not use user-specified predicate symbols.

5. Using the same counting rules as in the previous problem, write the shortest invalid $FO(\mathbb{Z})$ formula you can. Again, do not use user-specified predicate symbols.

1.14.4 For Section 1.10 on proof by induction

1. Let us write $[t/x]t'$ to be the term obtained by substituting term t for variable x in another term t'. We can define this function by terminating recursion as follows:

$$
\begin{aligned}
[t/x]x &= t \\
[t/x]x' &= x', \text{ where } x' \neq x \\
[t/x](t_1 \; op \; t_2) &= ([t/x]t_1) \; op \; ([t/x]t_2) \\
[t/x](-t') &= -([t/x]t')
\end{aligned}
$$

The first defining equation says that substituting t for x in x gives you t. The second says that if you are substituting into a term which is some variable x' that happens to be different from x, then the substitution has no effect: you just get the variable x' again. The next two equations state that to substitute into a bigger term, we just have to substitute into the immediate subterms, and then apply the appropriate operator to the result(s). So for example, $[3/x](2 * x)$ equals $(2 * 3)$. Note that it does not equal 6, because substitution as defined is just a syntactic operation. It does nothing more than textually replace the variable in question with another term.

Given this definition, prove the following theorem (hint: use structural induction). Be as explicit as possible about your reasoning: you should clearly state what you must prove and what you can assume, throughout your proof but especially when setting up the base case and step case of your induction.

$$\forall t.\ \forall t'.\ [[t/x]t']\sigma = [t']\sigma[x \mapsto [t]\sigma]$$

2. For this problem, we will use the following definition of addition:

$$
\begin{aligned}
0 + y &= y \\
S(x) + y &= S(x + y)
\end{aligned}
$$

Using that definition, and no other properties of addition (especially not commutativity, since we are proving that here), prove the following theorems (hint: you need the first two properties to prove the third).

(a) $\forall x.x + 0 = x$

(b) $\forall x.\forall y.x + S(y) = S(x + y)$

(c) $\forall x.\forall y.x + y = y + x$

Chapter 2
Denotational Semantics of WHILE

In this chapter, we will begin our study of semantics by considering a denotational semantics (as explained in the preceding chapter) for a simple programming language called WHILE. This is an *imperative* language: which value a variable holds can be changed by assignment. If the value of x is currently 3, then the assignment $x := 4$ will change the state of the program so that the value of x becomes 4. WHILE is intended to represent a familiar core part of many modern programming languages, including Java and C/C++. It certainly omits many features of such languages, notably procedures (and *a fortiori* object-orientation, etc.). The point of studying the semantics of a language with a minimal set of features is that it will make it feasible to consider denotational, operational (Chapter 4), and axiomatic (Chapter 3) semantics for a single, familiar language. Indeed, this is a standard approach to the study of programming languages: consider just a single minimalistic set of features, and analyze them in depth. The WHILE language is *Turing-complete*: in principle, any Turing machine can be simulated by a WHILE program. Since Turing machines are one of a group of equivalently powerful formalizations of the notion of computation, Turing-completeness shows that WHILE, though unworkably impractical for programming in practice, is an adequate representative of a computational language. So certain fundamental issues arising generally for computational languages will have to be considered in studying WHILE.

2.1 Syntax and informal semantics of WHILE

The syntax of the WHILE language is as follows:

commands c ::= skip $\mid x := t \mid c_1 ; c_2 \mid$ if t *pred* t' then c_1 else $c_2 \mid$
while t *pred* t' do c

The syntax of commands relies on the syntax of terms t (given in Section 1.1). There are five different forms of command in WHILE, corresponding to familiar programming-language statements. Here is an informal explanation of the semantics of commands, phrased in terms of how to execute the given command with respect to a given state. States will be taken just to be assignments σ, in the sense of the preceding chapter.

- skip. Executing this command does nothing to the state.

- $x := t$. Executing this **assignment** command changes the state so that it now assigns the value of term t to variable x.

- c_1 ; c_2. Executing this **sequencing** command first executes command c_1 and then, if that first execution halts, executes the command c_2.

- if t *pred* t' then c_1 else c_2. Executing this **conditional** command first tests whether the values of t and t' in the current state are in the relation corresponding to *pred*. If they are, then command c_1 is executed. Otherwise, command c_2 is executed.

- while t *pred* t' do c. Executing this command first tests whether the values of t and t' in the current state are in the relation corresponding to *pred*. If they are not, then execution of this command does nothing. Otherwise, command c is executed, and if that execution halts, we return to execute the entire while-command again.

The main task of this chapter is to give a formal, denotational semantics for WHILE commands, which we begin next.

2.2 Beginning of the formal semantics for WHILE

It is not difficult to set up the denotational semantics for WHILE, making use also of the semantics given in Section 1.6. We must interpret commands with respect to an assignment σ of integers to the variables x that appear in the program. We will allow σ to map other variables as well, but it must at least supply values for the variables used in the program. In this context, we will call such assignments σ **states**. What kind of thing should the interpretation *command*$[\![c]\!]\sigma$ of a command with respect to state σ be? It turns out that it works well to define the interpretation for commands which halt to be the state σ' which results from performing the command. For example, the meaning of the command $x := 3$ with respect to some state σ will be the overridden state $\sigma[x \mapsto 3]$. For commands which do not halt, we define the interpretation to be $\perp$ (pronounced "bottom", for reasons we will see below), which is just some mathematical object different from any state. So however we define our semantics, we expect equations like the following to be true, for all starting states σ:

$$[\![\texttt{while}\ 0 = 0\ \texttt{do}\ \texttt{skip}]\!]\sigma = \perp$$

Commands that (intuitively) do not halt are called **diverging**. Ones that do are called **converging**.

Based on this idea that the meaning of a command with respect to a starting state is either the ending state to which it converges or else $\perp$ if it diverges, we can easily define the syntax for all commands except `while`-commands:

$$
\begin{aligned}
[\![\texttt{skip}]\!]\sigma &= \sigma \\
[\![x := t]\!]\sigma &= \sigma[x \mapsto term[\![t]\!]\sigma] \\
[\![c_1 ; c_2]\!]\sigma &= \text{if } [\![c_1]\!]\sigma = \perp \text{ then } \perp; \text{ otherwise,} [\![c_2]\!]([\![c_1]\!]\sigma) \\
[\![\texttt{if } t \ pred \ t' \ \texttt{then } c_1 \ \texttt{else } c_2]\!]\sigma &= \text{if the relation for } pred \text{ holds of} \\
&\qquad term[\![t]\!]\sigma, term[\![t']\!]\sigma, \\
&\qquad \text{then } [\![c_1]\!]\sigma; \\
&\qquad \text{otherwise } [\![c_2]\!]\sigma
\end{aligned}
$$

2.3 Problem with the semantics of `while`-commands

Giving a semantics for `while`-commands turns out to raise problems we have not encountered up to now. A natural defining clause we might want to write is the following, which will turn out not to be allowable as part of the definition of the semantics:

$$
\begin{aligned}
[\![\texttt{while } t \ pred \ t' \ \texttt{do } c]\!]\sigma = \ &\text{if the relation for } pred \text{ does not hold of} \\
&\quad term[\![t]\!]\sigma, term[\![t']\!]\sigma, \\
&\text{then } \sigma; \\
&\text{otherwise, if } [\![c]\!]\sigma = \perp \text{ then } \perp ; \\
&\text{otherwise } [\![\texttt{while } t \ pred \ t' \ \texttt{do } c]\!]([\![c]\!]\sigma)
\end{aligned} \tag{2.1}
$$

Let us make sure, first, that it is clear what this equation says, and why that is intuitively plausible, even though it won't work as a defining clause. First, if the interpretation of the guard $t \ pred \ t'$ is false, then the meaning is just σ. That is, the command does not change the state in that situation, since the meaning of the command is the final state resulting from execution, and in this case, execution has not altered the state in any way. Next, the equation says that if the interpretation of the guard is true but the interpretation of the body c is $\perp$, meaning that the body has diverged; then in that case, the meaning of the whole `while`-command is $\perp$. Intuitively, this corresponds to the idea that if the first iteration of the body of the `while`-command diverges, and we actually do execute that iteration, then the `while`-command itself diverges. Finally, the equation says that if the interpretation of the guard is true, and if the first iteration of the body does terminate, then the meaning of the `while`-command is just the meaning of that same command, but with respect to state $[\![c]\!]\sigma$. This state is the one resulting from execution of the first iteration of the body. So intuitively, this last part of the equation corresponds to continuing the execution of the `while`-command recursively, following the converging execution of the first iteration of its body.

The problem with this equation is that adding it as a defining clause in the definition of the semantics of WHILE-commands will result in a definition which is not well-founded. This is because the right hand side appeals to the interpretation $[\![\texttt{while } t \ pred \ t' \ \texttt{do } c]\!]$, which is the same interpretation the equation is trying to define. Schematically, the equation looks like:

$$
[\![W]\!]\sigma = \cdots [\![W]\!]\sigma' \cdots
$$

That is, the interpretation of the while-command (schematically, W) is defined in terms of itself. If our definition of the semantics of WHILE included this equation, it would no longer be well-founded, because the argument to the interpretation function has not decreased where we recursively invoke that function on the right hand side.

This way of describing the problem may seem rather abstract, so let us consider a concrete manifestation of it by trying to compute the meaning of the diverging command while $0 = 0$ do skip in state σ, using the above equation. First, the interpretation of the guard $0 = 0$ is true. This is because the interpretation $[\![0]\!]\sigma$ of the first term 0 is equal to the interpretation of the second, which is also $[\![0]\!]\sigma$. Next, the interpretation $[\![\text{skip}]\!]\sigma$ of the body is not $\bot$. So we are in the third case of the above equation for while, which simplifies to:

$$[\![\text{while } 0 = 0 \text{ do skip}]\!]\sigma = [\![\text{while } 0 = 0 \text{ do skip}]\!]([\![\text{skip}]\!]\sigma)$$

But $[\![\text{skip}]\!]\sigma = \sigma$ by the definition of the semantics for skip, so this equation in turn can be simplified to:

$$[\![\text{while } 0 = 0 \text{ do skip}]\!]\sigma = [\![\text{while } 0 = 0 \text{ do skip}]\!]\sigma$$

Now this might seem innocuous, since this equation is merely stating a valid fact, of the form $W = W$. But we must be careful: the equation we have derived is equivalent to Equation 2.1 which we were considering as a natural candidate for the *definition* of the semantics of while-commands. In other words, that definition does not constrain the semantics of the while-command at all. To anthropomorphize, it is as if the definition is an oracle, whom we ask to tell us the meaning of while $0 = 0$ do skip. In reply, the oracle simply answers, in effect, "True". To tell someone "True" is to tell her nothing at all that she did not already reasonably know. That statement does not provide any non-trivial information about the way the world is. Hence, it is useless as a definition for the semantics of this while-command. Looking at the problem another way, we see that any value whatsoever for $[\![\text{while } 0 = 0 \text{ do skip}]\!]\sigma$ will satisfy the trivial equation we have derived. So the equation states that the meaning is $\bot$, as we would like. But it also states that the meaning is $\{x \mapsto 3\}$, and $\{y \mapsto 4, z \mapsto 5\}$. This implies that the interpretation is not a function. We could accept that by defining the interpretation as a relation between input states and possibly multiple output results. But this is incorrect in general: we expect execution to be deterministic for this particular language. And it is incorrect in particular, as stating that there is an output state σ' for while $0 = 0$ do skip violates the intuitive idea that this command is diverging. So in the end, even if we were somehow to justify using Equation 2.1 for the meaning of while, the resulting semantics would be wrong.

To repair this problem, we need a way to define the semantics of while-commands using a defining equation for the interpretation of while that does not violate well-foundedness of the recursive definition. To be able to state such an equation, we will take a brief (and standard) digression into the theory of a class of mathematical structures called domains. Domain theory will provide us with the technical tools we need to give a proper defining equation for the interpretation of while.

2.4 Domains

One part of the problem we encountered just above with trying to use Equation 2.1 to define the semantics of `while`-commands is that the equation leaves the semantics underconstrained: many different values for the interpretation of a diverging command like `while 0 = 0 do skip` are allowed by Equation 2.1. We will specify a single value out of these possibilities by thinking of $\perp$ as smaller than any state σ, and requiring our semantics to give us the smallest value. This idea of ordering (making $\perp$ smaller than states σ) will also play a central role in obtaining a well-founded defining equation for the interpretation of `while`.

Domains are certain kinds of mathematical structures with an ordering relation. As a short preview: in this section we build up to the definition of domain in three steps. First, we need to recall the basic definition, from discrete mathematics, of a partially ordered set. Then we define what an ω-chain is in such a set. Finally, using the concept of ω-chain, we can define what a predomain is (pronounced "pre-domain", as in something you get before you get a domain), and then what a domain is.

2.4.1 Partially ordered sets

Definition 2.4.1 (Partially ordered set). *A partially ordered set is a set X together with a binary relation $\sqsubseteq$ on X satisfying the following three conditions:*

1. *reflexivity:* $\forall x \in X.x \sqsubseteq x.$

2. *transitivity:* $\forall x, y, z \in X.(x \sqsubseteq y \wedge y \sqsubseteq z) \Rightarrow x \sqsubseteq z.$

3. *antisymmetry:* $\forall x, y \in X.(x \sqsubseteq y \wedge y \sqsubseteq x) \Rightarrow x = y.$

This definition is specifying what must be true in order for a set X with binary relation $\sqsubseteq$ to be a partially ordered set. The phrase "partially ordered set" is often abbreviated **poset** (pronounced like "Poe set"). It is standard to write the set X and the ordering $\sqsubseteq$ together in an ordered pair, like $(X, \sqsubseteq)$. There are many concrete examples of posets. We give some examples below. It will be helpful to visualize these posets as graphs. In general, if we have a binary relation $\sqsubseteq$ holding between elements of some set X, then whenever we have $x \sqsubseteq y$, for elements $x, y \in X$, we will have nodes x and y in the graph, and an edge from x to y:

Whenever an edge is required to exist by transitivity or reflexivity, we will omit it from the graphs below. This is just to avoid cluttering graphs with edges which can be inferred to exist.

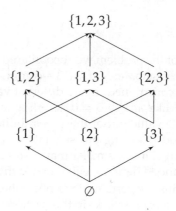

Figure 2.1: Graphical view of the poset $(\mathcal{P}(\{1,2,3\}), \subseteq)$

Example: the integers with the usual ordering $(\mathbb{Z}, \leq)$

The structure $(\mathbb{Z}, \leq)$ consisting of the integers with the standard ordering relation $\leq$ is a poset, since $\leq$ satisfies the three required properties: every integer is less than or equal to itself; if $x \leq y$ and $y \leq z$, then $x \leq z$; and the only way we can have $x \leq y$ and also $y \leq x$ is if $x = y$.

$$\cdots \longrightarrow -2 \longrightarrow -1 \longrightarrow 0 \longrightarrow 1 \longrightarrow 2 \longrightarrow \cdots$$

Example: the discrete poset $(X, =)$

The **discrete** partially ordered set $(X, =)$ consists of some set X, together with the equality relation on X. That is, the only relations we have are between an element $x \in X$ and itself. This relation is reflexive, since for all $x \in X$, we have $x = x$. It is transitive, because if $x_1 = x_2$ and $x_2 = x_3$, then $x_1 = x_3$. Finally, it is antisymmetric, because (just expanding the definition of antisymmetry) whenever we have $x = y$ and $y = x$, we certainly have $x = y$. Writing x_1, x_2 and so forth for elements of X, we can visualize this as the following graph with an empty set of edges:

$$\cdots \quad x_1 \quad x_2 \quad x_3 \quad x_4 \quad \cdots$$

Example: subsets ordered by inclusion $(\mathcal{P}(X), \subseteq)$

Recall from basic set theory that the **powerset** $\mathcal{P}(X)$ of a set X is the set of all subsets of X. If we order these subsets by the subset relation $\subseteq$, then this forms a partially ordered set. You can easily confirm that $\subseteq$ is reflexive, transitive, and antisymmetric. As an example, Figure 2.1 shows the graphical representation of the poset $(\mathcal{P}(\{1,2,3\}), \subseteq)$.

Example: natural numbers ordered by the divides relation $(\mathbb{N}, |)$

The set of natural numbers ordered by the divisibility relation $|$ is a poset, which we call the **divisibility poset**. The definition of divisibility is that $x \mid y$ iff there exists some $k \in \mathbb{N}$ such that $y = x \cdot k$. That is, x evenly divides y. This relation is reflexive (as every natural number divides itself), transitive (since if x divides y and y divides z, this implies that x divides z), and antisymmetric (as no two distinct natural numbers can divide each other).

2.4.2 Omega-chains

Definition 2.4.2 (Omega-chains). *An ω-chain in a partially ordered set $(X, \sqsubseteq)$ is a function f from $\mathbb{N}$ to X such that $f(n) \sqsubseteq f(n+1)$, for all $n \in \mathbb{N}$.*

We think of ω-chains as sequences of elements of X, ordered by $\sqsubseteq$; that is, elements later in the sequence are greater than or equal to elements earlier in the sequence. It is common to write f_n instead of $f(n)$, for the n'th element of the sequence.

Example: the identity function as a chain in $(\mathbb{Z}, \leq)$

The identity function is an ω-chain in the poset $(\mathbb{Z}, \leq)$ (the integers with the standard $\leq$ ordering; see Section 2.4.1). The n'th element of this chain is just n, since the identity function returns n as output when given n as input. We can write the chain as a sequence like this:

$$0, 1, 2, 3, \cdots$$

If we wish to emphasize the ordering, we can use this notation:

$$0 \leq 1 \leq 2 \leq 3 \leq \cdots$$

Example: constant chains

The constant function which always returns 3 is an ω-chain in $(\mathbb{Z}, \leq)$ (see Section 2.4.1). The n'th element of this chain is 3:

$$3 \leq 3 \leq 3 \leq 3 \leq \cdots$$

Indeed, the constant function which returns the same fixed element $x \in X$ for every input $n \in \mathbb{N}$ is always an ω-chain in $(X, \sqsubseteq)$, for every such partially ordered set (assuming X is non-empty, and so has some element $x \in X$ for the function to return).

2.4.3 Upper bounds

Definition 2.4.3 (Upper bound of a set). *Suppose we have some set $S \subseteq X$, where $(X, \sqsubseteq)$ is a poset. An **upper bound** of S is any element $u \in X$ such that for all elements $s \in S$, we have $s \sqsubseteq u$.*

Definition 2.4.4 (Least upper bound of a set). *A least upper bound of S is an upper bound $u \in X$ such that for any other upper bound $u' \in X$, we have $u \sqsubseteq u'$.*

Definition 2.4.5 (Upper and least upper bounds of a chain). *An upper bound of a chain f in poset $(X, \sqsubseteq)$ is an upper bound of the range $\mathrm{ran}(f)$ of f (that is, the set of outputs of f). Similarly, a least upper bound of chain f is a least upper bound of $\mathrm{ran}(f)$.*

Example: upper bound of a constant chain

In $(\mathbb{Z}, \leq)$, the chain $3 \leq 3 \leq 3 \cdots$ has least upper bound 3.

Example: upper bound of the identity chain

In $(\mathbb{Z}, \leq)$, the chain $0 \leq 1 \leq 2 \cdots$ does not have an upper bound (and hence, it cannot have a least upper bound): there is no non-negative integer greater than or equal to all the non-negative integers.

Theorem 2.4.6 (Uniqueness of least upper bounds). *If u and u' are both least upper bounds of S in a partially ordered set $(X, \sqsubseteq)$, then $u = u'$.*

Proof. Since u is a least upper bound of S, it is less than or equal to any other upper bound of u'. Since u' is such an upper bound of S by assumption, we have $u \sqsubseteq u'$. Similarly, we also have $u' \sqsubseteq u$. Then by antisymmetry of $\sqsubseteq$, we get the desired conclusion: $u = u'$. $\qquad\qquad\qquad\qquad\qquad\qquad\qquad\qquad\qquad\qquad\qquad\quad\square$

Definition 2.4.7 ($\sqcup$). *If a set S has a least upper bound, we will denote its unique (by Theorem 2.4.6) least upper bound as $\sqcup S$, and similarly for an ω-chain.*

As an aside, it is worth giving the following definition, even though we will not need it directly for the semantics of `while`-commands.

Definition 2.4.8 (Complete partial order). *A **complete partial order** (or "cpo") is a partially ordered set $(X, \sqsubseteq)$ where every $S \subseteq X$ has a least upper bound.*

Example: the powerset poset as a complete partial order

The powerset poset $(\mathcal{P}(X), \subseteq)$ is a complete partial order. The least upper bound of a set S of subsets of X is just the union $\cup S$ of S, which is the set containing all and only the elements of some element of S. This $\cup S$ clearly is an upper bound of S, since every set in S is included (i.e., is a subset of) $\cup S$. Also, there is no smaller upper bound than $\cup S$, since any smaller set A must exclude some element from one of the sets in S, and hence that set would not be a subset of A.

2.4.4   Predomains and domains

Definition 2.4.9 (Predomain). *A predomain is a partially ordered set $(X, \sqsubseteq)$ such that every ω-chain in $(X, \sqsubseteq)$ has a least upper bound. Predomains are also sometimes called ω-complete partial orders (or ω-cpos).*

Example: integers with ω element

Consider the structure $(\mathbb{Z} \cup \{\omega\}, \leq_\omega)$, where $\leq_\omega$ is just like the ordering $\leq$ on integers, except that it makes ω greater than or equal to itself and to all integers. This structure is a poset. Furthermore, any ω-chain has a least upper bound. If the chain has some maximal element, then that is the upper bound. For example, consider an **eventually constant** chain f, where at some point $n \in \mathbb{N}$, we have $f_{n'} = f_{n'+1}$ for all $n' \geq n$. Such a chain has maximal element f_n, and this is the least upper bound of the chain. Notice that f_n could be in $\mathbb{Z}$, or it could be ω. On the other hand, if the chain increases without a maximal element in the chain, then ω is the least upper bound (and hence must not occur in the chain itself).

Observation 2.4.10 (Cpos are predomains). *Every complete partial order is a predomain.*

Proof. Every chain c has a least upper bound, since every set has a least upper bound, by the definition of complete partial order (Definition 2.4.8). □

Observation 2.4.11 (Least upper bounds of constant chains). *For every partially ordered set $(X, \sqsubseteq)$, every constant chain $c, c, c, \cdots$ in $(X, \sqsubseteq)$ has a least upper bound, namely $c \in X$.*

Proof. We have c greater than or equal to every element in the chain, because it is equal to every element in the chain. There is no strictly smaller element that is equal to c, so this is indeed the least upper bound. □

Example: the discrete partially ordered set

The partially ordered set $(S, =)$ is a predomain, because all chains are constant chains.

Definition 2.4.12 (Eventually constant chains). *Let c be an ω-chain in poset $(X, \sqsubseteq)$. Then c is called **eventually constant** (as we used this term just above) iff there is some value v and some i, such that for every j greater than or equal to i, $c(j) = v$. That is, there is a point at which the chain just repeats the value v forever.*

Observation 2.4.13 (Least upper bounds of eventually constant chains). *Every eventually constant chain c has a least upper bound, namely the value v that is repeated infinitely.*

Proof. As for the preceding observation, the value v is greater than or equal to every element in the chain. Since it actually occurs in the chain, no lesser upper bound is possible. So v is the least upper bound. □

Definition 2.4.14 (Strictly increasing chains). *Let c an ω-chain in poset $(X, \sqsubseteq)$. Then c is called **strictly increasing** iff for all $i \in \mathbb{N}$, there exists a $j > i$ such that have $c(i) \neq c(j)$. This definition leaves open the possibility of finite repetitions of elements in the chain, but not infinite repetition of elements (as in eventually constant chains).*

Definition 2.4.15 (Least element). *A **least element** of a poset $(X, \sqsubseteq)$ is an element $\bot \in X$ such that for all elements $x \in X$, we have $\bot \sqsubseteq x$.*

Theorem 2.4.16 (Uniqueness of least element). *If poset $(X, \sqsubseteq)$ has a least element $\bot$, then $\bot$ is its only least element.*

Proof. We prove that all least elements $\bot'$ are equal to $\bot$. By the definition of least element, we have $\bot \sqsubseteq \bot'$ and also $\bot' \sqsubseteq \bot$, since both $\bot$ and $\bot'$ are least elements (so they must both be less than or equal to each other). But then by antisymmetry, $\bot = \bot'$ (since we have that each is less than or equal to the other). $\qquad\qquad\square$

Example: integers and naturals

The poset of integers ordered by $\leq$ does not have a least element. But if we consider the poset of natural numbers $\mathbb{N}$ ordered by $\leq$ then 0 is the least element.

Definition 2.4.17 (Domain). *A domain is a predomain $(X, \sqsubseteq)$ with a least element. We may write $(X, \sqsubseteq, \bot)$ to indicate the least element, which is unique by Theorem 2.4.16.*

Example: $(\mathbb{N} \cup \{\omega\}, \leq_\omega)$

The structure $(\mathbb{N} \cup \{\omega\}, \leq_\omega)$, which is like one considered in an example in Section 2.4.2 except that it does not include negative integers, is a domain. The least element is 0. We have already argued that ω-chains have least upper bounds in this structure.

Example: the divisibility poset

The divisibility poset is a domain. This is rather surprising, so let us look closely. First, we can consider what the least element of this poset is. It should be some natural number x which divides every other natural number. There is such a number, of course, namely 1. To show that the divisibility poset is a predomain, we must argue that every ω-chain c has a least upper bound. The central observation here is that since every number divides 0 (since for any number x, there exists a number y – namely 0 – such that $0 = x \cdot y$). So every chain has an upper bound. We know from Observation 2.4.13 that eventually constant chains have least upper bounds. So if we consider chains that increase forever, we can see there is no upper bound for the chain other than 0. So 0 is the least upper bound.

2.5   Continuous functions

We are very close to being able to prove the main theorem of this chapter, Theorem 2.6.6 (proved in the next section), which will enable us to solve the puzzle of how to give a well-founded recursive equation defining the interpretation of while-commands. The last technical concept we need for Theorem 2.6.6 is that of a continuous function, which is a special kind of monotonic function. The definitions follow.

Definition 2.5.1 (Monotonic function). *Suppose $(X_1, \sqsubseteq_1)$ and $(X_2, \sqsubseteq_2)$ are partially ordered sets. Then a function f from X_1 to X_2 is **monotonic** with respect to those partially ordered sets iff for elements $x_1, x_1' \in X_1$ (that is, for every two elements x_1 and x_1' of X_1), if $x_1 \sqsubseteq_1 x_1'$, then also $f(x_1) \sqsubseteq_2 f(x_1')$. In this case, we also speak of f being a monotonic function from the first partially ordered set (that is, the entire structure $(X_1, \sqsubseteq_1)$) to the second.*

This is a special case of the general algebraic idea of a structure-preserving function. The structure is preserved in the sense that elements related in a certain way in the first structure are mapped by the function to elements related in a corresponding way in the second structure. Here, the two structures are the partially ordered sets $(X_1, \sqsubseteq_1)$ and $(X_2, \sqsubseteq_2)$, and the structure which is being preserved is the ordering.

Example: finite cardinality function

The cardinality function for finite sets is a monotonic function from the partially ordered set $(\mathcal{P}(X), \subseteq)$ (see Section 2.4.1) to $(\mathbb{N}, \leq)$. This cardinality function, denoted $|\cdot|$, maps finite sets to their sizes (i.e., the number of elements in the set). For example, $|\{9, 16, 25\}| = 3$, and $|\varnothing| = 0$. To see that this function is monotonic for the given partially ordered sets, we must confirm that whenever we have subsets S_1 and S_2 of X, with $S_1 \subseteq S_2$, then we also have $|S_1| \leq |S_2|$. But this is certainly true: since S_2 has all the elements which S_1 has, and possibly some more, its cardinality must be at least as big as $|S_1|$.

Example: successor function

The function *Suc* which maps n to $n + 1$ for every $n \in \mathbb{N}$ is a monotonic function from $(\mathbb{N}, \leq)$ to $(\mathbb{N}, \leq)$. This is because of the elementary arithmetic fact that $n_1 \leq n_2$ implies $n_1 + 1 \leq n_2 + 1$.

For the statement of the next theorem to make sense, we need the following observation. Let $(X_1, \sqsubseteq_1)$ and $(X_2, \sqsubseteq_2)$ be predomains. Since a predomain is, by definition, also a partially ordered set, it makes sense to consider a monotonic function f from $(X_1, \sqsubseteq_1)$ to $(X_2, \sqsubseteq_2)$ (since those predomains are also partially ordered sets). Similarly, it also makes sense to speak of a monotonic function f from domain $(X_1, \sqsubseteq_1, \perp_1)$ to a domain $(X_2, \sqsubseteq_2, \perp_2)$, since domains are also partially ordered sets.

Theorem 2.5.2 (Preservation of chains). *If f is a monotonic function from predomain $(X_1, \sqsubseteq_1)$ to predomain $(X_2, \sqsubseteq_2)$, and if c is an ω-chain in $(X_1, \sqsubseteq_1)$, then $f \circ c$ (the composition of functions f and c) is an ω-chain in $(X_2, \sqsubseteq_2)$.*

Proof. First, we need to understand why it makes sense to write $f \circ c$ here. Recall from basic discrete mathematics the definition of function composition: the function $f \circ c$ returns $f(c(x))$ when called with input x. In our case, since c is an ω-chain in $(X_1, \sqsubseteq_1)$ by assumption, it is a function from $\mathbb{N}$ to X_1. Now function f maps X_1 to X_2. So given $n \in \mathbb{N}$, $f \circ c$ will return $f(c(n))$. This is well-defined, since $c(n) \in X_1$, and f accepts inputs in X_1. Thus, $f \circ c$ is a function mapping $\mathbb{N}$ to X_2.

We need to see now that this function is really an ω-chain in $(X_2, \sqsubseteq_2)$. From Definition 2.4.2, we just have to show that the elements in the sequence $f \circ c$ are ordered by $\sqsubseteq_2$. That is, we must show that for any $n \in \mathbb{N}$, we have $f(c(n)) \sqsubseteq_2 f(c(n+1))$. Because c is an ω-chain in $(X_1, \sqsubseteq_1)$, we have $c(n) \sqsubseteq_1 c(n+1)$ by the definition of ω-chain. Then because f is monotonic, $f(c(n)) \sqsubseteq_2 f(c(n+1))$. That is, f respects the structure of $(X_1, \sqsubseteq_1)$, so if we have elements x and y of X_1 – and here, those elements are $c(n)$ and $c(n+1)$ – such that $x \sqsubseteq_1 y$, then we also have $f(x) \sqsubseteq_2 f(y)$. So we have confirmed that $f \circ c$ is an ω-chain in $(X_2, \sqsubseteq_2)$. $\square$

Definition 2.5.3 (Continuous function). *Let f be a monotonic function from predomain $(X_1, \sqsubseteq_1)$ to predomain $(X_2, \sqsubseteq_2)$. Then f is **continuous** iff for every ω-chain c in $(X_1, \sqsubseteq_1)$, we have*

$$f(\sqcup c) = \sqcup(f \circ c)$$

*This latter condition is called the **continuity condition**.*

Let us translate this latter equation into English. The left hand side of the equation is $f(\sqcup c)$. If we think of this operationally, it says to apply f to the least upper bound of chain c. Since c is an ω-chain in predomain $(X_1, \sqsubseteq_1)$, it does have a least upper bound (again, by definition of predomain). The right hand side of the equation refers to the least upper bound of the chain $f \circ c$. Recall from Theorem 2.5.2 just above that this composition of functions f and c is indeed an ω-chain in $(X_2, \sqsubseteq_2)$. Since $(X_2, \sqsubseteq_2)$ is a predomain, by definition we know that any ω-chain in $(X_2, \sqsubseteq_2)$ has a least upper bound. So $\sqcup(f \circ c)$ is indeed defined.

To summarize: monotonic function f is continuous iff for every chain c, the value returned by f for the least upper bound of c is equal to the least upper bound of the chain obtained by applying f to each element of c. There is a common less precise but more memorable way to put this. We can refer more briefly to the least upper bound of a chain as the **limit** of the chain. Then continuity says: *"f of the limit equals the limit of the f's."*

A positive example

This example concerns the domain $(\mathbb{N} \cup \{\omega\}, \leq_\omega)$. Consider the function f defined on $\mathbb{N} \cup \{\omega\}$ by

$$f(x) = \begin{cases} x + 1 & \text{if } x \in \mathbb{N} \\ \omega & \text{if } x = \omega \end{cases}$$

This function is continuous from $(\mathbb{N} \cup \{\omega\}, \leq_\omega)$ to $(\mathbb{N} \cup \{\omega\}, \leq_\omega)$. We must show that for any chain c, $f(\sqcup c) = \sqcup(f \circ c)$. Suppose the chain is eventually constant, with least upper bound $n \in \mathbb{N}$. The chain $f \circ c$ is then also eventually constant, with least upper bound $n + 1$. Then we have:

$$f(\sqcup c) = f(n) = n + 1 = \sqcup(f \circ c)$$

If c is eventually constant with least upper bound ω, then the chain $f \circ c$ also is eventually constant with least upper bound ω, and we have

$$f(\sqcup c) = f(\omega) = \omega = \sqcup(f \circ c)$$

Finally, if c is strictly increasing (Definition 2.4.14), then it must consist solely of elements of $\mathbb{N}$. In that case, the least upper bound of f is ω. The chain $f \circ c$ is also strictly increasing, and so for the same reason also has least upper bound ω. So we have

$$f(\sqcup c) = f(\omega) = \omega = \sqcup(f \circ c)$$

A negative example

We again consider the domain $(\mathbb{N} \cup \{\omega\}, \leq_\omega)$, and now look at a function f which is not continuous:

$$f(x) = \begin{cases} 0 & \text{if } x \in \mathbb{N} \\ 1 & \text{if } x = \omega \end{cases}$$

Notice that this function is monotonic from $(\mathbb{N} \cup \{\omega\}, \leq_\omega)$ to $(\mathbb{N} \cup \{\omega\}, \leq_\omega)$: we have only to check that when $f(x) \leq_\omega f(y)$ and $f(x) \neq f(y)$ then we must have had $x \leq_\omega y$. We only have $f(x) \leq_\omega f(y)$ and $f(x) \neq f(y)$ when $x \in \mathbb{N}$ and $y = \omega$, in which case we indeed have $x \leq_\omega y$. To prove that f is not continuous, it suffices by the definition of continuity to exhibit a single chain c where the continuity condition is violated. Consider the identity function id as a chain in this poset (i.e., $0, 1, 2, \ldots$). The least upper bound is ω. On the other hand, the chain $f \circ id$ is just a constant chain, where all values are 0. We have:

$$f(\sqcup id) = f(\omega) = 1 \neq 0 = \sqcup(f \circ id)$$

So this function f is not continuous.

Theorem 2.5.4 (Continuity bound). *Suppose f is a monotonic function from predomain $(X_1, \sqsubseteq_1)$ to predomain $(X_2, \sqsubseteq_2)$. Then for every ω-chain c in $(X_1, \sqsubseteq_1)$, we have*

$$\sqcup(f \circ c) \sqsubseteq f(\sqcup c)$$

Proof. To prove that $f(\sqcup c)$ is greater than or equal to the least upper bound $\sqcup(f \circ c)$ of chain $f \circ t$, it suffices to prove that it is an upper bound of that chain. So prove, for an arbitrary $n \in \mathbb{N}$:

$$f(c(n)) \sqsubseteq f(\sqcup c)$$

But this follows easily, since $c(n) \sqsubseteq \sqcup c$ by definition of $\sqcup c$, and f is monotonic. □

Corollary 2.5.5 (Sufficient condition for continuity). *Let f be a monotonic function from predomain $(X_1, \sqsubseteq_1)$ to predomain $(X_2, \sqsubseteq_2)$. Then f is **continuous** iff for every ω-chain c in $(X_1, \sqsubseteq_1)$, we have*

$$f(\sqcup c) \sqsubseteq \sqcup(f \circ c)$$

Proof. This follows from Theorem 2.5.4 and the definition of continuity. □

2.6   The least fixed-point theorem

Definition 2.6.1 (Fixed point). *A fixed point of a function f is just some input x such that $f(x) = x$.*

Definition 2.6.2 (Least fixed point). *Suppose that $(X, \sqsubseteq)$ is a partially ordered set. A least fixed point in $(X, \sqsubseteq)$ of a function f is a fixed point $x \in X$ of f which is less than or equal to any other fixed point in X. That is, for any fixed point $x' \in X$ of f, we have $x \sqsubseteq x'$.*

Theorem 2.6.3 (Uniqueness of least fixed point). *If function f has least fixed points x and x' in $(X, \sqsubseteq)$, then $x = x'$.*

Proof. The proof is similar to that of Theorem 2.4.6 above: since x and x' are least fixed points by assumptions, we must have $x \sqsubseteq x'$ and $x' \sqsubseteq x$, and hence $x = x'$ by antisymmetry of $\sqsubseteq$.   □

Definition 2.6.4 (lfp). *We will denote the unique least fixed point of f, if that exists, by $lfp(f)$.*

Definition 2.6.5 ($f^n(x)$). *Suppose function f maps X to X. Then for $x \in X$ and $n \in \mathbb{N}$, we define the n-**fold iteration of** f **on** x, with notation $f^n(x)$, by recursion on n:*

$$
\begin{aligned}
f^0(x) &= x \\
f^{n+1}(x) &= f(f^n(x))
\end{aligned}
$$

Theorem 2.6.6 (Least Fixed Point). *Suppose f is a continuous function from a domain $(X, \sqsubseteq, \bot)$ to itself. Let c be the function which returns output $f^n(\bot)$ for input $n \in \mathbb{N}$. Then c is an ω-chain in $(X, \sqsubseteq)$, and $lfp(f) = \sqcup c$.*

Proof. We divide the proof into three parts. First, we show that the chain c is indeed an ω-chain in $(X, \sqsubseteq)$. Then we will prove that $\sqcup c$ is a fixed point of f. Finally, we will show that it is the least fixed point.

The chain c is an ω-chain in $(X, \sqsubseteq)$

First, let us confirm that c maps $n \in \mathbb{N}$ to an element of X. This is proved by induction on n:

<u>Base case.</u> If n is 0, then $c(n) = f^0(\bot) = \bot$, and $\bot \in X$ by the definition of domain.

<u>Step case.</u> Assume $f^n(\bot) \in X$ (this is the induction hypothesis), and show $f^{n+1}(\bot) \in X$. By definition, we have $f^{n+1}(\bot) = f(f^n(\bot))$. By the induction hypothesis, $f^n(\bot) \in X$, so then the output f returns for that value is also in X (since f maps X to X).

Next, we must show that c is ordered by $\sqsubseteq$: for all $n \in \mathbb{N}$, $c(n) \sqsubseteq c(n+1)$. This is also proved by induction on n.

Base case. If n is 0, then $c(n) = \bot$, and $c(n+1) = f(\bot)$. Since $\bot$ is the least element of X by the definition of domain, we have $\bot \sqsubseteq f(\bot)$, and so $c(n) \sqsubseteq c(n+1)$ in this case.

Step case. Assume that $f^n(\bot) \sqsubseteq f^{n+1}(\bot)$ (this is the induction hypothesis), and show that $f^{n+1}(\bot) \sqsubseteq f^{n+2}(\bot)$. By definition, this latter fact which we are supposed to prove can be written:

$$f(f^n(\bot)) \sqsubseteq f(f^{n+1}(\bot))$$

Since f is monotonic (because it is assumed to be continuous, which implies monotonicity), this fact follows from the induction hypothesis: we have two elements, $f^n(\bot)$ and $f^{n+1}(\bot)$, which are ordered by $\sqsubseteq$, so monotonicity tells us that the results of applying f to each of those elements will also be ordered by $\sqsubseteq$.

The value $\sqcup c$ is a fixed point of f

We have just completed the proof that the function c defined in the statement of the theorem is indeed an ω-chain of $(X, \sqsubseteq)$. So certainly $\sqcup c$ is defined, since $(X, \sqsubseteq, \bot)$ is a domain (and hence all ω-chains have least upper bounds in X). Now let us argue that $\sqcup c$ is a least fixed point of f. First we will prove it is a fixed point:

$$f(\sqcup c) = \sqcup c$$

By continuity of f, we know that

$$f(\sqcup c) = \sqcup(f \circ c)$$

So we only need to show the following fact to conclude $f(\sqcup c) = \sqcup c$:

$$\sqcup(f \circ c) = \sqcup c$$

This is sufficient, because we could then combine the two most recently displayed equations using transitivity of equality: $f(\sqcup c) = \sqcup(f \circ c) = \sqcup c$. To prove this last equation ($\sqcup(f \circ c) = \sqcup c$), it suffices to show (in other words, if we can prove what comes next, that will be enough, even if there are other ways to do the proof) that $\sqcup c$ is the least upper bound of $f \circ c$. Let us temporarily use the name c' for the chain $f \circ c$.

We'll first prove that $\sqcup c$ is an upper bound of c' (i.e., $f \circ c$), and then that it is the least such. For any $n \in \mathbb{N}$, we know

$$c'(n) = f(c(n)) = f(f^n(\bot)) = f^{n+1}(\bot) = c(n+1)$$

So the n'th element of c' is the $(n+1)$'th element of c. To prove that $\sqcup c$ is an upper bound of c', we just have to show that $c'(n) \sqsubseteq \sqcup c$. Since $\sqcup c$ is an upper bound of

c, we have for all $n' \in \mathbb{N}$ that $c(n') \sqsubseteq \sqcup c$. This is true if we instantiate n' with the $n+1$ we are currently considering:

$$c'(n) = c(n+1) \sqsubseteq \sqcup c$$

This shows that $\sqcup c$ is an upper bound of c'. To show it is the least such, suppose there is some $u \in X$ such that u is an upper bound of c' which is strictly smaller than $\sqcup c$. That is, suppose $u \neq \sqcup c$ but $u \sqsubseteq \sqcup c$. Since u is an upper bound of c', it is greater than $c'(n)$, for every $n \in \mathbb{N}$. But this implies that it is greater than $f^{n+1}(\bot)$ for every such n. So we have $f^{n'}(\bot) \sqsubseteq u$ for every $n' \in \mathbb{N}$ which equals $n+1$ for some $n \in \mathbb{N}$. That leaves only the case of $f^0(\bot)$ to consider. But by definition, this is equal to $\bot$, and since $\bot$ is the least element (since $(X, \sqsubseteq, \bot)$ is a domain by assumption), we also have $f^0(\bot) \sqsubseteq u$. So u is actually an upper bound of the original chain c, not just c'. But then it cannot be strictly smaller than $\sqcup c$, since $\sqcup c$ is the least upper bound of c.

The value $\sqcup c$ is the least fixed point of f

Suppose there is another fixed point a of f. We will show $\sqcup c \sqsubseteq a$ by showing that $f^n(\bot) \sqsubseteq a$, for all $n \in \mathbb{N}$. This is sufficient, by the definition of c. We will prove the claim by induction on n.

Base case. If n is 0, then $f^n(\bot) = \bot$, and we have $\bot \sqsubseteq a$ because $\bot$ is the least element of domain $(X, \sqsubseteq, \bot)$.

Step case. Assume that $f^n(\bot) \sqsubseteq a$ (this is the induction hypothesis), and show $f^{n+1}(\bot) \sqsubseteq a$. By the induction hypothesis, we have $f^n(\bot) \sqsubseteq a$. Since f is continuous by assumption, and hence monotonic, this latter equation implies:

$$f(f^n(\bot)) \sqsubseteq f(a)$$

But since we are assuming (for purposes of this part of the proof) that a is a fixed point of f, we have $f(a) = a$, and the displayed equation just above is then equivalent to:

$$f(f^n(\bot)) \sqsubseteq a$$

By definition of n-fold iteration (Definition 2.6.5), we have $f^{n+1}(\bot) = f(f^n(\bot))$, and so this latter displayed equation is equivalent to $f^{n+1} \sqsubseteq a$, as required for this step case.

This concludes the proof of Theorem 2.6.6. □

2.7 Completing the formal semantics of commands

Armed now with the Least Fixed Point Theorem, we can complete the definition we began in Section 2.2 of the denotational semantics for WHILE commands. For this, it is helpful to recast the definition of the semantics we have so far, which is:

$$
\begin{array}{lcl}
[\![\texttt{skip}]\!]\sigma & = & \sigma \\
[\![x := t]\!]\sigma & = & \sigma[x \mapsto term[\![t]\!]\sigma] \\
[\![c_1 \,; c_2]\!]\sigma & = & \text{if } [\![c_1]\!]\sigma =\bot \text{ then } \bot; \text{ otherwise,} [\![c_2]\!]([\![c_1]\!]\sigma) \\
[\![\texttt{if } t \ pred \ t' \ \texttt{then } c_1 \ \texttt{else } c_2]\!]\sigma & = & \text{if the relation for } pred \text{ holds of} \\
& & \quad term[\![t]\!]\sigma, term[\![t']\!]\sigma, \\
& & \quad \text{then } [\![c_1]\!]\sigma; \\
& & \quad \text{otherwise } [\![c_2]\!]\sigma
\end{array}
$$

As we will see next, it is more convenient to define $[\![c]\!]$ as a function that takes in the input state and produces the output state, rather than define $[\![c]\!]\sigma$ to be the output state, when σ is the input state. So the revised definition is the following, where I am writing $\sigma \mapsto e$ to indicate the mathematical function which maps any input state σ to the output state σ' described by meta-level expression e.

$$
\begin{array}{lcl}
[\![\texttt{skip}]\!] & = & \sigma \mapsto \sigma \\
[\![x := t]\!] & = & \sigma \mapsto \sigma[x \mapsto term[\![t]\!]\sigma] \\
[\![c_1 \,; c_2]\!] & = & \sigma \mapsto \text{if } [\![c_1]\!]\sigma =\bot \text{ then } \bot; \text{ otherwise,} [\![c_2]\!]([\![c_1]\!]\sigma) \\
[\![\texttt{if } t \ pred \ t' \ \texttt{then } c_1 \ \texttt{else } c_2]\!] & = & \sigma \mapsto \text{if the relation for } pred \text{ holds of} \\
& & \quad term[\![t]\!]\sigma, term[\![t']\!]\sigma, \\
& & \quad \text{then } [\![c_1]\!]\sigma; \\
& & \quad \text{otherwise } [\![c_2]\!]\sigma
\end{array}
$$

Now to describe the semantics of while-commands, we are going to use the Least Fixed Point Theorem to construct another mathematical function, like those described by the expressions $\sigma \mapsto e$ just above. These are functions from Σ to $\Sigma \cup \{\bot\}$. This mathematical function is going to be the least fixed point of a continuous function F, operating on elements of the set $\Sigma \to \Sigma \cup \{\bot\}$ of functions from Σ to $\Sigma \cup \{\bot\}$. Before we have a hope of defining a continuous function, we need to know that the set of functions $\Sigma \to \Sigma \cup \{\bot\}$ can be given the structure of a domain.

2.7.1 The domain of functions $(\Sigma \to \Sigma_\bot, \sqsubseteq_f, \bot_f)$

To give the set of functions $\Sigma \to \Sigma \cup \{\bot\}$ a domain structure, we start by defining the **lifted domain** $\Sigma_\bot$. Then we will show that the set of functions from Σ to $\Sigma_\bot$ is a domain. In general, a lifted domain is formed by adding a new least element to an existing predomain. In our case, we need only do this for the discrete predomain $(\Sigma, =)$. So the following less general definition is sufficient.

Definition 2.7.1 (The lifted domain $(S_\bot, =_\bot, \bot)$). *Let S be a set not containing the special object $\bot$. The lifted domain $(S_\bot, =_\bot, \bot)$ consists of the set $S_\bot$, which is defined to be $S \cup \{\bot\}$; the ordering $=_\bot$ which makes $\bot$ less than or equal to every element of $S \cup \{\bot\}$, and all elements of Σ less or equal to themselves; and has (therefore) least element $\bot$. This is easily confirmed to be a poset. It is also a predomain, because all chains contain a maximal element (either $\bot$ or else some element of S). And it has least element $\bot$ by construction.*

Now that we know that the range $\Sigma_\perp$ of the functions we are interested in forms a domain, we must show that $\Sigma \to \Sigma_\perp$ also forms a domain. We do this by considering a general construction for imposing a domain structure on a set of functions.

Theorem 2.7.2 (Domain of functions). *Suppose A is a set and $(X, \sqsubseteq, \perp)$ is a domain. Then so is $(A \to X, \sqsubseteq_f, \perp_f)$, where the "$f$" subscript is for "function", and the definitions of the components are:*

- *$A \to X$ is the set of all total functions from A to X.*

- *For all total functions f_1 and f_2 in $A \to X$, we define the **pointwise ordering** $\sqsubseteq_f$ by:*

$$f_1 \sqsubseteq_f f_2 \Leftrightarrow \forall a \in A.\ f_1(a) \sqsubseteq f_2(a)$$

- *$\perp_f$ is the function defined by:*

$$\forall a \in A.\ \perp_f(a) = \perp$$

Proof. Reflexivity, transitivity, and antisymmetry all follow easily from those properties for $\sqsubseteq$. We do one proof here as an example. To prove transitivity, suppose we have functions f_1, f_2, and f_3 with:

$$f_1 \sqsubseteq_f f_2 \sqsubseteq_f f_3$$

This implies that

$$\forall a \in A.\ f_1(a) \sqsubseteq f_2(a) \sqsubseteq f_3(a)$$

By transitivity of $\sqsubseteq$, we have:

$$\forall a \in A.\ f_1(a) \sqsubseteq f_3(a)$$

So we indeed have $f_1 \sqsubseteq_f f_3$.

Next, we must show that every ω-chain c has a least upper bound in $(A \to X, \sqsubseteq_f, \perp_f)$. Let us draw this chain of functions this way:

$$
\begin{array}{ccccccc}
\cdots & & \cdots & & \cdots & & \\
a' \mapsto c_0(a') & & a' \mapsto c_1(a') & & a' \mapsto c_2(a') & & \\
a \mapsto c_0(a) & \sqsubseteq & a \mapsto c_1(a) & \sqsubseteq & a \mapsto c_2(a) & \sqsubseteq & \cdots \\
a'' \mapsto c_0(a'') & & a'' \mapsto c_1(a'') & & a'' \mapsto c_2(a'') & & \\
\cdots & & \cdots & & \cdots & &
\end{array}
$$

Each function is depicted by a column showing a few of the mappings that function contains (the function might not contain any mappings, if A is empty, but let us not try to depict this case).

Now we want to construct the limit of this chain of functions. To do this, we need to observe that for any $a \in A$, the values of the functions $c_0, c_1, \ldots$ form an ω-chain in $(X, \sqsubseteq, \perp)$. In more detail: for any element $a \in A$, the function q_a defined as follows is an ω-chain in $(X, \sqsubseteq, \perp)$:

$$\forall n \in \mathbb{N}.\ q_a(n) = c_n(a)$$

This q_a maps each $n \in \mathbb{N}$ to the value given by the n'th function in the chain c. We can see that q_a is a chain in $(X, \sqsubseteq, \bot)$, because $c_n(a) \sqsubseteq c_{n+1}(a)$ follows from $c_n \sqsubseteq_f c_{n+1}$, by definition of the ordering $\sqsubseteq_f$. Graphically, we can depict the chain q_a by highlighting it in the previous diagram:

$$
\begin{array}{ccccccc}
\cdots & & \cdots & & \cdots & & \\
a' \mapsto c_0(a') & & a' \mapsto c_1(a') & & a' \mapsto c_2(a') & & \\
a \mapsto c_0(a) & \sqsubseteq & a \mapsto c_1(a) & \sqsubseteq & a \mapsto c_2(a) & \sqsubseteq & \cdots \\
a'' \mapsto c_0(a'') & & a'' \mapsto c_1(a'') & & a'' \mapsto c_2(a'') & & \\
\cdots & & \cdots & & \cdots & &
\end{array}
$$

Now the function which we will show is the least upper bound of c is the one which given any element $a \in A$, will return the least upper bound of the chain q_a (highlighted above). To define this formally, let $\hat{c}$ be the function defined by:

$$\forall a \in A.\ \hat{c}(a) = \bigsqcup q_a$$

Since q_a is a chain in domain $(X, \sqsubseteq, \bot)$, we know that it has a least upper bound $\bigsqcup q_a$. So the above definition for $\hat{c}$ is meaningful. It is this $\hat{c}$ which is the least upper bound of the original chain c in $(A \to X, \sqsubseteq_f, \bot_f)$. This follows, by the definition of $\sqsubseteq_f$, from the fact that for all $n \in \mathbb{N}$:

$$\forall a \in A.\ c_n(a) \sqsubseteq \hat{c}(a)$$

That is, for each input $a \in A$ to the functions in questions, $c_n(a) \sqsubseteq \hat{c}(a)$. This fact holds because $\hat{c}(a) = \bigsqcup q_a$, where $\bigsqcup q_a$ is the least upper bound of the chain containing $q_a(n)$, which is defined to be $c_n(a)$.

Finally, we must prove that $\bot_f$ is the least element. But this follows easily, because for all $a \in A$, and any element f of the set $A \to X$, we have:

$$\bot_f(a) = \bot \sqsubseteq f(a)$$

$\square$

One helpful way to think about the pointwise ordering is graphically. Imagine we have two functions f and g with a common poset as their range. Then f is less than or equal to g iff the graph of f is everywhere at or below the graph of g. An example is given in Figure 2.2.

2.7.2 The semantics of `while`-commands

We can now define:

$$[\![\texttt{while } t \text{ } pred \text{ } t' \text{ do } c]\!] \ = \ lfp(F)$$

$$
\text{where } F \quad = \quad w \mapsto (\sigma \mapsto \text{ if } [\![t]\!]\sigma \text{ is not related according to } pred
$$

with $[\![t']\!]\sigma$

then σ

else if $[\![c]\!]\sigma = \bot$ then $\bot$

else $w([\![c]\!]\sigma))$

Figure 2.2: Function f is pointwise less than or equal to function g

Note that here, the function F takes in a function $w \in (\Sigma \to \Sigma_\perp)$, and then returns a new function which takes in $\sigma \in \Sigma$ and returns an element of $\Sigma_\perp$. So F is a function operating on a set of functions: it takes a function as input and returns a function as output. Such a function is sometimes called a **functional**, or a higher-order function.

For our definition of the semantics of while-commands to be meaningful, we must prove that this functional F is continuous in the domain $(\Sigma \to \Sigma_\perp, \sqsubseteq_f, \perp_f)$. If it is, then the Least Fixed Point Theorem tells us it indeed has a least fixed point in that domain, and so $lfp(F)$ is defined.

2.7.3 Continuity of F

Let us confirm that F is continuous. We must first show that it is monotonic. If we have inputs w and w' with $w \sqsubseteq_f w'$, then we must show that $F(w) \sqsubseteq_f F(w')$. By the definition of the ordering $\sqsubseteq_f$, it is sufficient to assume some arbitrary state $\sigma \in \Sigma$, and prove that

$$F(w)(\sigma) =_\perp F(w')(\sigma) \tag{2.2}$$

If $[\![t]\!]\sigma$ is not related according to *pred* with $[\![t']\!]\sigma$, then both $F(w)(\sigma)$ and $F(w')(\sigma)$ are equal to σ. So in that case, we have Equation 2.2 by reflexivity of $=_\perp$. Similarly, if $[\![t]\!]\sigma$ is related according to *pred* with $[\![t']\!]\sigma$ but $[\![c]\!]\sigma =_\perp$, then we again have $F(w)(\sigma) = F(w')(\sigma)$, and hence Equation 2.2 by reflexivity of $=_\perp$. Finally, suppose that we are in the third case of the definition of $[\![\cdot]\!]$ on the while-command. In this case:

$$F(w)(\sigma) \quad = w([\![c]\!]\sigma) \tag{2.3}$$
$$F(w')(\sigma) \quad = w'([\![c]\!]\sigma) \tag{2.4}$$

But since $w \sqsubseteq_f w'$, we have $w(x) =_\perp w'(x)$, for any state $x \in \Sigma$. So we do have $w([\![c]\!]\sigma) =_\perp w'([\![c]\!]\sigma)$, and thus we get Equation 2.2 using Equations 2.3 and 2.4. This concludes the proof that F is monotonic.

Now let us confirm that F satisfies the continuity condition. Assume an arbitrary ω-chain d in domain $(\Sigma \to \Sigma_\perp, \sqsubseteq_f, \perp_f)$. (Just for clarity: since d is a chain in a domain of functions, each element d_n of d is a function from Σ to $\Sigma_\perp$.) We must show that

$$F(\sqcup d) = \sqcup(F \circ d)$$

The left and right hand sides of this equation both denote functions from Σ to $\Sigma_\perp$. It suffices to prove the following, for an arbitrary $\sigma \in \Sigma$:

$$F(\sqcup d)(\sigma) = (\sqcup(F \circ d))(\sigma) \tag{2.5}$$

From the proof of Theorem 2.7.2, we know that the least upper bound of a chain d of functions in this domain is a function $\hat{d}$ defined by:

$$\hat{d}(\sigma) = \sqcup d_\sigma$$

where d_σ is the chain defined by

$$\forall n \in \mathbb{N}.\ d_\sigma(n) = d_n(\sigma)$$

So if we temporarily define $\hat{d}$ to be $\sqcup(F \circ d)$, from the right hand side of Formula 2.5, we know that:

$$\forall \sigma \in \Sigma.\ \hat{e}(\sigma) = \sqcup d'_\sigma$$

where the function d'_σ is defined by

$$\forall n \in \mathbb{N}.\ d'_\sigma(n) = F(d_n)(\sigma)$$

So to show Equation 2.5, we just need to show

$$F(\sqcup d)(\sigma) = \sqcup d'_\sigma \tag{2.6}$$

We can complete the proof by considering which case of the definition of F we are in, for this σ. Recall the definition from Section 2.7.2 above:

$$F = w \mapsto (\sigma \mapsto \text{ if } [\![t]\!]\sigma \text{ is not related according to } pred \text{ with } [\![t']\!]\sigma \text{ then } \sigma$$
$$\text{else if } [\![c]\!]\sigma = \perp \text{ then } \perp$$
$$\text{else } w([\![c]\!]\sigma))$$

If we are in the first case, then the left hand side of Equation 2.6, namely $F(\sqcup d)(\sigma)$, is equal to σ. Also, for every $n \in \mathbb{N}$, we have

$$d'_\sigma(n) = F(d_n)(\sigma) = \sigma$$

So $\sqcup d'_\sigma = \sigma$ in this case, and the two sides of Equation 2.6 are both equal to σ. Similarly, in the second case of the definition for F, both sides of Equation 2.6 are equal to $\perp$. Finally, in the third case, we have these equations starting from the left hand side of Equation 2.6:

$$F(\sqcup d)(\sigma) = (\sqcup d)([\![c]\!]\sigma) = \sqcup d_{[\![c]\!]\sigma}$$

The final crucial fact is that the chains $d_{[\![c]\!]\sigma}$ and d'_σ are equal, since for all $n \in \mathbb{N}$, we have

$$d'_\sigma(n) = F(d_n)(\sigma) = d_n([\![c]\!]\sigma) = d_{[\![c]\!]\sigma}(n)$$

So, the left and right hand sides of Equation 2.6 both equal $\sqcup d_{[\![c]\!]\sigma}$ in this case.

2.7.4 Examples

Let us consider how the meaning of the trivial looping command while $0 = 0$ do skip is computed using the above semantics. We have the following equation (for F specialized to this particular while-command):

$$\llbracket \text{while } 0 = 0 \text{ do skip} \rrbracket = lfp(F)$$

To compute the least fixed point of F, we should consider the chain of elements which the Least Fixed Point Theorem (Theorem 2.6.6) tells us has the least fixed point of F as its least upper bound:

$$\bot_f, F(\bot_f), F(F(\bot_f)), \ldots$$

Let us consider these functions more closely. The function $\bot_f$ just returns $\bot$ for any input state σ. This is, in fact, what we expect the final semantics of while $0 = 0$ do skip to be. Now consider $F(\bot_f)$:

$$F(\bot_f)(\sigma) = \bot_f (\llbracket \text{skip} \rrbracket \sigma) = \bot$$

This is true because we are always going to fall into the third case of F, where the guard is true in state σ and execution of the body has not diverged. Indeed, we can easily prove that for all $n \in \mathbb{N}$, $F^n(\bot_f)(\sigma) = \bot$, by induction on n (a very similar case is considered in Exercise 2 of Section 2.11.3 below).

2.8 Connection to practice: static analysis using abstract interpretation

Denotational semantics provides an important theoretical tool for defining the meaning of languages, including logics and programming languages, as we have seen in this chapter. Denotational semantics is also used in practice as the basis for **static analysis** of programs. Static analysis aims to discover properties of all possible dynamic executions of a program, just by inspecting code statically (i.e., at compile-time, before actually executing the program on any inputs). Static analysis is, at the time of this writing, a very active area of research, with many papers written on advanced analyses for automatic bug-finding, verification, compiler optimizations, and other applications. See proceedings of conferences like Principles of Programming Languages (POPL), Computer-Aided Verification (CAV), Programming Language Design and Implementation (PLDI), to name just three prominent venues, for many examples of such work. Furthermore, static analysis is being applied in industry to improve code quality. For just one example, Microsoft has developed and applied static analysis tools internally for finding bugs in the Windows operating system [29].

The form of static analysis known as **abstract interpretation** can be developed as an alternative denotational semantics for programs, based on taking some domain other than $\Sigma_\bot$ as the basis for the domain of functions $(\Sigma \to \Sigma_\bot, \sqsubseteq_f, \bot_f)$

which we saw above (Section 2.7.1). This perspective is developed in the seminal paper "Abstract interpretation: a unified lattice model for static analysis of programs by construction or approximation of fixpoints", by P. Cousot and R. Cousot [10], upon which the large literature on abstract interpretation is based. An up-to-date tutorial treatment of abstract interpretation is difficult to find, but for more information, see Chapter 4 of the book by Nielson et al. [31].

Instead of basing our denotational semantics on the domain $\Sigma_\perp$ of (*concrete*) states, an abstract interpretation will instead use some other domain, of *approximate states*, based on some choice of abstract values for variables. Here, we will consider just one basic example, where abstract states tell us, for each variable, whether the value for that variable is positive or nonpositive (i.e., its polarity). In some cases we may lose information about the polarity. For example, subtracting two positive numbers can result in a positive or nonpositive number. To handle such situations, the set of abstract values is usually itself required to be an **upper semi-lattice**. This is a partially ordered set S where every two elements x and y in S have a least upper bound $x \sqcup y$ in S. In this case, we must just add a greatest element, which we will write $\pm$, and make the abstract values for "positive" and "nonpositive" less than $\pm$. We will then use $\pm$ as the value for cases like subtracting two positive numbers. The $\pm$ value represents the set of all possible concrete values (so $\mathbb{Z}$) for the variables. We still need the set of values to form a domain, so we also include a least element $\perp$. Based on this set of abstract values A, we then define the set of states $\mathcal{A}$ for interpretating WHILE programs to be the set of functions from the set of variables to A.

There is much more to be said about abstract interpretations. One important issue is how to state and prove that an abstract interpretation is sound with respect to the concrete denotational semantics (or for that matter, with respect to another abstract interpretation). Here, the theory of Galois connections is the primary technical tool. Intuitively, the idea is to define an abstraction function α which maps values from the concrete domain to the abstract domain, and a concretion function γ that maps from the abstract domain to the concrete domain. In practice, the concrete domain is often taken to be the powerset of a set of values. So for the signs example we will present in more detail below, an abstraction function can be used to map a set of numbers to either pos, nonpos, or $\pm$. In order for α and γ to form a Galois connection between two partially ordered sets – the set C of concrete values and the set A of abstract values – the requirement is that for all $x \in C$, whenever $\alpha(x)$ (which is an element of A) is less than some other element y of A, then $\gamma(y)$ should be greater than x in the ordering for C. This situation is shown in Figure 2.3, where dotted arrows in A and C indicate the ordering relation each of those ordered sets, and solid arrows indicate the action of α and γ. We can understand this intuitively as saying that if we abstract (with α), then move up in the ordering (on A), and then concretize (with γ), we should be higher in the ordering (on C) than where we started.

Another important point is algorithms for efficiently computing the least fixed-points in the semantics of while-commands. When the set of abstract values is finite, a least fixed-point can always be computed in finite time. When it is infinite, a technique called *widening* is used to guarantee that an approximation to the

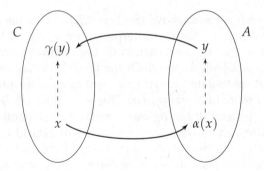

Figure 2.3: Graphical depiction of the essential property of a Galois connection

fixed point can be computed in finite time. And there are many very interesting abstract interpretations one can find in the literature. To take just one example, the paper "Smooth interpretation" by S. Chaudhuri and A. Solar-Lezama shows how to give an abstract interpretation of WHILE programs as smoothed mappings from states consisting of probability distributions for variables to other such states, with application to parameter synthesis for control problems [8]. But developing the current presentation to address these points is beyond the scope of this book.

2.8.1   Abstract states based on polarity of values

Let $\mathcal{A} = \{\text{pos}, \text{nonpos}, \pm, \bot_A\}$ be the set of abstract values, and define an ordering $\sqsubseteq_A$ by starting with the relation indicated by the following clauses, and then taking its reflexive transitive closure:

$$
\begin{array}{ccc}
\text{pos} & \sqsubseteq_A & \pm \\
\text{neg} & \sqsubseteq_A & \pm \\
\bot_A & \sqsubseteq_A & \text{pos} \\
\bot_A & \sqsubseteq_A & \text{neg}
\end{array}
$$

So $\pm$ is the greatest element, and $\bot_A$ the least. This follows the ideas sketched just above. The domain of all possible abstract states $\mathcal{A}$ is then the domain of functions from the set of variables to A, with the same ordering and least element as presented in Section 2.7.1 above (that is, we have the pointwise extension of $\sqsubseteq_A$ as our ordering on functions, and the least function is $\bot$ defined by $\bot(x) = \bot_A$). We will write σ_A as a meta-variable for an abstract state.

2.8.2   Abstract interpretation of terms

To give our abstract interpretation of WHILE programs, we must first define the abstract meaning of terms. In one clause below, I am writing $distinct(x_1, \ldots, x_n)$ to mean that $x_1, \ldots, x_n$ are pairwise different. This can be expressed precisely by simply saying that the cardinality of the set of $x_1, \ldots, x_n$ is equal to n:

$$distinct(x_1, \ldots, x_n) \Leftrightarrow |\{x_1, \ldots, x_n\}| = n$$

The abstract interpretation for terms is then:

$$
\begin{aligned}
[\![x]\!]\sigma_A &= \sigma_A(x) \\
[\![n]\!]\sigma_A &= \begin{cases} + & \text{if } n > 0 \\ - & \text{o.w.} \end{cases} \\
[\![t + t']\!]\sigma_A &= \begin{cases} [\![t]\!]\sigma_A & \text{if } [\![t]\!]\sigma_A = [\![t']\!]\sigma_A \\ \perp_A & \text{if } [\![t]\!]\sigma_A = \perp_A \text{ or } [\![t']\!]\sigma_A = \perp_A \\ \pm & \text{o.w.} \end{cases} \\
[\![t * t']\!]\sigma_A &= \begin{cases} + & \text{if } [\![t]\!]\sigma_A = [\![t']\!]\sigma_A = + \\ + & \text{if } [\![t]\!]\sigma_A = [\![t']\!]\sigma_A = - \\ - & \text{if } distinct([\![t]\!]\sigma_A, [\![t']\!]\sigma_A, \pm, \perp_A) \\ \perp_A & \text{if } [\![t]\!]\sigma_A = \perp_A \text{ or } [\![t']\!]\sigma_A = \perp_A \\ \pm & \text{o.w.} \end{cases} \\
[\![t - t']\!]\sigma_A &= [\![t + (-t')]\!]\sigma_A \\
[\![t \div t']\!]\sigma_A &= [\![t * t']\!]\sigma_A \\
[\![-t]\!]\sigma_A &= \begin{cases} + & \text{if } [\![t]\!]\sigma_A = - \\ - & \text{if } [\![t]\!]\sigma_A = + \\ \perp_A & \text{if } [\![t]\!]\sigma_A = \perp_A \\ \pm & \text{o.w.} \end{cases}
\end{aligned}
$$

As an example, we have the following meanings, where $\sigma_A(x) = +$:

$$
\begin{aligned}
[\![4 + (5 * 3)]\!]\sigma_A &= + \\
[\![-4 + (x * -3)]\!]\sigma_A &= - \\
[\![4 + (3 * -3)]\!]\sigma_A &= \pm
\end{aligned}
$$

The first equation holds because we have a positive (5) times a positive (3), added to a positive (4). The concrete result (19) is positive, and our abstract interpretation is able to figure that fact out. In the second example, we have a positive (x) times a negative, which is a negative. This is added to a negative, so the final result is negative. Finally, in the third example, even though we can see that the concrete result -5 is negative, our abstract interpretation cannot. All it sees is a positive added to a negative, and so is forced to conclude with $\pm$ as the value for the whole term.

2.8.3　Abstract interpretation of commands

Finally, we can give the semantics of commands:

$$
\begin{aligned}
[\![\texttt{skip}]\!]\sigma_A &= \sigma_A \\
[\![x := t]\!]\sigma_A &= \sigma_A[x \mapsto [\![t]\!]\sigma_A] \\
[\![c_1\,;\,c_2]\!]\sigma_A &= \text{if } [\![c_1]\!]\sigma_A = \bot \\
&\quad\ \text{then } \bot; \\
&\quad\ \text{otherwise,} [\![c_2]\!]([\![c_1]\!]\sigma_A) \\
[\![\texttt{if } t \text{ pred } t' \text{ then } c_1 \text{ else } c_2]\!]\sigma_A &= [\![c_1]\!]\sigma_A \sqcup [\![c_2]\!]\sigma_A \\
[\![\texttt{while } t \text{ pred } t' \text{ do } c]\!] &= \mathit{lfp}(F) \\
\text{where } F &= w \mapsto (\sigma_A \mapsto \text{if } [\![c]\!]\sigma_A = \bot \\
&\qquad\qquad\qquad\quad \text{then } \bot \\
&\qquad\qquad\qquad\quad \text{else } w([\![c]\!]\sigma_A))
\end{aligned}
$$

The defining equations for the semantics of skip-commands and assignments look exactly as for the concrete denotational semantics (Section 2.2). The clause for conditionals looks very strange, as it ignores the meaning of the guard entirely! It would be sound to take the guard into account in a conservative way, for example, by taking the meaning of the conditional to be $[\![c_1]\!]\sigma$ when the guard is something like $t < t'$ and the interpretation of t is $-$ and the interpretation of t' is $+$. But it is also sound just to ignore the guard, as we will anyway have to do in some cases (for example, if the meaning of one of the terms is $\pm$, of if the predicate in question is equality). So when we do not know which branch a concrete execution summarized by our abstract execution would have taken, then we just have to join the results of the two branches. Here, we are writing $\sigma_A' \sqcup \sigma_A''$ for the least upper bound of the functions, which is defined as the pointwise extension of the function computing the least upper bound of two abstract values. The least upper bound of x and y in A is the smallest element of A which is greater than or equal to both x and y in the ordering $\sqsubseteq_A$. For example, the least upper bound of $+$ and $-$ is $\pm$. If variable x is positive in each or negative in each, then certainly it will have that same polarity after completing the conditional, whichever branch is taken. If the two branches assign different polarity to x, then the whole conditional has to assign polarity $\pm$ to x. This is an example of the way abstract interpretation conservatively approximates the behavior of a set of possible concrete executions. Similarly, we ignore the guard in defining the semantics of the while-command.

2.8.4　Computability of abstract interpretations

The domain we use for the application of the least fixed-point theorem in the case of while-commands is $(\mathcal{A} \to \mathcal{A}, \sqsubseteq_f, \bot_f)$. This is the domain of functions from $\mathcal{A}$ to $\mathcal{A}$, as defined above (Section 2.7.1). Since any given program has just a finite set X of variables, we can in fact consider just a subset $\mathcal{A}_X$ of the set $\mathcal{A}$ of all abstract states, namely, the subset consisting of states σ_A with $dom(\sigma_A) = X$ (that is, states σ_A giving values just to the variables in X). This subset of abstract states is finite, as each state can map each variable to just four possible values ($+$, $-$, $\bot_A$, and $\pm$).

So instead of working with the infinite domain $(\mathcal{A} \to \mathcal{A}, \sqsubseteq_f, \bot_f)$, we can instead just use the finite domain $(\mathcal{A}_X \to \mathcal{A}_X, \sqsubseteq_f, \bot_f)$, for any command c with variables in X. Since this domain is finite, every ω-chain is eventually constant (Definition 2.4.12). So we can compute the least upper bound of the ω-chain $n \mapsto F^n(\bot_f)$, as required for the semantics of while-commands (Section 2.7.2) in a finite number of steps, just by iterating F on $\bot_f$ until we reach the fixed point. This implies that we can compute the abstract interpretation of any command c in some finite number of steps (of applying the equations defining the semantics).

This is different from the situation with the concrete semantics, where the domain $(\Sigma \to \Sigma_\bot, \sqsubseteq_f, \bot_f)$ is infinite, and hence interpretations of commands might not be computable in finite time by applying the semantic equations. It is typical for abstract interpretations to be designed so that they can always be effectively computed by applying the semantic equations. The chief benefit is that for any command c, some information about it, namely what is given by the abstract interpretation, is guaranteed to be computable. This information may be useful for understanding the behavior of the concrete executions of the command, assuming that our interpretation is indeed sound.

For example, with the abstract interpretation we have been considering, suppose that $\sigma_A(x) = \pm$ for all variables x in a given command c. Let $\sigma'_A = [\![c]\!]\sigma_A$. If $\sigma'_A(x) = +$, for example, we can conclude that the final value of x, if concrete execution of the command indeed terminates, is guaranteed to be positive. This is useful information we have gleaned about any possible concrete execution of the program.

2.9 Conclusion

We have seen how to define denotational semantics for the WHILE programming language, which is a simple imperative programming language, without procedural abstraction. Commands are either assignments, sequences of commands, conditional commands, the trivial skip command, or while-commands. We saw how to define the meaning of a command in a starting state σ (assigning integer values to the variables in the command) as either the final state σ' that is reached following execution of the command; or, if the command is not terminating, the special value $\bot$. Defining a compositional semantics for while-commands in particular turned out to be technically challenging. We took a significant detour into the theory of partially ordered sets (posets), predomains, and domains, in order to be able to state and prove the Least Fixed Point Theorem (Theorem 2.6.6). This theorem states the existence of a least fixed point for any continuous operation on a domain. Using that result, we were able to define the semantics of while-commands as the least fixed point of a functional F. We can see F as the functional which takes an approximation of the semantics of the while-command, and extends that approximation one step. The starting approximation is $\bot_f$, the function that returns $\bot$ for all input states. This is the trivial approximation that cannot compute anything at all: it always diverges. The next approximation will return (input state) σ if the guard is false, and otherwise $\bot$. The next approximation after that will return the expected final state, if that final state can be computed using at most one iteration of the loop. Subsequent approximations allow more and more iterations of the loop. The least upper bound of this sequence – and that is the least fixed point of F – allows any finite number of iterations of the loop to reach a final state. If no finite number of iterations is sufficient, then that least upper bound returns $\bot$, as expected. Finally, we have seen how to use denotational semantics to define abstract interpretations of programs, which can be used to derive static information about all the concrete executions of a program.

2.10 Basic exercises

2.10.1 For Section 2.1, on WHILE

1. Write a WHILE command that sets variable z to the maximum of x and y.

2. Write a WHILE command that sets variable z to x^y (x to the power y), assuming y is non-negative.

3. What is the meaning of command $x := y; y := z; z := x$ in the state $\{x \mapsto 0, y \mapsto 10, z \mapsto 20\}$?

4. What is the meaning of if $x > 0$ then $z := y - x$ else $z := y + x$ in the state $\{x \mapsto 3, y \mapsto 2, z \mapsto 1\}$?

5. Write down the meaning of $x := y; y := x$ in an arbitrary state σ. So the state you end up with will be described by some meta-language expression involving σ and the function overriding notation introduced in Section 1.6.

2.10.2 For Section 2.4, on domains

1. Write out the definitions of partially ordered set, predomain, and domain from memory.

2. Exactly one of the following structures is *not* a partially ordered set. Which one?

   (a) $(\emptyset, \emptyset)$ (that is, the set X is the empty set, and the binary relation $\sqsubseteq$ is also the empty set).

   (b) $(\mathbb{N}, =\text{mod}_2)$, where $x = \text{mod}_2 \, y$ means that x and y have the same remainder when divided by 2.

   (c) $(\mathbb{N}, R)$, where x is related by R to y iff $y = 0$ or $y = x$.

3. Which of the following chains is an ω-chain (according to Definition 2.4.2) in the partially ordered set $(\mathbb{Z}, \leq)$:

(a) $0, 0, 0, \cdots$

(b) $-10, 0, 10, 20, 30, \cdots$

(c) $0, 1, 0, 1, \cdots$

(d) $10, 9, 8, 7, \cdots$

2.10.3 For Section 2.5, on continuous functions

1. For this problem, we will work with functions mapping from the domain $(\mathbb{N} \cup \{\omega\}, \leq_\omega)$ (see Section 2.4.4) to that same domain. For each function f defined below, state whether it is non-monotonic, monotonic but not continuous, or continuous, and argue briefly and informally why (you do not need to give a formal proof).

(a) $f(n) = \begin{cases} 0 & \text{if } n \in \mathbb{N} \text{ is even,} \\ 1 & \text{if } n \in \mathbb{N} \text{ is odd,} \\ \omega & \text{if } n = \omega \end{cases}$

(b) $f(n) = \begin{cases} 2 * n & \text{if } n \in \mathbb{N} \\ \omega & \text{if } n = \omega \end{cases}$

(c) $f(n) = \omega$

2. For this problem, we will work with functions mapping from the domain $(\mathbb{N}, |, 1)$, for natural numbers ordered by divisibility (this example is discussed more in Section 2.4.4) to itself. For each function f defined below, state whether it is non-monotonic, monotonic but not continuous, or continuous, and argue informally why (again, you do not need to give a formal proof).

(a) $f(n) = n + 1$

(b) $f(n) = \begin{cases} n/2 & \text{if } n \text{ is even} \\ n * 2 & \text{if } n \text{ is odd} \end{cases}$

(c) $f(n) = \begin{cases} 0 & \text{if } n \text{ is even} \\ 1 & \text{if } n \text{ is odd} \end{cases}$

2.10.4 For Section 2.7, on semantics of `while`-commands

Consider the command `while x ≠ y do x := x + 1`. Write out the first three approximations to the meaning of this command; namely $\perp_f$, $F(\perp_f)$, $F(F(\perp_f))$, where the functional F is the one used in the semantics of `while`-commands (Section 2.7.2), specialized to this command.

2.10.5 For Section 2.8, on abstract interpretation

1. Compute the abstract interpretations, using the semantics defined in Section 2.8, for the following terms, with respect to an abstract state σ_A mapping x to $+$ and y to $-$.

(a) $x + (3 * y)$

(b) $(2 * x) - y$

2. Compute the abstract interpretation of the following commands, using the semantics of Section 2.8, with respect to an abstract state σ_A mapping x to $+$ and y to $\pm$.

(a) $x := -x; y := x * x$

(b) if $x > 0$ then $x := 3$ else $x := 4$

2.11   Intermediate exercises

2.11.1   For Section 2.1, on syntax and informal semantics of WHILE

1. In this problem, we will consider how to add support to WHILE for terms which change the state. The example we will use is the postfix ++ operator. Informally, evaluating the term x++ is supposed to return the current value $z \in \mathbb{Z}$ of variable x, but also change the state so that x is now associated with $z + 1$.

   (a) Write out the complete definition of the syntax of terms, with the new postfix-increment operation.

   (b) One way to define the formal semantics of terms with the new definition is to define two interpretation functions: one function which returns the integer value of the term, and one which returns the new state (taking into account any changes induced by evaluating ++-terms). So first define $[\![t]\!]_{\text{value}}\sigma$ to return just the integer value of t, and then define $[\![t]\!]_{\text{state}}\sigma$ to return the updated state. Each definition should be given as a set of recursive equations, as was done for the original kind of terms in Section 1.6.

2.11.2   For Section 2.4, on domains

1. Either prove the following or give a counterexample: if $(X, \sqsubseteq)$ is any partially ordered set, and if X is finite, then $(X, \sqsubseteq)$ is a pre-domain.

2. Prove that if $(X, \sqsubseteq)$ is a complete partial order (see Definition 2.4.8), then it must have a least element (hint: how can you define that element as the least upper bound of some subset of X?). Conclude that every cpo (i.e., complete partial order) is a domain.

2.11.3   For Section 2.7, on semantics of `while`-commands

1. Let $(A, \sqsubseteq_A, \perp_A)$ be the domain where:

- $A = \{0, 1, 2\}$
- $\forall a \in A.\, 0 \sqsubseteq_A a$
- $1 \sqsubseteq_A 2$
- $\forall a \in A.\, a \sqsubseteq_A a$
- $\bot_A = 0$

Also, let $(B, \sqsubseteq_B, \bot_B)$ be the domain where:

- $B = \{0, 1\}$
- $\forall b \in B.\, 0 \sqsubseteq_B b$
- $\forall b \in B.\, b \sqsubseteq_B b$
- $\bot_B = 0$

Consider the domain of functions from B to A, with the pointwise ordering and least element defined in Section 2.7.1.

(a) List the elements of $B \to A$. Each element should be described just in the format (a_1, a_2), which we temporarily define to mean the function

$$\{0 \mapsto a_1,\ 1 \mapsto a_2\}$$

(b) State which elements of $B \to A$ are related to which other ones by the pointwise ordering (Section 2.7.1). You do not need to include statements which are derivable by reflexivity or transitivity.

(c) State which elements are monotonic functions from $(B, \sqsubseteq_B)$ to $(A, \sqsubseteq_A)$, and which are not.

(d) Describe a monotonic function from $B \to A$ to $B \to A$. So this is a higher-order function that takes in a function from B to A as input and returns such a function as output.

(e) Compute the least fixed point of the function you wrote for the previous question.

2. Consider the functional F used in the semantics of while-commands (Section 2.7.2), specialized to the trivial looping command while $0 = 0$ do $x := x + 1$. Prove by induction on $n \in \mathbb{N}$ that for all such n, and all $\sigma \in \Sigma$, we have $F^n(\bot_f)(\sigma) = \bot$.

2.11.4 For Section 2.8, on abstract interpretation

Let σ_A be the abstract state mapping every variable to $\pm$, and suppose c is some command. Let σ'_A be $[\![c]\!]\sigma_A$. State conditions on the values of $\sigma'_A(x)$ and $\sigma'_A(y)$ that would be sufficient to guarantee that the following statements are true about the final state σ' of every concrete execution of c (starting from some arbitrary state σ); or else state that no conditions expressible in terms just of $\sigma'_A(x)$ and $\sigma'_A(y)$ would be sufficient.

1. $\sigma'(x) > 0$ and $\sigma'(y) \leq 0$
2. $\sigma'(x) = \sigma'(y)$
3. $\sigma'(x) > \sigma'(y)$

Chapter 3
Axiomatic Semantics of WHILE

Based on the denotational semantics we have considered in Chapter 2, we can now consider several axiomatic semantics for WHILE commands. The term "axiomatic semantics" appears to have arisen from famous papers of Floyd and Hoare [13, 19]. As the title of his paper "Assigning Meanings to Programs" suggests, Floyd proposes to define the meanings of programs in such a way as to facilitate proofs of their properties. He writes (italics his):

> "A *semantic definition* of a particular set of command types, then, is a rule for constructing, for any command c of one of these types, a verification condition $V_c(\mathbf{P}, \mathbf{Q})$ on the antecedents and consequents of c."

By "antecedents" (the vector of formulas $\mathbf{P}$), he means conditions that are assumed to hold before execution of the command c; by "consequents" (the vector $\mathbf{Q}$), he means conditions that will then be implied to hold, if the command c terminates normally. His paper also considers how to prove that commands terminate.

Where Floyd explicitly proposes his ideas as a way of defining the meaning of programs, Hoare's main goal is to propose methods for reasoning about the behavior of programs. He also formulates Floyd's verification condition $V_c(\mathbf{P}, \mathbf{Q})$ in a notationally more convenient form, which we will use below: $\{P\}\ c\ \{Q\}$, where P is the single antecedent, also called (by Hoare) the precondition; and Q is the single consequent, also called the postcondition.

Both Floyd and Hoare are concerned to give precise logical rules describing when verification conditions are true. The definition of their semantics (as Floyd views it) or verification rules (as Hoare views it) can be viewed as a set of axioms, and hence one can view the semantics determined by these rules as axiomatic. Hoare makes the interesting point that these axioms need not be complete, and hence can describe a partial semantics of programs, with certain aspects of program behavior left unspecified. Thus, we can see an axiomatic semantics more generally as constraining the meaning of expressions by stating properties that are true for those expressions. A property of the meaning of an expression, where that property is described precisely using a logical formula (or perhaps a set of logical formulas), serves to constrain that expression's meaning. If constraining enough, it can define that meaning. So we may take axiomatic semantics to be concerned with imposing constraints on the meaning of expressions in order to define, perhaps partially (as Hoare suggests) that meaning.

Hoare's set of axioms for proving Floyd's verification conditions for programs is known now as Hoare Logic. This logic and related ideas are used heavily in many contemporary approaches to program verification. We start with a simpler axiomatic semantics, however, which is based on the denotational semantics of the previous chapter. This semantics will further demonstrate the point that an axiomatic semantics – that is, a set of formulas constraining the meaning of programs – may be incomplete, even necessarily so. That is, fundamental limitations may prevent us from having a sound set of axioms which completely captures a certain aspect of the behavior of programs. This is true also for Hoare Logic, although we will note an important result of Cook's (Section 3.6.1) that mitigates this incompleteness.

As a historical note: Floyd won the Turing award in 1978, Hoare in 1980, and Cook in 1982.

3.1   Denotational equivalence

Let us define two commands to be **denotationally equivalent** iff they have the same interpretation, using the denotation semantics of Section 2.7, for any starting state. Since we are pursuing an axiomatic semantics, we will consider expressions of the form $c_1 =_{\text{den}} c_2$, with semantics defined as follows:

$$[\![c_1 =_{\text{den}} c_2]\!] \quad = \quad \text{forall } \sigma \in \Sigma, \text{ we have } [\![c_1]\!]\sigma \text{ equal to } [\![c_2]\!]\sigma$$

That is, the meaning of $c_1 =_{\text{den}} c_2$ is boolean value *True* if the meanings of commands c_1 and c_2 are the same in all states σ, and *False* otherwise. We can easily prove that denotational equivalence is indeed an equivalence relation (i.e., reflexive, symmetric, and transitive), since the equality (used in the definition) on elements of $\Sigma_\perp$ returned by the interpretation function is an equivalence relation.

Denotational equivalence as defined here is based solely on the input-output behavior of commands. Two commands whose denotations map input states to output states in the same way are considered denotationally equivalent. This makes denotational equivalence rather **coarse** as an equivalence relation: it equates rather more commands than you might expect. For example, we have the following denotational equivalences:

$$\texttt{while } 0 = 0 \texttt{ do skip} \quad =_{\text{den}} \quad \texttt{while } 0 = 0 \texttt{ do } x := x + 1$$

$$x := 0 \quad =_{\text{den}} \quad x := 3; x := 2; x := 1; x := 0$$

The two `while`-commands in the first line are denotationally equivalent, because no matter what the starting state, each has interpretation $\perp$, since each diverges. What is perhaps slightly surprising is that they do rather different things along the way to divergence: the first does nothing at all, while the second increments x forever. Depending on the situation, we might very well like to distinguish these two programs. If we were in a situation where looping programs can communicate with other programs by changing the value of a variable, then we might care about the difference in execution behavior of these two programs. Similarly, the programs in the second line both end up setting x to 0, but one does so in four (mostly useless) steps while the other does so in one step.

If we want an equivalence relation that can distinguish commands based on properties of their executions, rather than just their input-output behavior, we will either need a significantly more complex denotational semantics, or more likely, we will need to base our notion of equivalence on an operational semantics instead. Operational semantics, presented in Chapter 4, gives the meaning of programs by explaining how they evaluate step by step. It is natural to consider properties of that evaluation such as the number of steps taken, the set of variables written or read, and others. These could then be taken into account by an equivalence relation on commands. Pursuing this approach further is beyond the scope of this book, but for one pointer into the literature on resource-aware semantics of programming languages, see, for example, work by Jost et al. [23].

Once we have defined this notion of denotational equivalence, we can study the first-order logical theory which has denotational equivalence as its sole primitive non-logical concept. The language is similar to $FO(\mathbb{Z})$ (Chapter 1), except that it is based on $=_{\text{den}}$-formulas between commands, instead of arithmetic relational formulas between arithmetic terms. To study the theory of $=_{\text{den}}$, we can consider which formulas are **sound** with respect to the semantics of $=_{\text{den}}$ denotational equivalence. That is, formulas whose meanings (based on the meaning of $=_{\text{den}}$) are true. For example, formulas expressing that $=_{\text{den}}$ is an equivalence relation will certainly be sound:

$$\forall c.c =_{\text{den}} c$$
$$\forall c_1.\forall c_2. (c_1 =_{\text{den}} c_2) \Rightarrow (c_2 =_{\text{den}} c_1)$$
$$\forall c_1.\forall c_2.\forall c_3.(c_1 =_{\text{den}} c_2) \Rightarrow (c_2 =_{\text{den}} c_3) \Rightarrow (c_1 =_{\text{den}} c_3)$$

But of course, there will be many more sound formulas we could consider about $=_{\text{den}}$. So it would be very desirable to be able to write down a sound set of axioms about $=_{\text{den}}$ that is also **complete**, in the sense that every true formula of our $=_{\text{den}}$ theory can be derived from those axioms. The following theorem tells us that this desire cannot be fulfilled:

Theorem 3.1.1 (Incompleteness). *There is no finite sound and complete axiomatization for the set of true first-order formulas about $=_{\text{den}}$.*

Proof sketch. The proof makes use of Rice's Theorem, from computability theory. Rice's Theorem states that every nontrivial property of partial functions is undecidable. To understand this statement, we need to understand what a nontrivial property is, and what it means for a property to be decidable. A property of partial functions can just be identified with the set of partial functions that satisfy that property. So the property of returning the same natural-number output for every natural-number input would be identified with the set of partial functions that behave this way (like the function mapping every input to 6). Given this definition, a property is called trivial iff it is either the empty set or the set of all partial functions. Now for "undecidable": deciding a property S means applying some fixed program which, when presented with another program P as input, can report whether the partial function computed by P is in S (satisfies the property) or not. So a property S is undecidable iff no such fixed program exists for deciding S.

To prove Theorem 3.1.1, we first apply Rice's Theorem to the following property. Let us say that a partial function f is a constant $\bot$-function iff it is total and returns $\bot$ for all inputs. This property is nontrivial, since some functions are constant $\bot$-functions, while others are not. It follows by Rice's Theorem that the property of being a constant $\bot$-function is undecidable: there does not exist a program which can take an arbitrary program P as input and tell whether or not the partial function computed by P is uniformly undefined.

Now to prove our incompleteness theorem: suppose we had a finite sound and complete axiomatization for the first-order theory of denotational equivalence. That would mean that using just those finite axioms and the basic rules of logic, we could deduce any true fact about $=_{\text{den}}$. Now here is the crucial observation: a command c is a constant $\bot$-function iff it is denotationally equivalent to the trivial looping command `while 0 = 0 do skip`. Let us call this trivial looping command *loop*.

If we had a sound and complete finite axiomatization, we could iterate through the set of all proofs, looking for either a proof of $c =_{\text{den}}$ *loop* or a proof of $\neg(c =_{\text{den}}$ *loop*). One of these two facts is indeed a true fact about command c and $=_{\text{den}}$. Since our axiomatization is sound and complete by assumption, we must eventually find a proof of either the one fact or the other. But this would mean that given any command c we can algorithmically determine whether or not it is a constant $\bot$-function: our process of enumerating proofs looking for a proof of either $c =_{\text{den}}$ *loop* or $\neg(c =_{\text{den}}$ *loop*) is guaranteed to succeed after a finite number of steps. Certainly, the number of steps might be huge, but we are concerned here just about the theoretical possibility of finding a proof of one or the other formula, not how one might actually try to search efficiently for proofs in practice. This proof-enumerating algorithm is sufficient to decide the property of being a constant $\bot$-function, and so its existence contradicts the undecidability of being a constant $\bot$-function. Since that property really is undecidable by Rice's Theorem, there can be no such proof-enumerating algorithm, and hence no sound and complete finite axiomatization for the set of true first-order formulas about $=_{\text{den}}$ (or even for the set of true equations and disequations using $=_{\text{den}}$). ☐

As a small note: this proof works as long as we have any way to enumerate the axioms (in a computable way). So not only can there be no sound and complete finite axiomatization, even an infinite axiomatization is impossible if it is **recursively enumerable** (that is, if there is a program which can enumerate all the axioms by returning the n'th distinct axiom given any natural number n).

3.2   Partial correctness assertions

Hoare Logic is a system of rules for proving certain kinds of assertions about the behavior of programs. Many systems for program verification, for a variety of different programming languages and even paradigms, are based on Hoare Logic.

We will focus just on **partial correctness assertions** (pca), written as

$$\{F\} \, c \, \{F'\}$$

Partial correctness assertions like this are meant to assert that from any starting state satisfying F, execution of command c will either diverge or result in an ending state satisfying F'. We will not study total correctness assertions, often written $[F]c[F']$, which have a similar intended semantics except that divergence of c is not allowed: $[F]c[F']$ asserts that from any input state satisfying F, execution of c will terminate in an ending state satisfying F'. We will return to the question of program termination in Section 7.5, where we will see how types can be used to enforce program termination for lambda calculus. So for this chapter, we are considering partial correctness assertions with the following formal semantics:

Definition 3.2.1 (Semantics of a Pca). *The meaning* $[\![\{F\} \, c \, \{F'\}]\!]$ *of a pca* $\{F\} \, c \, \{F'\}$ *is defined by the following meta-language formula:*

$$\forall \sigma \in \Sigma. \; [\![F]\!]\sigma = True \; \Rightarrow \; (([\![c]\!]\sigma = \bot) \; \vee \; ([\![F']\!]([\![c]\!]\sigma) = True))$$

Let us read this definition in English. Recall from Section 1.7 that we say that σ satisfies F whenever $[\![F]\!]\sigma = True$. Then the formula says that for every state $\sigma \in \Sigma$ satisfying formula F, either the command c diverges from starting state σ, or else the resulting final state satisfies F'. The formula F is called the **pre-condition** of the pca, and formula F' is called the **post-condition**. So the idea is that starting the command in a state satisfying the pre-condition will either diverge or result in a state satisfying the post-condition. We will call a pca $\{F\} \, c \, \{F'\}$ **valid** iff this property of the meanings of F, c, and F' indeed holds. We can depict this situation as follows, where I am writing a dashed line to mean that either $[\![c]\!]$ diverges on a given input state satisfying the precondition, or else takes that input state to an output state satisfying the postcondition:

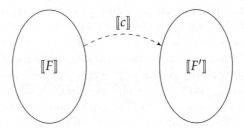

3.2.1 Examples of valid pca's

Here are some examples of valid pca's. I will write the pca first, and then explain why it is valid.

$$\{x > 0\} \, y := x \, \{y > 0\}$$

To show that this is a valid pca, we must show that for any state σ satisfying the pre-condition $x > 0$, then either the command $y := x$ either diverges (it does not, in fact), or else ends in a state satisfying the post-condition $y > 0$. And we can see that this is true: if $\sigma(x) > 0$, then assigning y to have the value of x will mean that the state σ' resulting from executing the command has $\sigma'(y) > 0$. This is just what is required by the post-condition, so this pca is valid.

$$\{x > y\} \; \texttt{if } y > 0 \texttt{ then } z := x \texttt{ else } z := 3 \; \{z > 0\}$$

This pca says that from any starting state σ where $\sigma(x) > \sigma(y)$, executing a certain command either diverges (it does not), or else results in a state σ' where $\sigma'(z) > 0$. The command in question checks if the value of y is greater than 0. If so, execution enters the then-branch of this conditional command, and the value of x is assigned to z; otherwise, execution proceeds to the else-branch, and 3 is assigned to z. Notice that in the situation where execution enters the then-branch, we know that $\sigma(y) > 0$. We are also assuming $\sigma(x) > \sigma(y)$. We can put these two facts together (by transitivity of $>$), to conclude that $\sigma(x) > 0$. When we assign the value of x to z, we are thus assigning a positive number ($\sigma(x)$) to z, and so the post-condition $z > 0$ is satisfied in the resulting state. And of course, it is obviously satisfied in the state resulting from executing the else-branch, since there z is assigned to the positive value 3.

$$\{\textit{True}\} \; \texttt{while } x \neq 0 \texttt{ do } x := x - 2 \; \{x = 0\}$$

This pca is also valid. Let us consider an arbitrary state σ satisfying the precondition. The precondition $\textit{True}$ is the weakest possible condition one can impose on a state. Imagine you are signing a contract with a software developer. You will pay them \$10,000 to produce software which satisfies the condition $\textit{True}$. Well, that is not a good deal for you, because they can give you any software they want, and the contractual condition will be satisfied. No matter what value $\sigma(x)$ we have in starting state σ, if the loop ever exits, the value of x will be 0. If $\sigma(x) > 0$ and $\sigma(x)$ is even, then the loop will eventually exit, since we will eventually count down (by 2s) to 0 from $\sigma(x)$. The pca is also valid by definition if the loop does not exit, since the semantics of pca's (Definition 3.2.1) says they are valid if the command diverges from the starting state. The loop diverges in the states where $\sigma(x) \leq 0$ or both $\sigma(x) > 0$ and $\sigma(x)$ is odd.

3.2.2   General examples of valid pca's

Here are some general examples of valid pca's, described by giving a pattern containing some meta-variables like F and c, for pca's. All pca's which match this pattern are valid.

$$\{F\}\ c\ \{\textit{True}\}$$

As noted, this is not a pca itself, but rather a pattern describing an infinite set of pca's: the ones which have any formula F for the pre-condition, any command c, and then *True* for the post-condition. An example of such a pca is $\{x > 0\}$ `skip` $\{\textit{True}\}$. All pca's matching the pattern are valid, because no matter what the starting state σ is from which we begin execution of command c, either that command will diverge or else it will terminate in some final state σ' which satisfies the post-condition. The post-condition is just *True*, which is satisfied by any state. So it does not matter what conditions have been imposed (by F) on the starting state, nor does it matter what the effect of the command c is. The final state, if any is reached, will always satisfy the post-condition, because the post-condition imposes only a trivial condition (*True*) which is always satisfied.

$$\{\textit{False}\}\ c\ \{F_1\}$$

All pca's matching this pattern – an example is $\{\textit{False}\}$ $x := 1$ $\{x > 0\}$ – are valid, because the pre-condition can never be satisfied. These pca's say that for any starting state σ where *False* is true, then executing c either diverges or results in a state σ' satisfying F_1. But there are no starting states σ which satisfy *False*, since no states can satisfy *False*. In this sense, *False* is the strongest possible condition one can require of a state. It is so strong no state can possibly satisfy it.

$$\{F\}\ \texttt{while}\ 1 > 0\ \texttt{do skip}\ \{\textit{False}\}$$

All pca's matching this pattern are valid, because the command in question diverges no matter what the starting state is. Since the semantics of a pca requires that the post-condition should be satisfied in the final state unless the command diverges, any pca with a command which diverges in any input state (or any input state satisfying the pre-condition), like this one, is valid.

3.3   Interlude: rules and derivations

In the next section, we will present a set of proof rules for Hoare Logic. Much of the Programming Languages literature is developed around sets of rules defining various aspects of the semantics of programming languages. The Hoare Logic rules are the first of many sets of rules we will encounter, just in this book. So we will digress briefly to consider some general concepts about sets of rules. Many of these come from proof theory; a starting reference is [39]. Rules are of the form:

$$\frac{P_1 \quad \cdots \quad P_n}{C}$$

The P_1 through P_n are the **premises** of the rule, and C is the **conclusion**. The meaning of a single rule is

$$(P_1 \wedge \cdots \wedge P_n) \Rightarrow C$$

That is, if the premises are true, then the conclusion is, too. For example, we might have formulas of the form A, B, C, D, E, F, and G, and rules like the following, which are not intended to have any interesting meaning, but to serve as a simple small example.

$$\frac{B \quad E}{A} \quad \frac{C \quad D}{B} \quad \frac{D \quad F}{A} \quad \frac{C \quad G}{E} \quad \frac{}{F} \quad \frac{}{C} \quad \frac{}{D}$$

A rule is called an **axiom** if it has no premises. So the two rightmost rules just shown are axioms. Sometimes rules have names, which are written on one side (or the other) of the horizontal bar separating premises and conclusion. These example rules do not have names.

3.3.1   Building proofs using rules

To build a proof using a set of rules, we connect instances of the rules by using an instance of one rule to derive the premise of another rule. For example, using the above example rules, we can build this proof:

$$\frac{\dfrac{C \quad D}{B} \quad E}{A}$$

This schematic example shows us applying one rule to premises C and D to conclude B, which then becomes the first premise of an another rule-instance, deriving A with second premise E. Instances of rules are sometimes called **inferences**. So our example proof here contains two inferences: one using the first of our rules listed above, and one using the second. If proof rules are named, one sometimes sees inferences written with the name, and sometimes without. A set of proof rules is often referred to as a **proof system**.

Proofs are almost always understood to be *finite* objects built in this way by applying rules. Rarely one will see proofs understood to be possibly infinite objects – but not in this book. The finiteness of proofs has the important consequence that we can reason by induction on their structure, as we will consider in Section 3.6 below.

Proofs viewed as formal objects like this one are sometimes also referred to as **derivations**. This terminology can be useful when one does a proof about the kinds of proofs that can be derived using a proof system. Then the proofs derived by the rules can be referred to as "derivations", and one can refer to the proof about the possible derivations as just a "proof". Derivations can be viewed as trees, where the root of the tree is the conclusion (at the very bottom of the derivation), and the leaves are the formulas at the end of the paths emanating from the root.

If a derivation contains some unproved premises, then it is sometimes called an **open** derivation. So the example schematic derivation given above is open. In contrast, the following one is **closed**:

$$\frac{\dfrac{\overline{C}\quad\overline{D}}{B}\quad\dfrac{\overline{C}}{E}}{A}$$

It is closed because there are no unproven assumptions: all the formulas at the leaves of the derivation are proved by axioms.

3.3.2 The judgments of a proof system

Rather than speaking of formulas, it is customary to speak of rules as deriving **judgments**. Judgments are just expressions intended to denote certain relations on various kinds of expressions. For example, the rules for Hoare Logic in the next section derive pca's, which express a certain relation on formulas and commands. So the judgments derived by the rules are those pca's. We will work just with rules which use judgments, in the premises and conclusions, matching one or more of a finite number of meta-expressions, called the **forms of judgment** of the proof system. We assume that no two of these meta-expressions have a common instance. In our example proof system, we could view it as having seven forms of judgment, namely $A, \cdots, G$; or else a single form of judgment X, if we have defined syntactic category X to contain $A, \cdots, G$. For most sets of rules, it will be quite clear what the forms of judgment are. For example, the form of judgment for the Hoare Logic rules in the next section is just the meta-expression $\{F\}\,c\,\{F'\}$.

3.3.3 Syntax-directed rules

It is sometimes the case that at most one inference that could possibly prove a given judgment. For example, the judgment C can only be derived in our sample proof system using the lone inference allowed by the sixth rule. For another example: if we were faced with the task of trying to prove F, there is only one inference that could possibly conclude F, namely an inference using the fifth rule. If there is always at most one inference which could apply to prove a given judgment, then the proof system is sometimes called **syntax-directed**. Similarly, for a particular rule if there is always at most once inference which could apply to prove a given judgment, then that rule is syntax-directed.

For syntax-directed proof systems, there is a simple approach for trying to prove a goal judgment G. If no inference could possibly prove G, then we report failure. Otherwise, apply the sole possible inference, and recursively try to prove the premises of that inference. This approach is not guaranteed to terminate. For a simple example, consider a proof system consisting of the rule

$$\frac{Q}{Q}$$

The algorithm just described will loop trying to prove Q by applying this rule's sole inference repeatedly. But the algorithm is deterministic. If instead of just one possible inference, every judgment has at most a finite number of inferences, then we could generalize the above search procedure to try the different possible rules in parallel, for example. Unfortunately, it often happens for proof systems of interest in programming languages (and logic) that an infinite number of inferences could apply to prove a given judgment. This is true even if there is only a finite number of rules, because a single rule can have an infinite number of instances.

3.3.4 Invertibility of rules and inversion on derivations

There are a few other pieces of terminology that we can consider now, even though they are not needed in this chapter. A rule is called **invertible** in a given system of rules if whenever the conclusion is derivable, so are the premises. For example, almost all our example rules are invertible:

$$\frac{B \quad E}{A} \qquad \frac{C \quad D}{B} \qquad \frac{C}{E} \qquad \frac{G}{F} \qquad \overline{C} \qquad \overline{D}$$

In each case, if we can derive the conclusion, we must have been able to derive the premises. Consider the third rule for a simple example. If we can derive E then we must be able to derive C, because there is no other rule that could possibly derive E except this one: it is the only one where E is the conclusion. The fourth rule is a somewhat subtle example. To be invertible, it must be the case that if we can derive the conclusion, then we can also derive the premises. Here, the conclusion is F, and the sole premise is G. But in this system of rules, it is impossible to derive F. And the definition of invertibility only requires us to be able to derive the premises when the conclusion is derivable. Since the conclusion is underivable, this rule is trivially invertible. The rule

$$\frac{D \quad F}{A}$$

is not invertible, because it is possible to derive the conclusion (as we did with our example closed derivation above), without deriving the premises. In particular, F is not derivable in this system of rules.

Sometimes, when reasoning about judgments derived using a particular proof system, it will happen that some judgment of interest could only possibly have been derived using some strict subset of all the rules, possibly just a single rule. For example, suppose we are assuming (for sake of argument) that A has been derived. The only rule which could possibly have been used to conclude A is our first example rule; all the other rules conclude with different judgments. In this case, the common terminology is to say that **by inversion** on the assumed derivation of A, we know that the premises of the rule (in this case, B and E) must also hold. If we had had another rule with A for the conclusion, then our reasoning by inversion would only be able to conclude that one or the other of the rules must have been applied, and hence one or the other set of premises must be true.

3.3.5 Admissibility and derivability

An additional piece of terminology (again, not needed in this chapter but often used) is "admissible". A rule is **admissible** in a system of rules if whenever the premises of that rule are derivable, so is the conclusion. Each rule r of a given system is trivially admissible in that system, since the rule itself can be used to derive the conclusion from the premises. So usually people are interested in whether a rule r which is not part of a given system of rules is admissible in that system. The following rule is one example of a rule which is admissible in our system:

$$\frac{B \quad C}{A}$$

This rule is admissible since if it should happen that B and C are derivable, then A is also derivable. In fact, B and C are actually derivable in this system, and thus the conclusion is, too. So the following rule is also admissible in our system (since the conclusion is derivable, as shown above):

$$\frac{}{A}$$

The following rule is admissible in our system for the trivial reason that the premise is underivable (thus making the requirement that the conclusion be derivable if the premises are, to be vacuously true):

$$\frac{F}{G}$$

And finally, the following rule is not admissible in our system, since we can derive the premise but not the conclusion, using our example system of rules:

$$\frac{A}{F}$$

Finally, we will call a rule **derivable** in a given system iff one can construct an open derivation which has the premises of the rule as the only unproved assumptions (one need not use them all in the open derivation), and the conclusion of the rule as the conclusion of the open derivation. So in our system, this rule is derivable:

$$\frac{B \quad C}{A}$$

That is because we can give this open derivation for it:

$$\frac{B \quad \dfrac{C}{E}}{A}$$

$$\frac{}{\{F\}\, \texttt{skip}\, \{F\}}\ \textit{Skip}$$

$$\frac{\models F_1' \Rightarrow F_1 \quad \{F_1\}\, c\, \{F_2\} \quad \models F_2 \Rightarrow F_2'}{\{F_1'\}\, c\, \{F_2'\}}\ \textit{Consequence}$$

$$\frac{}{\{[t/x]F\}\, x := t\, \{F\}}\ \textit{Assign}$$

$$\frac{\{F \wedge (t\ \textit{pred}\ t')\}\, c\, \{F\}}{\{F\}\, \texttt{while}\ t\ \textit{pred}\ t'\ \texttt{do}\ c\, \{F \wedge \neg(t\ \textit{pred}\ t')\}}\ \textit{While}$$

$$\frac{\{F\}\, c_1\, \{F'\} \quad \{F'\}\, c_2\, \{F''\}}{\{F\}\, c_1; c_2\, \{F''\}}\ \textit{Sequence}$$

$$\frac{\{F \wedge (t\ \textit{pred}\ t')\}\, c_1\, \{F'\} \quad \{F \wedge \neg(t\ \textit{pred}\ t')\}\, c_2\, \{F'\}}{\{F\}\, \texttt{if}\ t\ \textit{pred}\ t'\ \texttt{then}\ c_1\ \texttt{else}\ c_2\, \{F'\}}\ \textit{Conditional}$$

Figure 3.1: Hoare Logic Rules

In contrast, some of our admissible rules above are not derivable. For example, there is no open derivation of the conclusion from the premises for this rule:

$$\frac{F}{G}$$

3.4   Hoare Logic rules

Hoare Logic consists of a set of rules for proving pca's. These rules are given in Figure 3.1. One of the rules uses the notation $\models F$ to mean that formula F is valid, as defined in Chapter 1 (see Definition 1.9.1). The rules also use the notation $[t/x]F$ for **capture-avoiding substitution**:

Definition 3.4.1 (Capture-Avoiding Substitution). *For any expressions e_1 and e_2, we write $[e_1/x]e_2$ for the result of substituting e_1 for x in e_2. The substitution performed is capture-avoiding, in the sense that bound variables (see the informal explanation in Section 1.5 for bound variables) in e_2 are renamed away from the set of free variables in e_1.*

For a basic example, $[3/x](x = y)$ is the formula $3 = y$. For an example of capture avoidance: $[x/y](\forall x.y \leq x)$ is the formula $\forall z.x \leq z$. Notice that we renamed the x which was bound by $\forall x$ in the first formula to z. This ensured that we did not change the scope of the x which we were substituting for y. It was a global variable when we substituted it, and it still is after the substitution is finished. If we did not rename the bound x, we would have gotten the formula $\forall x.x \leq x$. In this formula, all the occurrences of x are for the local variable x introduced by $\forall x$. There are no global occurrences of x. So the formulas have quite different meanings. We will give a more formal definition of capture-avoiding substitution in Chapter 5 below.

To return to the Hoare Logic rules of Figure 3.1: there are several subtleties expressed in these rules, so we will consider them all now in turn. Our explanation will take the form of a proof that the rules are **sound** with respect to the semantics given in Definition 3.2.1. That is, if we consider the rule as a formula (as done in Section 3.3 just above), then that formula is valid, where we interpret each pca occurring in it according to Definition 3.2.1. We argue this informally here. We will a formal proof of a stronger result in Section 3.6 below.

The skip rule

$$\frac{}{\{F\} \, \texttt{skip} \, \{F\}} \; Skip$$

This rule is sound, because if $[\![F]\!]\sigma = \mathit{True}$, for an arbitrary $\sigma \in \Sigma$, then we also have $[\![F]\!]([\![\texttt{skip}]\!]\sigma) = \mathit{True}$. This is because $[\![\texttt{skip}]\!]\sigma = \sigma$.

The assignment rule

$$\frac{}{\{[t/x]F\} \, x := t \, \{F\}} \; Assign$$

This rule is formulated to achieve two goals:

- dropping old facts about the variable x from the pre-condition.

- porting facts about t to become facts about x in the post-condition.

To see why we have to drop old facts about x, consider the command $x := 0$. Suppose we start this command in a state σ satisfying the precondition $x > 1$. For example, such a state could be σ with $\sigma(x) = 2$. Executing this assignment will take us to a new state, namely $\sigma[x \mapsto 0]$, which does not satisfy $x > 1$. So we must somehow drop that fact, namely $x > 1$, from our precondition to compute the postcondition. Similarly, while we have to drop this fact, we should be allowed to add any fact we like about x that is true in states where $\sigma(x) = 0$, since we are guaranteed to be in such a state after executing this command.

The assignment rule drops old facts about x and ports facts about t to become facts about x in an elegant though somewhat tricky way. Suppose we have a post-condition F, which might (or might not) mention x. In order to reach a state satisfying F, we can start in any state we want which satisfies $[t/x]F$. This formula says the same things F does, but it says them about t instead of about x.

More formally, to see that this rule is sound, consider an arbitrary $\sigma \in \Sigma$ where $[\![[t/x]F]\!]\sigma = \mathit{True}$. Here we will make use of the following fact (proof omitted):

$$[\![[t/x]F]\!]\sigma = [\![F]\!]\sigma[x \mapsto [\![t]\!]\sigma] \tag{3.1}$$

This is quite similar to what we proved in Exercise 1 in Section 1.14.4 above substitution into terms. Let us make sure the meaning of this is clear. The expression on the left-hand side denotes the value of the substituted formula $[t/x]F$ in state

σ. The expression on the right-hand side denotes the value of the formula F in the state which is the same as σ except that it maps x to $[\![t]\!]\sigma$. Informally, these values are the same because the right-hand side requires us to use $[\![t]\!]\sigma$ for the value of x when interpreting F, while the formula in the left hand side has a t at exactly those same locations where F has x. We will interpret those occurrences of t as $[\![t]\!]\sigma$, of course. So the two interpretations will be equal.

To show soundness of the rule, we just need to show that $[\![F]\!]([\![x := t]\!]\sigma) = $ *True*. But $[\![x := t]\!]\sigma = \sigma[x \mapsto [\![t]\!]\sigma]$, so we have the desired conclusion using the assumption that $[\![[t/x]F]\!]\sigma = $ *True* and Equation 3.1.

It is instructive to see why alternative formulations of this rule fall short. Suppose we took instead this rule:

$$\overline{\{F\}\ x := t\ \{[x/t]F\}}$$

Let us assume we have defined $[x/t]F$ to mean the result of replacing the term t by x everywhere in F. With this version of the rule, we cannot prove the following obviously valid pca

$$\{3 = 3\}\ x := 3\ \{x = 3\}$$

This is because the rule requires replacing <u>every</u> occurrence of the term t in the precondition with x in the postcondition. So all we can prove with that rule is the uninformative pca

$$\{3 = 3\}\ x := 3\ \{x = x\}$$

With this rule, there will be pca's that we should be able to prove but cannot. But even worse, we can use this alternative rule to prove invalid pca's (so the rule is unsound). Consider this invalid pca:

$$\{x > 0\}\ x := x - 1\ \{x > 0\}$$

This is invalid because if we start in a state $\sigma[x \mapsto 1]$, then executing the assignment will take us to the state $\sigma[x \mapsto 0]$. The first state satisfies the precondition, but the second violates the postcondition. This shows the pca is invalid. But the alternative formulation of the assignment rule we are considering just says we need to replace any occurrences of the term t in the precondition. In this case, t is $x - 1$, and there are no occurrences of that term in the precondition. So replacing $x - 1$ with x when moving from the precondition to the postcondition does nothing, and we get $x > 0$ for the postcondition, too. The problem here is that the alternative rule failed to drop old facts about x. The actual assignment rule does this by substituting t for x in the precondition, so any facts that the precondition is expressing which involve x must actually be facts about t (which can contain x). This ensures soundness.

The `while` rule

$$\frac{\{F \wedge (t\ pred\ t')\}\ c\ \{F\}}{\{F\}\ \texttt{while}\ t\ pred\ t'\ \texttt{do}\ c\ \{F \wedge \neg(t\ pred\ t')\}}\ \textit{While}$$

The rule for `while`-commands is based on a simple idea. We do not attempt to reason about the number of times the loop will execute as a function of the starting state. Instead, we reason about the behavior of an unknown number of iterations of the `while`-loop by showing that no matter how many times it repeats, the state we are in when we reach the top of the loop (either initially or after iterating the body of the loop) satisfies the invariant formula F. Suppose we are really interested in the behavior of the `while` loop beginning from set of states S_0:

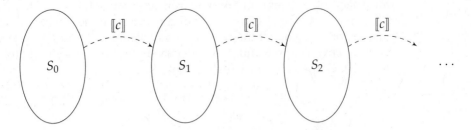

The `while` rule says instead to find a formula F such that $S_k \subseteq [\![F]\!]$ for all k:

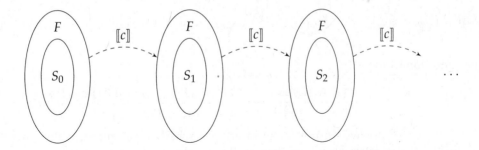

This formula F is called a **loop invariant**. It is something which is true after each iteration of the loop, and true initially. So however many times the loop is executed, the loop invariant will remain true. It truly does not *vary*, but remains *invariant* after all these executions. This idea is incorporated in the rule's premise, which says that if F is true before one execution of the body begins, then it will still be true after one execution of the body ends. Of course, the rule allows us to assume that the guard of the `while`-loop is true before the execution of the body begins. Similarly, in the conclusion, the rule allows us to conclude that the guard is false after execution of the whole `while`-loop completes.

Many trivial formulas are loop invariants, including *True* for example (which is always true), and also formulas that do not refer to variables used in the `while`-loop. It is not challenging to find a loop invariant. But it is often quite challenging, for both a human or a static-analysis program, to find a useful loop invariant that will allow a proof of some pca of interest to go through. We will work through this case in more detail when we prove a related theorem in Section 3.6 below.

The sequencing rule

$$\frac{\{F\}\ c_1\ \{F'\}\quad \{F'\}\ c_2\ \{F''\}}{\{F\}\ c_1;c_2\ \{F''\}}\quad Sequence$$

This rule reflects a kind of transitivity of pca's: if $\{F\}\ c_1\ \{F'\}$ and $\{F'\}\ c_2\ \{F''\}$, then also $\{F\}\ c_1;c_2\ \{F''\}$. The transitivity arises from the semantics of these pca's. Suppose execution of c_1 is guaranteed either to diverge or to take you from any state satisfying F to a state satisfying F'. Suppose similarly that execution of c_2 must also either diverge or take you from any state satisfying F' to a state satisfying F''. In that case, the rule says you can conclude that the command $c_1;c_2$ will either diverge or take you all the way from any state satisfying F to one satisfying F'', without any need to mention the intermediate state satisfying F' (or that formula F' itself). Graphically, the situation looks like this:

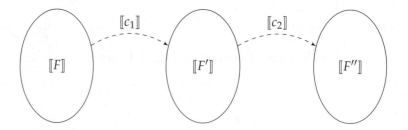

The conditional rule

$$\frac{\{F\ \wedge\ (t\ pred\ t')\}\ c_1\ \{F'\}\quad \{F\ \wedge\ \neg(t\ pred\ t')\}\ c_2\ \{F'\}}{\{F\}\ \texttt{if}\ t\ pred\ t'\ \texttt{then}\ c_1\ \texttt{else}\ c_2\ \{F'\}}\quad Conditional$$

Since we do not know in general whether the guard of the conditional is true or false, given an arbitrary state σ, this rule requires us to consider two cases, if we wish to prove the pca in the conclusion (about the conditional). We have to consider the case where the guard is true in the starting state, and separately, we have to consider the case where the guard is false. In each of these two cases, we must prove that the command we execute (in either the `then`- or the `else`-branch of the loop) will either diverge or take us from a state satisfying the pre-condition to a state satisfying the post-condition. Of course, the rule also allows us to add to the pre-condition the fact that the guard is true (in the first case), or else false (in the second).

The consequence rule

$$\frac{\models F_1'\Rightarrow F_1\quad \{F_1\}\ c\ \{F_2\}\quad \models F_2\Rightarrow F_2'}{\{F_1'\}\ c\ \{F_2'\}}\quad Consequence$$

To show that this rule is sound, suppose we have:

1. $\models F'\Rightarrow F$

2. $\{F\}\ c\ \{F_1\}$

3. $\models F_1 \Rightarrow F_1'$

We must prove $\{F'\}\ c\ \{F_1'\}$. To prove that pca, it is sufficient (by our semantics of pca's) to assume an arbitrary $\sigma \in \Sigma$ with $[\![F']\!]\sigma = \mathit{True}$, and prove that either $[\![c]\!]\sigma = \bot$ or else $[\![F_1']\!]([\![c]\!]\sigma) = \mathit{True}$. By assumption (i), we know that in any state where F' is true, F is also true. This is by the semantics of $FO(\mathbb{Z})$ formulas (see Section 1.7). So we know:

$$[\![F]\!]\sigma = \mathit{True}$$

But now using assumption (2), we know that in any state satisfying F – such as this state σ we have just shown to satisfy F – either c diverges or else F_1 is true in the resulting state. In the first situation, we can complete our proof, since then we can show $[\![c]\!]\sigma = \bot$ (and we had to prove either this or another fact). In the second situation, we have

$$[\![F_1]\!]\sigma = \mathit{True}$$

Now we can use assumption (3) to conclude that $[\![F_1']\!]\sigma = \mathit{True}$, which is sufficient to conclude the proof in this case (since we had to prove either that fact of $[\![c]\!]\sigma = \bot$). Graphically, the assumption of $\{F\}\ c\ \{F_1\}$ corresponds to this situation, where I am using different sizes just in anticipation of subsequent diagrams:

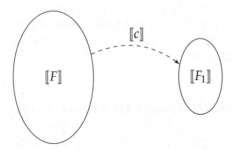

The entailment $\models F' \Rightarrow F$ corresponds to a subset relationship (and similarly for the other entailment):

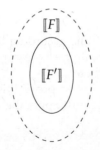

Putting these graphs together, we get the following graphical justification for the validity of the conclusion $\{F'\}\ c\ \{F'_1\}$, where the dashed nodes are for that pca, and the solid ones are for the assumed $\{F\}\ c\ \{F_1\}$:

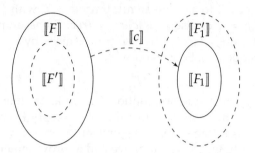

The consequence rule and the sequencing rule are not syntax-directed in the sense of Section 3.3.3. This is because there are meta-variables in the premises of those rules which do not appear in the conclusions. So to apply the sequencing rule to try to prove a pca, we have to guess nondeterministically the intermediate formula F' in the premise. We also have nondeterminism about whether to try to apply the consequence rule to prove a $\{F\}\ c\ \{F'\}$, or apply the the rule specific to the command c (e.g., the sequencing rule if c is $c_1; c_2$). When performing a Hoare Logic proof by hand, we often have to decide whether to apply the rule specific to the command c in the pca we are trying to prove, or else use the consequence rule to change the pre- and post-conditions of the pca. This makes it more difficult, unfortunately, to know how to proceed at any given point, when searching for such a proof.

3.5   Example derivations in Hoare Logic

To build a derivation of a pca using the proof rules of Hoare Logic, one has to apply the rules very carefully and precisely. Substitute values for the meta-variables (like F or c) in the rule, and make sure that you have proofs for exactly the premises that the rule requires. We are not allowed to fudge at all here: every inference must truly be an exact instance of a rule, with no modifications whatsoever, even if those modifications seem justified. For example, suppose we want to prove this pca:

$$\{z > 0\}\ y := z + 0\ \{y > 0\}$$

This is certainly valid according to the semantics for pca's (Definition 3.2.1), since for any starting state σ where $\sigma(x) > 0$, executing the command will indeed reach a final state σ' where
$sigma'(y) > 0$. But to prove this pca using the Hoare Logic rules, we must be careful. We cannot just apply the *Assign* rule:

$$\frac{}{\{[t/x]F\}\ x := t\ \{F\}}\ \textit{Assign}$$

The closest we could come with this rule is this inference:

$$\frac{}{\{z+0>0\}\, y := z+0 \,\{y>0\}} \; Assign$$

To construct this inference, we have instantiated the meta-variables of the *Assign* rule as follows:

$$
\begin{aligned}
t &\mapsto z+0 \\
x &\mapsto y \\
F &\mapsto y>0
\end{aligned}
$$

Here we see one subtle point: the *Assign* rule is written with a meta-variable x for whichever actual WHILE variable we are assigning to. To help see that our inference is really an instance of the rule, here is that inference written with the substitution in the pre-condition:

$$\frac{}{\{[z+0/y]y>0\}\, y := z+0 \,\{y>0\}} \; Assign$$

The pca we have derived with this inference is not exactly the same as what we are trying to prove, because the pre-condition is $z+0>0$, rather than $z>0$. Now, you could be forgiven for thinking this is exceptionally picky: isn't $z+0$ equal to 0 after all? Why can't we just use that fact in the proof? The answer is that we can, but we must do so explicitly. After all, proofs are intended as incontrovertible evidence, and so all details must be carefully accounted for in the proof itself. In our case, changing parts of a pre-condition or post-condition in a logically allowed way must be done using the *Consequence* rule. The derivation we need in this case is the following (omitting the "*Consequence*" label from the long horizontal bar, for typographic reasons):

$$\frac{\models z>0 \Rightarrow z+0>0 \quad \dfrac{}{\{z+0>0\}\, y := z+0 \,\{y>0\}}\; Assign \quad \models y>0 \Rightarrow y>0}{\{z>0\}\, y := z+0 \,\{y>0\}}$$

We are using the *Consequence* rule to change the pre-condition from the one which is permitted directly by the *Assign* to a logically equivalent pre-condition (though the *Consequence* rule only requires us to change to a logically stronger pre-condition, which implies the pre-condition in the premise). For the derivations we will write in Hoare Logic, we will just leave premises which are supposed to be $FO(\mathbb{Z})$ validities (the first and third premises of the *Consequence* rule) unproved. Of course, when you are writing out derivations, you should make sure that you only include valid formulas of $FO(\mathbb{Z})$ in such positions. But since we will not develop a proof system for $FO(\mathbb{Z})$ in this book, we will not require derivations of those formulas in our Hoare Logic derivations. So technically, we are writing *open derivations* (see the terminology in Section 3.3).

As a final note: we were forced to write the rather trivial premise $\models y>0 \Rightarrow y>0$ here, because the *Consequence* rule requires a $FO(\mathbb{Z})$ validity to change the post-condition, as well as one for the pre-condition. We are not allowed to omit one of those premises simply because we do not need to change that part of the pca. The solution is just to write a trivial implication of the form $F \Rightarrow F$ in such cases. Of course, we could always extend our Hoare Logic with new forms of the *Consequence* rule, like these:

$$\frac{\models F' \Rightarrow F \quad \{F\}\, c\, \{F_1\}}{\{F'\}\, c\, \{F_1\}} \; \textit{Consequence-Pre}$$

$$\frac{\{F\}\, c\, \{F_1\} \quad \models F_1 \Rightarrow F_1'}{\{F\}\, c\, \{F_1'\}} \; \textit{Consequence-Post}$$

Such rules are *derivable* in our system (see the terminology in Section 3.3). But for purposes of practicing writing formal derivations exactly correctly, we will not add these rules to our system.

3.5.1   An example with assignment, sequencing, and consequence

Consider the following pca:

$$\{2|x\}\; y := x * x; z := y - 1 \;\{z \geq -1\}$$

This formula says that starting in any state where 2 divides the value (in that state) of x, executing the assignments $y := x * x$ and then $z := y - 1$ will either diverge or else reach a state where the value of z is greater than or equal to -1. Doing a sequence of assignments can never diverge (as the only possibility for divergence in the WHILE language is with WHILE-loops). Informally, we can argue for the truth of this pca by noting that if we square the value of x we get a non-negative number, and hence if we subtract one from that value, we get a result (stored in variable z) that is at least -1.

Formally, we can derive this pca using the rules of Hoare Logic. The derivation is in Figure 3.2. For typographical reasons the names of the rules used have been omitted from the inferences in the derivation. The derivation P uses the consequence rule, and the part of the proof appearing in the top of the figure is an inference using the sequencing rule. The proof also makes use of the assignment rule, for the two inferences shown that do not have premises. The proof uses two validities from $FO(\mathbb{Z})$, in the inference using the consequence rule. The rightmost validity is trivially true, while the leftmost one follows directly from the obvious fact that $x * x \geq 0$: subtracting one from both sides of this inequality gives us the desired conclusion for that leftmost validity. This mirrors the informal argument for this pca just given.

3.5.2   An example with a while-command

We can give a proof of the following pca, which we argued in Section 3.2.2 above is valid based on its semantics:

$$\{F\}\; \texttt{while}\; 1 > 0 \;\texttt{do}\; \texttt{skip}\; \{\textit{False}\}$$

$$\frac{\dfrac{P}{\{2|x\}\, y := x*x\, \{(y-1) \geq -1\}} \qquad \overline{\{(y-1) \geq -1\}\, z := y-1\, \{z \geq -1\}}}{\{2|x\}\, y := x*x; z := y-1\, \{z \geq -1\}}$$

where the proof P is

$$\frac{\models 2|x \;\Rightarrow\; ((x*x)-1) \geq -1 \quad \overline{\{((x*x)-1) \geq -1\}\, y := x*x\, \{(y-1) \geq -1\}} \quad F}{\{2|x\}\, y := x*x\, \{(y-1) \geq -1\}}$$

and F is $\models (y-1) \geq -1 \;\Rightarrow\; (y-1) \geq -1$

Figure 3.2: The Hoare Logic derivation for Section 3.5.1

A derivation of this pca is given in Figure 3.3, again with rule names omitted from inferences for typographical reasons. Notice how we have to adjust the pre- and post-conditions at various points throughout the derivation, so that we can meet certain restrictions imposed by some of the rules. For example, we cannot use the *Skip* rule to derive the following pca which arises in the derivation:

$$\{\textit{True} \wedge 1 > 0\}\ \texttt{skip}\ \{\textit{True}\}$$

This is because here the pre- and post-conditions of the pca are slightly different, but the *Skip* rule requires that they be exactly the same. This is why in the derivation of Figure 3.3 we use the *Skip* rule to derive

$$\{\textit{True}\}\ \texttt{skip}\ \{\textit{True}\}$$

and then use *Consequence* to adjust the pre-condition to match what we need at that point in the derivation.

Stepping back a bit from these details, we see that here we are using *True* as the loop invariant when we apply the *While* rule. This is a rare situation: usually we must carefully determine a nontrivial loop invariant to apply the *While* rule. In this case, however, the negation of the loop's guard ($1 > 0$) is enough to prove the post-condition (*False*) of the loop. This reflects the fact that this loop will never terminate, since its guard is satisfied in all states. And the semantics of pca's tells us that a pca is valid if the command in question diverges.

3.5.3   An example of crafting a loop invariant

Let us now consider an example where some ingenuity is required to craft a loop invariant, for use with the *While* rule. As we have seen in the previous example, it is trivial to come up with *some* loop invariant: *True* is guaranteed to be preserved by the body of any `while`-loop, because *True* is trivially true in any state. So why can't we just always use *True* as the loop invariant for a `while`-loop? The answer is that we actually need a loop invariant to satisfy two conditions: it is preserved

$$\frac{\models (\mathit{True} \wedge 1 > 0) \Rightarrow \mathit{True} \quad \{\mathit{True}\} \, \texttt{skip} \, \{\mathit{True}\} \quad \models \mathit{True} \Rightarrow \mathit{True}}{\{\mathit{True} \wedge 1 > 0\} \, \texttt{skip} \, \{\mathit{True}\}}$$

$$\frac{\models F \Rightarrow \mathit{True} \qquad \dfrac{\{\mathit{True} \wedge 1 > 0\} \, \texttt{skip} \, \{\mathit{True}\}}{\{\mathit{True}\} \, \texttt{while} \, 1 > 0 \, \texttt{do} \, \texttt{skip} \, \{\mathit{True} \wedge \neg 1 > 0\}} \qquad F'}{\{F\} \, \texttt{while} \, 1 > 0 \, \texttt{do} \, \texttt{skip} \, \{\mathit{False}\}}$$

where F' is $\models (\mathit{True} \wedge \neg 1 > 0) \Rightarrow \mathit{False}$

Figure 3.3: The Hoare Logic derivation for Section 3.5.2

by the body of the `while`-loop, and it is strong enough (together with the negation of the loop's guard) to prove the post-condition of the `while`-loop.

For example, consider this pca:

$$\{x = x_0 \wedge y = 0\} \, \texttt{while} \, x \neq 0 \, \texttt{do} \, (y := y + 1; \, x := x - 1) \, \{y = x_0\}$$

We are using the extra variable x_0 (sometimes called a history variable) so that our post-condition can refer to the value that x had at the beginning of the loop. There is nothing special about this variable itself. It is just another variable which we state in the precondition is equal to x. So for a state σ to satisfy the pre-condition, we must have $\sigma(x) = \sigma(x_0)$.

Suppose we were to try to prove this pca using True as the invariant for the `while`-loop. Our proof could start out like this:

$$\frac{\dfrac{\{\mathit{True} \wedge x \neq 0\} \, y := y + 1; \, x := x - 1 \, \{\mathit{True}\}}{J_1 \quad \{\mathit{True}\} \, \texttt{while} \, x \neq 0 \, \texttt{do} \, (y := y + 1; \, x := x - 1) \, \{\mathit{True} \wedge \neg x \neq 0\} \quad J_2}}{\{x = x_0 \wedge y = 0\} \, \texttt{while} \, x \neq 0 \, \texttt{do} \, (y := y + 1; \, x := x - 1) \, \{y = x_0\}}$$

where:
$$J_1 \;=\; \models x = x_0 \wedge y = 0 \Rightarrow \mathit{True}$$
$$J_2 \;=\; \models (\mathit{True} \wedge \neg x \neq 0) \Rightarrow y = x_0$$

Of the unproved premises in this open derivation (see Section 3.3 above for the terminology), we will be able to prove the pca

$$\{\mathit{True} \wedge x \neq 0\} \, y := y + 1; \, x := x - 1 \, \{\mathit{True}\}$$

This is because as we have seen in the example in Section 3.5.2, True is trivially preserved across commands. But we will have problems with the premise J_2 of the application of the *Consequence* rule:

$$\mathit{True} \wedge \neg x \neq 0 \Rightarrow y = x_0$$

This premise is not provable: from the fact that $\sigma(x) = 0$ for an arbitrary state σ, we can conclude nothing about the relationship between $\sigma(y)$ and $\sigma(x_0)$. The problem is that our loop invariant True is too weak: it does not tell us enough about the relationships between the variables affected by the body of the `while`-loop.

To come up with a loop invariant which is strong enough to prove the post-condition, we have to understand the relationships between the variables at the beginning of every iteration of the `while`-loop. Listing out the variables' values for the first few iterations can help, since we are looking for a pattern to describe the relationship across all iterations, and we may be able to generalize from the first few iterations. Our pre-condition for the entire pca states that before the first iteration through the loop, $x = x_0$ and $y = 0$. For concreteness, just for purposes of trying to devise the loop invariant, let us pick some concrete value for x_0, like 4. Then at the start of each iteration through the loop, the variables x and y will have these values:

x	y
4	0
3	1
2	2
1	3
0	4

This pattern suggests an obvious relationship between x and y: $x + y = 4$. Now, we chose 4 just for purposes of exploration. More generally, we should have here x_0 instead of 4. So let us try out the formula $x + y = x_0$ as a loop invariant.

Before we go to the trouble of trying to prove that this formula is preserved by the body of the `while`-loop, it is advisable to confirm that it is true before the first iteration of the loop, and also that it is strong enough to prove the post-condition. This amounts to confirming that the following two formulas are $FO(\mathbb{Z})$ validities:

$$(x = x_0 \wedge y = 0) \Rightarrow x + y = x_0$$
$$x + y = x_0 \wedge \neg x \neq 0 \Rightarrow y = x_0$$

These formulas are both valid. For the second formula, the subformula $\neg x \neq 0$ is equivalent, of course, just to $x = 0$; and if $x = 0$, then $x + y = x_0$ is equivalent to $y = x_0$. It is now not difficult to prove that $x + y = x_0$ is indeed an invariant of the `while`-loop. The derivation is given in Figure 3.4, where some temporary abbreviations (of J_0, etc.) have been used for typographic reasons.

3.6 Soundness of Hoare Logic and induction on the structure of derivations

In Section 3.4 above, we informally argued that every rule of Hoare Logic (from Figure 3.1) is sound with respect to the semantics of pca's we gave in Definition 3.2.1: if we interpret each rule as a formula and interpret each pca according to Definition 3.2.1, then we obtain only valid formulas. But we would like to go one step further, and formally prove:

Theorem 3.6.1 (Soundness of Hoare Logic). *Whenever $\{F\}\ c\ \{F_1\}$ is derivable using the rules for Hoare Logic (in Figure 3.1), then $[\![\{F\}\ c\ \{F_1\}]\!]$ is valid.*

$$\frac{J_2 \quad J_3}{J_1 \quad \{(x-1)+(y+1)=x_0\}\, y:=y+1;\, x:=x-1\,\{x+y=x_0\} \quad J_4}$$
$$\frac{}{\{x+y=x_0 \land x \neq 0\}\, y:=y+1;\, x:=x-1\,\{x+y=x_0\}}$$
$$\frac{J_0 \quad \{x+y=x_0\}\, \texttt{while } x \neq 0 \texttt{ do } y:=y+1;\, x:=x-1\,\{x+y=x_0 \land \neg x \neq 0\} \quad J_5}{\{x=x_0 \land y=0\}\, \texttt{while } x \neq 0 \texttt{ do } y:=y+1;\, x:=x-1\,\{y=x_0\}}$$

where:

$$
\begin{aligned}
J_0 &= \models (x=x_0 \land y=0) \Rightarrow x+y=x_0 \\
J_1 &= \models (x+y=x_0 \land x \neq 0) \Rightarrow (x-1)+(y+1)=x_0 \\
J_2 &= \{(x-1)+(y+1)=x_0\}\, y:=y+1\,\{(x-1)+y=x_0\} \\
J_3 &= \{(x-1)+y=x_0\}\, x:=x-1\,\{x+y=x_0\} \\
J_4 &= \models x+y=x_0 \Rightarrow x+y=x_0 \\
J_5 &= \models (x+y=x_0 \land \neg x \neq 0) \Rightarrow y=x_0
\end{aligned}
$$

Figure 3.4: The Hoare Logic derivation for Section 3.5.3

How do we go from soundness of the rules interpreted as formulas to soundness of all the judgments provable using the rules? The answer is that we use induction on the structure of derivations built using the rules. Every derivation is a finite object, in particular a finite tree of a certain kind (as described above in Section 3.3). So just as we saw with induction on the structure of $FO(\mathbb{Z})$ terms (Section 1.11), we may do induction on the structure of derivations. We must consider each of the inferences which could possibly have proved a given pca, and prove that the semantics of the pca is valid in that case. In each case, we are allowed to use the property we are proving (soundness of derivable pca's), as long as we do so only for subderivations of the derivation we are considering in that case.

Proof of Theorem 3.6.1. The proof is by induction on the structure of the derivation, considering all cases.

Case:

$$\frac{}{\{F\}\,\texttt{skip}\,\{F\}}\ Skip$$

This rule is sound, because if $[\![F]\!]\sigma = True$, for an arbitrary $\sigma \in \Sigma$, then we also have $[\![F]\!]([\![\texttt{skip}]\!]\sigma) = True$, since $[\![\texttt{skip}]\!]\sigma = \sigma$.

Case:

$$\frac{}{\{[t/x]F\}\, x:=t\,\{F\}}\ Assign$$

Consider an arbitrary $\sigma \in \Sigma$ where $[\![[t/x]F]\!]\sigma = True$. By Equation 3.1 of Section 3.4 (proved in an exercise below), it suffices to show $[\![F]\!]([\![x:=t]\!]\sigma) = True$. But $[\![x:=t]\!]\sigma = \sigma[x \mapsto [\![t]\!]\sigma]$, so we have the desired conclusion using the assumption that $[\![[t/x]F]\!]\sigma = True$ and the fact that $[\![[t/x]F]\!]\sigma = [\![F]\!]\sigma[x \mapsto [\![t]\!]\sigma]$.

Case:

$$\frac{\{F \wedge (t \text{ pred } t')\} \, c \, \{F\}}{\{F\} \, \texttt{while } t \text{ pred } t' \, \texttt{do } c \, \{F \wedge \neg(t \text{ pred } t')\}} \quad \textit{While}$$

Consider an arbitrary $\sigma \in \Sigma$ where $[\![F]\!]\sigma = \textit{True}$. We know from our denotational semantics (Section 2.7.2) and from Theorem 2.6.6 (the Least Fixed Point Theorem) that the meaning of the $\texttt{while}$-loop in state σ is equal to $\sqcup(n \mapsto Q^n(\bot_f)(\sigma))$, where Q is the function from $\Sigma \rightarrow \Sigma_\bot$ to $\Sigma \rightarrow \Sigma_\bot$ determined by the $\texttt{while}$-loop (we used F as a meta-variable for this function in Section 2.7.2). Since all chains in the domain $\Sigma_\bot$ are finite, there must be some n where the chain $(n \mapsto Q^n(\bot_f)(\sigma))$ becomes constant. We will now proceed by an inner induction on this n. (The induction is called inner to contrast it with the outer induction we are doing, on the structure of the derivation of the pca.)

We first case split on whether or not the meaning of the $\texttt{while}$-loop starting in state σ is $\bot$. If it is $\bot$, then the pca is valid, since the semantics of pca's (Definition 3.2.1 makes the pca valid if the command diverges. This handles already the base case, where $n = 0$. So suppose it is not $\bot$, and $n = n' + 1$. Suppose $[\![t]\!]\sigma$ is not related according to the relation associated with $\textit{pred}$ with $[\![t']\!]\sigma$. Then the command ends in state σ, which satisfies the post-condition, since it satisfies F by assumption. The state σ also obviously satisfies $\neg t \text{ pred } t'$.

Now suppose $[\![t]\!]\sigma$ is indeed related to $[\![t']\!]\sigma$ according to the relation associated with $\textit{pred}$. Our outer induction hypothesis says that the interpretation of the pca $\{F \wedge t \text{ pred } t'\} \, c \, \{F\}$ is valid. So from this particular state σ, which satisfies the pre-condition of that pca, we know that this next execution of the loop body c will result in a state $[\![c]\!]\sigma$ satisfying F. We can now apply our inner induction hypothesis to conclude that $Q^{n'}([\![c]\!]\sigma)$ satisfies F. Since $Q^{n'+1}(\sigma) = Q^{n'}([\![c]\!]\sigma)$ in this case, this is sufficient.

Case:

$$\frac{\{F\} \, c_1 \, \{F'\} \quad \{F'\} \, c_2 \, \{F''\}}{\{F\} \, c_1; c_2 \, \{F''\}} \quad \textit{Sequence}$$

Consider an arbitrary $\sigma \in \Sigma$ satisfying F. We must show that starting in state σ, execution of $c_1; c_2$ either diverges or terminates in a state satisfying F''. We may apply the induction hypothesis to the derivations of $\{F\} \, c_1 \, \{F'\}$ and $\{F'\} \, c_2 \, \{F''\}$, which we have as subderivations of this inference. So we know $[\![\{F\} \, c_1 \, \{F'\}]\!]$ holds, and also $[\![\{F'\} \, c_2 \, \{F''\}]\!]$. From the first of these facts, and the fact that $[\![F]\!]\sigma$, we know that starting from state σ, execution of c_1 either diverges or else terminates in a state satisfying F'. For the first case: if c_1 diverges when executed from σ, then so does $c_1; c_2$, by the definition of the denotational semantics for sequencing commands, which is sufficient for what we have to prove in this case. So we can consider now the second case, and suppose that $[\![c_1]\!]\sigma = \sigma'$ for some $\sigma' \in \Sigma$, for which $[\![F']\!]\sigma' = \textit{True}$. Now we use the fact that $[\![\{F'\} \, c_2 \, \{F''\}]\!]$ holds, since this tells us that from state σ' (which satisfies F'), execution of c_2 either diverges or else terminates in a state σ'' satisfying F''. In the former case, just as we reasoned above, execution of $c_1; c_2$ will diverge, which suffices to prove our goal. So we can consider the second case, and then we have established that execution of c_1; c_2 starting from state σ will terminate in state σ'' satisfying F'', as required.

Case:

$$\frac{\{F \wedge (t\ pred\ t')\}\ c_1\ \{F'\} \quad \{F \wedge \neg(t\ pred\ t')\}\ c_2\ \{F'\}}{\{F\}\ \texttt{if}\ t\ pred\ t'\ \texttt{then}\ c_1\ \texttt{else}\ c_2\ \{F'\}}\ \textit{Conditional}$$

As for the previous cases, assume an arbitrary $\sigma \in \Sigma$ which satisfies F. By applying the induction hypothesis to the subderivations of this inference, we know:

$$\begin{aligned}
&1. \quad [\![\{F \wedge (t\ pred\ t')\}\ c_1\ \{F'\}]\!] \\
&2. \quad [\![\{F \wedge \neg(t\ pred\ t')\}\ c_2\ \{F'\}]\!]
\end{aligned}$$

We now case split on whether or not $[\![t\ pred\ t']\!]\sigma$ and is $True$ or $False$. If $True$, then we can use fact (1), since this says that starting from any state satisfying F and also interpreting t and t' in such a way that the relation associated with $pred$ does not hold for them; in such a state, executing c_1 either diverges or reaches a state satisfying F'. If $[\![t\ pred\ t']\!]\sigma$ is $False$, then we use fact (2) in a similar way.

Case:

$$\frac{\models F'_1 \Rightarrow F_1 \quad \{F_1\}\ c\ \{F_2\} \quad \models F_2 \Rightarrow F'_2}{\{F'_1\}\ c\ \{F'_2\}}\ \textit{Consequence}$$

Assume an arbitrary $\sigma \in \Sigma$ which satisfies F'. By the first premise of the inference, $F' \Rightarrow F$. So any state satisfying F' must also satisfy F. Now by the induction hypothesis, we know that $[\![\{F\}\ c\ \{F_1\}]\!]$ is valid. So from any state satisfying F, execution of c either diverges or terminates in a state satisfying F_1. Since σ is such a state, we can now case split on whether execution of c diverges or terminates in a state satisfying F_1. If execution of c diverges, then $[\![\{F'\}\ c\ \{F'_1\}]\!]$ is valid by definition of the semantics of pca's. So suppose execution of c terminates in a state σ' satisfying F_1. By the third premise of the inference, any state satisfying F_1 also satisfies F'_1, since F_1 implies F'_1. So execution of c from σ terminates in σ' satisfying F'_1. This is sufficient for validity of $[\![\{F'\}\ c\ \{F'_1\}]\!]$. $\qquad\square$

3.6.1   Incompleteness

We have just proved that Hoare Logic is sound: whenever a partial correctness assertion $\{F'\}\ c\ \{F\}$ is provable using the rules of Hoare Logic, then it is true, in the sense that the meta-language formula $[\![\{F'\}\ c\ \{F\}]\!]$ we defined in Definition 3.2.1 as its meaning is indeed true. It is natural to ask whether Hoare Logic is also complete, in the same sense we considered in Section 3.1 on denotational equivalence: any true formula is provable. Perhaps not surprisingly, the answer is no.

Theorem 3.6.2. *No sound, complete, and recursively enumerable proof system (set of rules) deriving partial correctness assertions exists.*

Proof. This again follows from a recursion-theoretic limitation: if such a proof system existed, we could use it to solve the (unsolvable) halting problem, as follows. Let us assume, for the sake of contradiction, that we have a sound, complete, and recursively enumerable proof system for pca's. Suppose we wish to tell whether or not WHILE command c terminates or not when run in starting state σ. Suppose that $\sigma = \{x_1 \mapsto n_1, \cdots, x_k \mapsto n_k\}$, and consider the pca $\{x_1 = \sigma(x_1) \wedge \cdots \wedge x_k = \sigma(x_k)\}\ c\ \{False\}$. The precondition of this pca exactly describes the values which the starting state σ gives to the variables $x_1, \ldots, x_k$. And the pca is true iff c diverges, because if c terminates in some final state σ', that final state cannot possibly satisfy the postcondition *False* (since *False* is never true, no matter what the state is). Now to decide whether or not c halts, all we have to do is perform two actions in parallel:

- run c from starting state σ, to see if it terminates in some final state σ';

- enumerate all possible proofs in the proof system, searching for a proof of $\{x_1 = \sigma(x_1) \wedge \cdots \wedge x_k = \sigma(x_k)\}\ c\ \{False\}$.

The next chapter will give a formal definition for running the program; here, we can just imagine executing it like a program in any imperative programming languages like C or Java. Since c either terminates or diverges when started from state σ, one or the other of these parallel actions must succeed in finite time. That is, either the first action succeeds, and we will find that c terminates in a final state; or else the second will succeed, and we will find a proof of the stated pca, showing that c diverges. This is where our assumption of completeness comes in: we are assuming, for the sake of deriving a contradiction, that we have a complete proof system for pca's. So if a pca is true (in this case, implying that c diverges), then we will eventually find a proof of that by enumerating all possible proofs. But parallel execution of these two actions would then constitute an algorithm for testing whether or not c halts in finite time, which we know from recursion theory is impossible. So our original assumption that we have a sound, complete, and recursively enumerable proof system for pca's is false. □

The first incompleteness theorem of the famous logician Kurt Gödel shows that there can be no sound, complete, and recursively enumerable proof system for semantic validity for $FO(\mathbb{Z})$. So in our consequence rule, where we appeal to semantic validity for $FO(\mathbb{Z})$, we are really appealing to a notion for which we lack a complete proof system. Cook's theorem shows that this is the only source of incompleteness in Hoare Logic:

Theorem 3.6.3 (Relative completeness). *Hoare Logic formulated (as we have done) with semantic validity for $FO(\mathbb{Z})$ in the Consequence rule is sound and complete.*

The theorem is called a relative completeness result because it shows that Hoare Logic is complete relative to the relation of semantic validity of arithmetic (which has no sound, complete, and recursively enumerable proof system by Gödel's theorem). For a detailed proof of Cooke's relative completeness theorem for the WHILE programming language, see [42]. In practice, we make do with sound but incomplete proof systems for $FO(\mathbb{Z})$, in order to have a (sound) recursively enumerable proof system for Hoare Logic.

3.7 Conclusion

In this chapter, we have seen two examples of axiomatic semantics: denotational equivalence of WHILE commands, and Hoare Logic for proving partial correctness assertions $\{F\} c \{F'\}$ about WHILE commands c. For the latter, the main challenge is identifying a loop invariant: a formula F which is satisfied by the program state, no matter how many times the body of the while-loop is executed. To be invariant under execution in this way, loop invariants have to be weak enough so that if they hold before the body of the loop is executed, they will hold again after the body is executed. They might fail to hold during execution, but they will hold once the beginning of the loop is reached again. And to be useful, loop invariants must imply whatever postcondition we wish to prove is satisfied after execution of the loop. So a trivial formula like *True*, while certainly a loop invariant (since it is true in every state), is not useful, since it cannot imply any nontrivial postcondition. We also proved that Hoare Logic is sound, but not complete.

3.8 Exercises

For several problems below, the following standard definition is used. Define F_1 to be **stronger** than F_2, which is then **weaker** than F_1, if the formula $F_1 \Rightarrow F_2$ is valid. This means that the weakest formula is *False* and the strongest is *True*.

3.8.1 Basic exercises for Section 3.2 on partial correctness assertions

1. Which of the following pca's are valid?

   - $\{x = 0\}\ x := x + x\ \{x > y\}$
   - $\{x > y\}\ x := x * x\ \{x > y\}$
   - $\{False\}\ x := z - 1; x := y + 1\ \{z > y\}$
   - $\{y < z\}\ x := y + z; x := y\ \{False\}$
   - $\{y < z\}\ x := y - z; z := x + z\ \{z = y\}$

2. For each of the following pca's, find the weakest precondition ϕ you can which makes the pca valid. By asking for the weakest precondition you can find, this problem is trying to rule out trivial answers like *False* for ϕ, unless there is no other formula ϕ' not equivalent to false which makes the pca valid.

   - $\{\phi\}\ x := x - 1\ \{x > y\}$
   - $\{\phi\}\ if\ x > 0\ then\ z := x * y\ else\ z := x - 1\ \{z < 0\}$

- $\{\phi\}$ *if* $x = y$ *then* $z := 0$ *else* $z := 1$ $\{x = z\}$
- $\{\phi\}$ $x := y; y := z$ $\{x = z\}$

3.8.2 Basic exercises for Section 3.3 on rules and derivations

Consider the following inference rules for reasoning with conjunction and *True*. These rules are formulated using an approach to proof systems for logical validity known as *natural deduction* (see the book by Troelstra and Schwichtenberg for much more on this topic [39]).

$$\frac{}{\models True} \; true\text{-}intro \qquad \frac{\models F_1 \qquad \models F_2}{\models F_1 \wedge F_2} \; and\text{-}intro$$

$$\frac{\models F_1 \wedge F_2}{\models F_1} \; and\text{-}elim1 \qquad \frac{\models F_1 \wedge F_2}{\models F_2} \; and\text{-}elim2$$

1. Some very basic questions:

    - What is the form of judgment for these rules?
    - What are the premises of the *and-intro* rule?
    - What is the conclusion of the *and-intro* rule?
    - Which rule is an axiom?

2. Give a derivation of $\models True \wedge (True \wedge True)$.

3. Show that the following inference rule is derivable:

$$\frac{\models F_2 \wedge F_1}{\models F_1 \wedge F_2} \; and\text{-}commute$$

4. Which of the following rules is admissible in this proof system (more than one might be)?

$$\frac{\models F_1}{\models F_1 \wedge F_1} \qquad \frac{\models False}{\models False \wedge False} \qquad \frac{\models True}{\models True \wedge F}$$

3.8.3 Basic exercises for Section 3.4 on Hoare Logic

Write out a proof in Hoare Logic for the following pca's. Be very careful to apply the rules exactly as they are defined, without taking any short cuts. This will generally require you to use the consequence rule.

1. $\{x > y \wedge y \geq 0\}$ $z := x + y$ $\{z * z > y * y\}$

2. $\{x > 0\}$ $y := x * x; z := y - 1$ $\{z \geq 0\}$

3. $\{x > y\}$ if $z < 0$ then $z := x - y$ else $z := z + 1$ $\{z > 0\}$

4. $\{x > y\}$ if $x - y < 0$ then $z := -1$ else $z := 1$ $\{z > 0\}$

5. $\{True\}$ if $x = y$ then $z := x * y; x := 1$ else $z := 1$ $\{z \geq 0\}$

3.8.4 Intermediate exercises for Section 3.4 on Hoare Logic

1. Write out a proof in Hoare Logic of the following pca:

   $$\{y_0 = y \wedge y \geq 0\} \; z := 1; \; \text{while } y > 0 \text{ do } (y := y - 1; \; z := z * x) \; \{z = x^{y_0}\}$$

   The critical challenge for this problem is to identify the correct loop invariant for this `while`-loop. What do you know must always be true about z every time this loop executes?

2. Find the weakest precondition ϕ you can which makes the following pca valid:

   $$\{\phi\} \; \text{while } x - y \geq 0 \text{ do } y := y + z; x := x - z; \; \{x = y\}$$

3. Prove Equation 3.1 from Section 3.4. Hint: the proof is by induction on the structure of the formula F mentioned in the equation. You can rename variables bound in F as needed, to avoid capturing variables in the term t which is being substituted for the variable x.

Chapter 4
Operational Semantics of WHILE

In this chapter, we will see another form of semantics, called **operational semantics**, where the meanings of programs are given by showing how to evaluate them in a step-by-step fashion. We have already seen how denotational semantics explains the meaning of WHILE programs by translating them into mathematical functions (Chapter 2). And axiomatic semantics gives a meaning for programs by writing down axioms describing some properties of their execution (Chapter 3). As powerful as those previous semantics are, operational semantics has certain advantages. The semantics seeks to give a direct mathematical description of how programs are executed, rather than of which mathematical functions they can be understood as denoting, or on how they lead from a set of states satisfying one property to one satisfying another. So it is more natural to use such a semantics as the basis for actually executing programs. Furthermore, the semantics does not require (relatively) complex mathematics to define (as did the denotational semantics), nor does it require justification in terms of another semantics, as did our Hoare Logic rules.

At the same time, the analysis of operational semantics can still be involved. For example, in this chapter we will define two different operational semantics. Big-step semantics shows how to evaluate a command from a starting state to reach a final state all at once, in one "big step" (for commands which terminate from that starting state). Small-step semantics will show how commands execute one small step at a time. We will prove a theorem (in Section 4.3) relating modified versions of these semantics, which use counters to keep track of the number of steps that have been executed. This proof is quite lengthy, due to the rather large number of cases that must be considered. Lengthy detailed proofs are very much the norm for programming languages theory, however, so in addition to presenting the operational semantics of WHILE, this chapter will serve as a good introduction to the practical work of detailed proofs of theorems about programming languages.

4.1   Big-step semantics of WHILE

We define when command c in starting state σ evaluates to final state σ', with notation $c, \sigma \Downarrow \sigma'$, by the rules in Figure 4.1. An operational semantics like this one, where the derivable judgments show directly how to perform a complete evaluation of a command (or some other kind of expression) is called a **big-step** semantics, or sometimes a **natural semantics**. In the next section, we will see the alternative, which is small-step semantics. Note that the second rule for `while-`

commands is non-compositional, as it defines the meaning of the `while`-command (in the conclusion) in terms again of the meaning of the `while`-command (in the third premise).

The rules in Figure 4.1 are syntax-directed, in the sense of Section 3.3.3: there is at most one inference which could possibly apply to prove any judgment. For example, if c is `skip`, there is only one rule that could apply. If c is a conditional or a `while`-command, then there are two rules which could apply, depending on whether the guard evaluates to *True* or *False*. But if the one rule applies, the other does not, as these conditions on the value of the guard are mutually exclusive. So there is at most one inference that could be used (and so the proof system is indeed syntax-directed). So we may apply the algorithm described in Section 3.3.1 to try to prove any evaluation judgment.

Going further: instead of trying to prove a judgment $c, \sigma \Downarrow \sigma'$ where all three components (c, σ, and σ) are given, we can start with just c and σ, and look for a rule which could possibly prove $c, \sigma \Downarrow \sigma'$ for some σ'. It can be confirmed that with c and σ given, there is still only one rule (but possibly many instances of that rule) that could apply to prove $c, \sigma \Downarrow \sigma'$ for some σ'. So we apply this rule. We will then need to prove the premises. If we do so in left-to-right order, we will always fill in the starting state of a premise further to the right using the ending state of the premise to its immediate left. Thus, the command and starting state will always be known, and we will just be using the rules to compute the ending state. This process can be seen as mimicking execution of c from starting state σ to ending state σ'. Of course, not every command terminates, and so sometimes this process will diverge.

Here is an example of using the rules in the way just described, to evaluate the command $x := x + 1; skip; y := x + x$ from starting state $\{x \mapsto 1, y \mapsto 2\}$. The only rule which could apply, with some final state σ', is the rule for sequencing. So we know the derivation (if there is one, as in this case) must end in an inference of this form, for some σ'':

$$\frac{x := x + 1, \{x \mapsto 1, y \mapsto 2\} \Downarrow \sigma'' \qquad skip; y := x + x, \sigma'' \Downarrow \sigma'}{x := x + 1; skip; y := x + x, \{x \mapsto 1, y \mapsto 2\} \Downarrow \sigma'}$$

So we recursively try to prove the first premise. Again, there is only one option:

$$\frac{}{x := x + 1, \{x \mapsto 1, y \mapsto 2\} \Downarrow \{x \mapsto 2, y \mapsto 2\}}$$

Notice that this inference has determined what σ'' has to be, since the inference can only be applied if $\sigma'' = \{x \mapsto 2, y \mapsto 2\}$. Since σ'' is known now, we can recursively try to prove the second premise of the first inference we found. There is again only one rule that could apply, namely the sequencing rule again, for some σ''':

$$\frac{skip, \{x \mapsto 2, y \mapsto 2\} \Downarrow \sigma''' \qquad y := x + x, \sigma''' \Downarrow \sigma'}{skip; y := x + x, \{x \mapsto 2, y \mapsto 2\} \Downarrow \sigma'}$$

We can prove the first premise using the axiom (from Figure 4.1) for `skip`:

$$\frac{}{skip, \{x \mapsto 2, y \mapsto 2\} \Downarrow \{x \mapsto 2, y \mapsto 2\}}$$

$$\overline{\text{skip}, \sigma \Downarrow \sigma} \qquad\qquad \overline{x := t, \sigma \Downarrow \sigma[x \mapsto [\![t]\!]\sigma]}$$

$$\frac{[\![t \; pred \; t']\!]\sigma = \mathit{True} \quad c_1, \sigma \Downarrow \sigma'}{\text{if } t \; pred \; t' \text{ then } c_1 \text{ else } c_2, \sigma \Downarrow \sigma'} \qquad \frac{[\![t \; pred \; t']\!]\sigma = \mathit{False} \quad c_2, \sigma \Downarrow \sigma'}{\text{if } t \; pred \; t' \text{ then } c_1 \text{ else } c_2, \sigma \Downarrow \sigma'}$$

$$\frac{c_1, \sigma \Downarrow \sigma' \quad c_2, \sigma' \Downarrow \sigma''}{c_1; c_2, \sigma \Downarrow \sigma''} \qquad\qquad \frac{[\![t \; pred \; t']\!]\sigma = \mathit{False}}{\text{while } t \; pred \; t' \text{ do } c, \sigma \Downarrow \sigma}$$

$$\frac{[\![t \; pred \; t']\!]\sigma = \mathit{True} \quad c, \sigma \Downarrow \sigma' \quad \text{while } t \; pred \; t' \text{ do } c, \sigma' \Downarrow \sigma''}{\text{while } t \; pred \; t' \text{ do } c, \sigma \Downarrow \sigma''}$$

Figure 4.1: Big-step rules for WHILE

Again, we have gained some information at this point, since the `skip`-rule can only be applied if the starting and ending states are the same. So we have learned that σ''' must equal $\{x \mapsto 2, y \mapsto 2\}$. We can now complete the derivation by proving

$$y := x + x, \{x \mapsto 2, y \mapsto 2\} \Downarrow \sigma'$$

This can be done using the axiom for assignments, as follows:

$$\overline{y := x + x, \{x \mapsto 2, y \mapsto 2\} \Downarrow \{x \mapsto 2, y \mapsto 2\}[y \mapsto [\![x + x]\!]\{x \mapsto 2, y \mapsto 2\}]}$$

We have again deduced something further about an unknown state. We learned that σ' must equal

$$\{x \mapsto 2, y \mapsto 2\}[y \mapsto [\![x + x]\!]\{x \mapsto 2, y \mapsto 2\}]$$

We can simplify that expression, of course, as follows:

$$\{x \mapsto 2, y \mapsto 2\}[y \mapsto [\![x + x]\!]\{x \mapsto 2, y \mapsto 2\}]$$
$$\{x \mapsto 2, y \mapsto 2\}[y \mapsto 4]$$
$$\{x \mapsto 2, y \mapsto 4\}$$

Since σ' was the state meta-variable we introduced for the final state of the whole evaluation, we have now proved

$$x := x + 1; skip; y := x + x, \{x \mapsto 1, y \mapsto 2\} \Downarrow \{x \mapsto 2, y \mapsto 4\}$$

4.2   Small-step semantics of WHILE

The goal of small-step semantics is to give a compositional definition of an operational semantics. The idea for doing this is due to Plotkin, who called the approach

$$\frac{}{\texttt{skip},\ \sigma\ \leadsto\ \sigma}$$

$$\frac{}{x := t,\ \sigma\ \leadsto\ \sigma[x \mapsto [\![t]\!]\sigma]}$$

$$\frac{c_1,\ \sigma\ \leadsto\ \sigma'}{c_1;c_2,\ \sigma\ \leadsto\ c_2,\sigma'}$$

$$\frac{c_1,\ \sigma\ \leadsto\ c_1',\sigma'}{c_1;c_2,\ \sigma\ \leadsto\ c_1';c_2,\ \sigma'}$$

$$\frac{[\![t\ pred\ t']\!]\sigma = \textit{True}}{\texttt{if}\ t\ pred\ t'\ \texttt{then}\ c_1\ \texttt{else}\ c_2,\ \sigma\ \leadsto\ c_1,\sigma}$$

$$\frac{[\![t\ pred\ t']\!]\sigma = \textit{False}}{\texttt{if}\ t\ pred\ t'\ \texttt{then}\ c_1\ \texttt{else}\ c_2,\ \sigma\ \leadsto\ c_2,\sigma}$$

$$\frac{[\![t\ pred\ t']\!]\sigma = \textit{False}}{\texttt{while}\ t\ pred\ t'\ \texttt{do}\ c,\ \sigma\ \leadsto\ \sigma}$$

$$\frac{[\![t\ pred\ t']\!]\sigma = \textit{True}}{\texttt{while}\ t\ pred\ t'\ \texttt{do}\ c,\ \sigma\ \leadsto\ c;\texttt{while}\ t\ pred\ t'\ \texttt{do}\ c,\sigma}$$

Figure 4.2: Small-step rules for WHILE

structural operational semantics [34]. Instead of directly defining the relation for evaluating a command from a starting state to a final state, we instead define a relation saying how to evaluate the command one small step further. To show how a program evaluates to a final state, we just chain together a sequence of small steps. Sometimes small-step semantics are called *reduction relations*; big-step semantics also get reduction relations, though some prefer to call them *evaluation relations*, since they show how a program is evaluated to a final value.

There are two forms of judgment for the rules of Figure 4.2. The first is

$$c,\sigma\ \leadsto\ c',\sigma'$$

This is intended to mean that command c will evaluate in one small step to intermediate command c', and the state will change from σ to intermediate σ'. The second form of judgment is

$$c,\sigma\ \leadsto\ \sigma'$$

This is for the special case when evaluating the command c one small step further actually leads to final state σ'.

4.2.1 Determinism

Both big- and small-step semantics are deterministic: starting from the same initial configuration (starting state and command to execute), there is only one way which computation can proceed. This is intuitively obvious, since the language does not have any constructs for nondeterministic computation (we will consider some nondeterministic constructs in Chapter 8). But how do we state and prove this fact? We can formulate determinism for small-step reduction as follows. We will see how this is extended to big-step semantics below (Section 4.3.7).

Theorem 4.2.1 (Determinism of small-step reduction). *The following are all true:*

1. *If $c, \sigma \leadsto \sigma'$ and $c, \sigma \leadsto \sigma''$, then $\sigma' = \sigma''$.*

2. *If $c, \sigma \leadsto c', \sigma'$ and $c, \sigma \leadsto c'', \sigma''$, then $c' = c''$ and $\sigma' = \sigma''$.*

3. *If $c, \sigma \leadsto \sigma'$, then we cannot have $c, \sigma \leadsto c', \sigma'$ for any c' and any σ'.*

This is saying that if computation leads to two resulting configurations, then those configurations must be, in fact, identical. So computation cannot yield two distinct results. Our results below relating big-step and small-step reduction (Section 4.3) will show how to extend this result to big-step semantics.

Proof of Theorem 4.2.1. The proof is by mutual induction on the structure of the first assumed derivation (cf. the proof of Theorem 3.6.1). We will just consider two representative cases: one for an axiom, and one for an inference rule with a small-step reduction for a premise. The others all follow the patterns of these two cases.

Case:

$$\overline{\texttt{skip}, \sigma \leadsto \sigma}$$

For part (1): the command c in question is $\texttt{skip}$, and the resulting configuration is just σ. Now we will use inversion on the form of the second assumed derivation; that is, we will consider cases for the derivation of the judgment $c, \sigma \leadsto \sigma''$, given that c is $\texttt{skip}$ (see Section 3.3.4 for more on inversion). There is, in fact, only one possibility:

$$\overline{\texttt{skip}, \sigma \leadsto \sigma}$$

Clearly the resulting configurations are equal in this case. This also shows part (3) of the lemma.

Case:

$$\frac{c_1, \sigma \leadsto \sigma'}{c_1; c_2, \sigma \leadsto c_2, \sigma'}$$

We apply inversion to the second assumed derivation. There are two possibilities, which we consider in the following subcases:

Subcase:

$$\frac{c_1, \sigma \leadsto \sigma''}{c_1; c_2, \sigma \leadsto c_2, \sigma''}$$

In this case, we can apply the induction hypothesis, part (1), to the derivation of $c_1, \sigma \leadsto \sigma'$ which we have for the premise in the inference considered in this case, together with the one for the premise of the inference in the subcase:

$$\frac{c_1, \sigma \leadsto \sigma' \qquad c_1, \sigma \leadsto \sigma''}{\sigma' = \sigma''} \ IH$$

This gives us the desired conclusion.

Subcase:

$$\frac{c_1, \sigma \leadsto c_1', \sigma''}{c_1; c_2, \sigma \leadsto c_1'; c_2, \sigma''}$$

We can apply our induction hypothesis, part (3) to the derivations in the premises of the inferences for the case and subcase, respectively. This induction hypothesis tells us that it is impossible to have both $c_1, \sigma \leadsto \sigma'$ and $c_1, \sigma \leadsto c_1', \sigma''$. So this subcase simply cannot arise, and there is thus nothing further to prove. This concludes our consideration of representative cases for this theorem.

$$\square$$

4.2.2   Multi-step reduction

With the small-step rules of Figure 4.2, we can prove individual statements of the form $c, \sigma \leadsto \sigma'$. For example, we could prove statements like these two:

$$1. \quad x := 1; y := 2, \sigma \quad \leadsto \quad y := 2, \sigma[x \mapsto 1]$$

$$2. \quad y := 2, \sigma[x \mapsto 1] \quad \leadsto \quad \sigma[x \mapsto 1, y \mapsto 2]$$

But the rules of Figure 4.2 do not give us any way to connect these two proofs, of the two separate small steps, into a complete proof showing how $x := 1; y := 2$ in the given starting step transitions, in two steps, to the final state. To do this, we need to use rules for **multi-step reduction**, given in Figure 4.3. These rules derive judgments of the form $c, \sigma \leadsto^* c', \sigma'$ and $c, \sigma \leadsto^* \sigma'$, which are similar to the judgments defined in the previous section, except allowing multiple steps of computation, instead of just a single step. We can connect the example small steps above as follows, using those rules, to derive a multi-step reduction:

$$\frac{\dfrac{\dfrac{x := 1, \sigma \leadsto \sigma[x \mapsto 1]}{x := 1; y := 2, \sigma \leadsto y := 2, \sigma[x \mapsto 1]}}{x := 1, \sigma \leadsto^* \sigma[x \mapsto 1]} \qquad \dfrac{y := 2, \sigma[x \mapsto 1] \leadsto \sigma[x \mapsto 1, y \mapsto 2]}{y := 2, \sigma[x \mapsto 1] \leadsto^* \sigma[x \mapsto 1, y \mapsto 2]}}{x := 1; y := 2, \sigma \leadsto^* \sigma[x \mapsto 1, y \mapsto 2]}$$

$$\frac{c,\sigma \leadsto \sigma'}{c,\sigma \leadsto^* \sigma'} \qquad\qquad \frac{c,\sigma \leadsto c',\sigma'}{c,\sigma \leadsto^* c',\sigma'}$$

$$\frac{c,\sigma \leadsto^* c',\sigma' \quad c',\sigma' \leadsto^* \sigma''}{c,\sigma \leadsto^* \sigma''} \qquad \frac{c,\sigma \leadsto^* c',\sigma' \quad c',\sigma' \leadsto^* c'',\sigma''}{c,\sigma \leadsto^* c'',\sigma''}$$

$$\frac{}{c,\sigma \leadsto^* c,\sigma}$$

Figure 4.3: Rules for multi-step reduction

$$\frac{a\ R\ a'}{a\ R^*\ a'} \qquad \frac{a_1\ R^*\ a_2 \quad a_2\ R^*\ a_3}{a_1\ R^*\ a_3} \qquad \frac{}{a\ R^*\ a}$$

Figure 4.4: Rule for the reflexive-transitive closure of binary relation R

4.2.3 Reflexive-transitive closure

Multi-step reduction is similar to the **reflexive transitive closure** of R^* of a binary relation R. Semantically, this is the least relation containing R which is also reflexive and transitive. Here when we speak of "the least relation", the ordering we have in mind is the subset ordering $\subseteq$, operating on relations viewed as sets (i.e., sets of ordered pairs). And where this definition says "the least relation containing R", it means the smallest (in the subset ordering) relation which has R as a subset. So if X is any other reflexive and transitive relation containing R (i.e., for which $R \subseteq X$), then we have the following fact about R^*, since it is the least such set by definition:

$$R \subseteq R^* \subseteq X$$

The rules of Figure 4.4 define the reflexive transitive closure R^* of R, writing both relations in infix notation (so $a\ R\ a'$ means that a is related to a' by R). We will make use of this notion in subsequent operational semantics, particularly for lambda calculus (Chapter 5).

4.3 Relating the two operational semantics

The two operational semantics we have defined above are both supposed to describe the execution of WHILE programs. In this section, we will prove a theorem relating them. While we could prove such a theorem directly, with the relations as we have defined them above, we will actually digress slightly to refine our definitions to keep track of exactly how many steps of computation have taken place. We will then be able to get a tighter connection between the two semantics.

If we sought to relate the two semantics as defined above, we would run into one incompatibility right away: the small-step semantics is more expressive when it comes to describing the execution of diverging commands. Suppose we want to describe the execution of the trivial looping command `while 0 = 0 do skip` (let us call this command *loop* for the moment). With the big-step semantics, we cannot derive any judgment of the form *loop*$, \sigma \Downarrow \sigma'$. This is because the big-step semantics can only be used to prove such judgments when the command in question terminates. On the other hand, we can prove that *loop*$, \sigma \leadsto^*$ *loop*$, \sigma$, using the small-step semantics. The reduction steps involved are:

$$\textit{loop}, \sigma \leadsto \texttt{skip}; \textit{loop}, \sigma \leadsto \textit{loop}, \sigma$$

So there is a mismatch between big-step and small-step semantics in the case of diverging commands. This mismatch is not terribly fundamental, however. If we want a big-step semantics which we can use to describe diverging computations, we can simply limit the number of steps the big-step semantics is allowed to take. This can be done by changing the form of big-step judgments to $c, \sigma \Downarrow_n \sigma'$ and adding a new judgment form $c, \sigma \Downarrow_n c', \sigma'$. The subscript n is just a natural number, which we will use as a counter which keeps track of the number of steps of computation. If evaluation would run for more than n steps in the big-step rules without counters, the rules with counters will cut it off before it reaches a final state. We will refine our multi-step reduction judgments to $c, \sigma \leadsto^n \sigma'$ and $c, \sigma \leadsto^n c', \sigma'$. The latter form is for evaluations that were cut off early: there is still a residual command c' that has not completed. The theorem we prove in this section is then that n-step big-step reduction is exactly equivalent to n-step small-step reduction.

4.3.1   Extending the relations with counters

Figures 4.5, 4.6, and 4.7 give the new rules for our judgments with counters n. The multi-step rules are straightforward to adapt with counters, but the big-step rules require more work, to handle the situations where the counter reaches 0 before we have reached a final state. The new rules for this situation are in Figure 4.7.

Let us consider an example of a big-step derivation with counters, for the following command (which we will temporarily abbreviate $\hat{c}$ below):

$$\texttt{while } 0 = 0 \texttt{ do } x := x + 1; y := x$$

This command would diverge, from any starting state, using the big-step rules without counters (Figure 4.1). Using counters, its evaluation will be cut off early, without reaching a final state. For example, if we use a counter value of 2 and start the command from state $\sigma = \{x \mapsto 0, y \mapsto 0\}$, we have this derivation, where we write σ' for $\sigma[x \mapsto 1]$:

$$\cfrac{\llbracket 0 = 0 \rrbracket \sigma = \textit{True} \qquad \cfrac{\cfrac{}{x := x+1, \sigma \Downarrow_1 \sigma[x \mapsto 1]} \quad \cfrac{}{y := x, \sigma' \Downarrow_0 y := x, \sigma'}}{x := x+1; y := x, \sigma \Downarrow_1 y := x, \sigma'}}{\texttt{while } 0 = 0 \texttt{ do } x := x+1; y := x, \sigma \Downarrow_2 y := x; \hat{c}, \sigma'}$$

$$\frac{c,\sigma \rightsquigarrow \sigma'}{c,\sigma \rightsquigarrow^1 \sigma'} \qquad\qquad \frac{c,\sigma \rightsquigarrow c',\sigma'}{c,\sigma \rightsquigarrow^1 c',\sigma'}$$

$$\frac{c,\sigma \rightsquigarrow^n c',\sigma' \quad c',\sigma' \rightsquigarrow^m \sigma''}{c,\sigma \rightsquigarrow^{n+m} \sigma''} \qquad \frac{c,\sigma \rightsquigarrow^n c',\sigma' \quad c',\sigma' \rightsquigarrow^m c'',\sigma''}{c,\sigma \rightsquigarrow^{n+m} c'',\sigma''}$$

$$\frac{}{c,\sigma \rightsquigarrow^0 c,\sigma}$$

Figure 4.5: Rules for multi-step reduction, keeping track of reduction length

$$\frac{}{\texttt{skip},\sigma \Downarrow_1 \sigma}$$

$$\frac{}{x := t,\sigma \Downarrow_1 \sigma[x \mapsto [\![t]\!]\sigma]}$$

$$\frac{c_1,\sigma \Downarrow_n \sigma' \quad c_2,\sigma' \Downarrow_m \sigma''}{c_1;c_2,\sigma \Downarrow_{n+m} \sigma''}$$

$$\frac{[\![t\ pred\ t']\!]\sigma = True \quad c_1,\sigma \Downarrow_n \sigma'}{\texttt{if}\ t\ pred\ t'\ \texttt{then}\ c_1\ \texttt{else}\ c_2,\sigma \Downarrow_{n+1} \sigma'}$$

$$\frac{[\![t\ pred\ t']\!]\sigma = False \quad c_2,\sigma \Downarrow_n \sigma'}{\texttt{if}\ t\ pred\ t'\ \texttt{then}\ c_1\ \texttt{else}\ c_2,\sigma \Downarrow_{n+1} \sigma'}$$

$$\frac{[\![t\ pred\ t']\!]\sigma = False}{\texttt{while}\ t\ pred\ t'\ \texttt{do}\ c,\sigma \Downarrow_1 \sigma}$$

$$\frac{[\![t\ pred\ t']\!]\sigma = True \quad c,\sigma \Downarrow_n \sigma' \quad \texttt{while}\ t\ pred\ t'\ \texttt{do}\ c,\sigma' \Downarrow_m \sigma''}{\texttt{while}\ t\ pred\ t'\ \texttt{do}\ c,\sigma \Downarrow_{n+m+1} \sigma''}$$

Figure 4.6: Big-step rules with counters for WHILE. These are the rules where computation reaches a final state. See Figure 4.7 for rules for when computation does not reach a final state.

$$c,\sigma \Downarrow_0 c,\sigma$$

$$\frac{c_1,\sigma \Downarrow_n c_1',\sigma'}{c_1;c_2,\sigma \Downarrow_n c_1';c_2,\sigma'}$$

$$\frac{[\![t\ pred\ t']\!]\sigma = True \quad c_1,\sigma \Downarrow_n c',\sigma'}{\texttt{if}\ t\ pred\ t'\ \texttt{then}\ c_1\ \texttt{else}\ c_2,\sigma \Downarrow_{n+1} c',\sigma'}$$

$$\frac{c_1,\sigma \Downarrow_n \sigma' \quad c_2,\sigma' \Downarrow_m c_2',\sigma''}{c_1;c_2,\sigma \Downarrow_{n+m} c_2',\sigma''}$$

$$\frac{[\![t\ pred\ t']\!]\sigma = False \quad c_2,\sigma \Downarrow_n c',\sigma'}{\texttt{if}\ t\ pred\ t'\ \texttt{then}\ c_1\ \texttt{else}\ c_2,\sigma \Downarrow_{n+1} c',\sigma'}$$

$$\frac{[\![t\ pred\ t']\!]\sigma = True \quad c,\sigma \Downarrow_n c',\sigma'}{\texttt{while}\ t\ pred\ t'\ \texttt{do}\ c,\sigma \Downarrow_{n+1} c';\texttt{while}\ t\ pred\ t'\ \texttt{do}\ c,\sigma'}$$

$$\frac{[\![t\ pred\ t']\!]\sigma = True \quad c,\sigma \Downarrow_n \sigma'}{\texttt{while}\ t\ pred\ t'\ \texttt{do}\ c,\sigma \Downarrow_{n+1} \texttt{while}\ t\ pred\ t'\ \texttt{do}\ c,\sigma'}$$

$$\frac{[\![t\ pred\ t']\!]\sigma = True \quad c,\sigma \Downarrow_n \sigma' \quad \texttt{while}\ t\ pred\ t'\ \texttt{do}\ c,\sigma' \Downarrow_m c'',\sigma''}{\texttt{while}\ t\ pred\ t'\ \texttt{do}\ c,\sigma \Downarrow_{n+m+1} c'',\sigma''}$$

Figure 4.7: Big-step rules with counters for WHILE. These are the rules where computation does not reach a final state (because the counter reaches 0 before that).

4.3.2   Proving equivalence of the counter-based systems

In this section, we will prove the following theorem:

Theorem 4.3.1. *The following both hold, for all natural numbers k:*

1. *$c, \sigma \Downarrow_k \sigma'$ iff $c, \sigma \leadsto^k \sigma'$.*

2. *$c, \sigma \Downarrow_k c', \sigma'$ iff $c, \sigma \leadsto^k c', \sigma'$.*

The proof relies on the following three lemmas, which we prove in Sections 4.3.3, 4.3.4, and 4.3.5 below. These lemmas reveal some of the central technical ideas needed in the proof of Theorem 4.3.1.

Lemma 4.3.2 (Compatibility of multi-step reduction with sequencing). *The following both hold:*

1. *If $c_1, \sigma \leadsto^n c_1', \sigma'$, then $c_1; c_2, \sigma \leadsto^n c_1'; c_2, \sigma'$.*

2. *If $c_1, \sigma \leadsto^n \sigma'$, then $c_1; c_2, \sigma \leadsto^n c_2, \sigma'$.*

Lemma 4.3.3 (Transitivity of big-step evaluation with counters). *Suppose $c, \sigma \Downarrow_n c', \sigma'$. Then the following both hold:*

1. *$c', \sigma' \Downarrow_m \sigma''$ implies $c, \sigma \Downarrow_{n+m} \sigma''$.*

2. *$c', \sigma' \Downarrow_m c'', \sigma''$ implies $c, \sigma \Downarrow_{n+m} c'', \sigma''$.*

Lemma 4.3.4 (Relating small-step reduction and big-step reduction with counters). *The following both hold:*

1. *If $c, \sigma \leadsto \sigma'$ then $c, \sigma \Downarrow_1 \sigma'$.*

2. *If $c, \sigma \leadsto c', \sigma'$ then $c, \sigma \Downarrow_1 c', \sigma'$.*

About detailed proofs. Like many proofs in Programming Languages theory, the proofs below are not difficult, but there are a lot of detailed cases to work through. In the course of writing this proof down, I found and corrected numerous small bugs in the exact formulations of the rules with counters. It is a common observation in Programming Languages that writing detailed proofs helps improve the quality of the languages about which one is reasoning. At the same time, such proofs have sometimes been called "write-only": they usually make for rather dry reading. You may find that it is more profitable to try to prove some parts of this theorem, or of the lemmas, yourself, and then compare your proofs with what is written below. Even the effort to understand the statements of the theorems and lemmas will yield significant insight into how the multi-step and big-step relations with counters work.

Note on meta-variables. Before we begin the proof, it is worth discussing a somewhat annoying issue: the choice of meta-variables when considering cases on the form of a derivation. Below, we will often be considering all possible forms a derivation could have. In particular, we will consider what the last inference of the derivation is. The proof rule in question is defined using its own meta-variables. For example, a rule like the following (from Figure 4.7) uses 10 different meta-variables:

$$\frac{[\![t \; pred \; t']\!]\sigma = True \quad c,\sigma \Downarrow_n \sigma' \quad \texttt{while} \; t \; pred \; t' \; \texttt{do} \; c,\sigma' \Downarrow_m c'',\sigma''}{\texttt{while} \; t \; pred \; t' \; \texttt{do} \; c,\sigma \Downarrow_{n+m+1} c'',\sigma''}$$

Sometimes some of these meta-variables are already being used in the surrounding context of one's proof. In the case of this rule for `while`-commands, the left-to-right direction of part (2) of Theorem 4.3.1 already uses 4 of those meta-variables (c, σ, c', and σ'). Sometimes those uses are the same as in the rule. For example, in this case σ is used in the same way in the rule as in the left-to-right direction of the theorem: the theorem uses σ as the starting state for the assumed big-step evaluation, and the rule happens to use σ for that starting state, too. But sometimes the uses are different. Here, the left-to-right direction of part (2) the theorem uses σ' for the ending state of the assumed big-step evaluation, but the rule uses σ'' for the ending state. Also, the statement of the theorem uses c for the name of the whole command, while the `while`-rule uses it for the body of the `while`-command. In such cases, one can always change the meta-variables in the rule so that they use different meta-variables from those used in the statement of the theorem or the surrounding context of the proof, to help avoid confusion. For example, we could use this renamed rule:

$$\frac{[\![t \; pred \; t']\!]\sigma = True \quad c_1,\sigma \Downarrow_n \sigma_1 \quad \texttt{while} \; t \; pred \; t' \; \texttt{do} \; c_1,\sigma_1 \Downarrow_m c',\sigma'}{\texttt{while} \; t \; pred \; t' \; \texttt{do} \; c_1,\sigma \Downarrow_{n+m+1} c',\sigma'}$$

This rule is the same as the one shown above, except that we have renamed meta-variables so that the rule's usage and the theorem's are consistent. This can help reduce confusion in proofs, at the cost of using a renamed rule. Using a renamed rule can make it a little harder on the reader to follow the proof, since s/he must match up the renamed rule with the original one to confirm they are equivalent. Furthermore, for the person writing the proof, it is easy to make a mistake in carrying out the renaming (if this is done by hand, as it most often is). An alternative to renaming is simply to understand the meta-variables used in the rule as shadowing those in the surrounding context. That is, we understand that the new meta-variables have been introduced by our case-analysis on the form of the derivation, and we take subsequent uses of those meta-variables (in that case) to be the ones introduced in the rule. This may induce some refinements of meta-variables in the surrounding proof context using those in the rule. For example, if we used the original (unrenamed) rule, we would know that the c in the statement of the theorem has been refined to `while` $t \; pred \; t$ `do` c. Sometimes there is too much danger of confusion with this approach, and then using a renamed rule is the clearest way to go. We will see both approaches in the following proof. A final alternative is to choose meta-variables in the statement of the theorem which do not conflict with the meta-variables in the rules (though this may make the theorem harder to read, since it will be using different meta-variables than used elsewhere).

Proof of Theorem 4.3.1. We will prove the forward directions of the equivalences stated in Theorem 4.3.1 by mutual induction, and then the reverse directions. Each direction will be proved by induction on the structure of the assumed derivation. Each direction of the proof is constructive: it can be thought of as showing, for example, how to transform a proof of $c, \sigma \Downarrow_k \sigma'$ into a proof of $c, \sigma \leadsto^k \sigma'$. So in each of the cases below, we will show how to build a proof of the desired result judgment from a proof of the assumed judgment.

Proof of left-to-right direction of part (1) of Theorem 4.3.1. Assume $c, \sigma \Downarrow_k \sigma'$, and prove $c, \sigma \leadsto^k \sigma'$. The proof now proceeds by considering all the different cases for deriving the assumed big-step judgment.

Case:

$$\frac{}{\texttt{skip}, \sigma \Downarrow_1 \sigma}$$

The following derivation proves the desired judgment:

$$\frac{\texttt{skip}, \sigma \leadsto \sigma}{\texttt{skip}, \sigma \leadsto^1 \sigma}$$

That is, we have $\texttt{skip}, \sigma \leadsto \sigma$ using the rule for $\texttt{skip}$-commands in Figure 4.2, and hence we can use the appropriate rule of Figure 4.5 to conclude $\texttt{skip}, \sigma \leadsto^1 \sigma$.

Case:

$$\frac{}{x := t, \sigma \Downarrow_1 \sigma[x \mapsto [\![t]\!]\sigma]}$$

The following derivation suffices:

$$\frac{x := t, \sigma \leadsto \sigma[x \mapsto [\![t]\!]\sigma]}{x := t, \sigma \leadsto^1 \sigma[x \mapsto [\![t]\!]\sigma]}$$

Case:

$$\frac{c_1, \sigma \Downarrow_n \sigma' \quad c_2, \sigma' \Downarrow_m \sigma''}{c_1; c_2, \sigma \Downarrow_{n+m} \sigma''}$$

The following derives the required $c_1; c_2, \sigma \leadsto^{n+m+1} \sigma''$, appealing to the lemma stated at the start of this section (and proved below, Section 4.3.3), as well as the induction hypothesis (IH), which we apply as part of the derivation:

$$\frac{\dfrac{\dfrac{c_1, \sigma \Downarrow_n \sigma'}{c_1, \sigma \leadsto^n \sigma'} \ \text{IH}}{c_1; c_2, \sigma \leadsto^n c_2, \sigma'} \ \text{Lemma 4.3.2} \quad \dfrac{c_2, \sigma' \Downarrow_m \sigma''}{c_2, \sigma' \leadsto^m \sigma''} \ \text{IH}}{c_1; c_2, \sigma \leadsto^{n+m} \sigma''}$$

Case:

$$\frac{[\![t \ pred \ t']\!]\sigma = True \quad c_1, \sigma \Downarrow_n \sigma'}{\texttt{if } t \ pred \ t' \texttt{ then } c_1 \texttt{ else } c_2, \sigma \Downarrow_{n+1} \sigma'}$$

We use the following derivation of the desired judgment:

$$
\cfrac{
  \cfrac{
    \cfrac{[\![t \; pred \; t']\!]\sigma = True}{\texttt{if } t \; pred \; t' \texttt{ then } c_1 \texttt{ else } c_2, \sigma \rightsquigarrow c_1, \sigma}
  }{\texttt{if } t \; pred \; t' \texttt{ then } c_1 \texttt{ else } c_2, \sigma \rightsquigarrow^1 c_1, \sigma}
  \qquad
  \cfrac{c_1, \sigma \Downarrow_n \sigma'}{c_1, \sigma \rightsquigarrow^n \sigma'} \; IH
}{\texttt{if } t \; pred \; t' \texttt{ then } c_1 \texttt{ else } c_2, \sigma \rightsquigarrow^{n+1} \sigma'}
$$

Case:

$$
\cfrac{[\![t \; pred \; t']\!]\sigma = False \qquad c_2, \sigma \Downarrow_n \sigma'}{\texttt{if } t \; pred \; t' \texttt{ then } c_1 \texttt{ else } c_2, \sigma \Downarrow_{n+1} \sigma'}
$$

The derivation in this case is just like the one for the previous case, except choosing c_2, since the guard of the if-command has value *False* in state σ:

$$
\cfrac{
  \cfrac{
    \cfrac{[\![t \; pred \; t']\!]\sigma = False}{\texttt{if } t \; pred \; t' \texttt{ then } c_1 \texttt{ else } c_2, \sigma \rightsquigarrow c_2, \sigma}
  }{\texttt{if } t \; pred \; t' \texttt{ then } c_1 \texttt{ else } c_2, \sigma \rightsquigarrow^1 c_2, \sigma}
  \qquad
  \cfrac{c_2, \sigma \Downarrow_n \sigma'}{c_2, \sigma \rightsquigarrow^n \sigma'} \; IH
}{\texttt{if } t \; pred \; t' \texttt{ then } c_1 \texttt{ else } c_2, \sigma \rightsquigarrow^{n+1} \sigma'}
$$

Case:

$$
\cfrac{[\![t \; pred \; t']\!]\sigma = False}{\texttt{while } t \; pred \; t' \texttt{ do } c, \sigma \Downarrow_1 \sigma}
$$

The following derivation suffices:

$$
\cfrac{
  \cfrac{[\![t \; pred \; t']\!]\sigma = False}{\texttt{while } t \; pred \; t' \texttt{ do } c, \sigma \rightsquigarrow \sigma}
}{\texttt{while } t \; pred \; t' \texttt{ do } c, \sigma \rightsquigarrow^1 \sigma}
$$

Case:

$$
\cfrac{[\![t \; pred \; t']\!]\sigma = True \quad c, \sigma \Downarrow_n \sigma' \quad \texttt{while } t \; pred \; t' \texttt{ do } c, \sigma' \Downarrow_m \sigma''}{\texttt{while } t \; pred \; t' \texttt{ do } c, \sigma \Downarrow_{n+m+1} \sigma''}
$$

We use the following derivation, where we are abbreviating $\texttt{while } t \; pred \; t' \texttt{ do } c$ as $\hat{c}$, for typographic reasons:

$$
\cfrac{
  \cfrac{
    [\![t \; pred \; t']\!]\sigma = True \qquad \cfrac{\cfrac{c, \sigma \Downarrow_n \sigma'}{c, \sigma \rightsquigarrow^n \sigma'} \; IH}{c; \hat{c}, \sigma \rightsquigarrow^n \hat{c}, \sigma'} \; Lemma \; 4.3.2 \qquad \cfrac{\hat{c}, \sigma' \Downarrow_m \sigma''}{\hat{c}, \sigma' \rightsquigarrow^m \sigma''} \; IH
  }{
    \cfrac{\hat{c}, \sigma \rightsquigarrow c; \hat{c}, \sigma}{\hat{c}, \sigma \rightsquigarrow^1 c; \hat{c}, \sigma} \qquad c; \hat{c}, \sigma \rightsquigarrow^{n+m} \sigma''
  }
}{\hat{c}, \sigma \rightsquigarrow^{n+m+1} \sigma''}
$$

End proof of left-to-right direction of part (1) of Theorem 4.3.1.

Proof of left-to-right direction of part (2) of Theorem 4.3.1. Assume $c, \sigma \Downarrow_k c', \sigma'$, and prove $c, \sigma \rightsquigarrow^k c', \sigma'$ by considering all the different cases for deriving the assumed big-step judgment.

Case:

$$\overline{c, \sigma \Downarrow_0 c, \sigma}$$

The last rule of Figure 4.5 gives us $c, \sigma \leadsto^0 c, \sigma$, as required.

Case:

$$\frac{c_1, \sigma \Downarrow_n c_1', \sigma'}{c_1; c_2, \sigma \Downarrow_n c_1'; c_2, \sigma'}$$

The following derives the desired judgment:

$$\frac{\dfrac{c_1, \sigma \Downarrow_n c_1', \sigma'}{c_1, \sigma \leadsto^n c_1', \sigma'} \; IH}{c_1; c_2, \sigma \leadsto^n c_1'; c_2, \sigma'} \; Lemma \; 4.3.2$$

Case:

$$\frac{c_1, \sigma \Downarrow_n \sigma' \quad c_2, \sigma' \Downarrow_m c_2', \sigma''}{c_1; c_2, \sigma \Downarrow_{n+m} c_2', \sigma''}$$

We use this derivation:

$$\frac{\dfrac{\dfrac{c_1, \sigma \Downarrow_n \sigma'}{c_1, \sigma \leadsto^n \sigma'} \; IH}{c_1; c_2, \sigma \leadsto^n c_2, \sigma'} \; Lemma \; 4.3.2 \qquad \dfrac{c_1, \sigma' \Downarrow_n c_2', \sigma''}{c_2, \sigma' \leadsto^m c_2', \sigma''} \; IH}{c_1; c_2, \sigma \leadsto^{n+m} c_2, \sigma'}$$

Case:

$$\frac{[\![t \; pred \; t']\!]\sigma = True \quad c_1, \sigma \Downarrow_n c', \sigma'}{\texttt{if } t \; pred \; t' \texttt{ then } c_1 \texttt{ else } c_2, \sigma \Downarrow_{n+1} c', \sigma'}$$

The derivation of the required judgment is similar to the one we had for this big-step rule, in the proof of part (1) of the theorem:

$$\frac{\dfrac{[\![t \; pred \; t']\!]\sigma = True}{\texttt{if } t \; pred \; t' \texttt{ then } c_1 \texttt{ else } c_2, \sigma \leadsto c_1, \sigma}}{\texttt{if } t \; pred \; t' \texttt{ then } c_1 \texttt{ else } c_2, \sigma \leadsto^1 c_1, \sigma} \qquad \dfrac{c_1, \sigma \Downarrow_n c', \sigma'}{c_1, \sigma \leadsto^n c', \sigma'} \; IH}{\texttt{if } t \; pred \; t' \texttt{ then } c_1 \texttt{ else } c_2, \sigma \leadsto^{n+1} c', \sigma'}$$

Case:

$$\frac{[\![t \; pred \; t']\!]\sigma = False \quad c_2, \sigma \Downarrow_n c', \sigma'}{\texttt{if } t \; pred \; t' \texttt{ then } c_1 \texttt{ else } c_2, \sigma \Downarrow_{n+1} c', \sigma'}$$

The following derivation is similar to the one for the previous case:

$$\frac{\dfrac{[\![t \; pred \; t']\!]\sigma = False}{\texttt{if } t \; pred \; t' \texttt{ then } c_1 \texttt{ else } c_2, \sigma \leadsto c_2, \sigma}}{\texttt{if } t \; pred \; t' \texttt{ then } c_1 \texttt{ else } c_2, \sigma \leadsto^1 c_2, \sigma} \qquad \dfrac{c_2, \sigma \Downarrow_n c', \sigma'}{c_2, \sigma \leadsto^n c', \sigma'} \; IH}{\texttt{if } t \; pred \; t' \texttt{ then } c_1 \texttt{ else } c_2, \sigma \leadsto^{n+1} c', \sigma'}$$

Case:

$$\frac{[\![t \ pred \ t']\!]\sigma = True \quad c,\sigma \Downarrow_n c',\sigma'}{\texttt{while} \ t \ pred \ t' \ \texttt{do} \ c,\sigma \Downarrow_{n+1} c'; \texttt{while} \ t \ pred \ t' \ \texttt{do} \ c,\sigma'}$$

Abbreviating `while` $t \ pred \ t'$ `do` c as $\hat{c}$ for typographic reasons, we have this derivation:

$$\frac{\dfrac{[\![t \ pred \ t']\!]\sigma = True}{\dfrac{\hat{c},\sigma \rightsquigarrow c;\hat{c},\sigma}{\hat{c},\sigma \rightsquigarrow^1 c;\hat{c},\sigma}} \qquad \dfrac{\dfrac{c,\sigma \Downarrow_n \sigma'}{c,\sigma \rightsquigarrow^n \sigma'} \ IH}{c;\hat{c},\sigma \rightsquigarrow^n \hat{c},\sigma'} \ Lemma \ 4.3.2}{\hat{c},\sigma \rightsquigarrow^{n+1} \hat{c},\sigma'}$$

Case:

$$\frac{[\![t \ pred \ t']\!]\sigma = True \quad c,\sigma \Downarrow_n \sigma'}{\texttt{while} \ t \ pred \ t' \ \texttt{do} \ c,\sigma \Downarrow_{n+1} \texttt{while} \ t \ pred \ t' \ \texttt{do} \ c,\sigma'}$$

Again abbreviating `while` $t \ pred \ t'$ `do` c as $\hat{c}$, we have:

$$\frac{\dfrac{[\![t \ pred \ t']\!]\sigma = True}{\dfrac{\hat{c},\sigma \rightsquigarrow c;\hat{c},\sigma}{\hat{c},\sigma \rightsquigarrow^1 c;\hat{c},\sigma}} \qquad \dfrac{\dfrac{c,\sigma \Downarrow_n c',\sigma'}{c,\sigma \rightsquigarrow^n c',\sigma'} \ IH}{c;\hat{c},\sigma \rightsquigarrow^n c';\hat{c},\sigma'} \ Lemma \ 4.3.2}{\hat{c},\sigma \rightsquigarrow^{n+1} c';\hat{c},\sigma'}$$

Case:

$$\frac{[\![t \ pred \ t']\!]\sigma = True \quad c,\sigma \Downarrow_n \sigma' \quad \texttt{while} \ t \ pred \ t' \ \texttt{do} \ c,\sigma' \Downarrow_m c'',\sigma''}{\texttt{while} \ t \ pred \ t' \ \texttt{do} \ c,\sigma \Downarrow_{n+m+1} c'',\sigma''}$$

Again abbreviating `while` $t \ pred \ t'$ `do` c as $\hat{c}$, we have:

$$\frac{\dfrac{[\![t \ pred \ t']\!]\sigma = True}{\dfrac{\hat{c},\sigma \rightsquigarrow c;\hat{c},\sigma}{\hat{c},\sigma \rightsquigarrow^1 c;\hat{c},\sigma}} \quad \dfrac{\dfrac{\dfrac{c,\sigma \Downarrow_n \sigma'}{c,\sigma \rightsquigarrow^n \sigma'} \ IH}{c;\hat{c},\sigma \rightsquigarrow^n \hat{c},\sigma'} \ Lemma \ 4.3.2 \quad \dfrac{\hat{c},\sigma' \Downarrow_m c'',\sigma''}{\hat{c},\sigma' \rightsquigarrow^m c'',\sigma''} \ IH}{c;\hat{c},\sigma \rightsquigarrow^{n+m} c'',\sigma''}}{\hat{c},\sigma \rightsquigarrow^{n+m+1} c'',\sigma''}$$

End proof of left-to-right direction of part (2) of Theorem 4.3.1.

Proof of right-to-left direction of part (1) of Theorem 4.3.1. Assume $c, \sigma \rightsquigarrow^k \sigma'$, and prove $c,\sigma \Downarrow_k \sigma'$. There are only two possibilities for the form of the derivation in this case, since the multi-step reduction ends with a final state only (and not a command and a final state):

Case:

$$\frac{c,\sigma \rightsquigarrow \sigma'}{c,\sigma \rightsquigarrow^1 \sigma'}$$

The result follows from Lemma 4.3.4, proved in Section 4.3.5 below.

Case:

$$\frac{c,\sigma \leadsto^n c',\sigma' \quad c',\sigma' \leadsto^m \sigma''}{c,\sigma \leadsto^{n+m} \sigma''}$$

We can use the following derivation (the lemma is proved in Section 4.3.4 below):

$$\frac{\dfrac{c,\sigma \leadsto^n c',\sigma'}{c,\sigma \Downarrow_n c',\sigma'}\;IH \qquad \dfrac{c',\sigma' \leadsto^m \sigma''}{c',\sigma' \Downarrow_m \sigma''}\;IH}{c,\sigma \Downarrow_{n+m} \sigma''}\;Lemma\ 4.3.3$$

End proof of right-to-left direction of part (1) of Theorem 4.3.1.

Proof of right-to-left direction of part (2) of Theorem 4.3.1. Assume $c,\sigma \leadsto^k c',\sigma'$, and prove $c,\sigma \Downarrow_k c',\sigma'$. There are several cases to consider for the derivation of the assumed multi-step reduction:

Case:

$$\frac{c,\sigma \leadsto c',\sigma'}{c,\sigma \leadsto^1 c',\sigma'}$$

The result follows from Lemma 4.3.4, proved in Section 4.3.5 below.

Case:

$$\frac{c,\sigma \leadsto^n c',\sigma' \quad c',\sigma' \leadsto^m c'',\sigma''}{c,\sigma \leadsto^{n+m} c'',\sigma''}$$

We have the following derivation:

$$\frac{\dfrac{c,\sigma \leadsto^n c',\sigma'}{c,\sigma \Downarrow_n c',\sigma'}\;IH \qquad \dfrac{c',\sigma' \leadsto^m c'',\sigma''}{c',\sigma' \Downarrow_m c'',\sigma''}\;IH}{c,\sigma \Downarrow_{n+m} c'',\sigma''}\;Lemma\ 4.3.3$$

Case:

$$\frac{}{c,\sigma \leadsto^0 c,\sigma}$$

This suffices:

$$\frac{}{c,\sigma \Downarrow_0 c,\sigma}$$

End proof of right-to-left direction of part (2) of Theorem 4.3.1.

This concludes the proof of Theorem 4.3.1. $\qquad\qquad\square$

4.3.3 Proof of Lemma 4.3.2 (used in the proof of Theorem 4.3.1)

Proof. The proof is by mutual induction on the structure of the assumed multi-step reduction derivations. For part (1) of the lemma: assume $c_1,\sigma \leadsto^n c_1',\sigma'$, and prove $c_1;c_2,\sigma \leadsto^n c_1';c_2,\sigma'$. There are three possibilities, given that the derived judgment ends in a paired command and final state (as opposed to just a final state):

Case:

$$\frac{c_1,\sigma \rightsquigarrow c_1',\sigma'}{c_1,\sigma \rightsquigarrow^1 c_1',\sigma'}$$

The following derives the desired judgment in this case:

$$\frac{\dfrac{c_1,\sigma \rightsquigarrow c_1',\sigma'}{c_1;c_2,\sigma \rightsquigarrow c_1';c_2,\sigma'}}{c_1;c_2,\sigma \rightsquigarrow^1 c_1';c_2,\sigma'}$$

Case:

$$\frac{c_1,\sigma \rightsquigarrow^j c_1'',\sigma_1 \quad c_1'',\sigma_1 \rightsquigarrow^k c_1',\sigma'}{c_1,\sigma \rightsquigarrow^{j+k} c_1',\sigma'}$$

We can use this derivation, where we are applying the IH to the derivations we have from the premises of the derivation in this case:

$$\frac{\dfrac{c_1,\sigma \rightsquigarrow^j c_1'',\sigma_1}{c_1;c_2,\sigma \rightsquigarrow^j c_1'';c_2,\sigma_1}\ IH \quad \dfrac{c_1'',\sigma_1 \rightsquigarrow^k c_1',\sigma'}{c_1'';c_2,\sigma_1 \rightsquigarrow^k c_1';c_2,\sigma'}\ IH}{c_1;c_2,\sigma \rightsquigarrow^{j+k} c_1';c_2,\sigma'}$$

Case:

$$\frac{}{c_1,\sigma \rightsquigarrow^0 c_1,\sigma}$$

This derivation suffices:

$$\frac{}{c_1;c_2,\sigma \rightsquigarrow^0 c_1;c_2,\sigma}$$

For part (2) of the lemma: assume $c_1,\sigma \rightsquigarrow^n \sigma'$ and prove $c_1;c_2,\sigma \rightsquigarrow^n c_2,\sigma'$. There are two possible cases for the assumed derivation:

Case:

$$\frac{c_1,\sigma \rightsquigarrow \sigma'}{c_1,\sigma \rightsquigarrow^1 \sigma'}$$

We can derive the desired judgment this way:

$$\frac{\dfrac{c_1,\sigma \rightsquigarrow \sigma'}{c_1;c_2,\sigma \rightsquigarrow c_2,\sigma'}}{c_1;c_2,\sigma \rightsquigarrow^1 c_2,\sigma'}$$

Case:

$$\frac{c_1,\sigma \rightsquigarrow^j c_1',\sigma_1 \quad c_1',\sigma_1 \rightsquigarrow^k \sigma'}{c_1,\sigma \rightsquigarrow^{j+k} \sigma'}$$

As in the proof of the first part of the lemma, we apply the IH to the derivations of the premises:

$$\frac{\dfrac{c_1,\sigma \rightsquigarrow^j c_1',\sigma_1}{c_1;c_2,\sigma \rightsquigarrow^j c_1';c_2,\sigma_1}\ IH \quad \dfrac{c_1',\sigma_1 \rightsquigarrow^k \sigma'}{c_1';c_2,\sigma_1 \rightsquigarrow^k c_2,\sigma'}\ IH}{c_1;c_2,\sigma \rightsquigarrow^{j+k} c_2,\sigma'}$$

□

4.3.4   Proof of Lemma 4.3.3 (used in the proof of Theorem 4.3.1)

Proof. The proof is by induction on the structure of the first assumed big-step reduction derivation. We must consider the following cases (for the rules from Figure 4.7). In each case, we must show that a big-step evaluation which has been prematurely cut off can be extended. The first assumed derivation is for the prematurely ended evaluation, and the second assumed derivation is for an evaluation which picks up where the prematurely halted evaluation left off. We will refer to these two evaluations as the prematurely ended evaluation and the resuming evaluation, respectively. We will call the evaluation which extends the prematurely ended one using the resuming one the extended evaluation.

Case:
$$c, \sigma \Downarrow_0 c, \sigma$$

Here, what we have to prove for each part is trivial: we must show that if $c, \sigma \Downarrow_m \sigma''$ (this is the resuming evaluation), then $c, \sigma \Downarrow_m \sigma''$ (this is the extended evaluation); and similarly, if $c, \sigma \Downarrow_m c'', \sigma''$, then $c, \sigma \Downarrow_m c'', \sigma''$. But these implications are trivially true: what we must prove for each implication is exactly what we are allowed to assume.

Case:
$$\frac{c_1, \sigma \Downarrow_n c_1', \sigma'}{c_1; c_2, \sigma \Downarrow_n c_1'; c_2, \sigma'}$$

Here we need to consider subcases for the form of the derivation of the resuming evaluation. Since we are resuming the evaluation of a sequencing command, the form of the command limits the possibilities to the following (we consider the subcases for both parts of the lemma):

Subcase:
$$\frac{c_1', \sigma \Downarrow_j \sigma_1 \quad c_2, \sigma_1 \Downarrow_k \sigma''}{c_1'; c_2, \sigma' \Downarrow_{j+k} \sigma''}$$

We can construct the following derivation. Note that the derivations given as premises to the induction hypothesis (IH) are the premise $c_1, \sigma \Downarrow_n c_1', \sigma'$ of the inference for the case we are currently in, together with the premise $c_1', \sigma' \Downarrow_j \sigma_1$ for the subcase:

$$\frac{\dfrac{c_1, \sigma \Downarrow_n c_1', \sigma' \quad c_1', \sigma' \Downarrow_j \sigma_1}{c_1, \sigma \Downarrow_{n+j} \sigma_1} \; IH \quad c_2, \sigma_1 \Downarrow_k \sigma''}{c_1; c_2, \sigma \Downarrow_{n+j+k} \sigma''}$$

Subcase:
$$\frac{c_1', \sigma' \Downarrow_m c_1'', \sigma''}{c_1'; c_2, \sigma' \Downarrow_m c_1''; c_2, \sigma''}$$

In this case, we can use this derivation, where as for the previous subcase, we are using the IH to combine the derivation of the premise of the inference for this case, with the derivation for the first premise of the inference for the subcase:

$$\dfrac{\dfrac{c_1,\sigma \Downarrow_n c_1',\sigma' \qquad c_1',\sigma' \Downarrow_m c_1'',\sigma''}{c_1,\sigma \Downarrow_{n+m} c_1'',\sigma''}\ IH}{c_1;c_2,\sigma \Downarrow_{n+m} c_1'';c_2,\sigma''}$$

Subcase:

$$\dfrac{c_1',\sigma' \Downarrow_j \sigma_1 \qquad c_2,\sigma_1 \Downarrow_k c_2',\sigma''}{c_1';c_2,\sigma' \Downarrow_{j+k} c_2',\sigma''}$$

This derivation suffices, again using the derivations of premises of the inference for the case and the subcase, as in the proofs in the previous subcases:

$$\dfrac{\dfrac{c_1,\sigma \Downarrow_n c_1',\sigma' \qquad c_1',\sigma' \Downarrow_j \sigma_1}{c_1,\sigma \Downarrow_{n+j} \sigma_1}\ IH \qquad c_2,\sigma_1 \Downarrow_k c_2',\sigma''}{c_1;c_2,\sigma \Downarrow_{n+j+k} c_2',\sigma''}$$

This completes the subcases of this case, and we can return to consider other cases for the derivation of the prematurely ended evaluation.

Case:

$$\dfrac{c_1,\sigma \Downarrow_j \sigma_1 \qquad c_2,\sigma_1 \Downarrow_k c_2',\sigma'}{c_1;c_2,\sigma \Downarrow_{j+k} c_2',\sigma'}$$

In this case, for part (1) of the lemma the resuming evaluation is $c_2',\sigma' \Downarrow_m \sigma''$, and for part (2) it is $c_2',\sigma' \Downarrow_m c'',\sigma''$. For the former case, we have the following, where the derivations given to the IH are, respectively, from the second premise of the inference for this case, and the derivation of the resuming evaluation:

$$\dfrac{c_1,\sigma \Downarrow_j \sigma_1 \qquad \dfrac{c_2,\sigma_1 \Downarrow_k c_2',\sigma' \qquad c_2',\sigma' \Downarrow_m \sigma''}{c_2,\sigma_1 \Downarrow_{k+m} \sigma''}\ IH}{c_1;c_2,\sigma \Downarrow_{j+k+m} \sigma''}$$

In the latter case, the derivation is similar:

$$\dfrac{c_1,\sigma \Downarrow_j \sigma_1 \qquad \dfrac{c_2,\sigma_1 \Downarrow_k c_2',\sigma' \qquad c_2',\sigma' \Downarrow_m c'',\sigma''}{c_2,\sigma_1 \Downarrow_{k+m} c'',\sigma''}\ IH}{c_1;c_2,\sigma \Downarrow_{j+k+m} c'',\sigma''}$$

Case:

$$\dfrac{[\![t\ pred\ t']\!]\sigma = True \qquad c_1,\sigma \Downarrow_j c',\sigma'}{\texttt{if}\ t\ pred\ t'\ \texttt{then}\ c_1\ \texttt{else}\ c_2,\sigma \Downarrow_{j+1} c',\sigma'}$$

In this case, we use this derivation for part (1) of the lemma:

$$\frac{\quad\quad\quad \dfrac{c_1,\sigma \Downarrow_j c',\sigma' \quad c',\sigma' \Downarrow_m \sigma''}{c_1,\sigma \Downarrow_{j+m} \sigma''}\; \text{IH}}{\text{if } t \text{ pred } t' \text{ then } c_1 \text{ else } c_2, \sigma \Downarrow_{j+m+1} \sigma''}$$

$$[\![t \text{ pred } t']\!]\sigma = True$$

For part (2) of the lemma, we use this very similar derivation:

$$[\![t \text{ pred } t']\!]\sigma = True \quad \frac{\dfrac{c_1,\sigma \Downarrow_j c',\sigma' \quad c',\sigma' \Downarrow_m c'',\sigma''}{c_1,\sigma \Downarrow_{j+m} c'',\sigma''}\; \text{IH}}{\text{if } t \text{ pred } t' \text{ then } c_1 \text{ else } c_2, \sigma \Downarrow_{j+m+1} c'',\sigma''}$$

Case:

$$\frac{[\![t \text{ pred } t']\!]\sigma = False \quad c_2,\sigma \Downarrow_j c',\sigma'}{\text{if } t \text{ pred } t' \text{ then } c_1 \text{ else } c_2, \sigma \Downarrow_{j+1} c',\sigma'}$$

The derivations for parts (1) and (2) of the lemma are almost exactly the same as in the previous case, just with *False* and c_2 in place of *True* and c_1. For part (1):

$$[\![t \text{ pred } t']\!]\sigma = False \quad \frac{\dfrac{c_2,\sigma \Downarrow_j c',\sigma' \quad c',\sigma' \Downarrow_m \sigma''}{c_2,\sigma \Downarrow_{j+m} \sigma''}\; \text{IH}}{\text{if } t \text{ pred } t' \text{ then } c_1 \text{ else } c_2, \sigma \Downarrow_{j+m+1} \sigma''}$$

For part (2):

$$[\![t \text{ pred } t']\!]\sigma = False \quad \frac{\dfrac{c_2,\sigma \Downarrow_j c',\sigma' \quad c',\sigma' \Downarrow_m c'',\sigma''}{c_2,\sigma \Downarrow_{j+m} c'',\sigma''}\; \text{IH}}{\text{if } t \text{ pred } t' \text{ then } c_1 \text{ else } c_2, \sigma \Downarrow_{j+m+1} c'',\sigma''}$$

Case:

$$\frac{[\![t \text{ pred } t']\!]\sigma = True \quad c_1,\sigma \Downarrow_j c_1',\sigma'}{\text{while } t \text{ pred } t' \text{ do } c_1, \sigma \Downarrow_{j+1} c_1'; \text{while } t \text{ pred } t' \text{ do } c, \sigma'}$$

Let us abbreviate while t *pred* t' do c_1 as $\hat{c}$. In this case, the resuming evaluations are for command $c_1'; \hat{c}$. We must now consider subcases for the derivation of the resuming evaluation. This is similar to what we did in the case above for sequencing commands.

Subcase:

$$\frac{c_1',\sigma \Downarrow_k \sigma_1 \quad \hat{c},\sigma_1 \Downarrow_\ell \sigma''}{c_1';\hat{c},\sigma' \Downarrow_{k+\ell} \sigma''}$$

We use this derivation, where as in the subcases above for the sequencing case, we take derivations from the prematurely ended evaluation and from the resuming evaluation, to which we apply the IH.

$$\llbracket t \text{ } pred \text{ } t' \rrbracket \sigma = True \quad \dfrac{\dfrac{c_1, \sigma \Downarrow_j c_1', \sigma' \quad c_1', \sigma' \Downarrow_k \sigma_1}{c_1, \sigma \Downarrow_{j+k} \sigma_1} IH \quad \hat{c}, \sigma_1 \Downarrow_\ell \sigma''}{\text{while } t \text{ } pred \text{ } t' \text{ do } c_1, \sigma \Downarrow_{j+k+\ell+1} \sigma''}$$

Subcase:

$$\dfrac{c_1', \sigma' \Downarrow_m c_1'', \sigma''}{c_1'; \hat{c}, \sigma' \Downarrow_m c_1''; \hat{c}, \sigma''}$$

We use this derivation:

$$\llbracket t \text{ } pred \text{ } t' \rrbracket \sigma = True \quad \dfrac{\dfrac{c_1, \sigma \Downarrow_j c_1', \sigma' \quad c_1', \sigma' \Downarrow_m c_1'', \sigma''}{c_1, \sigma \Downarrow_{j+m} c_1'', \sigma''} IH}{\text{while } t \text{ } pred \text{ } t' \text{ do } c_1, \sigma \Downarrow_{j+m+1} c_1'', \sigma''}$$

Subcase:

$$\dfrac{c_1', \sigma' \Downarrow_k \sigma_1 \quad \hat{c}, \sigma_1 \Downarrow_\ell c'', \sigma''}{c_1'; \hat{c}, \sigma' \Downarrow_{k+\ell} c'', \sigma''}$$

We use this derivation, which is similar to the one for the first subcase:

$$\llbracket t \text{ } pred \text{ } t' \rrbracket \sigma = True \quad \dfrac{\dfrac{c_1, \sigma \Downarrow_j c_1', \sigma' \quad c_1', \sigma' \Downarrow_k \sigma_1}{c_1, \sigma \Downarrow_{j+k} \sigma_1} IH \quad \hat{c}, \sigma_1 \Downarrow_\ell c'', \sigma''}{\text{while } t \text{ } pred \text{ } t' \text{ do } c_1, \sigma \Downarrow_{j+k+\ell+1} c'', \sigma''}$$

Case:

$$\dfrac{\llbracket t \text{ } pred \text{ } t' \rrbracket \sigma = True \quad c, \sigma \Downarrow_n \sigma'}{\text{while } t \text{ } pred \text{ } t' \text{ do } c, \sigma \Downarrow_{n+1} \text{while } t \text{ } pred \text{ } t' \text{ do } c, \sigma'}$$

In this case, the derivation of the extended evaluation just places the resuming evaluation in the premise of an inference of one of the rules for while-commands, and no appeal to the induction hypothesis is needed. For part (1) of the lemma, we use this derivation:

$$\dfrac{\llbracket t \text{ } pred \text{ } t' \rrbracket \sigma = True \quad c, \sigma \Downarrow_n \sigma' \quad \text{while } t \text{ } pred \text{ } t' \text{ do } c, \sigma' \Downarrow_m \sigma''}{\text{while } t \text{ } pred \text{ } t' \text{ do } c, \sigma \Downarrow_{n+m+1} \sigma''}$$

For part (2), the derivation is similar:

$$\dfrac{\llbracket t \text{ } pred \text{ } t' \rrbracket \sigma = True \quad c, \sigma \Downarrow_n \sigma' \quad \text{while } t \text{ } pred \text{ } t' \text{ do } c, \sigma' \Downarrow_m c'', \sigma''}{\text{while } t \text{ } pred \text{ } t' \text{ do } c, \sigma \Downarrow_{n+m+1} c'', \sigma''}$$

Case:

$$\dfrac{\llbracket t \text{ } pred \text{ } t' \rrbracket \sigma = True \quad c, \sigma \Downarrow_j \sigma' \quad \text{while } t \text{ } pred \text{ } t' \text{ do } c, \sigma' \Downarrow_k c_1, \sigma_1}{\text{while } t \text{ } pred \text{ } t' \text{ do } c, \sigma \Downarrow_{j+k+1} c_1, \sigma_1}$$

We again abbreviate `while` t *pred* t' `do` c by $\hat{c}$. For part (1), we use this derivation:

$$\cfrac{[\![t\ pred\ t']\!]\sigma = \textit{True} \qquad c,\sigma \Downarrow_j \sigma' \qquad \cfrac{\hat{c},\sigma' \Downarrow_k c_1,\sigma_1 \qquad c_1,\sigma_1 \Downarrow_m \sigma''}{\hat{c},\sigma' \Downarrow_{k+m} \sigma''}\ IH}{\hat{c},\sigma \Downarrow_{j+k+m+1} \sigma''}$$

For part (2), the derivation is similar:

$$\cfrac{[\![t\ pred\ t']\!]\sigma = \textit{True} \qquad c,\sigma \Downarrow_j \sigma' \qquad \cfrac{\hat{c},\sigma' \Downarrow_k c_1,\sigma_1 \qquad c_1,\sigma_1 \Downarrow_m c'',\sigma''}{\hat{c},\sigma' \Downarrow_{k+m} c'',\sigma''}\ IH}{\hat{c},\sigma \Downarrow_{j+k+m+1} c'',\sigma''}$$

$\square$

4.3.5   Proof of Lemma 4.3.4 (used in the proof of Theorem 4.3.1)

Proof. We must prove that $c,\sigma \rightsquigarrow \sigma'$ implies $c,\sigma \Downarrow_1 \sigma'$ and $c,\sigma \rightsquigarrow c',\sigma'$ implies $c,\sigma \Downarrow_1 c',\sigma'$. The proof is by induction on the structure of the assumed derivation, either of $c,\sigma \rightsquigarrow \sigma'$ or $c,\sigma \rightsquigarrow c',\sigma'$. We consider both cases simultaneously, showing how to translate derivations for the small-step reductions into big-step derivations with counters, where the counter value is just 1.

Case:

$$\overline{\texttt{skip},\sigma \rightsquigarrow \sigma}$$

In this case, we can just use this inference:

$$\overline{\texttt{skip},\sigma \Downarrow_1 \sigma}$$

Case:

$$\overline{x := t,\ \sigma \rightsquigarrow \sigma[x \mapsto [\![t]\!]\sigma]}$$

This suffices:

$$\overline{x := t,\sigma \Downarrow_1 \sigma[x \mapsto [\![t]\!]\sigma]}$$

Case:

$$\cfrac{c_1,\ \sigma \rightsquigarrow \sigma'}{c_1;c_2,\ \sigma \rightsquigarrow c_2,\sigma'}$$

We can use this derivation, where we are using a big-step derivation with counter value 0 in order to have a legal application of the appropriate rule for sequencing. This and the next case are the only ones which need to use the induction hypothesis (since the small-step rules in question are the only ones which have small-step reductions in their premises).

$$\cfrac{\cfrac{c_1,\sigma \rightsquigarrow \sigma'}{c_1,\sigma \Downarrow_1 \sigma'}\ IH \qquad \overline{c_2,\sigma' \Downarrow_0 c_2,\sigma'}}{c_1;c_2,\sigma \Downarrow_1 c_2,\sigma'}$$

Case:

$$\frac{c_1, \sigma \rightsquigarrow c_1', \sigma'}{c_1; c_2, \sigma \rightsquigarrow c_1'; c_2, \sigma'}$$

We can use this derivation:

$$\frac{\dfrac{c_1, \sigma \rightsquigarrow c_1', \sigma'}{c_1, \sigma \Downarrow_1 c_1', \sigma'} \; IH}{c_1; c_2, \sigma \Downarrow_1 c_1'; c_2, \sigma'}$$

Case:

$$\frac{[\![t \; pred \; t']\!]\sigma = True}{\text{if } t \; pred \; t' \text{ then } c_1 \text{ else } c_2, \; \sigma \rightsquigarrow c_1, \sigma}$$

This suffices:

$$\frac{[\![t \; pred \; t']\!]\sigma = True \qquad c_1, \sigma \Downarrow_0 c_1, \sigma}{\text{if } t \; pred \; t' \text{ then } c_1 \text{ else } c_2, \sigma \Downarrow_1 c_1, \sigma}$$

Case:

$$\frac{[\![t \; pred \; t']\!]\sigma = False}{\text{if } t \; pred \; t' \text{ then } c_1 \text{ else } c_2, \; \sigma \rightsquigarrow c_2, \sigma}$$

The proof is just like in the previous case, except with *False* and c_2 in place of *True* and c_1:

$$\frac{[\![t \; pred \; t']\!]\sigma = False \qquad c_2, \sigma \Downarrow_0 c_2, \sigma}{\text{if } t \; pred \; t' \text{ then } c_1 \text{ else } c_2, \sigma \Downarrow_1 c_2, \sigma}$$

Case:

$$\frac{[\![t \; pred \; t']\!]\sigma = False}{\text{while } t \; pred \; t' \text{ do } c, \; \sigma \rightsquigarrow \sigma}$$

This suffices:

$$\frac{[\![t \; pred \; t']\!]\sigma = False}{\text{while } t \; pred \; t' \text{ do } c, \sigma \Downarrow_1 \sigma}$$

Case:

$$\frac{[\![t \; pred \; t']\!]\sigma = True}{\text{while } t \; pred \; t' \text{ do } c, \; \sigma \rightsquigarrow c; \text{while } t \; pred \; t' \text{ do } c, \sigma}$$

This derivation suffices:

$$\frac{[\![t \; pred \; t']\!]\sigma = True \qquad c, \sigma \Downarrow_0 c, \sigma}{\text{while } t \; pred \; t' \text{ do } c, \sigma \Downarrow_1 c; \text{while } t \; pred \; t' \text{ do } c, \sigma}$$

$\square$

4.3.6 Relating the original small-step and big-step semantics

Using Theorem 4.3.1, whose proof we just completed, we can relate our original big- and small-step semantics, without counters. We could have done this without considering the counter-based systems, but now that we have – in order to be able to relate small-step reductions $c, \sigma \leadsto^n c', \sigma'$ resulting in an intermediate state with a prematurely ending big-step reduction $c, \sigma \Downarrow_n c', \sigma'$ – we can relate the original systems just by relating them to the counter-based ones. This is done by the following lemmas, whose proofs are left as exercises:

Lemma 4.3.5. $c, \sigma \Downarrow \sigma'$ holds iff $c, \sigma \Downarrow_k \sigma'$ holds.

Lemma 4.3.6. *The following are both true:*

1. $c, \sigma \leadsto^* \sigma'$ holds iff there exists a k such that $c, \sigma \leadsto^k \sigma'$ holds.

2. $c, \sigma \leadsto^* c', \sigma'$ holds iff there exists a k such that $c, \sigma \leadsto^k c', \sigma'$ holds.

Using these two facts and Theorem 4.3.1, it is easy to prove the following:

Theorem 4.3.7. $c, \sigma \Downarrow \sigma'$ holds iff $c, \sigma \leadsto^* \sigma'$ holds.

4.3.7 Determinism for multi-step and big-step semantics

Theorem 4.2.1 shows that small-step reduction is deterministic. We can extend this multi-step reduction with counters in the following lemma, whose proof we leave as an exercise.

Lemma 4.3.8. *The following are all true:*

1. *If $c, \sigma \leadsto^j \sigma'$ and $c, \sigma \leadsto^k \sigma''$, then $j = k$ and $\sigma' = \sigma''$.*

2. *If $c, \sigma \leadsto^j c', \sigma'$ and $c, \sigma \leadsto^j c'', \sigma''$, then $c' = c''$ and $\sigma' = \sigma''$.*

3. *If $c, \sigma \leadsto^j \sigma'$, then we cannot have $c, \sigma \leadsto^k c', \sigma'$ for any $k \geq j$, any c', and any σ'.*

The following states determinism for big-step reduction (the proof is also left as an exercise):

Theorem 4.3.9. *If $c, \sigma \Downarrow \sigma'$ and $c, \sigma \Downarrow \sigma''$, then $\sigma' = \sigma''$.*

This could be proved using the connections we have established in the theorems of this chapter between multi-step reduction with counters and big-step reduction. Alternatively, we could prove this directly, by induction on the structure of the first assumed derivation.

4.4   Conclusion

In this chapter, we have considered two forms of operational semantics for WHILE commands: big-step and small-step semantics. With big-step semantics, the rules describe, in a recursive fashion, when a command and a starting state evaluate to a final state: $c, \sigma \Downarrow \sigma'$. The small-step rules, in contrast, specify how a command and a state transition to either a final state or a new command and a new (intermediate) state: $c, \sigma \leadsto \sigma'$ or $c, \sigma \leadsto c', \sigma'$. We need additional rules, related to those for the reflexive-transitive closure of a relation, to connect many individual small steps into a multi-step reduction: $c, \sigma \leadsto^* \sigma'$ or $c, \sigma \leadsto^* c', \sigma'$. In order to relate these two semantics, we extended both with natural-number counters, and added a judgment form $c, \sigma \Downarrow_n c', \sigma'$, representing a big-step evaluation that has been cut off after n steps of computation, with resulting intermediate command c' and state σ'. We were then able to work through a rather lengthy proof that the big-step semantics with counters and the small-step one are equivalent. The result is not too surprising, but carefully working through all the details of such a proof almost always reveals bugs (hopefully, and often enough, easily fixed) in one's semantics. This is standard practice in Programming Languages theory, and so it is worthwhile to gain experience reading and writing such proofs.

4.5   Basic exercises

4.5.1   For Section 4.1, big-step semantics of WHILE

1. Write a derivation using the rules of Figure 4.1 proving the following judgment, where $\sigma = \{\, x \mapsto 10,\ y \mapsto 20 \,\}$:

$$(\texttt{if } x = y \texttt{ then } z := 1 \texttt{ else } z := -1); x := x * z, \sigma \Downarrow \sigma[z \mapsto -1]$$

2. Write a derivation using the rules of Figure 4.1 proving the following judgment, for some output state σ' (which your derivation should identify):

$$\texttt{while } x > 0 \texttt{ do } (x := x - 1; y := y * 2), \{\, x \mapsto 2,\ y \mapsto 1 \,\} \Downarrow \sigma'$$

4.5.2   For Section 4.2, small-step semantics of WHILE

1. Write a derivation using the rules of Figure 4.2 proving the following judgment:

$$\texttt{if } x < 100 \texttt{ then } x := x * 10 \texttt{ else skip}, \{\, x \mapsto 9 \,\} \ \leadsto\ \{\, x \mapsto 90 \,\}$$

2. Write a derivation using the rules of Figure 4.2 proving the following judgment:

$$x := x * 2;\ y := y - 2, \{\, x \mapsto 7\, y \mapsto 3 \,\} \ \leadsto\ y := y - 2, \{\, x \mapsto 14\, y \mapsto 1 \,\}$$

3. Write a derivation using the rules of Figure 4.2 proving the following judgment, for some c' and some σ', where $\sigma = \{ x \mapsto 10,\ y \mapsto 1 \}$:

$$(\texttt{if } x > 0 \texttt{ then } (x := x - 1; y := y + 1) \texttt{ else skip}); \texttt{skip}, \sigma \rightsquigarrow c', \sigma'$$

4. Write a derivation using the rules of Figure 4.2 proving the following judgment, for some c' and some σ':

$$\texttt{while } x > 0 \texttt{ do } (y := x * y;\ x := x - 2),\ \{ x \mapsto 3, y \mapsto 5 \} \rightsquigarrow c, \sigma'$$

5. Write a derivation using the rules of Figures 4.2 and 4.3 for the following judgment (note that this is a multi-step reduction), where $\sigma = \{ x \mapsto 9,\ y \mapsto 1 \}$ and $\sigma' = \{ x \mapsto 27,\ y \mapsto 0 \}$:

$$\texttt{if } y > 0 \texttt{ then } (x := x * 3; y := y - 1) \texttt{ else skip}, \sigma \rightsquigarrow^* \sigma'$$

6. Write a derivation using the rules of Figures 4.2 and 4.3 for the following judgment, for some output state σ' (note that this is a multi-step reduction):

$$\texttt{while } x > 0 \texttt{ do } (x := x - 1; y := y * 2),\ \{ x \mapsto 2, y \mapsto 1 \} \rightsquigarrow^* \sigma'$$

4.5.3 For Section 4.3, relating big- and small-step semantics

1. Write out a derivation of the following judgements, where $\sigma_1 = \{ x \mapsto 3, y \mapsto 0 \}$ and $\sigma_2 = \{ x \mapsto 10, y \mapsto 1, z \mapsto 0 \}$:

   (a) $(\texttt{if } x > 0 \texttt{ then } y := -x \texttt{ else } y := x); x := 0, \sigma_1 \rightsquigarrow^3 \{ x \mapsto 0, y \mapsto -3 \}$

   (b) $(\texttt{if } x = 0 \texttt{ then } y := 1 \texttt{ else } y := 2), \sigma_1 \Downarrow_1 y := 2, \{ x \mapsto 3, y \mapsto 0 \}$

   (c) $x := 2; y := x; z := 3, \sigma_2 \Downarrow_2 z := 3, \{ x \mapsto 2, y \mapsto 2, z \mapsto 0 \}$

2. For each value of k from 0 to 5 inclusive, show a derivation of one or the other of the following two judgments, for some σ' and c':

$$\texttt{while } x < 8 \texttt{ do } (x := x * 3),\ \{ x \mapsto 1 \} \Downarrow_k c', \sigma'$$
$$\texttt{while } x < 8 \texttt{ do } (x := x * 3),\ \{ x \mapsto 1 \} \Downarrow_k \sigma'$$

3. Determine a value for k and σ' such that the following judgment is derivable, where σ is $\{ x \mapsto 2, y \mapsto 3 \}$:

$$(\texttt{if } x = y \texttt{ then skip else } (z := x * y; y := x)); x := 1, \sigma \rightsquigarrow^k \sigma'$$

4. Write out a detailed proof of Theorem 4.3.7. Hint: this should not require you to carry out any inductions, since this just follows from Theorem 4.3.1 and the lemmas stated just before the lemma in Section 4.3.

4.6   Intermediate exercises

4.6.1   For Section 4.1, big-step semantics of WHILE

1. For purposes of this problem, let us temporarily define the notation $\texttt{skip}^n$ as follows:

$$\begin{aligned} \texttt{skip}^0 &= \texttt{skip} \\ \texttt{skip}^{n+1} &= \texttt{skip}; \texttt{skip}^n \end{aligned}$$

   (a) Write out the value of $\texttt{skip}^2$ by applying the above defining equations.
   (b) Prove by induction on n that for any $\sigma \in \Sigma$, and for all $n \in \mathbb{N}$, $\texttt{skip}^n, \sigma \Downarrow \sigma$ is derivable using the rules of Figure 4.1. Your proof is essentially going to show how to construct a derivation of that judgment, for any $n \in \mathbb{N}$.

4.6.2   For Section 4.2, small-step semantics of WHILE

1. Find a command c such that for all starting states σ, we have $c, \sigma \leadsto^* \sigma'$, where:

$$\sigma' = \{x \mapsto \sigma(y), \ y \mapsto \sigma(x)\}$$

   Note that since the final state has values only for variables x and y, your command c can only assign to those variables.

2. An alternative way to define the reflexive transitive closure of binary relation R is with the following rules:

$$\frac{a_1 \ R \ a_2 \quad a_2 \ R^* \ a_3}{a_1 \ R^* \ a_3} \qquad \frac{}{a \ R^* \ a}$$

   If we compare this to the rules of Figure 4.4, we can see that here we only have 2 rules, compared with 3 in Figure 4.4. So let us temporarily call the alternative set of rules the 2-rule system for reflexive transitive closure, and the system in Figure 4.4 the 2-rule system. One important detail to note: the first rule in the 2-rule system has R in the first premise. The similar (two-premise) rule in the 3-rule system (Figure 4.4) has R^* in that first premise.

   (a) Prove that every rule of the 2-rule system is derivable in the 3-rule system.
   (b) Show that the first rule of the 3-rule system is derivable in the 2-rule system.
   (c) Prove that if we can derive $a_1 \ R^* \ a_2$ and $a_2 \ R^* \ a_3$ in the 2-rule system, then we can also derive $a_1 \ R^* \ a_3$ in the 2-rule system. Hint: prove this by induction on the structure of the first assumed derivation.
   (d) Using these results (from the previous parts of this problem), argue that the two systems are equivalent (that is, $a \ R^* \ b$ can be derived in the 2-rule system iff it can be derived in the 3-rule system).

4.6.3   For Section 4.3, relating big- and small-step semantics

1. Write out detailed proofs (both directions) of the equivalence in Lemma 4.3.5 (Section 4.3). Hint: use induction on the structure of the assumed derivation in each case.

2. Write out a detailed proof of Theorem 4.3.9 in Section 4.3.7, using induction on the structure of the assumed derivation (but see the next problem).

3. Write out a detailed proof of Theorem 4.3.9 in Section 4.3.7, but this time, do not use induction on the structure of the assumed derivation. Rather, use the other lemmas and theorems established in this chapter, to make the connection between determinism of multi-step reduction with counters and big-step reduction.

4. Write out a detailed proof of Lemma 4.3.8 in Section 4.3.7.

5. Write out detailed proofs of both directions of Lemma 4.3.6 in Section 4.3.6, again using induction on the structure of the assumed derivation in each case.

Chapter 5
Untyped Lambda Calculus

The lambda calculus is a very small but very expressive programming language. It is based on the idea of defining the behavior of functions by textually substituting arguments for input variables. It is also Turing complete: any function that can be computed with a Turing machine can be computed with a lambda calculus program.

The lambda calculus is due to Alonzo Church (see [9]). Its ideas are incorporated in modern functional programming languages like OCAML and HASKELL, and also used crucially in many branches of logic, particularly constructive logic, as well as in theorem provers and computer-checked proofs.

In this chapter, we study the syntax and various operational semantics of untyped lambda calculus. Later chapters will consider programming in untyped lambda calculus (Chapter 6) and type systems for lambda calculus (Chapters 7 and 10).

5.1 Abstract syntax of untyped lambda calculus

Lambda calculus expressions are called terms. The syntax for terms t is:

$$terms\ t\ ::=\ x \mid t\,t' \mid \lambda x.\,t$$

Here, x is for variables, $t\,t'$ is for **applications** of t as a function to t' as an argument, and $\lambda x.\,t$ is a **lambda-abstraction**, an anonymous function which takes input x and returns output t. The λ in $\lambda x.t$ is said to bind x in t. It introduces local variable x within t. We will use x, y, z, and other names as both variables (within the language of lambda calculus) and meta-variables ranging over variables. When they are used in concrete example terms, they will serve as variables; when they are used in general definitions, they should be understood to be meta-variables. The difference is only important because as meta-variables, x and y might refer to the same variable, and hence cannot be assumed to have distinct values. But as variables, x and y will be considered distinct. Syntactically, it is not a bad idea to write parentheses around applications and lambda-abstractions as one is getting used to the language. We will see several conventions in the next subsection which will allow us to drop some parentheses.

5.1.1 Examples

- Assuming we have defined *mult* somehow (we'll see how in Chapter 6) to multiply numbers encoded as lambda terms, then the following term defines

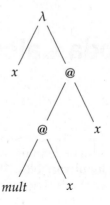

Figure 5.1: A lambda-calculus term shown in tree format

the squaring function:
$$\lambda x.\,((mult\ x)\ x)$$

Note that applications of a function like *mult* to two arguments must be written in left-nested form: we apply *mult* to the first argument x, and then apply the application $(mult\ x)$ to the second argument x. Because it is a bit cumbersome to write all these parentheses, by convention parentheses associate to the left, so we can write $(mult\ x\ x)$ or just *mult* x x instead of $((mult\ x)\ x)$. The sample lambda term above can be rendered as a tree using λ and @ for the tree labels corresponding to lambda-abstractions and applications, as in Figure 5.1.

- The following term applies argument x as a function to itself:

$$\lambda x.(x\ x)$$

So x is both the function and the argument in the application. We may use a second parsing convention here, that the scope of $\lambda x.$ extends as far to the right as possible. With this convention, we can write the above term as $\lambda x.x\ x$. Because the scope of $\lambda x.$ extends as far to the right as possible, we know that this term may be fully parenthesized as $(\lambda x.(x\ x))$, as opposed to $((\lambda x.x)\ x)$.

- The following term takes a function f and argument x as inputs, and returns $(f\ (f\ x))$:

$$\lambda f.\,\lambda x.\,(f\ (f\ x))$$

Using this second parsing convention, we can write this as $\lambda f.\lambda x.f\ (f\ x)$. But note that the remaining parentheses are required. If we dropped them, we would have $\lambda f.\lambda x.f\ f\ x$, and because application is left-associative (as mentioned above), this would be fully parenthesized as $(\lambda f.(\lambda x.((f\ f)\ x)))$, which is a different term. (In it, f is applied first to f and then to x, while in

$$\frac{}{(\lambda x.\,t)\,t' \rightsquigarrow [t'/x]t}\ \beta \qquad \frac{t \rightsquigarrow t'}{\lambda x.\,t \rightsquigarrow \lambda x.\,t'}\ lam$$

$$\frac{t_1 \rightsquigarrow t_1'}{(t_1\,t_2) \rightsquigarrow (t_1'\,t_2)}\ app1 \qquad \frac{t_2 \rightsquigarrow t_2'}{(t_1\,t_2) \rightsquigarrow (t_1\,t_2')}\ app2$$

Figure 5.2: Rules defining full β-reduction

our term, f is applied to $(f\ x)$.) We see in this example how lambda calculus supports the idea of **higher-order functions**, where functions can be inputs or outputs for other functions. This lambda term is higher-order because it takes in a function f as input, and then returns the function $\lambda x.\,f\ (f\ x)$ as output.

- The following term can be thought of as defining the composition of functions f and g:

$$\lambda f.\,\lambda g.\,\lambda x.\,(f\ (g\ x))$$

Let us call that term *compose*. Then the following term behaves just the way the composition of functions f and g should:

$$(compose\ f\ g)$$

This term, if given now any argument a, will return:

$$(f\ (g\ a))$$

The application $(compose\ f\ g)$ can itself be used as a function, which is just waiting for the argument a in order to return $(f\ (g\ a))$. So *compose* is another example of a higher-order function: the functions f and g are inputs, and the function $\lambda x.\,(f\ (g\ x))$ is then an output.

5.2 Operational semantics: full β-reduction

We begin our study of the semantics of lambda-calculus using a small-step reduction relation. We will relate this to a big-step evaluation relation in Section 5.5 below. We will actually consider several different small-step semantics for lambda-calculus. The first of these is a non-deterministic reduction semantics called full β-reduction ("beta-reduction"), defined by the rules of Figure 5.2.

The first rule in Figure 5.2 is called the β-reduction rule, and passing from $(\lambda x.\,t)\ t'$ to $[t'/x]t$ is called β-reduction. We will define the notation $[t'/x]t$ for capture-avoiding substitution formally just below: roughly speaking, it just replaces variable x by term t' in term t, avoiding violations of scoping that might arise if two differently scoped variables have the same name. The other rules specify that reduction is compatible with the other term-forming operations. As a bit of further terminology: any term of the form $((\lambda x.t)\ t')$ is called a β-redex ("reducible expression"), and one sometimes speaks of **contracting** the redex to its **contractum** $[t'/x]t$.

5.2.1   Capture-avoiding substitution

The notation $[t'/x]t$ is standard for **capture-avoiding substitution** of t' for x in t. This means to replace all free occurrences of x in t with t', renaming bound variables if necessary to avoid capturing free variables of t'. An occurrence of x in t is **free** iff it is not beneath a lambda-abstraction introducing x. So the leftmost occurrence of x is free in the following term, while the rightmost is not:

$$(\lambda y.x)\ \lambda x.x$$

Substitution is capture-avoiding in the sense that we do not allow it to change the scoping of variables (that is, whether they are global or local, and if local, which lambda-abstraction introduced them). For example, below we rename the lambda-bound x to z, in order to avoid having that lambda capture the underlined x:

$$[\underline{x}/y]\lambda x.\,(x\ y)\ =\ \lambda z.\,(z\ \underline{x})$$

This result preserves the scoping of variables, since $\underline{x}$ is still globally scoped in the contractum. In contrast, if substitution were not capture-avoiding, we would get the term $\lambda x.(x\ \underline{x})$, where the underlined x has been captured: its scope has changed from global to local.

Formally, we can define capture-avoiding substitution as follows:

$$
\begin{aligned}
[t/x]x &= t \\
[t/x]y &= y,\ \text{if } x \neq y \\
[t/x](t_1\ t_2) &= ([t/x]t_1)\ ([t/x]t_2) \\
[t/x]\lambda x.t_1 &= \lambda x.t_1 \\
[t/x]\lambda y.t_1 &= \lambda y.[t/x]t_1,\ \text{if } x \neq y \text{ and } y \notin FV(t)
\end{aligned}
$$

This definition relies on a function $FV(\cdot)$, for computing the set of free variables of a term:

$$
\begin{aligned}
FV(x) &= \{x\} \\
FV(t_1\ t_2) &= FV(t_1)\ \cup\ FV(t_2) \\
FV(\lambda x.t) &= FV(t)\ \setminus\ \{x\}
\end{aligned}
$$

The definition of $FV(\cdot)$ just removes the bound variable x when passing from the body of the λ-abstraction to the λ-abstraction itself. (Recall that $S_1 \setminus S_2$, also written $S_1 - S_2$, denotes the difference of two sets; see the review of sets and operations on sets in the "Mathematical Background" section.) The definition of capture-avoiding substitution omits a third case for substituting into a λ-abstraction, namely the case where we are substituting t for x in $\lambda y.t_1$, and $y \in FV(t_1)$. We explain next why this is justified.

α-**equivalence.** When we wish to apply capture-avoiding substitution, we can always ensure that we have renamed bound variables in such a way that we are never blocked from applying the last defining equation above for substitution. One way to justify this practice is to stipulate that we are not actually going to work with terms, but rather with equivalence classes of terms with respect to so-called α-equivalence. This is the equivalence relation determined by equating any two terms which are the same except that one term has $\lambda x.t$ at a position where the other term has $\lambda y.[y/x]t$, where the result $[y/x]t$ of capture-avoiding substitution is indeed defined. So we are allowed to rename λ-bound variables, as long as we do so in a scope-preserving way. We write $t =_\alpha t'$ in this case. For example, we have these positive instances of α-equivalence:

- $\lambda x.x\ x =_\alpha \lambda y.y\ y$

- $(\lambda x.x)\ x =_\alpha (\lambda y.y)\ x$

- $(\lambda x.x\ \lambda y.y) =_\alpha (\lambda x.x\ \lambda x.x)$

And here are some negative instances:

- $\lambda x.x\ y \neq_\alpha \lambda y.y\ y$, because the y in the first term has been captured moving to the second term.

- $(\lambda x.x)\ y =_\alpha (\lambda x.x)\ z$, because we are only allowed to rename bound variables, and here we renamed the free occurrence of variable y to z.

In some situations, for example when doing computer-checked proofs, it is necessary to work out even more formal details of these definitions, but this level of formalization will suffice for our purposes in this book.

Here are some further examples of capture-avoiding substitution:

$$
\begin{aligned}
{[x\ x/y]\lambda x.y\ x} &= \lambda z.x\ x\ z \\
{[\lambda x.x\ x/y]\lambda x.y\ x} &= \lambda x.(\lambda x.\ x\ x)\ x \\
{[x\ \lambda x.x/y]\lambda x.y\ x} &= \lambda z.(x\ \lambda x.\ x)\ z
\end{aligned}
$$

In the first example, we must rename the bound x to z, to avoid capturing the free x in $x\ x$, which is being substituted for y. In the second example, there is no need for such renaming, since the term being substituted for y does not contain x free (though it does contain x bound). In the final example, the term being substituted for y contains x free and x bound. In this case, we must rename the bound x in the term into which we are doing the substitution (namely, $\lambda x.y\ x$), but we do not need to rename the bound x in the term which we are substituting for y.

5.2.2   Example reductions

Here is an example derivation using the rules above to show that $\lambda x.x \, ((\lambda z.z \, z) \, x)$ reduces to $\lambda x.x \, (x \, x)$.

$$\cfrac{\cfrac{\cfrac{}{(\lambda z.z \, z) \, x \rightsquigarrow x \, x} \; \beta}{x \, ((\lambda z.z \, z) \, x) \rightsquigarrow x \, (x \, x)} \; app2}{\lambda x.x \, ((\lambda z.z \, z) \, x) \rightsquigarrow \lambda x.x \, (x \, x)} \; lam$$

As an alternative to writing out such derivations for reductions, we can simply underline the redex that is being reduced:

$$\lambda x.x \, \underline{((\lambda z.z \, z) \, x)} \rightsquigarrow \lambda x.x \, (x \, x)$$

Underlining notation is convenient when we chain reduction steps. The underlined redex is always the one being reduced by the next reduction. So for a simple example, consider the term $((\lambda w.w) \, x) \, ((\lambda w.w) \, y) \, ((\lambda w.w) \, z)$. There are three redexes here. If we reduce first the left one, then the middle one, and then the right one, we get this sequence of reductions:

$$\begin{aligned}
\underline{((\lambda w.w) \, x)} \, ((\lambda w.w) \, y) \, ((\lambda w.w) \, z) & \rightsquigarrow \\
x \, \underline{((\lambda w.w) \, y)} \, ((\lambda w.w) \, z) & \rightsquigarrow \\
x \, y \, \underline{((\lambda w.w) \, z)} & \rightsquigarrow \\
x \, y \, z &
\end{aligned}$$

We will use the term **reduction sequence** to refer to a sequence of steps like this one just shown (whether or not we choose to underline the redexes). A **maximal** reduction sequence is one which is either infinite or ends in a normal form.

5.2.3   Nontermination

For another example, the following reduction sequence shows that the term involved has no **normal form** . A normal form is a term t which cannot reduce; that is, for which $t \rightsquigarrow t'$ is not derivable for any t'. Terms without a normal form are also said to **diverge** .

$$\begin{aligned}
(\lambda x.x \, x) \, (\lambda x.x \, x) & \rightsquigarrow \\
(\lambda x.x \, x) \, (\lambda x.x \, x) & \rightsquigarrow \\
(\lambda x.x \, x) \, (\lambda x.x \, x) & \rightsquigarrow \\
\cdots &
\end{aligned}$$

This infinite maximal reduction sequence shows that $\rightsquigarrow$ is a nonterminating relation: not every reduction sequence is finite. This example is an example of a **looping** term, which is one that can reduce to a term containing (possibly a substitution instance of) itself. An example of a nonlooping nonterminating term is

$(\lambda x.x\ x)\ (\lambda x.x\ x\ x)$, with the following reduction sequence:

$$
\begin{array}{ll}
\underline{(\lambda x.x\ x)\ (\lambda x.x\ x\ x)} & \rightsquigarrow \\
\underline{(\lambda x.x\ x\ x)\ (\lambda x.x\ x\ x)} & \rightsquigarrow \\
\underline{(\lambda x.x\ x\ x)\ (\lambda x.x\ x\ x)}\ (\lambda x.x\ x\ x) & \rightsquigarrow \\
\underline{(\lambda x.x\ x\ x)\ (\lambda x.x\ x\ x)}\ (\lambda x.x\ x\ x)\ (\lambda x.x\ x\ x) & \rightsquigarrow \\
\cdots
\end{array}
$$

Every term in this sequence after the first one, though, is a looping term, since each such term appears in all the following terms in the sequence. Let us call a term **persistently** nonlooping nonterminating if both it and all terms to which it reduces using the reflexive transitive closure $\rightsquigarrow^*$ of $\rightsquigarrow$ (see Section 4.2.2) are also nonlooping nonterminating. For an example of a persistently nonlooping nonterminating term, first define:

$$
F \;=\; \lambda y.\lambda x.\ x\ (\lambda z.\ y)\ x
$$

Now the term $F\ (\lambda z.z)\ F$ is persistently nonlooping nonterminating:

$$
F\ (\lambda z.z)\ F \;\rightsquigarrow^*\; F\ (\lambda z.\lambda z.z)\ F \;\rightsquigarrow^*\; F\ (\lambda z.\lambda z.\lambda z.z)\ F \;\rightsquigarrow^*\; \cdots
$$

It is a basic fact of recursion theory that if a programming language is recursive and every program written in it is guaranteed to terminate, then there are terminating functions which cannot be written in that language. So to get a Turing-complete language, it is necessary to accept the possibility of divergence of programs.

5.2.4 Nondeterminism

The reduction relation defined by the rules above is non-deterministic, in the sense that there are terms t, t_1, and t_2, with t_1 and t_2 distinct, such that $t \rightsquigarrow t_1$ and $t \rightsquigarrow t_2$. The example just above hints at this: there are three redexes, and we can reduce them in any order. Here is another example:

$$
\begin{array}{ll}
\underline{(\lambda x.x\ x)}\ ((\lambda y.y)\ z)) & \rightsquigarrow \quad ((\lambda y.y)\ z)\ ((\lambda y.y)\ z) \\
((\lambda x.x\ x)\ \underline{((\lambda y.y)\ z)}) & \rightsquigarrow \quad ((\lambda x.x\ x)\ z)
\end{array}
$$

This means that a single term may have multiple maximal reduction sequences that begin with that term. Now it happens that even though full β-reduction is non-deterministic, it is still **confluent**: whenever we have $t \rightsquigarrow^* t_1$ and $t \rightsquigarrow^* t_2$, then there exists a $\hat{t}$ such that $t_1 \rightsquigarrow^* \hat{t}$ and $t_2 \rightsquigarrow^* \hat{t}$. This means that however differently we reduce t (to get t_1 and t_2), we can always get back to a common term $\hat{t}$. In the above example, $\hat{t}$ is $(z\ z)$. Section 9.1 discusses confluence and related concepts in more detail, and gives a proof that lambda calculus is confluent.

5.2.5 Some congruence properties of multi-step reduction

We can easily prove the following lemmas about multi-step reduction. We just prove one of them, as the proofs of the others are completely similar.

Lemma 5.2.1 (Congruence of multi-step reduction, body of λ-abstractions). *If $t' \rightsquigarrow^*$ t', then $\lambda x.t \rightsquigarrow^* \lambda x.t'$.*

Lemma 5.2.2 (Congruence of multi-step reduction, functional part of applications). *If $t_1 \rightsquigarrow^* t_1'$, then $t_1\, t_2 \rightsquigarrow^* t_1'\, t_2$.*

Lemma 5.2.3 (Congruence of multi-step reduction, argument part of applications). *If $t_2 \rightsquigarrow^* t_2'$, then $t_1\, t_2 \rightsquigarrow^* t_1\, t_2'$.*

Proof. The proof is by induction on the structure of the derivation of $t_2 \rightsquigarrow^* t_2'$.

<u>Case:</u>

$$\frac{t_2 \rightsquigarrow t_2'}{t_2 \rightsquigarrow^* t_2'}$$

We can construct this derivation:

$$\frac{\dfrac{t_2 \rightsquigarrow t_2'}{t_1\, t_2 \rightsquigarrow t_1\, t_2'}\; app1}{t_1\, t_2 \rightsquigarrow^* t_1\, t_2'}$$

<u>Case:</u>

$$\frac{t_2 \rightsquigarrow^* t_2'' \quad t_2'' \rightsquigarrow^* t_2'}{t_2 \rightsquigarrow^* t_2'}$$

By the induction hypothesis applied separately to each of the premises of this derivation, we have $t_1\, t_2 \rightsquigarrow^* t_1\, t_2''$ and also $t_1\, t_2'' \rightsquigarrow^* t_1\, t_2'$. So we can construct this derivation:

$$\frac{t_1\, t_2 \rightsquigarrow^* t_1\, t_2'' \quad t_1\, t_2'' \rightsquigarrow^* t_1\, t_2'}{t_1\, t_2 \rightsquigarrow^* t_1\, t_2'}$$

<u>Case:</u>

$$\frac{}{t_2 \rightsquigarrow^* t_2}$$

We can construct this derivation:

$$\frac{}{t_1\, t_2 \rightsquigarrow^* t_1\, t_2}$$

$\square$

5.3 Defining full β-reduction with contexts

Since any given lambda-term can contain many different β-redexes (giving rise to different reductions of the term, as explained in the previous section), we may define different operational semantics by specifying different orders for reduction of the β-redexes in a term. One technical device for doing this is using **contexts**.

A context is a term containing a single occurrence of a special variable denoted $*$, and called the hole of the context. Often people use $\mathcal{C}$ as a meta-variable for contexts. If C is a context, then $C[t]$ is the term obtained by inserting the term t into the context's hole. More formally, $C[t]$ is obtained by **grafting** the term t in for $*$. Grafting is simply a form of substitution which allows variables in t to be captured by lambda-abstractions in C. For example, if C is $\lambda x.*$, then $C[x]$ is actually $\lambda x.x$. In contrast, using capture-avoiding substitution, we would have

$$[x/*]\lambda x.* = \lambda y.x \; .$$

To define reduction using a particular order, we use a set of contexts to specify where reductions may take place. For example, for full β-reduction, the contexts are all possible ones:

$$\text{contexts } C \; ::= \; * \mid (C \; t) \mid (t \; C) \mid \lambda x.C$$

Wherever the $*$ is, a reduction is allowed. So as an alternative to the definition in Section 5.2, we can define the operational semantics of full β-reduction using just the single following rule:

$$\frac{}{C[(\lambda x.t) \; t'] \; \rightsquigarrow \; C[[t'/x]t]} \; \textit{ctxt-}\beta$$

This rule decomposes a reduced term into context C and redex $(\lambda x.t) \; t'$.

5.3.1   Examples

Consider the following reduction, written with underlining notation:

$$\begin{array}{ll}
\underline{\lambda x.(\lambda y.x \; y) \; ((\lambda z.z) \; x)} & \rightsquigarrow \\
\lambda x.(\lambda y.x \; y) \; \underline{x} & \rightsquigarrow \\
\lambda x.x \; x &
\end{array}$$

Here are the contexts used for the two reductions (C_0 for the first reduction, C_1 for the second):

$$\begin{array}{lll}
C_0 & = & \lambda x.(\lambda y.x \; y) \; * \\
C_1 & = & \lambda x.*
\end{array}$$

These are obtained just by replacing the underlined redex with a $*$, as you can confirm. For a second example, consider this different reduction sequence from the same starting term:

$$\begin{array}{ll}
\lambda x.\underline{(\lambda y.x \; y)} \; ((\lambda z.z) \; x) & \rightsquigarrow \\
\lambda x.x \; \underline{((\lambda z.z) \; x)} & \rightsquigarrow \\
\lambda x.x \; x &
\end{array}$$

The contexts used for these reductions are:

$$\begin{array}{lll}
C_0 & = & \lambda x.* \\
C_1 & = & \lambda x.x \; *
\end{array}$$

5.4   Specifying other reduction orders with contexts

Different operational semantics can now be defined by specifying different sets of contexts. These semantics are also called reduction strategies or reduction orders. They are all restrictions of full β-reduction: every reduction step allowed by one of the operational semantics below is also allowed by full β-reduction.

5.4.1   Left-to-right call-by-value

$$contexts\ \mathcal{C}\quad ::=\quad * \mid (\mathcal{C}\ t) \mid (v\ \mathcal{C})$$

$$values\ v\quad ::=\quad \lambda x.t$$

We are also specifying here a set of values v, which will turn out to be normal forms with respect to left-to-right, call-by-value operational semantics. For untyped lambda calculus, the values are just the λ-abstractions, but for extensions of lambda calculus, the set of values will be extended to include other normal forms, which are intended to be the final results of reduction.

The central idea in call-by-value operational semantics is that we will only allow β-reductions where the argument is a value. This is expressed using a restricted form of the $\mathtt{ctxt-}\beta$ rule (β_v is for "β value"):

$$\frac{}{\mathcal{C}[(\lambda x.t)\ v] \rightsquigarrow \mathcal{C}[[v/x]t]}\ \ ctxt\text{-}\beta_v$$

The "left-to-right" part of the name for this reduction order comes from the fact that we will first reduce the function-part t of an application $t\ t'$ to a value, before we attempt to reduce the argument-part. This restriction is expressed by writing $(v\ \mathcal{C})$ in the grammar for contexts. The semantics does not allow reduction inside a lambda-abstraction. Left-to-right call-by-value is a deterministic reduction strategy: for each term t, there is at most one t' such that $t \rightsquigarrow t'$.

Usually we consider call-by-value strategies only for terms t which are **closed**; that is, when $FV(t) = \varnothing$ (see the definition of FV in Section 5.2.1). For closed terms, the set of values is the same as the set of normal forms. For open terms (i.e., ones which may contain free variables), we can have normal forms like just x or $(x\ \lambda y.y)$, which are not values.

As an example, here is a left-to-right call-by-value reduction sequence, with redexes underlined:

$$
\begin{array}{ll}
\underline{(\lambda x.x)\ (\lambda y.y)}\ ((\lambda w.w)\ (\lambda z.(\lambda a.a)\ z)) & \rightsquigarrow \\
(\lambda y.y)\ \underline{((\lambda w.w)\ (\lambda z.(\lambda a.a)\ z))} & \rightsquigarrow \\
\underline{(\lambda y.y)\ (\lambda z.(\lambda a.a)\ z)} & \rightsquigarrow \\
\lambda z.(\lambda a.a)\ z &
\end{array}
$$

Notice that we cannot reduce this final term $\lambda z.(\lambda a.a)\ z$. That is because the context we would need to reduce the redex is $\lambda z.*$. But that context is disallowed by the grammar for contexts $\mathcal{C}$, given at the start of this section. So we see here that this operational semantics gives us different normal forms from those of full β-reduction. In full β-reduction, we would extend the above reduction sequence one more step to get $\lambda z.z$ as our normal form. But in call-by-value, $\lambda z.(\lambda a.a)\ z$ is the (unique) normal form for the starting term.

5.4.2   Right-to-left call-by-value

$$contexts\ C\quad ::=\quad *\mid (t\ C)\mid (C\ v)$$

$$values\ v\quad ::=\quad \lambda x.t$$

We again use the ctxt$-\beta_v$ rule. This is just like the previous operational semantics, except now we evaluate applications $(t\ t')$ by first evaluating t' and then t. So if we use the same example term as in the previous section, we will get this different reduction sequence:

$$
\begin{array}{ll}
(\lambda x.x)\ (\lambda y.y)\ \underline{((\lambda w.w)\ (\lambda z.(\lambda a.a)\ z))} & \rightsquigarrow \\
(\lambda x.x)\ (\lambda y.y)\ \underline{(\lambda z.(\lambda a.a)\ z)} & \rightsquigarrow \\
\underline{(\lambda y.y)\ (\lambda z.(\lambda a.a)\ z)} & \rightsquigarrow \\
\lambda z.(\lambda a.a)\ z &
\end{array}
$$

5.4.3   Normal order (leftmost-outermost)

This semantics is not as conveniently describable with contexts. Suppose S is a set of redexes, all of which occur in term t. We define the **leftmost** of these redexes in t to be the one which occurs furthest left in t. So for example, $(\lambda x.x)\ (\lambda y.y)$ is the leftmost redex in the following term. The underlining makes this clear, as the line beneath the leftmost redex starts furthest to the left of any such lines.

$$\underline{(\lambda x.x)\ (\lambda y.y)}\ \underline{((\lambda w.w)\ (\lambda w.w))}$$

In the following term, the leftmost redex contains a smaller redex, which is to the right of it (since the line beneath the smaller redex starts to the right of the starting point of the bigger redex's line):

$$\underline{(\lambda x.\underline{(\lambda y.y)}\ x)\ (\lambda y.y)}$$

A redex of t is **outermost** if it is not contained in another redex. For example, if we abbreviate $(\lambda x.x)\ (\lambda y.(\lambda z.z)\ y)$ as X, then $X\ X$ has two outermost redexes.

The usual definition of normal-order reduction states that we always reduce the leftmost of the outermost redexes. In fact, it is equivalent just to say the leftmost of all the redexes in the term (more briefly, "the leftmost redex"), since the leftmost of the outermost redexes must be the leftmost redex. Normal-order reduction is a deterministic strategy. It gives us this reduction sequence for $X\ X$:

$$\frac{(\lambda x.x)\ (\lambda y.(\lambda z.z)\ y)\ ((\lambda x.x)\ (\lambda y.(\lambda z.z)\ y))}{\ }\ \rightsquigarrow$$
$$\frac{(\lambda y.(\lambda z.z)\ y)\ ((\lambda x.x)\ (\lambda y.(\lambda z.z)\ y))}{\ }\ \rightsquigarrow$$
$$\frac{(\lambda z.z)\ ((\lambda x.x)\ (\lambda y.(\lambda z.z)\ y))}{\ }\ \rightsquigarrow$$
$$\frac{(\lambda x.x)\ (\lambda y.(\lambda z.z)\ y)}{\ }\ \rightsquigarrow$$
$$\frac{\lambda y.(\lambda z.z)\ y}{\ }\ \rightsquigarrow$$
$$\lambda y.y$$

It is instructive to compare this sequence with the one we would get in left-to-right call-by-value reduction:

$$\frac{(\lambda x.x)\ (\lambda y.(\lambda z.z)\ y)\ ((\lambda x.x)\ (\lambda y.(\lambda z.z)\ y))}{\ }\ \rightsquigarrow$$
$$(\lambda y.(\lambda z.z)\ y)\ \frac{((\lambda x.x)\ (\lambda y.(\lambda z.z)\ y))}{\ }\ \rightsquigarrow$$
$$\frac{(\lambda y.(\lambda z.z)\ y)\ (\lambda y.(\lambda z.z)\ y)}{\ }\ \rightsquigarrow$$
$$\frac{(\lambda z.z)\ (\lambda y.(\lambda z.z)\ y)}{\ }\ \rightsquigarrow$$
$$\lambda y.(\lambda z.z)\ y$$

Note that the call-by-value reduction ends in a term which is not a normal form with respect to normal-order reduction, because it contains a redex beneath a lambda-abstraction.

The normal-order reduction strategy gets its name from the fact that for any term t, if t reduces to a normal form n using full β-reduction, then it also does so using normal-order reduction. This is a consequence of a result called the Standardization Theorem, which is not covered in this book (see Section 11.4 of [5]). A definition of contexts for this reduction strategy is possible, but a bit complicated (and not standard, to my knowledge):

$$\text{contexts } \mathcal{C} \quad ::= \quad \mathcal{D} \mid \lambda x.\mathcal{C}$$

$$\text{application contexts } \mathcal{D} \quad ::= \quad * \mid (\mathcal{D}\ t) \mid (n\ \mathcal{C})$$

$$\text{head-normal terms } n \quad ::= \quad x \mid n\ N$$

$$\text{normal terms } N \quad ::= \quad \lambda x.N \mid n$$

5.4.4   Call-by-name

$$\text{contexts } \mathcal{C} \quad ::= \quad * \mid (\mathcal{C}\ t)$$

This strategy does not reduce inside lambda-abstractions (so it differs in that respect from normal order), and unlike call-by-value strategies, it does not require arguments to be evaluated before doing β-reductions with them. Call-by-name is related to lazy evaluation, which we will explore in more detail in Section 11.3. An

$$\frac{t_1 \Downarrow \lambda x.\, t_1' \qquad t_2 \Downarrow t_2' \qquad [t_2'/x]t_1' \Downarrow t}{t_1\, t_2 \Downarrow t} \qquad\qquad \overline{\lambda x.\, t \Downarrow \lambda x.\, t}$$

Figure 5.3: Big-step call-by-value operational semantics

example reduction sequence is:

$$\frac{(\lambda x.\lambda y.\lambda z.x)\; ((\lambda x.x\; x)\; (\lambda x.x\; x))\; ((\lambda z.z)\; \lambda z.z)}{\frac{(\lambda y.\lambda z.((\lambda x.x\; x)\; (\lambda x.x\; x)))\; ((\lambda z.z)\; \lambda z.z)}{\lambda z.((\lambda x.x\; x)\; (\lambda x.x\; x))}} \quad \begin{array}{c}\rightsquigarrow \\ \rightsquigarrow\end{array}$$

The starting term of this reduction diverges with all the other reduction orders above, while here it converges (although the term to which it converges is not a normal form with respect to full β-reduction).

5.5 Big-step call-by-value operational semantics

In this section and the next, we study a big-step operational semantics corresponding to the call-by-value small-step relations above. Figure 5.3 defines this big-step, call-by-value evaluation relation for closed terms. The reason this is just intended for closed terms is that the relation is undefined when the first term is a variable. This also makes the relation undefined on applications whose functional parts evaluate to variables, for example. Note that the first rule, for applications, takes three premises: one for evaluating the functional part t_1 of the application to a value $\lambda.\, t_1'$; one for evaluating the argument part t_2 to a value t_2'; and one more for evaluating the contractum $[t_2'/x]t_1'$ to a final value t. Here is an example derivation using these rules:

$$\frac{\dfrac{\overline{(\lambda x.\,\lambda y.\, x) \Downarrow (\lambda x.\,\lambda y.\, x)} \quad \overline{\lambda z.\, z \Downarrow \lambda z.\, z} \quad \overline{\lambda y.\,\lambda z.\, z \Downarrow \lambda y.\,\lambda z.\, z}}{(\lambda x.\,\lambda y.\, x)\, (\lambda z.\, z) \Downarrow \lambda y.\,\lambda z.\, z} \quad D_1 \quad D_2}{(\lambda x.\,\lambda y.\, x)\, (\lambda z.\, z)\, (\lambda w.\, w\, w) \Downarrow \lambda z.\, z}$$

where:

$$D_1 = \overline{\lambda w.\, w\, w \Downarrow \lambda w.\, w\, w}$$
$$D_2 = \overline{\lambda z.\, z \Downarrow \lambda z.\, z}$$

A first observation we can make about this relation is that if $t \Downarrow t'$, then t' is a value, in the sense of Section 5.4.1 above (i.e., it is a λ-abstraction).

Theorem 5.5.1 (Results of evaluation are values). *If $t \Downarrow t'$, then $t' = \lambda x.t''$, for some x and t''.*

Proof. The proof is by induction on the structure of the derivation of $t \Downarrow t'$.

<u>Case:</u>

$$\frac{t_1 \Downarrow \lambda x.\, t_1' \qquad t_2 \Downarrow t_2' \qquad [t_2'/x]t_1' \Downarrow t}{t_1\, t_2 \Downarrow t}$$

By the induction hypothesis for the derivation given for the third premise, $t = \lambda x'.\, t'$, for some x' and t'. This is sufficient to conclude that the final result, in the conclusion of this inference, has that same required form.

<u>Case:</u>

$$\frac{}{\lambda x.\, t \Downarrow \lambda x.\, t}$$

The result of the evaluation has the required form.

$\square$

5.6   Relating big-step and small-step operational semantics

We can now relate our big-step semantics with the left-to-right call-by-value small-step semantics we defined above (Section 5.4.1). This section provides a good example of a nontrivial proof about operational semantics. The proof is rather involved, and not every reader will wish to wade through all the details. The main theorem, though, is an important one. As a small note: we could easily modify the proof below to relate the big-step semantics with right-to-left call-by-value small-step semantics. As a corollary, this would serve to relate the left-to-right and right-to-left small-step relations to each other.

Theorem 5.6.1 (Equivalence of big-step and small-step CBV semantics). *We have* $t \Downarrow v$ *iff* $t \rightsquigarrow^* v$ *(using the small-step semantics of Section 5.4.1).*

Proof ($\Rightarrow$). We will first prove the left-to-right implication. So suppose $t \Downarrow v$. We will now prove $t \rightsquigarrow^* v$ by induction on the structure of the derivation of $t \Downarrow v$. Since we know that results of big-step evaluation are values by Theorem 5.5.1, we will use meta-variables for values below, for the results of evaluation.

<u>Case:</u>

$$\frac{t_1 \Downarrow \lambda x.\, t_1' \qquad t_2 \Downarrow v_2 \qquad [v_2/x]t_1' \Downarrow v}{t_1\, t_2 \Downarrow v}$$

By the induction hypotheses for the derivations given for the three premises of this rule, we have:

$$\begin{aligned}
t_1 \quad &\rightsquigarrow^* \quad \lambda x.\, t_1' \\
t_2 \quad &\rightsquigarrow^* \quad v_2 \\
[v_2/x]t_1' \quad &\rightsquigarrow^* \quad v
\end{aligned}$$

Our goal is now to use these facts to construct the reduction sequence indicated by:

$$t_1\, t_2 \rightsquigarrow^* (\lambda x.\, t_1')\, t_2 \rightsquigarrow^* (\lambda x.\, t_1')\, v_2 \rightsquigarrow [v_2/x]t_1' \rightsquigarrow^* v$$

Notice that the step $(\lambda x.\, t_1')\, v_2 \rightsquigarrow [v_2/x]t_1'$ is a legal CBV step, since the argument v_2 is a value. To construct the sequence, we just use the following two lemmas (and transitivity of $\rightsquigarrow^*$), which we will prove after we complete the current proof of Theorem 5.6.1.

Lemma 5.6.2 (Congruence of multi-step reduction, functional part of applications). *If $t \rightsquigarrow^* v$, then $t\, t' \rightsquigarrow^* v\, t'$.*

Lemma 5.6.3 (Congruence of multi-step reduction, argument part of applications). *If $t' \rightsquigarrow^* v'$, then $v\, t' \rightsquigarrow^* v\, v'$.*

Case:

$$\frac{}{\lambda x.\, t \Downarrow \lambda x.\, t}.$$

We have $\lambda x.\, t \rightsquigarrow^* \lambda x.\, t$.

End proof $(\Rightarrow)$.

Proof $(\Leftarrow)$. We will now assume $t \rightsquigarrow^* v$, and prove $t \Downarrow v$. From the derivation of $t \rightsquigarrow^* v$, we can extract the ordered list of single steps taken to get from t to v:

$$t = t_1 \rightsquigarrow t_2 \rightsquigarrow t_3 \rightsquigarrow \cdots \rightsquigarrow t_n = v$$

This extraction can be easily defined by recursion on the structure of the derivation, based on the rules for reflexive transitive closure in Section 4.2.2. The definition is in Figure 5.4. We proceed now by induction on the number n of single steps in this extracted list $t_1 \rightsquigarrow \cdots \rightsquigarrow t_n$. For the base case, if there are no single steps, this implies that $t = v$. In that case, we obtain $v \Downarrow v$ using the big-step rule for evaluating λ-abstractions (since values v are just λ-abstractions).

For the step case, we have at least one single step between t and v. We will now argue that there must be some step of the form $(\lambda x.\, t')\, v' \rightsquigarrow [v'/x]t'$ in our sequence $t_1 \rightsquigarrow \cdots \rightsquigarrow t_n$. That is, there is some reduction in the sequence which uses context $*$. If not, then all steps must take place inside some context $\mathcal{C}$ other than $*$. This would imply that the final result v is of the form $\mathcal{C}[t']$, for some such $\mathcal{C}$ and t. This in turn would imply, by the definition of left-to-right call-by-value contexts $\mathcal{C}$ (Section 5.4.1), that v is an application, which is impossible, since values are just λ-abstractions.

So consider the first such top-level (i.e., with just $*$ for the context $\mathcal{C}$) β-reduction step in our sequence. Our sequence must look like:

$$t \rightsquigarrow^* (\lambda x.\, t')\, v' \rightsquigarrow [v'/x]t' \rightsquigarrow^* v$$

Since all reduction steps between t and the displayed β-redex occur with context $\mathcal{C}$ other than $*$, we know that t must be some application $t_a\, t_b$, and what we know about our reduction sequence can be further refined to:

$$t_a\, t_b \rightsquigarrow^* (\lambda x.\, t')\, t_b \rightsquigarrow^* (\lambda x.\, t')\, v' \rightsquigarrow [v'/x]t' \rightsquigarrow^* v$$

This is justified by the following lemma, proved in Section 5.6.2 below.

$$\frac{a \rightsquigarrow a'}{a \rightsquigarrow^* a'} \qquad \text{yields} \quad a \rightsquigarrow a'$$

$$\frac{a_1 \rightsquigarrow^* a_2 \quad a_2 \rightsquigarrow^* a_3}{a_1 \rightsquigarrow^* a_3} \qquad \text{yields} \quad \begin{array}{l} L_1 \text{ concatenated with } L_2 \\ \textit{where } L_1 \textit{ is extracted from first subproof} \\ \textit{and } L_2 \textit{ is extracted from second subproof} \end{array}$$

$$a \rightsquigarrow^* a \qquad \text{yields} \quad \textit{empty list}$$

Figure 5.4: Translating multi-step derivations to multiple single-steps

Lemma 5.6.4. *If $t_a\ t_b \rightsquigarrow^* t'_a\ t'_b$ using only single steps where the context C is not $*$, then we have $t_a \rightsquigarrow^* t'_a$ and $t_b \rightsquigarrow^* t'_b$.*

Consider now these three multi-step reductions:

$$\begin{array}{rcl} t_a & \rightsquigarrow^* & \lambda x.\,t' \\ t_b & \rightsquigarrow^* & v' \\ [v'/x]t' & \rightsquigarrow^* & v \end{array}$$

In each case, we know that the length of the reduction sequence is less than the length of our original reduction sequence, because that sequence contains one additional step, namely $(\lambda x.\,t')\ v' \rightsquigarrow [v'/x]t'$, that is omitted from all of these sequences. So we may apply our induction hypothesis to the sequences of steps corresponding to each of these three displayed facts, to obtain:

$$\begin{array}{rcl} t_a & \Downarrow & \lambda x.\,t' \\ t_b & \Downarrow & v' \\ [v'/x]t' & \Downarrow & v \end{array}$$

We can now assemble these pieces as follows to complete the proof:

$$\frac{t_a \Downarrow \lambda x.\,t' \quad t_b \Downarrow v' \quad [v'/x]t' \Downarrow v}{t_a\ t_b \Downarrow v}$$

End proof.

5.6.1 Proofs of Lemmas 5.6.2 and 5.6.3 above

Proof of Lemma 5.6.2. First, assume $t \rightsquigarrow^* v$. We must prove that $t\ t' \rightsquigarrow^* v\ t'$. The proof is by induction on the structure of the derivation of $t \rightsquigarrow^* v$.

Case:

$$\frac{t \rightsquigarrow v}{t \rightsquigarrow^* v}$$

Suppose that the context used for $t \rightsquigarrow v$ is C, the redex R, and the contractum C. Then we have this derivation for the required reduction:

$$\frac{t\,t' \rightsquigarrow v\,t'}{t\,t' \rightsquigarrow^* v\,t'}$$

The premise is justified using context $C\,t'$, which is a legal left-to-right CBV context, and again redex R and contractum C.

Case:

$$\frac{t \rightsquigarrow^* \hat{t} \quad \hat{t} \rightsquigarrow^* v}{t \rightsquigarrow^* v}$$

We use the induction hypothesis for the two subproofs to obtain the two premises in the derivation below, which is sufficient for this case:

$$\frac{t\,t' \rightsquigarrow^* \hat{t}\,t' \quad \hat{t}\,t' \rightsquigarrow^* v\,t'}{t\,t' \rightsquigarrow^* v\,t'}$$

Case:

$$\frac{}{v \rightsquigarrow^* v}$$

The required derivation is just:

$$\frac{}{v\,t' \rightsquigarrow^* v\,t'}$$

$\square$

Proof of Lemma 5.6.3. The last two cases of this proof are very similar to those for Lemma 5.6.2, so we just consider the first case:

Case:

$$\frac{t' \rightsquigarrow v'}{t' \rightsquigarrow^* v'}$$

Suppose that the context used for $t \rightsquigarrow v$ is C, the redex R, and the contractum C. Then we have this derivation for the required reduction:

$$\frac{v\,t' \rightsquigarrow v\,v'}{v\,t' \rightsquigarrow^* v\,v'}$$

The premise is justified using context $v\,C$, which is a legal left-to-right CBV context, and again redex R and contractum C.

$\square$

5.6.2   Proof of Lemma 5.6.4

Proof. Assume that $t_a\ t_b \leadsto^* t'_a\ t'_b$ using only single steps where the context $\mathcal{C}$ is not $*$. We must show that $t_a \leadsto^* t'_a$ and $t_b \leadsto^* t'_b$. The proof is by induction on the structure of the derivation of $t_a\ t_b \leadsto^* t'_a\ t'_b$.

Case:

$$\frac{t_a\ t_b \leadsto t'_a\ t'_b}{t_a\ t_b \leadsto^* t'_a\ t'_b}$$

By assumption, the single step in the premise has some context $\mathcal{C}$ other than $*$. It must either be of the form $\mathcal{C}'\ t_b$ or else $t_a\ \mathcal{C}'$. In the latter case, t_a must be a value, or else the context is not a legal left-to-right CBV context. In the former, we have $t_a \leadsto t'_a$ and $t'_b = t_b$; while in the latter case we have $t_b \leadsto t'_b$ and $t'_a = t_a$. Either way, we then obtain $t_a \leadsto^* t'_a$ and $t_b \leadsto^* t'_b$ using the same inference rule for reflexive transitive closure as for this case (for whichever of t_a and t_b takes a step here), and also the reflexivity rule for reflexive transitive closure (for whichever of t_a and t_b does not take a step here).

Case:

$$\frac{t_a\ t_b \leadsto^* t''_a\ t''_b \quad t''_a\ t''_b \leadsto^* t'_a\ t'_b}{t_a\ t_b \leadsto^* t'_a\ t'_b}$$

By the induction hypothesis for the two subproofs, we have these facts:

$$t_a \leadsto^* t''_a$$
$$t''_a \leadsto^* t'_a$$
$$t_b \leadsto^* t''_b$$
$$t''_b \leadsto^* t'_b$$

Using the transitivity rule for the reflexive transitive closure, we can glue together the proofs corresponding to the top two and the bottom two facts, respectively, to obtain the desired facts:

$$t_a \leadsto^* t'_a$$
$$t_b \leadsto^* t'_b$$

Case:

$$\frac{}{t_a\ t_b \leadsto^* t_a\ t_b}$$

In this case, $t_a = t'_a$ and $t_b = t'_b$. We just use reflexivity again to get $t_a \leadsto^* t_a$ and $t_b \leadsto^* t_b$.

$\square$

5.7   Conclusion

In this chapter, we have seen the abstract syntax and operational semantics of untyped lambda calculus. We obtain different **reduction relations** (i.e., small-step evaluation relations) by restricting where the β-reduction steps – which substitute arguments for input variables when functions are applied – can occur. We saw also how to relate one small-step semantics (namely, left-to-right call-by-value semantics) with a big-step semantics.

Unlike the WHILE language studied previously, lambda calculus is not based on an idea of implicit state. Rather, it provides a model of computable mathematical functions without implicit state. In the next chapter, we will see how to program in untyped lambda calculus, and then consider how to add a type system and support for other features of practical programming.

See [12] for further development of the idea of reduction using contexts, in particular to so-called **abstract machines**, which are reduction semantics optimized for practical efficiency.

5.8   Basic Exercises

5.8.1   For Section 5.1, syntax of lambda terms

1. Draw the syntax trees for the following terms of lambda calculus. You need to follow the parsing conventions described in Section 5.1, for example to understand that $x\, y\, x$ is just less parenthesized notation for $((x\, y)\, x)$ [3 points each]:

   (a) $\lambda x.\lambda y.(x\, y)$

   (b) $\lambda x.x\, (\lambda y.y\, y)$

   (c) $x\, \lambda x.x\, y\, x$

2. Find the most specific pattern you can which matches the following lambda terms [3 points]. That is, you are looking for the most informative expression you can find in our meta-language, where that expression consists of lambda-calculus operators and meta-variables t, t', etc., and where both terms below are instances of that meta-language expression:

   - $\lambda x.(\lambda y.y)\, (x\, x)$
   - $\lambda x.x\, (x\, \lambda y.y)$

3. Write a closed lambda term (that is, one with no free variables) with at least three lambda-binders in it and where every bound variable is used at least once in the body of its lambda abstraction [2 points].

4. Fully parenthesize the following terms:

   (a) $\lambda x.\lambda y.x$

   (b) $x\, x\, x$

   (c) $x\, \lambda x.x\, x$

5. Drop as many parentheses as possible from the following fully parenthe-sized terms, according to the conventions in Section 5.1.1. The resulting term should have the same structure as the original one, but with as few paren-theses as possible.

(a) $((\lambda x.(x\ x))\ x)$

(b) $((\lambda y.y)\ (\lambda x.(x\ (x\ x))))$

(c) $((\lambda x.(\lambda y.((x\ y)\ x)))\ z)$

6. Rename variables in the following terms so that global variables (i.e., ones free in the term) have different names from local ones (i.e., ones introduced by λ), and so that different uses of λ introduce variables with different names. This should be done without changing the names of global variables. For ex-ample $x\ \lambda x.x$ could be renamed to $x\ \lambda y.y$, but not $y\ \lambda x.x$ (because we are not allowing global variables to be renamed).

(a) $x\ y\ \lambda x.\lambda y.z$

(b) $(\lambda x.x\ x)\ (\lambda x.x\ x)$

(c) $(\lambda x.x)\ y\ (\lambda x.x\ y)$

5.8.2   For Section 5.2.1, capture-avoiding substitution

1. Using the definition in Section 5.2.1, compute the set of free variables of the following terms [2 points each]:

(a) $x\ y\ \lambda x.x\ y$

(b) $\lambda x.y\ x\ x$

(c) $\lambda x.(\lambda y.y)\ y\ \lambda x.x$

2. Compute the result of the following substitutions, renaming bound variables as necessary so that the substitution is defined:

(a) $[x/y](\lambda z.z\ y)$

(b) $[(x\ x)/x](\lambda z.x\ y\ z)$

(c) $[(z\ x)/x](\lambda z.x\ z)$

5.8.3   For Section 5.2, full β-reduction

1. Using the proof rules given at the start of Section 5.2 for full β-reduction, write out derivation trees for each of the following facts (similar to the one shown at the start of Section 5.2.2):

(a) $y\ ((\lambda x.x\ x)\ \lambda z.z) \rightsquigarrow y\ ((\lambda z.z)\ \lambda z.z)$

(b) $\lambda x.\lambda y.(\lambda x.x)\ y \rightsquigarrow \lambda x.\lambda y.y$

(c) $(\lambda x.x)\ ((\lambda y.x\ y)\ \lambda z.z) \rightsquigarrow (\lambda x.x)\ (x\ (\lambda z.z))$

2. Which of the following terms are in normal form (see Section 5.2.3 for the definition)?

   - $\lambda x.x \; \lambda y.y \; x$
   - $x \; (\lambda y.y) \; \lambda z.z$
   - $x \; ((\lambda y.x) \; y)$
   - $\lambda x.\lambda y.y \; \lambda z.z$
   - $\lambda x.\lambda y.(\lambda z.z) \; y$

3. For each of the following terms, write out a single maximal reduction sequence, with redexes underlined (similar to the one shown at the end of Section 5.2.2), that begins with that term. Some of these terms may have more than one sequence possible. You just need to pick a single reduction sequence and write it out (which one you choose does not matter). All of the terms reach a normal form no matter which sequence you use. You do not need to give derivations, as in the previous problem, to justify the steps of the reduction sequence.

   (a) $(\lambda x.(\lambda y.y) \; x) \; (\lambda z.z)$

   (b) $\lambda x.(\lambda y.y \; y) \; ((\lambda z.z) \; x)$

   (c) $z \; ((\lambda y.y \; x) \; (\lambda z.y \; z))$

4. List all the β-redexes (i.e., terms of the form $(\lambda x.t) \; t'$) in each of the following terms:

   (a) $(\lambda x.(\lambda x.x) \; x) \; \lambda y.y$

   (b) $(\lambda x.(\lambda y.y) \; \lambda z.z) \; (\lambda x.x) \; (\lambda y.y)$

   (c) $(\lambda x.\lambda y.y) \; ((\lambda x.x) \; (\lambda y.y))$

5. List all the full β-reduction sequences possible (by reducing redexes in all the different possible orders) for each of the following terms, using underlining notation:

   (a) $(\lambda w.w) \; (\lambda x.x) \; ((\lambda y.y) \; (\lambda z.z))$

   (b) $(\lambda x.\lambda y.x) \; (\lambda x.x) \; ((\lambda x.x) \; (\lambda y.y))$

5.8.4 For Section 5.3, full β-reduction and contexts

1. Compute the result of the following graftings, for the given context $\mathcal{C}$:

   (a) $\mathcal{C}[(x \; y)]$, where $\mathcal{C} = \lambda x.x \; *$.

   (b) $\mathcal{C}[\lambda x.x]$, where $\mathcal{C} = x \; *$.

   (c) $\mathcal{C}[(\lambda x.x) \; \lambda y.y]$, where $\mathcal{C} = *$.

2. For each of the reduction steps shown (with redexes underlined), write down the corresponding context:

(a) $\lambda x.(\lambda y.y\ y)\ (\underline{(\lambda z.z\ z)\ x}) \rightsquigarrow \lambda x.(\lambda y.y\ y)\ (x\ x)$

(b) $(\lambda x.x)\ ((\lambda y.y\ y)\ \lambda z.\underline{(\lambda w.w)\ z}) \rightsquigarrow (\lambda x.x)\ ((\lambda y.y\ y)\ \lambda z.z)$

(c) $\underline{(\lambda x.x)\ (\lambda y.y)}\ \lambda z.z\ z \rightsquigarrow (\lambda y.y)\ \lambda z.z\ z$

3. Write down all the full β-reduction contexts for which the following terms can be decomposed into context and redex:

    (a) $(\lambda x.(\lambda y.x)\ x)\ (\lambda z.(\lambda y.y)\ z)$

    (b) $(\lambda x.x\ x)\ ((\lambda y.\lambda z.y)\ \lambda y.\lambda z.z)$

    (c) $(\lambda s.\lambda z.(\lambda x.x)\ (s\ z))\ (\lambda x.\lambda y.((\lambda z.y)\ x))$

5.8.5   For Section 5.4, other reduction orders

1. For each of the following expressions, list all the reduction orders (including full β-reduction) for which they are legal contexts.

    (a) $\lambda x. * x$

    (b) $* (\lambda x.x)\ \lambda y.y$

    (c) $(\lambda x.x)\ * (\lambda y.y)$

    (d) $(\lambda x.x)\ (\lambda y.y)\ *$

    (e) $(\lambda x.x)\ \lambda y.*$

2. Consider the following term:

$$(\lambda x.\lambda y.x)\ (\lambda z.z)\ ((\lambda x.x)\ (\lambda y.y))$$

    (a) For this term, show both the left-to-right and the right-to-left call-by-value reduction sequences which end in values, using underlining notation.

    (b) Write down the contexts used for each step in those reduction sequences, and confirm that all the contexts are accepted by the appropriate grammar in the chapter.

3. Consider the following term:

$$(\lambda x.\lambda y.\lambda z.y)\ ((\lambda x.x\ x)\ (\lambda x.x\ x))\ ((\lambda x.x)\ (\lambda x.x))$$

    (a) For this term, show the normal-order reduction sequence ending in a normal form, using underlining notation.

    (b) Write down the contexts used for each step in that reduction sequence, and confirm that they are accepted by the appropriate grammar in the chapter.

5.9   Intermediate Exercises

1. Find a lambda-calculus term t and an infinite reduction sequence $t_1 \leadsto^* t_2 \leadsto^* \cdots$ where again t_{i+1} is on the order of twice the size of t_i, for all $i \in \mathbb{N}$.

2. For purposes of this problem, define $t \downarrow t'$ to mean $\exists t''.t \leadsto^* t'' \wedge t' \leadsto^* t''$, where $\leadsto$ is normal-order reduction (where the outermost β-redex is reduced, and reduction proceeds under λ-binders). As usual, variables can be safely renamed, so that we consider $\lambda x.x$ equivalent to $\lambda y.y$, for example.

   For which of the following terms do we have $t \downarrow \lambda x.\lambda y.y$? Please indicate all terms which satisfy this property.

   (a) $\lambda x.\lambda y.y$

   (b) $(\lambda x.x)\, \lambda y.y$

   (c) $(\lambda x.x\; x)\, (\lambda y.y)\, \lambda x.\lambda y.y$

   (d) $\lambda x.(\lambda x.\lambda y.y\; y)\, (\lambda x.x)$

   (e) $\lambda x.\lambda x.(\lambda y.y)\; x$

5.10   More Challenging Exercises

1. Prove that if n is the normal form of t using left-to-right call-by-value reduction, then it is also the normal form of t using right-to-left call-by-value reduction.

2. Prove for all terms t, that if each local variable x is used at most once after being introduced by its lambda-abstraction in t, then t has a normal form using full β-reduction.

3. **Complete developments.** This problem is based on material in Section 11.2 of Barendregt's book [5]. We will work with a modified syntax for terms:

   $$terms\; t \;::=\; x \mid \lambda x.t \mid x\, t \mid (t\, t')\, t'' \mid (\lambda x.t)\, t' \mid (\lambda x.t)^l\, t'$$

   We have variables and lambda-abstractions as usual. For applications, we have three different main cases, depending on the form of the function-part of the application. And if the function part is a lambda-abstraction, it is either labeled with l, drawn from some countably infinite set of labels; or else unlabeled.

   Using the contexts for full β-reduction in the chapter, we give this modified definition for reduction:

   $$\frac{}{\mathcal{C}[(\lambda x.t)^l\, t'] \;\leadsto\; \mathcal{C}[[t'/x]t]}\; ctxt\text{-}\beta^l$$

That is, we only allow reduction of labeled redexes, and hence we call this **labeled reduction**.

We can erase all the labels in any term t to obtain a term $|t|$ in our original (unlabeled) syntax. Furthermore, suppose we have a labeled-reduction sequence ρ, beginning with a term t. We can erase all the labels from the terms in ρ, and we will obtain a reduction sequence $|\rho|$ using full β-reduction (with unlabeled terms). Such a reduction sequence is called a **development** of $|t|$. If ρ ends in a normal form (with respect to $\texttt{ctxt-}\beta^l$), then $|\rho|$ is called a **complete development**.

(a) Give a labeled term t where all β-redexes are labeled, and where $|t| = (\lambda x.x\,((\lambda y.y)\,x))\,(\lambda x.x\,((\lambda y.y)\,x))$.

(b) Show a complete development of the term $|t|$ of the previous problem.

(c) Prove that every labeled term t has a normal form with respect to labeled reduction. Hint: this is not hard to prove if you pick the right reduction strategy.

Chapter 6
Programming in Untyped Lambda Calculus

The previous chapter introduced the lambda calculus, and demonstrated some of its power. In this chapter, we will go further, and see how to implement familiar data structures and algorithms using lambda calculus. The basic idea is to encode data as terms in the lambda calculus. In particular, data will be encoded as certain lambda-abstractions. So every piece of data, including numbers and lists, for example, will be encoded as a function. There really is no alternative, unless we wish to extend the language with new primitive constructs (as we will do in Section 11.1). Since the only closed normal forms in lambda calculus are lambda abstractions, every piece of data will have to be encoded as one of these. We will consider two different lambda encodings in this chapter: one due to Alonzo Church, and the other to Dana Scott. The different encodings have different advantages and disadvantages, which we will discuss.

6.1 The Church encoding for datatypes

For any encoding of data like natural numbers, lists, or booleans as pure lambda terms (and we say *pure* here to emphasize that we have not added any additional constructs to the lambda calculus; it is exactly as presented in the previous chapter), the central issue is how to view the data as a function. What is the central functional abstraction that we use when programming with data? The Church encoding takes iteration through the data as the central operation we will perform with data. Note that in this section, we will need to assume we are using either full β-reduction or else normal order reduction. This is because we will need to reduce under λ-bindings, in order to get the expected results of basic arithmetic operations on Church-encoded numbers.

6.1.1 Unary natural numbers

For what is hopefully an intuitive starting example, let us consider the natural numbers in unary notation, also known as **Peano** numbers:

0	1	2	3	4	$\cdots$
|	||	|||	||||		$\cdots$
Z	$(S\,Z)$	$(S\,(S\,Z))$	$(S\,(S\,(S\,Z)))$	$(S\,(S\,(S\,(S\,Z))))$	$\cdots$

Here, I am listing the usual decimal numbers in the first line, the number in unary (where we have just one digit, written |) on the second line, and then the number using constructor notation (explained next). The sole piece of subdata for a number is the predecessor of that number. If the number is 0, there are no subdata (and nothing to write in unary notation on the second line).

In constructor notation, we generate the natural numbers from Z (a constructor with no arguments, also called a 0-ary constructor) by applying S, a unary constructor. Constructors build bigger data elements from smaller ones: given subdata, they create data. They are also injective functions: given different subdata as inputs, they will produce different data as outputs. Each element of the datatype is generated by a finite number of applications of the constructors.

An often used operation we can perform with a natural number is iteration. For a mathematical function f and starting value a, let us define the n-fold iteration of f on a by:

$$\begin{aligned} f^0(a) &= a \\ f^{n+1}(a) &= f(f^n(a)) \end{aligned}$$

For example, let *double* be the function which doubles its natural-number input. Then we can define the function *pow2* which takes natural number x and returns 2^x by:

$$pow2(x) = double^x(1)$$

For example, expanding the definition of n-fold iteration, we have

$$\begin{aligned} &pow2(3) \\ =\ &double^3(1) \\ =\ &double(double^2(1)) \\ =\ &double(double(double^1(1))) \\ =\ &double(double(double(double^0(1)))) \\ =\ &double(double(double(1))) \\ =\ &double(double(2)) \\ =\ &double(4) \\ =\ &8 \end{aligned}$$

We will overload our iteration notation to apply also to terms, and not just mathematical functions. If f and a are lambda terms, we recursively define another lambda term $f^n\ a$ by:

$$\begin{aligned} f^0\ a &= a \\ f^{n+1}\ a &= f\ (f^n\ a) \end{aligned}$$

For example, $x^3\ y$ equals $x\ (x\ (x\ y))$. The concept of iteration is central to the Church encoding for unary natural numbers, as we will now see.

6.1.2   Church encoding for unary natural numbers

Any lambda encoding is charged with representing data, like unary natural numbers, as pure lambda terms. Assuming those lambda terms are to be closed and have a normal form (reasonable assumptions, one would think, for an encoding), then this means that encoded data will always be a λ-abstraction of some form. So all lambda-encoded data become (lambda calculus) functions. The only question is, which functions?

The Church encoding answers this question in an intuitive and compelling way: iteration functions. The number n is going to be encoded as a function which iterates another function f a total of n times on a starting value a. So we want the following statement to be true for a Church-encoded number n:

$$n\, f\, a \leadsto^* f^n a$$

So we will have:

$$3\, x\, y \leadsto^* x^3\, y = x\, (x\, (x\, y))$$

Based on this idea, we have the following encoding for unary natural numbers:

$$
\begin{aligned}
0 &:= \lambda f.\lambda a.a \\
1 &:= \lambda f.\lambda a.f\, a \\
2 &:= \lambda f.\lambda a.f\, (f\, a) \\
&\quad \cdots \\
n &:= \lambda f.\lambda a.f^n\, a \\
&\quad \cdots
\end{aligned}
$$

Another way to view this definition is that each number is a function giving an interpretation to the constructors S and Z, based on an interpretation of S and an interpretation of Z. As a constructor term, 2 is $S\ (S\ Z)$. If one applies 2 to f and a, one gets $f\ (f\ a)$. This expression has the same structure as the constructor term $S\ (S\ Z)$, but with S replaced by f and Z by a. Perhaps for this reason, one often sees variables s and z used in place of f and a:

$$
\begin{aligned}
0 &:= \lambda s.\lambda z.z \\
1 &:= \lambda s.\lambda z.s\, z \\
2 &:= \lambda s.\lambda z.s\, (s\, z) \\
&\quad \cdots \\
n &:= \lambda s.\lambda z.s^n\, z \\
&\quad \cdots
\end{aligned}
$$

Given that these are the encodings of the numbers, we can define the constructors as follows:

$$
\begin{aligned}
Z &:= \lambda s.\lambda z.z \\
S &:= \lambda n.\lambda s.\lambda z.s\, (n\, s\, z)
\end{aligned}
$$

The term $s\ (n\ s\ z)$ in the definition of S can be thought of as iterating s one more time after iterating s a total of n times starting from z – exactly what $(n\ s\ z)$ computes. Here is an example to see the definitions of the constructors in action:

$$
\begin{aligned}
& S\,(S\,Z) \\
=\ & S\,((\lambda n.\lambda s.\lambda z.s\,(n\,s\,z))\,Z) \\
\rightsquigarrow\ & S\,(\overline{(\lambda n.\lambda s.\lambda z.s\,(n\,s\,z))\,Z}) \\
\rightsquigarrow\ & S\,\lambda s.\lambda z.s\,(Z\,s\,z) \\
=\ & S\,\lambda s.\lambda z.s\,((\lambda s.\lambda z.z)\,s\,z) \\
\rightsquigarrow\ & S\,\lambda s.\lambda z.s\,(\overline{(\lambda z.z)\,z}) \\
\rightsquigarrow\ & S\,\lambda s.\lambda z.s\,z \\
=\ & S\,1 \\
=\ & (\lambda n.\lambda s.\lambda z.s\,(n\,s\,z))\,1 \\
\rightsquigarrow\ & \lambda s.\lambda z.s\,(1\,s\,z) \\
=\ & \lambda s.\lambda z.s\,((\lambda s.\lambda z.s\,z)\,s\,z) \\
\rightsquigarrow\ & \lambda s.\lambda z.s\,(\overline{(\lambda z.s\,z)\,z}) \\
\rightsquigarrow\ & \lambda s.\lambda z.s\,\overline{(s\,z)} \\
=\ & 2
\end{aligned}
$$

6.1.3 Encoding basic arithmetic functions

Basic arithmetic functions are easy and elegant to define on Church-encoded natural numbers. One must only be able to view the function as an iteration, in order to define it in a direct way on Church-encoded numbers. For example, we can think of addition as iterated successor:

$$3 + 4 = S\,(S\,(S\,4))$$

In other words (and switching to prefix notation), we could view addition this way:

$$plus\ n\ m = S^n\ m$$

In other words, just iterate the S function n times starting from m. That is easy to do with Church encodings:

$$plus := \lambda n.\lambda m.n\,S\,m$$

Multiplication can also be viewed as an iteration:

$$3 * 4 = 4 + (4 + (4 + 0))$$

We are iterating the "plus 4" function 3 times, starting with 0. So we can view multiplication (again, switching to prefix notation) this way:

$$mult\ n\ m = (plus\ n)^m\ 0$$

This leads to the following definition in lambda calculus on Church-encoded natural numbers:

$$mult := \lambda n.\lambda m.m\,(plus\ n)\,Z$$

Exponentiation can also be defined as iterated multiplication (this is left as an exercise below).

Encoding functions as iterations is working so beautifully, you might wonder if it ever runs aground. The answer, sadly, is yes, for a very trivial function, which we consider next.

6.1.4 Encoding the predecessor function

The predecessor operation, which given 4 will return 3, is quite unnatural to define as iteration, though it is a basic and useful function. It takes quite some creativity to find a way to view the predecessor as an iteration. The standard solution is to base predecessor on the following transformation on pairs of natural numbers:

$$(n, m) \implies (m, m + 1)$$

For look what happens when we iterate this transformation three times, for example, starting from $(0,0)$:

$$(0,0) \implies (0,1) \implies (1,2) \implies (2,3)$$

We end up with the pair $(2,3)$, which amazingly has the predecessor 2 of 3 (the number of times we iterated the transformation) as its first component.

To implement this on Church-encoded natural numbers, we first need a Church encoding of pairs.

6.1.5 Church encoding of pairs

We can Church-encode pairs of elements (x, y) using this definition:

$$(x, y) = \lambda f. f \, x \, y$$

This has exactly the desired effect: when a pair is applied to a function f, that function will be called with the two components x and y of the pair. There is no iteration here, because the datatype of pairs is not recursive: in general, pairs just contain elements of other datatypes. A function to construct the pair from the components is then:

$$mkpair = \lambda x. \lambda y. \lambda f. f \, x \, y$$

So for example, if we wish to make a pair of the two (Church-encoded) numbers 1 and 2, we just apply $mkpair$, which will then compute the pair. Here I am underlining the current left-to-right call-by-value redex:

$$
\begin{aligned}
& \underline{mkpair \, 1} \, 2 \\
= \; & \underline{(\lambda x. \lambda y. \lambda f. f \, x \, y) \, 1} \, 2 \\
\rightsquigarrow \; & \underline{(\lambda y. \lambda f. f \, 1 \, y) \, 2} \\
\rightsquigarrow \; & \lambda f. f \, 1 \, 2
\end{aligned}
$$

The final result is the pair, which is itself a function (as all data are with the Church encoding), that is waiting for a function f to call with the two elements of the pair, 1 and 2.

To select the first element of a pair, we just apply the pair to the function $\lambda x.\lambda y.x$. For example:

$$
\begin{array}{ll}
 & (\lambda f.\, f\, 1\, 2)\ \lambda x.\lambda y.x \\
\rightsquigarrow & \overline{(\lambda x.\lambda y.x)\, 1\, 2} \\
\rightsquigarrow & \overline{(\lambda y.1)\, 2} \\
\rightsquigarrow & 1
\end{array}
$$

So we have extracted the first component of the pair. To extract the second, apply the pair to $\lambda x.\lambda y.y$:

$$
\begin{array}{ll}
 & (\lambda f.\, f\, 1\, 2)\ \lambda x.\lambda y.y \\
\rightsquigarrow & \overline{(\lambda x.\lambda y.y)\, 1\, 2} \\
\rightsquigarrow & \overline{(\lambda y.y)\, 2} \\
\rightsquigarrow & 2
\end{array}
$$

6.1.6 Completing the encoding of predecessor

Armed with the Church encoding of pairs, we can now define the predecessor function on Church-encoded natural numbers, which we began above (Section 6.1.4). First, let us implement the transformation we considered above:

$$(n, m) \;\Rightarrow\; (m, m + 1)$$

We will implement this by a function called *pairshift*, as follows:

$$\textit{pairshift} = \lambda p.\textit{mkpair}\ (p\ \lambda x.\lambda y.y)\ (S\ (p\ \lambda x.\lambda y.y))$$

This function takes in a pair p, and returns a new pair (constructed by *mkpair*), whose first element is the second element of p (computed by the term $(p\ \lambda x.\lambda y.y)$), and whose second element is the successor of the second element of p.

Now the idea is to define the predecessor of n by iterating *pairshift* n times starting from (Z, Z), and then extracting the first component of the resulting pair:

$$\textit{pred} = \lambda n.(n\ \textit{pairshift}\ (\textit{mkpair}\ Z\ Z))\ \lambda x.\lambda y.x$$

The n-fold iteration of *pairshift* is performed by the term $(n\ \textit{pairshift}\ (\textit{mkpair}\ Z\ Z))$. Applying this term to $\lambda x.\lambda y.x$ then extracts the first component of the resulting pair, which we have seen will be the predecessor of n. If n happens to be zero, then no iteration will take place, and we will extract the first component of the starting pair (Z, Z). This is acceptable, because the natural-number predecessor of zero is often (when dealing with total functions) simply defined to be zero again.

Of course, in addition to being complicated, this definition has the unattractive feature that to compute the predecessor of n requires the n-fold iteration of a function. So it will take $O(n)$ β-reduction steps to compute. This is generally true for Church-encoded datatypes: extracting the immediate subdata of some Church-encoded piece d of data will take time proportional to the size of d. This is unfortunate, as we might reasonably expect this operation to take constant time.

6.1.7   Booleans

Before we turn to the Scott encoding, let us see one more example of the Church encoding. Many other datatypes can be Church-encoded. Let us look at the Church encoding for booleans. Like pairs, booleans are non-recursive datatypes, so there is no real iteration to perform. The degenerate form of iteration for booleans is to give the boolean b a value to return in case b is *false*, and another in case b is *true*. So each boolean b must accept two arguments: the value to return in the *false* case, and the one to return in the *true* case. So the Church-encoded boolean values are:

$$\begin{aligned} true &= \lambda t.\lambda f.t \\ false &= \lambda t.\lambda f.f \end{aligned}$$

The order in which each boolean accept its two arguments is not important, as long, of course, as a single order is used consistently. We could just as well have defined *true* and *false* to take in f first and then t. The same is true for all datatypes encoded with the Church encoding.

6.1.8   Boolean operations: conjunction, disjunction, negation

To implement conjunction on Church-encoded booleans, we will write a function that takes in two such boolean values b_1 and b_2, and first checks whether b_1 is *true* or *false*. If it is *false*, then the entire conjunction should be *false*. If it is *true*, then we can just return b_2, as the truth or falsity of b_2 will now determine the truth-value of the conjunction. The definition is:

$$and = \lambda b_1.\lambda b_2.b_1\ b_2\ false$$

In the body of this λ-abstraction, we performing degenerate iteration over b_1 by applying it as a function to two arguments, corresponding to the two cases. If b_1 is false, the first argument (*false*) is returned, and if b_1 is true, we return the second (b_2). This matches the informal description given above.

Similarly, if to implement disjunction, our function should again take in b_1 and b_2, but now return *true* if b_1 is *true*, and b_2 otherwise. The definition is:

$$or = \lambda b_1.\lambda b_2.b_1\ true\ b_2$$

This is quite similar to the definition of conjunction, just with arguments reversed and *false* replaced by *true*. Finally, for negation, we write a function taking in a single boolean b, and just need to return *true* if b is *false*, and *false* if b is *true*:

$$not = \lambda b.b\ false\ true$$

Here is an example reduction using these definitions:

$$
\begin{array}{l}
not\ (and\ true\ false) = \\
\underline{not\ ((\lambda b_1.\,\lambda b_2.\,b_1\ b_2\ false)\ true\ false)} \rightsquigarrow \\
not\ (\underline{(\lambda b_2.\,true\ b_2\ false)\ false}) \rightsquigarrow \\
not\ (true\ false\ false) = \\
not\ (\underline{(\lambda t.\,\lambda f.\,t)\ false\ false}) \rightsquigarrow \\
not\ (\underline{(\lambda f.\,false)\ false}) \rightsquigarrow \\
\underline{not\ false} = \\
\underline{(\lambda b.\,b\ false\ true)\ false} \rightsquigarrow \\
false\ false\ true = \\
\underline{(\lambda t.\,\lambda f.\,f)\ false\ true} \rightsquigarrow \\
\underline{(\lambda f.\,f)\ true} \rightsquigarrow \\
true
\end{array}
$$

6.2 The Scott encoding for datatypes

Let us turn now to another lambda encoding, attributed to Dana Scott. The Scott encoding is developed from the perspective that the central functional abstraction we use for programming with data is case-analysis. The basic functional operation is to determine which kind of data we have, and simultaneously access its subdata. In effect, this is pattern matching on the data. The Scott encoding will encode each piece of data as a function that lets a user of that data do pattern matching on the data. This sounds a bit abstract and cryptic. We will see how it works now through several examples. Before we go further: for this section, we will use left-to-right call-by-value reduction (see Section 5.4.1 above). This will be important when it comes to defining recursive functions using *fix* in Section 6.5 below.

6.2.1 Another view of unary natural numbers

Let us again consider the Peano numbers generated with constructors Z and S. To do pattern matching on an arbitrary Peano number, we need to handle two cases: one where the constructor is Z, and the other where it is S. In the former case there are no subdata. In the latter, the sole piece of subdata is the predecessor of the number. In functional languages like OCAML and HASKELL, such pattern matching is provided directly by the language. In OCAML, for example, we could write the following:

```
match n with
  S p -> case1
| Z -> case2
```

Operationally, this expression is evaluated by evaluating case1 if the constructor of n is S, and case2 if it is Z. In the former case, the variable p will be set to the predecessor of n (so 4 if n is 5). The term upon which we are pattern matching (here n) is sometimes called the **scrutinee** of the match-term. Note that the order of cases does not matter in a language like OCAML, as long as the patterns cover disjoint sets of values for the scrutinee (as they do here, since every number n is constructed either with S or with Z, but not both). So we could just as well have written:

```
match n with
  Z -> case2
| S p -> case1
```

6.2.2 Scott encoding for unary natural numbers

As mentioned, the Scott encoding encodes every piece of data as a lambda-abstraction that implements pattern matching for that data. With the Scott encoding, a pattern-matching construct like the one we just saw from OCAML,

```
match n with
  S p -> case1
| Z -> case2
```

can be implemented by simply dropping everything except the scrutinee and the two cases (shown in boxes):

```
match n with
  S p -> case1
| Z -> case2
```

That is, we will have just the following for pattern matching on n: an application of n as a function to case1 and case2 as arguments.

```
n case1 case2
```

So every natural number n is going to be encoded as a function that takes in a function to use in each of the two cases: one function (let us call it s) for if n is S p for some predecessor number p, and another (z) for if it is Z. In the former case, the number n will call the function s on p. In the latter case, the number n will just return z; so in practice, for the zero case we don't supply a function to call in that case, but rather a value to return. We could indeed supply a function to call, but traditionally the Scott encoding just returns a value in the Z case.

So here are the first few Scott-encoded numerals:

$$
\begin{aligned}
0 &= \lambda s.\, \lambda z.\, z \\
1 &= \lambda s.\, \lambda z.\, (s\, 0) \\
2 &= \lambda s.\, \lambda z.\, (s\, 1) \\
3 &= \lambda s.\, \lambda z.\, (s\, 2)
\end{aligned}
$$

The lambda-term we use for 0 just takes in s and z and returns z, as explained above. The lambda-term for 1 takes in s and z and calls s on the predecessor of 1 (namely, 0). In general, the number $p + 1$ takes in s and z and returns $s\,p$. This gives us the ability to do pattern matching on a number n by calling n as a function with the functions to use in the S and Z case.

6.3   Other datatypes: lists

Other datatypes can be Scott-encoded in the same way. The Scott encoding of booleans and pairs is exactly the same as the Church encoding. Indeed, the Church and Scott encodings agree on non-recursive datatypes. So here is another example of a recursive datatype, in the Scott encoding.

Lists l are encoded as either the empty list with no elements, or else a list containing some element a, followed by the rest of the elements of the list. In constructor notation, the empty list is traditionally called *nil*, and the operation of building a bigger list by putting an element a on the front of a smaller list l' is called *cons*. These names go back to Lisp. So the list "1,2,3" is written in constructor notation as:

$$cons\ 1\ (cons\ 2\ (cons\ 3\ nil))$$

Given this representation of lists, pattern matching must deal with two cases: one where the list is *nil*, and another where it is a *cons*-list with data a and sublist l'. So we implement the list constructors using the Scott encoding like this:

$$
\begin{aligned}
nil &= \lambda c.\,\lambda n.\,n \\
cons &= \lambda a.\,\lambda l'.\,\lambda c.\,\lambda n.\,c\ a\ l'
\end{aligned}
$$

The *cons* constructor takes in the data a to put at the head of the list, and the sublist l' to use for the tail, and returns a new list. That new list is $\lambda c.\,\lambda n.\,c\ a\ l'$. This is indeed a list, since our encoding has all lists begin by taking in two arguments. In this case, the list will call the first argument with the head and tail of the list.

6.4   Non-recursive operations on Scott-encoded data

It will take a bit more work to be able to write recursive operations like addition and multiplication on Scott-encoded natural numbers. But with what we currently have, we can implement non-recursive operations on unary natural numbers, as well as boolean operations.

6.4.1   Arithmetic operations: predecessor and is-zero

To compute the predecessor of a number n, we will return 0 if n is 0, and p if n is $S\,p$. This means we can define the predecessor function to take in the number n, and then apply it to the appropriate values for the two cases:

$$pred \;=\; \lambda n.\, n\,(\lambda p.\, p)\,0$$

Since we want *pred* $(S\ p)$ to return p, we call n with $\lambda p.\, p$ as the function to call when n is $S\ p$. So n will call that function with argument p. Since the function is just the identity function, p will be returned as desired.

We can implement a function to test whether or not a natural number is zero by returning *false* in the S-case and *true* in the Z-case:

$$is\text{-}zero \;=\; \lambda n.\, n\,(\lambda p.\, false)\,true$$

The S-case is still going to be given the predecessor number p when it is called, but for this function, we just ignore that value, since it is not needed once we know the number is a successor number.

6.4.2   List operations: is-nil, head, and tail

Let us define several non-recursive operations on lists. First, a function that tests whether or not a list is *nil*:

$$is\text{-}nil \;=\; \lambda l.\, l\,(\lambda a.\, \lambda l'.\, false)\,true$$

This function takes in an input list l, and applies it to two arguments. If the list l is a *cons*-list, l will call the first argument with its head and tail. That is why our first argument is a λ-abstraction which first takes in arguments a (for the head) and l' (for the tail), and then returns *false*, as l is not *nil* in this case. The second argument given to l will simply be returned by l, if l is, in fact, *nil*.

For *head* and *tail*, we will write similar functions, except that for *head*, the first argument to l we want to give a function which, when called with head a and tail l', returns a. Similarly, for *tail*, the first argument to l should be a function which, when called with head a and tail l', returns l'. We do not expect these functions to be called with a list which is *nil*, so we will return something arbitrary (*false*) in that case. Here are the definitions:

$$\begin{aligned}
head &= \lambda l.\, l\,(\lambda a.\, \lambda l'.\, a)\,false \\
tail &= \lambda l.\, l\,(\lambda a.\, \lambda l'.\, l')\,false
\end{aligned}$$

Now, since we are working in a completely untyped language, it is worth pointing out that some of the definitions we have available for other datatypes can somewhat abusively (but totally legally) be used for lists, too. For example, we already have defined functions that have the behavior of the first arguments we have given above for *head* and *tail*. The functions are:

$$\lambda a.\, \lambda l'.\, a$$
$$\lambda a.\, \lambda l'.\, l'$$

But if we just rename the bound variables (as of course, we can always do), we can see these functions a little differently:

$$\lambda t.\, \lambda f.\, t$$
$$\lambda t.\, \lambda f.\, f$$

These are none other than the terms we have defined to equal *true* and *false*, respectively. So while it would certainly make for some confusing code, we can just as well use these definitions for *head* and *tail*:

$$
\begin{aligned}
head &= \lambda l.\, l \; true \; false \\
tail &= \lambda l.\, l \; false \; false
\end{aligned}
$$

This somewhat startling use of functions across datatypes is often possible, if not advisable, in untyped languages.

6.5 Recursive equations and the *fix* operator

To define recursive functions, we start with recursive equations. For example, here is a definition of addition on unary natural numbers using recursive equations:

$$
\begin{aligned}
add \; Z \; m &= m \\
add \; (S \; p) \; m &= add \; p \; (S \; m)
\end{aligned}
$$

If we rewrite these equations with standard infix notation (also writing $S \; m$ as $m + 1$), we will see they are valid for our usual notion of addition:

$$
\begin{aligned}
0 + m &= m \\
(p + 1) + m &= p + (m + 1)
\end{aligned}
$$

But we can use these equations as the actual definition of *add*, since we can argue they define a total function. Every case for the first argument is covered by one of the equations, since every natural number is either Z or $(S \; p)$ for some natural number p. Also, the recursive call to *add* on the right-hand side of the second equation has a strictly smaller value for the first argument: the left-hand side has $(S \; p)$, while the right-hand side has just p. So the equations use well-founded recursion.

Using our Scott encoding of natural numbers, we can almost turn these equations into a lambda-term:

$$
add = \lambda n.\, \lambda m.\, n \; (\lambda p.\, add \; p \; (S \; m)) \; m
$$

The pattern matching on n has been implemented by just applying n, as we already have seen, to the S-case, which is $(\lambda p.\, add \; p \; (S \; m))$; and the Z-case, which is just m. The only hitch here is that the above equation is circular: we are defining *add* to be some lambda-term that contains *add*. So this is not yet a legal definition, and we seem to be stuck.

6.5.1 Definition of *fix*

Fortunately, at this point we can use the same technique that we did when we encountered a circular equation back in Chapter 2 on the denotational semantics of

WHILE. We can solve the circular equation using least fixed points. For WHILE, we had to use domain theory to define the operator *lfp* for computing the least fixed point of a continuous function on a domain. Here, amazingly, we can actually define that operator as a λ-term, which is traditionally called *fix* in this setting (rather than *lfp*). Here it is:

$$fix \; = \; \lambda f. \, (\lambda x. \, f \, (\lambda y. \, x \, x \, y)) \, (\lambda x. \, f \, (\lambda y. \, x \, x \, y))$$

Now this is a rather formidable term, so we have to look at it carefully to understand what it is doing. First, if we define

$$F \; = \; (\lambda x. \, f \, (\lambda y. \, x \, x \, y))$$

then we can recast the above definition in this simpler form:

$$fix \; = \; \lambda f. \, F \, F$$

We see self-application here, and in the $x \, x$ subterm of the term we have defined F to be above. And as we saw in Section 5.2.3 in the preceding chapter, self-application gives us computational rocket-fuel, so to speak: we get divergence from the self-applicative term $(\lambda x. \, x \, x) \, (\lambda x. \, x \, x)$, and without the power to diverge, we cannot have a Turing-complete language.

Let us try to understand now why we have $\lambda y. \, x \, x \, y$. This term is what is called the (one-step) η-**expansion** ("eta expansion" – η is lowercase long "e" in Greek) of $x \, x$. The η-expansion of a term behaves just like that term when applied to an argument. For example, if we apply $x \, x$ to a term like 3 (just for example), then we will get $x \, x \, 3$. Similarly, if we apply the η-expansion of that term to 3, we will end up with the same result:

$$(\lambda y. \, x \, x \, y) \, 3 \; \leadsto_{\beta_v} \; x \, x \, 3$$

But in a call-by-value (or call-by-name) language, the effect of eta-expanding a term t is to prevent it from evaluating until it is called. For example, if we eta-expand $(\lambda x.x) \, (\lambda y.y)$, we will get the following lambda-abstraction, which is a value and hence in normal form with call-by-value reduction:

$$\lambda z. \, (\lambda x.x) \, (\lambda y.y) \, z$$

To see that *fix* computes a fixed point of a function f, let us see how *fix* f computes (where F is as defined above):

$$fix \, f \; \leadsto_{\beta_v} \; F \, F \; \leadsto_{\beta_v} \; f \, (\lambda y. \, F \, F \, y)$$

So we can see that $F \, F$ reduces to f applied to the eta-expansion of $F \, F$. That eta-expansion is used to prevent $F \, F$ from reducing again at this point, until f decides to make a recursive call by applying it to an argument. Leaving aside this eta-expansion, we essentially have:

$$F \, F \; \leadsto \; f \, (F \, F)$$

If we define an equivalence relation $\approx_\beta$ by the reflexive, transitive and symmetric closure of $\leadsto$ (which is similar to the reflexive, transitive closure of $\leadsto$ as in Section 4.2.2, except also symmetric, as the name says), then we would have that

$$F\, F \approx_\beta f\, (F\, F)$$

or more suggestively

$$f\, (F\, F) \approx_\beta F\, F$$

This is the sense in which *fix* has computed a fixed point of f: it has given us a term, $F\, F$, such that f applied to that term is equivalent again to that term.

6.6   Another recursive example: multiplication

We can define multiplication by iterated addition as follows:

$$mult \;=\; fix \lambda mult.\, \lambda n.\, \lambda m.\, n\, (\lambda p.\, add\, m\, (mult\, p\, m))\, Z$$

This definition is based on the following recursive equations:

$$
\begin{aligned}
mult\; Z\; m &= Z \\
mult\; (S\; p)\; m &= add\; m\; (mult\; p\; m)
\end{aligned}
$$

We can see the idea behind this definition in a small example, by applying these equations enough times to eliminate the *mult* symbol, without applying the equations for *add*:

$$
\begin{aligned}
mult\; 3\; 10 &= add\; 10\; (mult\; 2\; 10) \\
&= add\; 10\; (add\; 10\; (mult\; 1\; 10)) \\
&= add\; 10\; (add\; 10\; (add\; 10\; (mult\; 0\; 10))) \\
&= add\; 10\; (add\; 10\; (add\; 10\; 0))
\end{aligned}
$$

We can see here that multiplying 3 and 10 has the effect of adding 10 three times to 0. Similarly, multiplying n and m adds the number m n times to 0. So multiplication is defined by iterated addition.

6.7   Conclusion

In this chapter we have seen how to program with lambda-encoded data. With the Church encoding, each piece of data is encoded as its own iteration function, or equivalently, as its own interpretation function. For the Scott encoding, data are implemented as functions which implement a basic pattern-matching operation on that data. We worked through several examples of these encodings: unary natural numbers, booleans, tuples, and lists. For Scott-encoded data, we also saw how to define recursive functions using a fixed-point operator, implemented by a somewhat large λ-term, and we got some insight into how that λ-term uses self-application to support recursion.

6.8   Basic exercises

6.8.1   For Section 6.1, Church encoding

1. For each of the following terms, write out a small-step reduction sequence leading from that term to a normal form, using the definitions given in Section 6.1 (so, for Church-encoded natural numbers and the operations defined on them). You should confirm, of course, that you get the expected answer.

   - *S Z*

   - *plus* 1 2

   - *mult* 2 2

2. Write a function *add-components* that takes in a pair (x, y) and returns the pair $x + y$.

3. Write a function *swap-pair* that takes in a pair (x, y) and returns the pair (y, x).

4. Give a definition of the exclusive-or function on Scott-encoded booleans, which takes in booleans b_1 and b_2, and returns *true* iff exactly one of those booleans is *true*.

6.8.2   For Section 6.2, Scott encoding

1. Write down the lambda terms, in normal form, which encode the following data in the Scott encoding. Do not use any of the abbreviations we defined above, but just write a pure lambda term.

   (a) 2

   (b) *cons true (cons false nil)*

   (c) *(nil, (false, 0))*

   (d) *cons (0,1) (cons true nil)*

2. Suppose we wish to encode a datatype consisting of basic colors *red* and *blue*, with possibly repeated modifier *light*. So example data elements are: *red, blue, light blue, light (light red)*, etc.

   Give definitions for the three constructors, *red, blue,* and *light*, using the Scott encoding.

3. Give definitions using the Scott encoding for constructors *node* and *leaf* for a datatype of binary trees, with data stored at the nodes but not the leaves. So a tree like this,

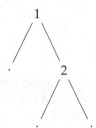

will be built by this constructor term: (*node* 1 *leaf* (*node* 2 *leaf leaf*)).

6.9   Intermediate exercises

6.9.1   For Section 6.1, Church encoding

1. Define a function *exp* on Church-encoded numbers, such that *exp n m* reduces to the (Church-encoded) value of *n* raised to the power *m*. So *exp* 2 2 should reduce to Church-encoded 4. Your definition may use previous definitions, like the definition for *mult*, from Section 6.1.

2. Give a Church encoding of lists defined by the following grammar, where *d* is an element of some other datatype *D* (for example, *D* might be *nat*):

$$lists\ L ::= nil\ |\ cons\ d\ L$$

To define the encoding, it is enough to define the constructors *nil* and *cons* so that they will return lists that are their own interpretation functions. For example, if *L* is the list *cons* 1 (*cons* 2 *nil*), then applying *L* to *f* and *a* should compute

$$f\ 1\ (f\ 2\ a)$$

Notice that this expression has the same structure as the data *cons* 1 (*cons* 2 *nil*), except that *cons* has been replaced by *f*, and *nil* has been replaced by *a*.

6.9.2   For Section 6.2, Scott encoding

1. One way to write a function *eqnat* to test whether two Peano numbers are equal is to remove a successor from each of them, until either both numbers are zero, in which case we return *true*; or else one is zero and the other is not, in which case we return *false*.

   (a) Based on this idea, define *eqnat* using recursive equations.

   (b) Translate your encoding into a lambda term using the Scott encoding.

2. Write a function *lt* which tests whether one number is strictly smaller than another. First do this with recursive equations, and then as a lambda term using the Scott encoding.

3. Write a function *append* operating on Scott-encoded lists, which takes as input two lists, and returns their concatenation.

4. Write a function *reverse* operating on Scott-encoded lists, which takes as input one list, and returns the reversed version of the list. This can be rather easily done in quadratic time by repeatedly appending the head of the list to the result of recursively reversing the tail:

$$
\begin{aligned}
reverse\ nil &= nil \\
reverse\ (cons\ a\ l) &= append\ (reverse\ l)\ (cons\ a\ nil)
\end{aligned}
$$

It is much better, of course, to write a *reverse* function that takes only linear time in the length of the input list. Doing this is somewhat tricky. Hint: use an extra argument to *reverse* (or a helper function *reverse-h*) to hold the part of the list which has been reversed so far.

Chapter 7
Simple Type Theory

In this chapter, we begin our study of typed lambda calculi. Types play a central organizing role for many applications of lambda calculus. Within Computer Science, checking types at compile time is one of the most effective methods known for guaranteeing the absence of certain kinds of bugs in programs. Types are just abstractions of data values. For example, the type *int* is an abstraction of the integer value 3. Similarly, function types like *int* $\rightarrow$ *int* are abstractions of functions that map integer inputs to integer outputs. We will also see an important application of types to logic in this chapter, in the form of the Curry-Howard isomorphism (Section 7.7). Within Linguistics, *categorial grammars* are based on ideas close to those of simply typed lambda calculus [25].

In this chapter, we study a basic system of types for lambda calculus, called **simple types**. We will define the syntax of simple types, and then define a set of rules which assign a simple type to a term of untyped lambda calculus (Chapter 5). This gives us the simply typed lambda calculus (STLC). Our set of typing rules will turn out not to determine a deterministic algorithm either for computing a type for a term ("type computation"), or checking that a term has a given type ("type checking"). We will then see several different approaches for achieving deterministic algorithms for both these operations. One basic approach is to annotate the terms so that at points where the typing rules would face a nondeterministic choice, the nondeterminism is resolved by an annotation of the term. The second basic approach is to compute a set of constraints on the typing of the (unannotated) untyped lambda-calculus term, and then solve those constraints to determine a most general type for the term. The constraints are solved using an algorithm known as **unification**.

7.1 Abstract syntax of simple type theory

Syntax. The syntax of simple types T is given by

$$\begin{array}{ll} \textit{base types } b & \\ \textit{simple types } T & ::= \quad b \mid T_1 \rightarrow T_2 \end{array}$$

The intuition is that $T_1 \rightarrow T_2$ is supposed to be the type for functions with domain T_1 and range T_2. The base types b are some otherwise unspecified types, which might be things like `int` or `char`. By convention, the $\rightarrow$ construct associates to the right. So $T_1 \rightarrow T_2 \rightarrow T_3$ is fully parenthesized as $(T_1 \rightarrow (T_2 \rightarrow T_3))$. Note that this means that we cannot drop the parentheses from a type like $(b_1 \rightarrow b_2) \rightarrow b_3$, because if we do, the parsing convention will place the parentheses on the right, giving us a syntactically different expression.

7.2   Semantics of types

We can make the above informal intuitions about the meaning of simple types precise by defining a mathematical semantics for them. The basic idea is that the interpretation of a type will be a set of terms of (untyped) lambda calculus, namely the terms which have the behavior specified by the type. We will not choose any particular semantics for base types, since we have left open which base types we actually have, and do not wish to commit to a particular collection of them. So we will define the interpretation of types relative to an assignment I of semantics to base types. So let I be any function from base types to sets of terms. Then we define the semantics of types this way, by recursion on the structure of the type:

$$
\begin{array}{rcl}
[\![b]\!]\, I & = & I(b) \\
[\![T_1 \to T_2]\!]\, I & = & \{t \in terms \mid \forall t' \in [\![T_1]\!]\, I.\, (t\, t') \in [\![T_2]\!]\, I\}
\end{array}
$$

The definition says first that the interpretation $[\![b]\!]\, I$ of a base type b is whatever the assignment I says it should be (I maps base types b to sets of terms, so we are indeed specifying a set of terms as the value of $[\![b]\!]\, I$). The second defining equation says that the interpretation $[\![T_1 \to T_2]\!]\, I$ of a function type $T_1 \to T_2$ is a set of terms t with the following property. For any input term t' in the interpretation $[\![T_1]\!]\, I$ of T_1, the application of t to t' is in the interpretation $[\![T_2]\!]\, I$ of T_2. This definition formalizes the above informal intuition for the semantics of function types.

We should prove one important lemma about this interpretation of types before we proceed. Let us call a set S of terms **inverse-reduction closed** if whenever we have $t \leadsto t'$ and $t' \in S$, we have also $t \in S$.

Lemma 7.2.1 (Inverse-reduction closed). *Suppose $I(b)$ is inverse-reduction closed for all base-types b. Then so is $[\![T]\!]\, I$ for all types T.*

Proof. The proof is by induction on the structure of T. For the base case, suppose T is a base type b. Then $[\![T]\!]\, I$ equals $I(b)$, which is inverse-reduction closed by assumption. For the step case, suppose T is a function type of the form $T_1 \to T_2$. We must prove that $[\![T_1 \to T_2]\!]\, I$ is inverse-reduction closed. To do that, let us assume we have arbitrary terms t and t' where $t \leadsto t'$ and $t' \in [\![T_1 \to T_2]\!]\, I$. It suffices, by the definition of inverse-reduction closed, to prove $t \in [\![T_1 \to T_2]\!]\, I$. To prove that statement, we use the definition of the interpretation of function types. The definition says that $t \in [\![T_1 \to T_2]\!]\, I$ holds iff for all $t'' \in [\![T_1]\!]\, I$, the term $(t\, t'')$ is in $[\![T_2]\!]\, I$. So consider an arbitrary $t'' \in [\![T_1]\!]\, I$. By assumption, we know $t \leadsto t'$, and so by the definition of full β-reduction, we have $t\, t'' \leadsto t'\, t''$. Now since we are also assuming $t' \in [\![T_1 \to T_2]\!]\, I$, we know that $t'\, t''$ is in $[\![T_2]\!]\, I$. We can now apply our induction hypothesis: we know $t\, t'' \leadsto t'\, t'' \in [\![T_2]\!]\, I$. This is an instance of our induction hypothesis, with a smaller type T_2 than we started this case with. So we can conclude $t\, t'' \in [\![T_2]\!]\, I$, which is what we had to prove at this point. $\square$

$$\frac{\Gamma(x) = T}{\Gamma \vdash x : T} \quad \frac{\Gamma, x : T_1 \vdash t : T_2}{\Gamma \vdash \lambda x.t : T_1 \to T_2} \quad \frac{\Gamma \vdash t_1 : T_2 \to T_1 \quad \Gamma \vdash t_2 : T_2}{\Gamma \vdash t_1\, t_2 : T_1}$$

Figure 7.1: Type-assignment rules for simply typed lambda calculus

7.3 Type-assignment rules

We would like to come up with a sound set of rules for proving that a term has a simple type. For example, $\lambda x.x$ can be assigned any simple type of the form $T \to T$, since the identity function can be considered to have domain T and range T for any simple type T. Figure 7.1 inductively defines the **simple type-assignment relation**. In the notation $\Gamma \vdash t : T$, t is a lambda term to be assigned simple type T, and Γ is a **context** assigning simple types to the free variables of t:

$$\textit{typing contexts } \Gamma \quad ::= \quad \cdot \mid \Gamma, x : T$$

The context $\cdot$ is the empty context. It is common to view contexts as functions from variables to simple types. So in the first rule below, the notation $\Gamma(x) = T$ is used to mean that the result of looking up the type for variable x in context Γ is T (i.e., the function Γ returns type T for x). We write $dom(\Gamma)$ for the set of variables x where $x : T$ is in Γ.

Example. The following derivation shows that $\lambda x.\lambda y.(x\, y)$ can be assigned the type $(T_1 \to T_2) \to (T_1 \to T_2)$, for any types T_1 and T_2:

$$\frac{\dfrac{x : T_1 \to T_2, y : T_1 \vdash x : T_1 \to T_2 \quad x : T_1 \to T_2, y : T_1 \vdash y : T_1}{x : T_1 \to T_2, y : T_1 \vdash (x\, y) : T_2}}{\dfrac{x : T_1 \to T_2 \vdash \lambda y.(x\, y) : T_1 \to T_2}{\cdot \vdash \lambda x.\lambda y.(x\, y) : (T_1 \to T_2) \to (T_1 \to T_2)}}$$

7.4 Semantic soundness for type-assignment rules

We can prove that the type-assignment rules of the previous section are indeed sound for the semantics for types we defined in Section 7.2 above. We need one further piece of notation. Suppose Γ is a typing context, and σ is a substitution mapping $dom(\Gamma)$ to terms in such a way that $\sigma(x) \in [\![\Gamma(x)]\!]\, I$, for all $x \in dom(\Gamma)$. Then we will write $\sigma \in [\![\Gamma]\!]\, I$, and say that σ **satisfies** Γ. Also, we will write $\sigma\, t$ to denote the result of applying the substitution σ to t, to replace all variables $x \in dom(\Gamma)$ with $\sigma(x)$. This is a simple extension of our notion of capture-avoiding substitution from Chapter 5.

Theorem 7.4.1 (Semantic Soundness). *Suppose $I(b)$ is inverse-reduction closed for all base types b, and suppose $\Gamma \vdash t : T$. Suppose further that $\sigma \in [\![\Gamma]\!]\, I$. Then we have $\sigma\, t \in [\![T]\!]\, I$.*

Proof. The proof is by induction on the structure of the derivation of $\Gamma \vdash t : T$.
Case:

$$\frac{\Gamma(x) = T}{\Gamma \vdash x : T}$$

In this case, we must prove $\sigma(x) \in \llbracket T \rrbracket \, I$. But this holds because $\Gamma(x) = T$, and we are assuming that $\sigma(x) \in \llbracket \Gamma(x) \rrbracket \, I$ for all $x \in dom(\Gamma)$.

Case:

$$\frac{\Gamma \vdash t_1 : T_2 \to T_1 \quad \Gamma \vdash t_2 : T_2}{\Gamma \vdash t_1 \, t_2 : T_1}$$

By our induction hypothesis, we know:

- $\sigma \, t_1 \in \llbracket T_2 \to T_1 \rrbracket \, I$

- $\sigma \, t_2 \in \llbracket T_2 \rrbracket \, I$

The first of these facts implies that for any input $t' \in \llbracket T_2 \rrbracket \, I$, $(\sigma \, t_1) \, t'$ is in $\llbracket T_1 \rrbracket \, I$. We can instantiate this universal statement with $\sigma \, t_2$ for t', since we indeed have $\sigma \, t_2 \in \llbracket T_2 \rrbracket \, I$, by the second of these facts. So we can deduce $(\sigma \, t_1) \, (\sigma \, t_2) \in \llbracket T_1 \rrbracket \, I$. By the definition of applying a substitution to an application, this is equivalent to $\sigma \, (t_1 \, t_2) \in \llbracket T_1 \rrbracket \, I$, which is what we had to prove in this case.

Case:

$$\frac{\Gamma, x : T_1 \vdash t : T_2}{\Gamma \vdash \lambda x.t : T_1 \to T_2}$$

We assume here that variables have been renamed appropriately so that $x \notin dom(\Gamma)$. We must prove that $\sigma \, \lambda x.t$ is in $\llbracket T_1 \to T_2 \rrbracket \, I$. We also assume that x is not free in $\sigma(y)$ for any $y \in dom(\Gamma)$. By the definition of the interpretation of function types, it suffices to prove that for any input $t' \in \llbracket T_1 \rrbracket \, I$, the term $(\sigma \lambda x.t) \, t'$ is in $\llbracket T_2 \rrbracket \, I$. So consider an arbitrary such t', and let σ' be the substitution $\sigma[x \mapsto t']$. By the induction hypothesis, we know:

$$\sigma' \, t \in \llbracket T_2 \rrbracket \, I$$

This is because σ' is a substitution satisfying the requirements of the theorem, for the extended context $\Gamma, x : T_1$. We have

$$(\sigma \, \lambda x.t) \, t' \rightsquigarrow [t'/x](\sigma t) = \sigma' \, t$$

By Lemma 7.2.1 (Section 7.2 above), the fact that $\sigma' \, t$ is in $\llbracket T_2 \rrbracket \, I$ then implies that $(\sigma \, \lambda x.t) \, t'$ is in $\llbracket T_2 \rrbracket \, I$, since the latter term reduces in one step to the former. $\square$

7.5   Applying semantic soundness to prove normalization

The Semantic Soundness Theorem is a powerful tool for studying typed lambda calculus. We can also use it to obtain an important result for our current type-assignment system (with no extensions). This result is called Normalization. It says that every lambda term t is guaranteed to reduce to some normal form, if $\Gamma \vdash t : T$ holds for some Γ and some T. We will prove this result in this section.

7.5.1   Normalization and termination

A **normal form** is a term t which cannot be reduced further. This definition applies to any notion of reduction, although we will work here with full β-reduction. A **normalizing** term is one which reduces to a normal form using some reduction sequence. A **terminating** term is one which reduces to a normal form no matter which reduction sequence is used. Termination certainly implies normalization, but not vice versa. An example of a normalizing term which is not terminating is:

$$(\lambda x.\lambda y.y)\,((\lambda x.x\ x)\,(\lambda x.x\ x))$$

We can reduce the outermost redex to obtain just $\lambda y.y$, which is a normal form. So the term is normalizing. But it is not terminating, because it has an infinite reduction sequence, namely the one that reduces $((\lambda x.x\ x)\,(\lambda x.x\ x))$ forever.

Note that the terminology *normalizing* and *terminating* is used in the term rewriting literature (see Section 9.1.1 for more on concepts from rewriting). In the type theory literature, one often finds the terms **weakly normalizing** and **strong normalizing**, respectively, for *normalizing* and *terminating*.

In what follows, we will write *Norm* for the set of all normalizing terms (with full β-reduction). In the type theory literature, one sees the notation *WN* for this set, and *SN* for the set of strongly normalizing terms.

7.5.2   Deriving Normalization from Semantic Soundness

To prove Normalization using Semantic Soundness (Theorem 7.4.1), we first define an appropriate assignment I, by making $I(b) = Norm$ for all base types b. To apply Semantic Soundness, we must just observe that $I(b)$ is inverse-reduction closed, which it is: if a term t' is normalizing (so a member of *Norm*, which we have defined $I(b)$ to equal), and if $t \leadsto t'$, then t is also normalizing. It has a reduction sequence to a normal form, by first stepping to t' and then following the reduction sequence which t' has, by assumption, to a normal form.

With this choice of assignment I, we immediately obtain the result that if $\sigma \in [\![\Gamma]\!]$ and $\Gamma \vdash t : b$, then $\sigma t \in [\![b]\!]\,I$. Since $[\![b]\!]\,I = I = Norm$, this says that σt is normalizing. As a special case, $\cdot \vdash t : b$ implies t is normalizing. So any closed term (i.e., with no free variables, so requiring only an empty typing context for Γ) which is typable at base type is normalizing. This is quite remarkable, except that you may have noticed that we actually do not have any way to assign a base type to a term in the empty context, as we prove in Section 7.7.4 below. So this direct consequence of Semantic Soundness is not as interesting as we might like.

But an interesting result is right around the corner. We can actually prove that with $I(b) \subseteq Norm$, we have $\llbracket T \rrbracket I \subseteq Norm$. This implies that if $\sigma \in \llbracket \Gamma \rrbracket$ and $\Gamma \vdash t : T$, then σt is normalizing. In particular, it tells us that every typable closed term is normalizing. This is a remarkable result. Any typable term is guaranteed to normalize! This is certainly not true for general programming languages, but it is for the (unextended) simply typed lambda calculus. To prove this, all we need to prove is:

Lemma 7.5.1. *If $I(b) = Norm$ for all base types b, then $\llbracket T \rrbracket I \subseteq Norm$.*

Now it turns out that to prove this by induction on the structure of the type T, we need to strengthen our induction hypothesis a bit. Let us define a subset of the normalizing terms as follows. First, let us use w as a meta-variable to range over *Norm* (so w always denotes a normalizing term). Then define:

$$var\text{-}headed\text{-}normalizing \; n \; ::= \; x \mid n \, w$$

A var-headed normalizing term is one which is **headed** by a variable, and is normalizing. Being headed by a variable means that the syntax tree for the term is either a variable itself or an application where a variable is the leftmost non-application node of the syntax tree. We will write *vhNorm* for the set of var-headed normalizing terms. The lemma we need to prove is:

Lemma 7.5.2 (Interpretations are normalizing). *If $I(b) = Norm$ for all base types b, then:*

$$vhNorm \subseteq \llbracket T \rrbracket I \subseteq Norm$$

Proof. The proof is by induction on the structure of T. For the base case, we have T equal to some base type b. Then $\llbracket T \rrbracket I = I(b)$, and $I(b) \subseteq Norm$ by assumption. So we get $\llbracket T \rrbracket I \subseteq Norm$ in this case as required. It is also clear that $vhNorm \subseteq \llbracket T \rrbracket I$, because, all var-headed normalizing terms are normalizing.

For the step case, we have $T = T_1 \to T_2$. To prove that $\llbracket T_1 \to T_2 \rrbracket I \subseteq Norm$, assume an arbitrary $t \in \llbracket T_1 \to T_2 \rrbracket I$ and prove that t is normalizing. By the induction hypothesis, we know that any var-headed normalizing term is in $\llbracket T_1 \rrbracket I$ (note that the type involved has decreased from $T_1 \to T_2$ to just T_1). So we know, for example, that $x \in \llbracket T_1 \rrbracket I$, where x is a variable. By the definition of the interpretation of function types, we know that $t \, x \in \llbracket T_2 \rrbracket I$ (because $x \in \llbracket T_1 \rrbracket I$). We can now apply the induction hypothesis to deduce that $t \, x \in Norm$. Now if $t \, x$ is normalizing, t must also be normalizing, which we can argue as follows. Choose a normalizing reduction sequence for $t \, x$. Either this sequence does not involve a top-level β-reduction, or else it does. If it does not, then $t \, x$ reduces to a normal form $t' \, x$, where t' is a normal form of t, as required. If the normalizing reduction sequence for $t \, x$ does involve a top-level β-reduction, that means we must have reduces t to a λ-abstraction, say $\lambda x.t'$. It is convenient and legal to assume that the bound variable is x. For this means that the top-level β-reduction step is $(\lambda x.t') \, x \rightsquigarrow t'$. Now t' reduces to a normal form, t'' say, since the reduction sequence is normalizing.

This means that we have $t \leadsto^* \lambda x.t' \leadsto \lambda x.t''$, where the latter term is a normal form.

To complete the step case, we still have to prove that when T is $T_1 \to T_2$ and n is var-headed and normalizing, then $n \in [\![T]\!]\ I$. To prove this, it suffices, by the definition of the interpretation of function types, to assume an arbitrary $t' \in [\![T_1]\!]\ I$, and prove $n\ t' \in [\![T_2]\!]\ I$. By the induction hypothesis, t' is normalizing, so $n\ t'$ is again var-headed and normalizing. This means that we can again apply our induction hypothesis to conclude $n\ t' \in [\![T_2]\!]\ I$, as required. $\qquad\square$

Corollary 7.5.3 (Closed Typable Terms Normalizing). *If $\cdot \vdash t : T$, then t is normalizing.*

Proof. This follows from Semantic Soundness (Theorem 7.4.1) and Lemma 7.5.2.
$\qquad\square$

7.6   Type preservation

An important property of a type system is described in this theorem:

Theorem 7.6.1 (Type Preservation). *If $\Gamma \vdash t : T$ and $t \leadsto_\beta t'$ (full β-reduction), then $\Gamma \vdash t' : T$.*

The proof makes use of this lemma, proved in Section 7.6.1 below:

Lemma 7.6.2 (Substitution). *If $\Gamma_1, y : T_b, \Gamma_2 \vdash t_a : T_a$ and $\Gamma_1 \vdash t_b : T_b$, then $\Gamma_1, \Gamma_2 \vdash [t_b/y]t_a : T_a$.*

Proof of Theorem 7.6.1. To begin our proof of Type Preservation, recall the definition of $t \leadsto_\beta t'$ from Figure 5.2 of Chapter 5:

$$\frac{t_1 \leadsto t_1'}{(t_1\ t_2) \leadsto (t_1'\ t_2)}\ app1 \qquad \frac{t_2 \leadsto t_2'}{(t_1\ t_2) \leadsto (t_1\ t_2')}\ app2$$

$$\frac{t \leadsto t'}{\lambda x.t \leadsto \lambda x.t'}\ lam \qquad \frac{}{(\lambda x.t)\ t' \leadsto [t'/x]t}\ \beta$$

We proceed by induction on the structure of the derivation of $t \leadsto_\beta t'$.

Case:

$$\frac{t_1 \leadsto t_1'}{(t_1\ t_2) \leadsto (t_1'\ t_2)}\ app1$$

By inversion on the typing derivation (that is, the only possibility for proving the derivation gives us the following; see Section 3.3.4 for more on proof by inversion), we have:

$$\frac{\Gamma \vdash t_1 : T_2 \to T_1 \quad \Gamma \vdash t_2 : T_2}{\Gamma \vdash t_1\ t_2 : T_1}$$

We may apply our induction hypothesis to the proof of $t_1 \rightsquigarrow t_1'$ and the proof in the first premise of this inference, to get:

$$\Gamma \vdash t_1' : T_2 \rightarrow T_1$$

Putting this together with our proof of $\Gamma \vdash t_2 : T_2$ (from the second premise of the typing proof above), we have

$$\frac{\Gamma \vdash t_1' : T_2 \rightarrow T_1 \quad \Gamma \vdash t_2 : T_2}{\Gamma \vdash t_1'\, t_2 : T_1}$$

The case for the other application rule is similar, so we omit the details.

Case:

$$\frac{t \rightsquigarrow t'}{\lambda x.t \rightsquigarrow \lambda x.t'} \; lam$$

By inversion on the typing derivation, we also have:

$$\frac{\Gamma, x : T_1 \vdash t : T_2}{\Gamma \vdash \lambda x.t : T_1 \rightarrow T_2}$$

Then by our induction hypothesis applied to the derivation in the premise of the reduction inference and the derivation in the premise of the typing inference, we obtain:

$$\Gamma, x : T_1 \vdash t' : T_2$$

Now we may apply *t-lam* to that to get:

$$\frac{\Gamma, x : T_1 \vdash t' : T_2}{\Gamma \vdash \lambda x.t' : T_1 \rightarrow T_2}$$

Case:

$$\frac{}{(\lambda x.t)\, t' \rightsquigarrow [t'/x]t} \; \beta$$

By inversion on the typing derivation, we also have:

$$\frac{\dfrac{\Gamma, x : T_2 \vdash t : T_1}{\Gamma \vdash (\lambda x.t) : T_2 \rightarrow T_1} \quad \Gamma \vdash t' : T_2}{\Gamma \vdash (\lambda x.t)\, t' : T_1}$$

To complete this case, it suffices to apply Lemma 7.6.2 to the premises of the above derivation:

$$\frac{\Gamma, x : T_2 \vdash t : T_1 \quad \Gamma \vdash t' : T_2}{\Gamma, \vdash [t'/x]t : T_1} \; Lemma\ 7.6.2$$

$\square$

7.6.1   Proofs of Weakening and Substitution Lemmas

The proof of Lemma 7.6.2 (Substitution) relies on the following lemma, which we prove first.

Lemma 7.6.3 (Weakening). *If $\Gamma_1, \Gamma_3 \vdash t_a : T_a$ then $\Gamma_1, \Gamma_2, \Gamma_3 \vdash t_a : T_a$, assuming that the variables declared in Γ_2 are disjoint from those declared in Γ_1 and Γ_3.*

Proof. The proof is by induction on the structure of the assumed derivation.

Case:

$$\frac{(\Gamma_1, \Gamma_3)(x) = T}{\Gamma_1, \Gamma_3 \vdash x : T}$$

We can use this inference:

$$\frac{(\Gamma_1, \Gamma_2 \Gamma_3)(x) = T}{\Gamma_1, \Gamma_2, \Gamma_3 \vdash x : T}$$

Case:

$$\frac{\Gamma_1, \Gamma_3, x : T_1 \vdash t : T_2}{\Gamma_1, \Gamma_3 \vdash \lambda x.t : T_1 \to T_2}$$

We can use this derivation, where we are writing (as in Chapter 4) applications of the induction hypothesis *IH* as inferences in a derivation:

$$\frac{\dfrac{\Gamma_1, \Gamma_3, x : T_1 \vdash t : T_2}{\Gamma_1, \Gamma_2, \Gamma_3, x : T_1 \vdash t : T_2}\ IH}{\Gamma_1, \Gamma_2, \Gamma_3 \vdash \lambda x.t : T_1 \to T_2}$$

Case:

$$\frac{\Gamma_1, \Gamma_3 \vdash t_1 : T_2 \to T_1 \quad \Gamma_1, \Gamma_3 \vdash t_2 : T_2}{\Gamma_1, \Gamma_3 \vdash t_1\, t_2 : T_1}$$

We can use this derivation:

$$\frac{\dfrac{\Gamma_1, \Gamma_3 \vdash t_1 : T_2 \to T_1}{\Gamma_1, \Gamma_2, \Gamma_3 \vdash t_1 : T_2 \to T_1}\ IH \quad \dfrac{\Gamma_1, \Gamma_3 \vdash t_2 : T_2}{\Gamma_1, \Gamma_2, \Gamma_3 \vdash t_2 : T_2}\ IH}{\Gamma_1, \Gamma_3 \vdash t_1\, t_2 : T_1}$$

$\square$

Now we can prove the Substitution Lemma:

Proof of Lemma 7.6.2 (Substitution). The proof is by induction on the structure of the first assumed derivation.

Case:

$$\frac{\Gamma(x) = T_a}{\Gamma_1, y : T_b, \Gamma_2 \vdash x : T_a}$$

Here, $t_a = x$. We must case split on whether or not $x = y$. If so, then $[t_b/y]t_a = [t_b/y]y = t_b$, and $T_a = T_b$. We construct this derivation, where we are applying Lemma 7.6.3 (Weakening) as part of the derivation:

$$\frac{\Gamma_1 \vdash t_b : T_b}{\Gamma_1, \Gamma_2 \vdash t_b : T_b} \; \textit{Lemma 7.6.3}$$

If $x \neq y$, then we use the following derivation, where we know x is declared in Γ_1, Γ_2 since it is declared in $\Gamma = \Gamma_1, y : T_2, \Gamma_2$ and $x \neq y$:

$$\frac{(\Gamma_1, \Gamma_2)(x) = T_a}{\Gamma_1, \Gamma_2 \vdash x : T_a}$$

Case:

$$\frac{\Gamma_1, y : T_b, \Gamma_2, x : T_1 \vdash t : T_2}{\Gamma_1, y : T_b, \Gamma_2 \vdash \lambda x.t : T_1 \to T_2}$$

We construct this derivation, where we may assume $x \neq y$, and so the term in the conclusion, $\lambda x.[t_b/y]t$, equals the desired term $[t_b/y]\lambda x.t$:

$$\frac{\dfrac{\Gamma_1, y : T_b, \Gamma_2, x : T_1 \vdash t : T_2}{\Gamma_1, \Gamma_2, x : T_1 \vdash [t_b/y]t : T_2} \; IH}{\Gamma_1, \Gamma_2 \vdash \lambda x.[t_b/y]t : T_1 \to T_2}$$

Case:

$$\frac{\Gamma_1, y : T_b, \Gamma_2 \vdash t_1 : T_2 \to T_1 \quad \Gamma_1, y : T_b, \Gamma_2 \vdash t_2 : T_2}{\Gamma_1, y : T_b, \Gamma_2 \vdash t_1 \, t_2 : T_1}$$

We construct this derivation, where the term in the conclusion equals the desired $[t_b/y](t_1 \, t_2)$:

$$\frac{\dfrac{\Gamma_1, y : T_b, \Gamma_2 \vdash t_1 : T_2 \to T_1}{\Gamma_1, \Gamma_2 \vdash [t_b/y]t_1 : T_2 \to T_1} \quad \dfrac{\Gamma_1, y : T_b, \Gamma_2 \vdash t_2 : T_2}{\Gamma_1, \Gamma_2 \vdash [t_b/y]t_2 : T_2}}{\Gamma_1, \Gamma_2 \vdash [t_b/y]t_1 \, [t_b/y]t_2 : T_1}$$

$\square$

7.7   The Curry-Howard isomorphism

The fact that simply typed terms are normalizing has important applications in logic, thanks to a surprising connection between typed lambda calculus and logic known as the Curry-Howard isomorphism. Volumes (literally) have been written about this connection [36], but the central insight is easy to grasp: terms of typed lambda calculus can be seen as being in 1-1 correspondence with logical proofs. A proof that A implies B is seen as a lambda-calculus term of type $A \to B$. Also, the logical inference which concludes B from $A \to B$ and A is seen as an application

$$\frac{T \in \Gamma}{\Gamma \vdash T} \; Assump \qquad \frac{\Gamma, T_1 \vdash T_2}{\Gamma \vdash T_1 \rightarrow T_2} \; ImpIntro \qquad \frac{\Gamma \vdash T_1 \rightarrow T_2 \quad \Gamma \vdash T_1}{\Gamma \vdash T_2} \; ImpElim$$

Figure 7.2: Proof rules for minimal implicational logic

of a function of type $A \rightarrow B$ to an argument of type A. So typed lambda calculus terms can be viewed as notations for logical proofs.

This correspondence between logical proofs and terms of typed lambda calculus can be developed for many different logics based on corresponding different lambda calculi, sometimes requiring significant technical sophistication. In this section, we will consider the basic example of this: simply typed lambda calculus and what is called minimal implicational logic. Since we understand reasonably well our simply typed lambda calculus, the first thing to consider here is the definition of minimal implicational logic.

7.7.1   Minimal implicational logic

The formulas of minimal implicational logic are defined this way:

$$atomic\ formulas\ b$$
$$formulas\ T \quad ::= \quad b \mid T_1 \rightarrow T_2$$

We assume there is some set of atomic formulas, and then build formulas from these using the implication operator $\rightarrow$. We associate $\rightarrow$ to the right, just as we did for simple types (see Section 7.1). An example formula is the following, assuming we have atomic formulas *is_raining*, *no_umbrella*, and *get_wet*:

$$is\_raining \; \rightarrow \; (no\_umbrella \; \rightarrow \; get\_wet)$$

This formula might be interpreted as saying that if it is raining, and if you have no umbrella, then you will get wet. Of course, whether or not such a formula is true depends entirely on the interpretation of the atomic formulas *is_raining* and the other two (and even then the formula might not be considered true: imagine you are not outside, or are under a thickly leaved tree). Minimal implicational logic is not the most elegant for expressing facts like this, as atomic formulas are completely unstructured. First-order logic, as studied in Chapter 1, is more expressive. Nevertheless, this example suggests that interesting problems can be formulated in propositional logic, a fact born out by the NP-completeness of the (classical) propositional satisfiability problem, and success encoding many important examples in practice.

Minimal implicational logic is concerned with validity of implicational formulas without any specific interpretation of the atomic formulas. It is a fragment of minimal propositional logic, which is similar but includes the other standard propositional connectives $\wedge$ (conjunction) and $\vee$ (disjunction). Negation $\neg T$ is usually defined to be just $T \rightarrow \bot$, where $\bot$ is for falsity. Minimal logic does not give any special meaning to $\bot$ (though see Section 7.7.2 below).

The logic is formulated using judgments of the form $\Gamma \vdash T$, where Γ is a list of atomic formulas. The interpretation we have in mind is that if all the atomic formulas in Γ are provable, then so is T. The proof rules for this logic are given in Figure 7.2. This is not the only way to define this logic. In fact, there are many different proof systems even for this very simple system. The one in Figure 7.2 is in the style known as **natural deduction** (mentioned also in Section 3.8.2). For each logical connective, the proof system has rules for introducing the connective, and also for eliminating it. A connective is introduced by a rule when it appears below the line in the rule (but not above), and eliminated when it appears above the line (but not below). Here, the logical connective is $\rightarrow$, and the introduction and elimination rules are the second and third from the left in the figure.

For an example derivation, here is a proof of $(a \rightarrow b) \rightarrow (a \rightarrow b)$, in the empty context Γ. This proof just uses the *Assump* and *ImpIntro* rules.

$$\frac{\cdot, a \rightarrow b \vdash a \rightarrow b}{\cdot \vdash (a \rightarrow b) \rightarrow (a \rightarrow b)}$$

Proving that $a \rightarrow b$ implies $a \rightarrow b$ is not terribly illuminating, since we well believe that T implies T for any formula T. As trivial as this fact is, it has (infinitely) many other derivations in minimal implicational logic. Here is one more:

$$\frac{\dfrac{\cdot, a \rightarrow b, a \vdash a \rightarrow b \qquad \cdot, a \rightarrow b, a \vdash a}{\cdot, a \rightarrow b, a \vdash b}}{\dfrac{\cdot, a \rightarrow b \vdash a \rightarrow b}{\cdot \vdash (a \rightarrow b) \rightarrow (a \rightarrow b)}}$$

7.7.2 A note on other propositional logics

Intuitionistic propositional logic is an extension of minimal propositional logic with a special atomic formula $\bot$ for falsity, and a new inference rule:

$$\frac{\Gamma \vdash \bot}{\Gamma \vdash T} \; FalseElim$$

This rule says that if we can prove false from a list of assumed atomic formulas Γ, then we are allowed to conclude any formula T we want. This embodies the idea that from a contradiction, anything follows.

Classical propositional logic is an extension of intuitionistic propositional logic with the following axiom:

$$\frac{}{\Gamma \vdash ((T \rightarrow \bot) \rightarrow \bot) \rightarrow T} \; Dne$$

The name *Dne* is for "double negation elimination". It can be read as saying that if you can derive a contradiction by assuming T implies false, then you can conclude T must be true. One can show that using this rule, even some formulas without $\perp$ can be derived that could not be derived in minimal propositional logic. An example is what is called Peirce's law: $((a \to b) \to a) \to a$. Interestingly, it is possible to formulate a minimal classical logic which lacks false elimination but satisfies Peirce's law [2].

7.7.3 The Curry-Howard correspondence for minimal implicational logic

Formulas of minimal implicational logic and types of simply typed lambda calculus, as we presented them above, have exactly the same syntax. Let us now compare the proof rules in Figure 7.2 with the type-assignment rules for simple types, which we saw in Section 7.3. Figure 7.3 compares the two systems of rules. In the first row we have the rules of minimal implicational logic, and in the second, the type-assignment rules for simply typed lambda calculus. The striking thing is that if we just erase all the term parts of the type-assignment rules, we have exactly the proof rules of minimal implicational logic. For example, the premises of the type-assignment rule for applications are:

- $\Gamma \vdash t_1 : T_2 \to T_1$

- $\Gamma \vdash t_2 : T_2$

Suppose we erase the variables from the context Γ, leaving only the types. This can be done with a function $|\cdot|$ defined by:

$$|\cdot| \quad = \quad \cdot$$
$$|\Gamma, x : T| \quad = |\Gamma|, T$$

Then we can erase the term parts of those premises to get

- $|\Gamma| \vdash T_2 \to T_1$

- $|\Gamma| \vdash T_2$

These exactly match the premises of the corresponding rule of minimal implicational logic. The conclusions also match up if we erase the application term $t_1 \, t_2$ from the conclusion of the type-assignment rule (and erase the variables from the context). The same is true for the type-assignment rules for variables and for λ-abstractions.

This correspondence is quite informative if we use it to pass from minimal implicational logic to lambda calculus. Take the sample derivation from the end of Section 7.7.1:

$$\frac{\dfrac{\cdot, a \to b, a \vdash a \to b \qquad \cdot, a \to b, a \vdash a}{\cdot, a \to b, a \vdash b}}{\dfrac{\cdot, a \to b \vdash a \to b}{\cdot \vdash (a \to b) \to (a \to b)}}$$

$\dfrac{T \in \Gamma}{\Gamma \vdash T}$	$\dfrac{\Gamma, T_1 \vdash T_2}{\Gamma \vdash T_1 \to T_2}$	$\dfrac{\Gamma \vdash T_1 \to T_2 \qquad \Gamma \vdash T_1}{\Gamma \vdash T_2}$
$\dfrac{\Gamma(x) = T}{\Gamma \vdash x : T}$	$\dfrac{\Gamma, x : T_1 \vdash t : T_2}{\Gamma \vdash \lambda x.t : T_1 \to T_2}$	$\dfrac{\Gamma \vdash t_1 : T_2 \to T_1 \qquad \Gamma \vdash t_2 : T_2}{\Gamma \vdash t_1\, t_2 : T_1}$

Figure 7.3: Comparison of implicational logic rules and simple typing rules

Here is the corresponding type-assignment derivation:

$$\dfrac{\dfrac{\dfrac{\cdot, f : a \to b,\ x : a \vdash f : a \to b \qquad \cdot, f : a \to b,\ x : a \vdash x : a}{\cdot, f : a \to b,\ x : a \vdash f\, x : b}}{\cdot, f : a \to b \vdash (\lambda x.f\ x) : a \to b}}{\cdot \vdash (\lambda f.\lambda x.f\ x) : (a \to b) \to (a \to b)}$$

Erasing the term parts of this type-assignment derivation gives back the derivation in minimal implicational logic. The lambda term that is being typed is $\lambda f.\lambda x.f\ x$. This term exactly captures the structure of the logical proof. In the logical proof we assume $a \to b$, then assume a, and apply the first assumption to the second to obtain b. The lambda term captures this structure by introducing the name f for the assumption of $a \to b$, and the name x for the assumption of a. The application of the first assumption to the second is written with an application term of lambda calculus: $f\ x$. The Curry-Howard correspondence can be summarized in this way:

Theorem 7.7.1 (Curry-Howard Isomorphism). *Let Γ be a context of simply typed lambda calculus where no variable is declared twice (so Γ can be viewed as a function from variables to their types). Then the following are equivalent:*

1. *$|\Gamma| \vdash T$ in minimal implicational logic.*

2. *there exists t such that $\Gamma \vdash t : T$*

Proof. The proof, which is quite straightforward, is by induction on the structure of the assumed derivation, for each direction of the stated equivalence. As an aside, we can observe that the proof is constructive in each case: given a derivation in one system, the proof shows how to construct a derivation in the other. The proof for the implication from (1) to (2) is as follows.

<u>Case</u>:

$$\dfrac{T \in |\Gamma|}{|\Gamma| \vdash T}$$

We can apply the type-assignment rule for variables to obtain $\Gamma \vdash x : T$, where $\Gamma(x) = T$. We can prove that there must be such an x in Γ, by induction on Γ. The case where Γ is empty cannot arise, since we are assuming $|\Gamma|$ contains T. So suppose Γ is $\Gamma', y : T'$ for some Γ', y, and T'. If $T' = T$, then take y for x and we are done. Otherwise, we may apply the inner induction hypothesis.

Case:

$$\frac{|\Gamma'|, T_1 \vdash T_2}{|\Gamma'| \vdash T_1 \to T_2}$$

Here, we must have $\Gamma = \Gamma', x : T_1$, for some x. By the IH, we then have a term t such that $\Gamma', x : T_1 \vdash t : T_2$. We may apply the type-assignment rule for λ-abstractions to conclude $\Gamma' \vdash \lambda x.t : T_1 \to T_2$, which suffices for what we needed to prove.

Case:

$$\frac{|\Gamma| \vdash T_1 \to T_2 \qquad |\Gamma| \vdash T_1}{|\Gamma| \vdash T_2}$$

By the IH, there are terms t_1 and t_2 such that $\Gamma \vdash t_1 : T_1$ and $\Gamma \vdash t_2 : T_2$. We may apply the type-assignment rule for applications to conclude $\Gamma \vdash t_1 \, t_2 : T_2$.

The proof for the implication from (2) to (1) is then the following.

Case:

$$\frac{\Gamma(x) = T}{\Gamma \vdash x : T}$$

We can easily prove by induction on Γ that we have $T \in |\Gamma|$, so we can apply the *Assump* rule to get $|\Gamma| \vdash T$.

Case:

$$\frac{\Gamma, x : T_1 \vdash t : T_2}{\Gamma \vdash \lambda x.t : T_1 \to T_2}$$

By the IH, $|\Gamma|, T_1 \vdash T_2$, and we may apply the *ImpIntro* rule to obtain $|\Gamma| \vdash T_1 \to T_2$.

Case:

$$\frac{\Gamma \vdash t_1 : T_2 \to T_1 \qquad \Gamma \vdash t_2 : T_2}{\Gamma \vdash t_1 \, t_2 : T_1}$$

By the IH, we have $|\Gamma| \vdash T_2 \to T_1$ and $|\Gamma| \vdash T_2$. We may apply the *ImpElim* rule to obtain $|\Gamma| \vdash T_1$. $\qquad\square$

7.7.4   Using normalization to prove logical consistency

Proof theorists of the 20th century developed a method for establishing the logical consistency of various formal logical theories, based on transformations of proofs. To understand this, we first need to define logical consistency.

Definition 7.7.2 (Logical Consistency). *If $\mathcal{L}$ is a logic of some kind, then it is consistent iff there is at least one formula which it does not accept as a theorem.*

A more familiar definition is that a logic is consistent if it does not derive a contradiction (like $0 = 1$ or *False*). The definition above is more broadly applicable, since some logics do not have a single formula like *False* representing a contradiction. Our minimal implicational logic is a good example: the only formulas are atomic formulas b and implications $T_1 \rightarrow T_2$. It would not be useful to define consistency as unprovability of *False* in this case, since *False* is not a formula. For this system, it is more informative to know that not all formulas are provable. In particular, we will show that atomic formulas b are not provable in the empty context. The basic proof-theoretic strategy for proving consistency of a logical theory is the following:

1. Prove (in the meta-language) that for every proof p of formula F, there exists a proof p' in a certain restricted form of the same formula F.

2. Prove that there is some formula that no proof p' in that restricted form could possibly prove.

The approach used for showing (1) is to rewrite proofs to remove certain patterns of inference that make (2) difficult to prove. The technically challenging part of this approach is then to show that the rewriting of proofs is indeed guaranteed to terminate.

For logics like minimal implicational logic for which we have a Curry-Howard correspondence betweens proofs and typed lambda-calculus terms, the rewriting of proofs turns out to correspond to small-step reduction of terms. Using this idea, we can prove:

Theorem 7.7.3. *Minimal implicational logic is consistent: that is, there is a formula which is not provable (in the empty context).*

Proof. We will show that b is not provable, for an atomic formula b, by assuming that it is provable and deriving a contradiction. So assume $\cdot \vdash b$. By the Curry-Howard isomorphism (Theorem 7.7.1), there must then be some lambda-calculus term t such that $\cdot \vdash t : b$. By Normalization for closed simply typable terms (Theorem 7.5.3), t has some normal form n. By iterating Type Preservation (Theorem 7.6.1), we can conclude that $\cdot \vdash n : b$. At this point we have achieved step (1) in the general proof-theoretic strategy for proving consistency: we have identified a restricted class of proofs (ones corresponding to normal forms of lambda calculus), and shown that for every unrestricted proof p of a formula F (here, the proof corresponds to t and the formula is b), there exists a proof in restricted form of F (namely, the one corresponding to n).

Now we follow step (2) in the general strategy for proving consistency: show that proofs in restricted form cannot possibly prove the formula we claim is unprovable. So here, we are going to prove that if n is in normal form, then we cannot possibly have $\cdot \vdash n : b$. More specifically, we will prove that whenever we have $\cdot \vdash n : T$ with n in normal form, then n must be a λ-abstraction. The proof is by induction on the derivation (which we are assuming exists) of $\cdot \vdash n : T$.

$$\frac{\cdot(x) = T}{\cdot \vdash x : T}$$

This case is impossible since $\cdot(x)$ cannot possibly equal T (since $\cdot$ is the empty context).

Case:

$$\frac{\cdot, x : T_1 \vdash t : T_2}{\cdot \vdash \lambda x.t : T_1 \to T_2}$$

The term in the conclusion is a λ-abstraction, so the claim holds in this case.

Case:

$$\frac{\cdot \vdash t_1 : T_2 \to T_1 \quad \cdot \vdash t_2 : T_2}{\cdot \vdash t_1\, t_2 : T_1}$$

By the IH, t_1 must be a λ-abstraction. But then $t_1\, t_2$ is not in normal form as assumed. So we derive a contradiction and the claim holds in this case, too. $\square$

Semantic Soundness (Theorem 7.4.1) actually gives us a more direct way to derive a contradiction, as done in the proof just above, from the assumption that we have a term t with $\cdot \vdash t : b$. Let us define an assignment I of sets of terms to base types by $I(b) = \emptyset$, for all base types b. To apply Semantic Soundness, we must confirm that $I(b)$ is inverse-reduction closed for all base types b, but this holds vacuously: we must show that if $t \rightsquigarrow t'$ and $t' \in I(b)$ then $t \in I(b)$, but since $I(b) = \emptyset$ by definition, there are no terms t' in $I(b)$. Now Semantic Soundness tells us that $\cdot \vdash t : b$ implies $t \in [\![b]\!]\, I$. But $[\![b]\!]\, I = I(b) = \emptyset$ by definition of the semantics of base types and the definition of I. So $t \notin [\![b]\!]\, I$, and hence we cannot have $\cdot \vdash t : b$. So although the proof of consistency above used Type Preservation and then an induction on the structure of derivations of $\cdot \vdash n : T$ for normal n, this was not actually needed, since Semantic Soundness already gives us enough information to conclude that no term can have type b in the empty context.

7.8   Algorithmic typing

We can try to use the type-assignment rules algorithmically by starting with some goal type assignment to prove, and matching the conclusion of a rule to that goal. The appropriately instantiated premises then become the new goals, and we proceed recursively. If you are familiar with logic programming as in Prolog, this is a similar idea. There are two ways we might try to use these rules in this way, depending on which of Γ, t, and T we consider to be inputs, and which outputs. Unfortunately, both of which end up being infinitarily non-deterministic (and hence unusable). So we will have to refine the rules in some way to get a deterministic algorithm.

1. **Type checking.** On this approach, we take Γ, t, and T as inputs (and there are no outputs). So the judgment expresses that we check whether t can be assigned simple type T in context Γ. The problem with this reading is that when we apply the application rule, we must non-deterministically guess type T_2 as we pass from its conclusion to its premises. There are an infinite number of choices, since there are infinitely many simple types. Note, however, that the other rules can both be executed deterministically.

2. **Type computation.** We can also take Γ and t as inputs, and T as output. In this case, the judgment expresses the idea that simple type T can be computed for t in context Γ. The application rule is completely deterministic on this reading: if we have computed type $T_2 \rightarrow T_1$ for t_1 and type T_2 for t_2, then we compute type T_1 for the application of t_1 to t_2. The problem with the type computation reading shows up in the rule for typing λ-abstractions. There, we must non-deterministically guess the type T_1 to give to x in the extended context in the premise of the rule. So once again, the rules are infinitarily non-deterministic.

We now consider different ways to obtain a deterministic algorithm for typing:

1. **Annotated applications for type checking.** If we wish to use the typing rules for type checking, then we can annotate applications to remove the non-determinism in the application rule (described above). We may add annotations to applications by the syntax of λ-terms t:

$$t \quad ::= \quad x \mid (t_1 \, t_2) \, [T] \mid \lambda x.t$$

The typing rules above are then modified as follows (note that only the application rule has changed):

$$\frac{\Gamma(x) = T}{\Gamma \vdash x : T} \quad \frac{\Gamma \vdash t_1 : T_2 \rightarrow T_1 \quad \Gamma \vdash t_2 : T_2}{\Gamma \vdash t_1 \, t_2 \, [T_2] : T_1} \quad \frac{\Gamma, x : T_1 \vdash t : T_2}{\Gamma \vdash \lambda x.t : T_1 \rightarrow T_2}$$

This approach is admittedly not commonly used in practice, though it is theoretically sufficient.

2. **Annotated abstractions for type computation.** More commonly, if we wish to use the typing rules for type computation, then we can annotate λ-abstractions to remove the non-determinism in the abstraction rule:

$$t \quad ::= \quad x \mid (t_1 \, t_2) \mid \lambda x : T.t$$

The typing rules above are then modified as follows (only the λ-abstraction rule has changed):

$$\frac{\Gamma(x) = T}{\Gamma \vdash x : T} \qquad \frac{\Gamma \vdash t_1 : T_2 \rightarrow T_1 \quad \Gamma \vdash t_2 : T_2}{\Gamma \vdash t_1\, t_2 : T_1} \qquad \frac{\Gamma, x : T_1 \vdash t : T_2}{\Gamma \vdash \lambda x : T_1.t : T_1 \rightarrow T_2}$$

In both cases, since the subject t of the typing judgment $\Gamma \vdash t : T$ is structurally decreased from conclusion to premises of every rule, the rules are not only algorithmic but also terminating. We can therefore use them as effective tests for typability.

7.8.1 Examples

Let us consider how our three different systems for algorithmic typing (type checking, type computation,, and constraint generation) handle the example type assignment $\cdot \vdash \lambda x.\lambda y.(x\, y) : (T_1 \rightarrow T_2) \rightarrow (T_1 \rightarrow T_2)$.

Type checking. For type checking, we must annotate applications with the type of the argument. So our term $\lambda x.\lambda y.(x\, y)$ becomes $\lambda x.\lambda y.(x\, y)[T_1]$. We then have this derivation using our type-checking rules:

$$\frac{\dfrac{x : T_1 \rightarrow T_2, y : T_1 \vdash x : T_1 \rightarrow T_2 \quad x : T_1 \rightarrow T_2, y : T_1 \vdash y : T_1}{x : T_1 \rightarrow T_2, y : T_1 \vdash (x\, y)[T_1] : T_2}}{\dfrac{x : T_1 \rightarrow T_2 \vdash \lambda y.(x\, y)[T_1] : T_1 \rightarrow T_2}{\cdot \vdash \lambda x.\lambda y.(x\, y)[T_1] : (T_1 \rightarrow T_2) \rightarrow (T_1 \rightarrow T_2)}}$$

Notice that every expression written directly above a line is determined by expressions written directly below that line. So we do not need to choose (nondeterministically) any expression as we use the type-checking rules algorithmically. In particular, we do not need to guess the domain type for the function x (and the type for the argument y) when checking the application $(x\, y)$.

Type computation. For type computation, we need to annotate λ-abstractions with the type of the input. So our example term becomes $\lambda x : T_1 \rightarrow T_2.\lambda y : T_1.(x\, y)$, and we have this derivation:

$$\frac{\dfrac{x : T_1 \rightarrow T_2, y : T_1 \vdash x : \mathbf{T_1} \rightarrow \mathbf{T_2} \quad x : T_1 \rightarrow T_2, y : T_1 \vdash y : \mathbf{T_1}}{x : T_1 \rightarrow T_2, y : T_1 \vdash (x\, y) : \mathbf{T_2}}}{\dfrac{x : T_1 \rightarrow T_2 \vdash \lambda y : T_1.(x\, y) : \mathbf{T_1} \rightarrow \mathbf{T_2}}{\cdot \vdash \lambda x : T_1 \rightarrow T_2.\lambda y : T_1.(x\, y) : (\mathbf{T_1} \rightarrow \mathbf{T_2}) \rightarrow (\mathbf{T_1} \rightarrow \mathbf{T_2})}}$$

Here I have written the inputs to type computation in the regular font, and outputs in bold. Notice that all inputs directly above a line are determined by inputs below that line, and similarly, all outputs directly below a line are determined by outputs above that line. This tells us that inputs to recursive calls are determined by inputs to surrounding calls, and outputs from surrounding calls are determined by outputs from recursive calls. So information is flowing properly for this to compute the type T as an output from the term t and the context Γ as inputs.

7.9 Algorithmic typing via constraint generation

We saw that the above typing rules are not algorithmic. Whether one is computing a type or checking a type, one must make a non-deterministic choice of a type in the premise of one rule. One solution is to add annotations to the program that specify this type, thus removing the need for the non-deterministic choice.

Another way to get a typing algorithm without adding any annotations is to modify our type-assignment rules so they generate constraints. This idea can be implemented based on an interpretation of the typing judgment as expressing type checking, as well as on an interpretation as type computation. Here, we pursue the latter. The rules now operate on judgments of the form $\Gamma \vdash t : T > C$, where Γ and t are inputs, and T and C are outputs. C is a set of constraints which must be satisfied in order for the type assignment to hold. A constraint is an equation between simple types with meta-variables X, which we call here **type schemes**, defined by the following syntax:

$$\text{type schemes } T \quad ::= \quad b \mid X \mid T_1 \rightarrow T_2$$

The constraint generation rules are the following (where $\cdot$ denotes the empty set of constraints, and comma is used for unioning sets of constraints). In the rule for λ-abstractions and the rule for applications, X is a new meta-variable (not occurring in any other term, type, or context listed).

$$\frac{\Gamma(x) = T}{\Gamma \vdash x : T > \cdot} \qquad \frac{\Gamma \vdash t_1 : T_1 > C_1 \quad \Gamma \vdash t_2 : T_2 > C_2}{\Gamma \vdash t_1\, t_2 : X > C_1, C_2, T_1 = T_2 \rightarrow X} \qquad \frac{\Gamma, x : X \vdash t : T > C}{\Gamma \vdash \lambda x.t : X \rightarrow T > C}$$

So to compute a type for a term, one applies these rules bottom-up (from conclusion to premises). This will generate a set of constraints. If these have a common solution, then the original term is typable. We will see how to solve these constraints using **unification** in Section 7.9.2 below. First, though, let us consider an example of constraint generation.

7.9.1 Example

For constraint-based typing, we do not need to annotate our term at all. Instead, we are computing a type possibly containing some meta-variables, and a set of constraints on meta-variables. If the constraints are solvable, they determine a substitution that we can apply to the computed type, to get a final type for the term. This type can still have meta-variables in it, so it will actually be a type scheme, describing an infinite set of types that can be assigned to the term. Here is the constraint-based typing derivation for the example term we considered in Section 7.8.1.

$$\frac{\dfrac{x:X,y:Y\vdash x:X>\cdot\quad x:X,y:Y\vdash y:Y>\cdot}{x:X,y:Y\vdash (x\,y):Z>X=Y\to Z}}{\dfrac{x:X\vdash \lambda y.(x\,y):Y\to Z>X=Y\to Z}{\cdot\vdash \lambda x.\lambda y.(x\,y):X\to (Y\to Z)>X=Y\to Z}}$$

We have not yet studied how to solve sets of constraints, but in this case, the set is already in **solved form**: each equation is of the form $X = T$, where X occurs nowhere else in the set of constraints. This constitutes an explicit definition for X. Applying this definition as a substitution means replacing X by what it is defined to equal, in this case $Y \to Z$. So the final type (scheme) we get is $(Y \to Z) \to (Y \to Z)$, which matches what we derived above with other approaches.

7.9.2 Solving constraints using unification

Now let us see an algorithm for solving constraints. The syntactic unification problem is the following: given two expressions e_1 and e_2, which may use unification variables X (in our case, meta-variables), find a substitution σ for those variables such that σe_1 and σe_2 are exactly the same expression. This substitution is a **unifier** of the two expressions. More generally, we are looking for a substitution which simultaneously unifies a set of pairs of expressions (e_1, e_2).

It is helpful to be a bit more detailed about what a substitution is. In general, in a setting where we have some set of expressions containing variables drawn from some other set, a substitution is a total function σ from the set of variables to expressions, where $\sigma(X) = X$ for all but a finite number of variables X. The idea is that the substitution should only replace a finite number of variables with some other expression; all other variables X are left unmodified by the substitution, which is captured by having $\sigma(X) = X$. Such a substitution can be denoted as a finite function $\{X_1 \mapsto e_1, \cdots, X_n \mapsto e_n\}$, where we need only show the mappings for variables X where $\sigma(X) \neq X$. In our setting of constraint solving for simple types, the set of variables in question is the set of type meta-variables, and the expressions to which these variables are being mapped are type schemes. Applying a substitution like $\{X \mapsto Y \to Y\}$ to a type scheme like $X \to Z$ results in $(Y \to Y) \to Z$, since the substitution does not modify Z.

An algorithm for solving constraints by unification is given by the rules of Figure 7.4. The rules are to be applied top-down (from premises to conclusion) to transform a set of constraints C, where each constraint is an equation $e_1 = e_2$. In the figure, we write $e_1 = e_2, C$ to mean $\{e_1 = e_2\} \cup C$, where the equation $e_1 = e_2$ is not already a member of the set C. For constraint-based simple typing, we have just one function symbol f that could appear in the *decompose* rule: this is the $\to$-construct, for forming function types. This is because our constraint-based typing rules will generate equations between type expressions. It is these equations that will be solved by the above unification algorithm.

A variable is called **solved** in C if it occurs exactly once in C, on the left hand side of an equation. If all constraints are of the form $X = t$, where X is a solved

$$\frac{t = t, C}{C} \quad delete$$

$$\frac{t = X, C \quad X \notin Vars(t) \quad t \text{ is not a variable}}{X = t, C} \quad orient$$

$$\frac{f(t_1, \ldots, t_n) = f(s_1, \ldots, s_n)}{t_1 = s_1, \ldots, t_n = s_n, C} \quad decompose$$

$$\frac{X = t, C \quad X \notin Vars(t) \quad X \in Vars(C)}{X = t, [t/X]C} \quad solve$$

Figure 7.4: A simple non-deterministic unification algorithm

variable, then C is said to be in solved form. Such a C determines a substitution, namely, the one which maps X to t for each such constraint.

A number of important properties of this algorithm can be shown. One property is that it terminates with a solved form, no matter what order the rules are applied in, iff the original unification problem is solvable. Another important property is that it computes a **most general** unifier. We take a brief digression to discuss this property, after seeing first an example.

7.9.3   Example

Suppose C is $\{(Y \to Z) \to W = (X \to X), W = A \to A\}$. Then the following derivation represents a run of the unification algorithm:

$$\frac{\{(Y \to Z) \to W = (X \to X),\ W = (A \to A)\}}{\cfrac{\{(Y \to Z) = X,\ W = X,\ W = (A \to A)\}}{\cfrac{\{X = (Y \to Z),\ W = X,\ W = (A \to A)\}}{\cfrac{\{X = (Y \to Z),\ W = (Y \to Z),\ W = (A \to A)\}}{\cfrac{\{X = (Y \to Z),\ W = (Y \to Z),\ (Y \to Z) = (A \to A)\}}{\cfrac{\{X = (Y \to Z),\ W = (Y \to Z),\ Y = A,\ Z = A\}}{\cfrac{\{X = (A \to Z),\ W = (A \to Z),\ Y = A,\ Z = A\}}{\{X = (A \to A),\ W = (A \to A),\ Y = A,\ Z = A\}} \ solve} \ solve} \ decompose} \ solve} \ solve} \ orient} \ decompose}$$

Notice that the variables W, X, Y, and Z are all solved in the final (i.e., lowest printed) constraint set. The variable A is not solved in that constraint set. This does not prevent the final constraint set from being in solved form, because each constraint in that set is of the form $X = t$, where X is solved.

7.9.4 Generality of substitutions

In general, for substitutions mapping from variables to some class of expressions, we can define a notion of generality as follows. Substitution σ is more general than σ' if there exists a substitution σ'' such that $\sigma' = \sigma'' \circ \sigma$ (the composition of σ'' and σ, where σ is applied first, and then σ''). Intuitively, this means that σ' acts like σ, followed by some additional instantiating of variables (by σ''). So σ instantiates variables less than σ' does. For example, the following σ is more general than the following σ':

$$\sigma = \{X \mapsto f(Y), Z \mapsto a\}$$
$$\sigma' = \{X \mapsto f(g(Y))), Z \mapsto a, W \mapsto a\}$$

We have $\sigma(X) = f(Y)$, but $\sigma'(X) = f(g(Y))$. Also, $\sigma(W) = W$, but $\sigma'(W) = a$. The substitution σ'' showing that σ is more general than σ' as defined above is:

$$\sigma'' = \{Y \mapsto g(Y), W \mapsto a\}$$

Substitutions are **equivalently general** iff each is more general than the other according to the above definition. An example of a pair of equivalently general substitutions is

$$\sigma_1 = \{X \mapsto f(Y)\}$$
$$\sigma_2 = \{X \mapsto f(Z)), Z \mapsto Y, Y \mapsto Z\}$$

In each case, we can compose the substitution with the **renaming** (which is a finite permutation of variables) $\{Z \mapsto Y, Y \mapsto Z\}$ to get the other. The composition

$$\{Z \mapsto Y, Y \mapsto Z\} \circ \{X \mapsto f(Y)\}$$

maps X first to $f(Y)$, and then to $f(Z)$; and it maps Y to Z and Z to Y. The composition

$$\{Z \mapsto Y, Y \mapsto Z\} \circ \{X \mapsto f(Z), Z \mapsto Y, Y \mapsto Z\}$$

maps X first to $f(Z)$ and then to $f(Y)$; and it maps Z first to Y and then back to Z, and similarly Y to Z and then back to Y. So the composition is really

$$\{Z \mapsto Z, Y \mapsto Y, X \mapsto f(Y)\}$$

which is equivalent to just $\{X \mapsto f(Y)\}$ (since our notation for substitutions allows us to hide mapping of variables to themselves). Finally, substitutions may be **incomparable** in this generality ordering. That is, it can happen that neither is more general than the other. An example is $\{X \mapsto f(X)\}$ and $\{X \mapsto g(X)\}$.

7.9.5 Termination

We show here that the algorithm terminates, by reducing a certain measure: (# unsolved variables, size of constraint set, # unoriented equations), where (recall that) a variable is solved iff it occurs exactly once, on the left-hand side of an equation;

the size of the constraint set is the sum of the number of symbols except equality in its members; and an equation is unoriented if *orient* could be applied to it. We compare elements of this measure using the threefold **lexicographic combination** of the usual natural-number ordering with itself. If we have two strict orders $<_1$ on set A and $<_2$ on set B, then the lexicographic combination $<_{lex(1,2)}$ of the orders is a strict ordering where $(a, b) <_{lex(1,2)} (a', b')$ iff

$$a <_1 a' \lor (a = a' \land b <_2 b')$$

So we decrease in $<_{lex(1,2)}$ iff either the first element of the pair decreases (and the second element can change arbitrarily, including increasing), or else the first element is unchanged and the second decreases. It is not hard to prove that if $<_1$ and $<_2$ are terminating, then so is $<_{lex(1,2)}$.

In the table below, a dash indicates a value that could possibly increase, but since it is to the right of a value that decreases, the measure is still decreased in the lexicographic combination of orderings. You can confirm that the rules in question decrease these quantities as stated, thus showing that each rule decreases the measure. Since the ordering is terminating, the measure cannot be decreased forever, and hence the algorithm terminates.

Rule	# unsolved variables	size of constraint set	# unoriented
delete	$\leq$	$<$	-
decompose	$\leq$	$<$	-
orient	$\leq$	$=$	$<$
solve	$<$	-	-

7.10   Subtyping

In some situations it is desirable to allow a term of type T_1 where a term of type T_2 is required, when T_1 and T_2 are related in a certain way. For example, we might want to allow every boolean to be used as an integer, by identifying *true* and *false* with 1 and 0, respectively. To do this, we will allow a term of type *bool* (playing the role of T_1) to be used wherever a term of type *int* (T_2) is required. The standard terminology is that we are treating *bool* as a **subtype** of *int*. For more on subtyping for other type systems, including polymorphic ones, see [33].

The way that subtyping enters into the type-assignment system for STLC (Section 7.3) is through the addition of a so-called subsumption rule, where $T_1 <: T_2$ means that T_1 is a subtype of T_2 (the formal definition is given below):

$$\frac{\Gamma \vdash t : T_1 \quad T_1 <: T_2}{\Gamma \vdash t : T_2}$$

This rule says that if in context Γ we have t of type T_1, then we can just as well assign the type T_2 to t, if we know that T_1 is a subtype of T_2. Intuitively, this is justified by a semantics for $T_1 <: T_2$ which says that every value of type T_1 is also

$$\frac{}{b <: b} \qquad \frac{SubBase(b_1, b_2)}{b_1 <: b_2} \qquad \frac{T_1' <: T_1 \quad T_2 <: T_2'}{T_1 \to T_2 <: T_1' \to T_2'}$$

Figure 7.5: Rules for subtyping

a value of type T_2. Let us define this semantics. Recall the interpretation $[\![T]\!] \, I$ of a type T with respect to an assignment I, defined in Section 7.2, where I maps base types to sets of terms. We define the semantics for subtyping judgments $T_1 <: T_2$ with respect to I as follows:

$$[\![T_1 <: T_2]\!] \, I \; := \; [\![T_1]\!] \, I \subseteq [\![T_2]\!] \, I$$

We will see below that with this interpretation, we can easily extend our proof of Theorem 7.4.1 (Semantic Soundness) to handle the subsumption rule. But first we need to give rules for the subtyping judgment.

7.10.1 Subtyping rules

Figure 7.5 gives rules for the subtyping judgment $T_1 <: T_2$. The first rule expresses reflexivity of subtyping for base types: we are surely allowed to use a b wherever a b is required. The second rule presupposes a primitive subtyping relation $SubBase$ on base types. For the example mentioned above, we would make $SubBase(bool, nat)$ true, and all other subtypings of base types false. This enforces an asymmetric relationship between the two types T_1 and T_2: we want to use *bool*s as *int*s, but let us say we will not allow using *int*s as *bool*s (although that can certainly also be sensible). Other situations could use a different primitive subtyping relation on base types.

The third rule of Figure 7.5 expresses subtyping for function types. Note that the first premise is really $T_1' <: T_1$, with the T_1' first and the T_1 second (this is not a typo). This is the phenomenon known as **contravariance** of subtyping for the domain part of function types. In contrast, we do have the $T_2 <: T_2'$, with the T_2 first and T_2' second, for the range parts, and subtyping is said to exhibit **covariance** in this case. We will give a formal proof below that this is sound with respect to our semantics, but let us consider the situation informally. Suppose we want to use a term t of type $T_1 \to T_2$ where a term t' of type $T_1' \to T_2'$ is required. When is this sound? Well, we know that t' might be applied to an argument of type T_1'. So to use t in place of t', we need to be sure that every argument of type T_1' is also acceptable as an argument of type T_1. For after all, we know only that t accepts arguments of T_1. This is why the subtyping rule for function types requires $T_1' <: T_1$. Now after applying t to such an argument, we know we will get back a result of type T_2. But in the place where t' of type $T_1' \to T_2'$ is used, all results obtained by applying t' are required to be of type T_2'. We can satisfy that requirement if we know $T_2 <: T_2'$, as required by the second premise of the subtyping rule for function types.

7.10.2   Examples

Here are some example derivable subtypings, where we assume $SubBase(bool, nat)$.

$$1. \quad nat \rightarrow bool \qquad <: \quad bool \rightarrow nat$$

$$2. \quad nat \rightarrow bool \qquad <: \quad bool \rightarrow bool$$

$$3. \quad bool \rightarrow bool \qquad <: \quad bool \rightarrow bool$$

$$4. \quad (bool \rightarrow nat) \rightarrow b \quad <: \quad (bool \rightarrow bool) \rightarrow b$$

(1) is derivable using the function-subtyping rule, since we have $bool <: nat$, which is needed for both the first and second premise of that rule in this case. (2) is derivable using $bool <: nat$ for the first premise of the function-subtyping rule, and $bool <: bool$ for the second. (3) is derivable using $bool <: bool$, which holds by the second rule of Figure 7.5, for both premises of the function-subtyping rule. (4) is derivable since we have the following subtyping for the first premise of the function-subtyping rule, and $b <: b$ for the second:

$$bool \rightarrow bool <: bool \rightarrow nat$$

7.10.3   Extending semantic soundness to subtyping

Recall from Section 7.4 that $\sigma \in [\![\Gamma]\!]\, I$ means that $\sigma(x) \in [\![\Gamma(x)]\!]\, I$, for every x in the domain of substitution σ, where that domain is assumed to be equal to the domain of Γ. Our goal now is to extend Theorem 7.4.1 (Semantic Soundness) to include the subsumption rule and subtyping rules introduced just above. The first step for this is to prove that the subtyping rules are semantically sound, as expressed in this lemma:

Lemma 7.10.1 (Soundness of subtyping rules). *Suppose that whenever $SubBase(b_1, b_2)$ holds (using the rules of Figure 7.5), we have $I(b_1) \subseteq I(b_2)$. If $T_1 <: T_2$ is derivable (Figure 7.5), then $[\![T_1 <: T_2]\!]\, I$ holds.*

Proof. The proof is by induction on the structure of the assumed subtyping derivation:

Case:

$$\frac{SubBase(b_1, b_2)}{b_1 <: b_2}$$

We have $I(b_1) \subseteq I(b_2)$ from our assumption relating $SubBase$ and I.

Case:

$$\frac{}{b <: b}$$

The interpretation of the conclusion is $I(b) \subseteq I(b)$, but this holds by basic set theory.

Case:

$$\frac{T_1' <: T_1 \quad T_2 <: T_2'}{T_1 \to T_2 <: T_1' \to T_2'}$$

The interpretation of the conclusion is $I(T_1 \to T_2) \subseteq I(T_1' \to T_2')$. To prove this, it suffices to assume an arbitrary term $t \in I(T_1 \to T_2)$, and show $t \in I(T_1' \to T_2')$. For the latter, it suffices to assume an arbitrary $t' \in I(T_1')$, and show $t\,t' \in I(T_2')$. By the IH applied to the first premise, we know that $I(T_1') \subseteq I(T_1)$, so $t' \in I(T_1)$. Since we are assuming $t \in I(T_1 \to T_2)$, we may now deduce that $t\,t' \in I(T_2)$. By the IH applied to the second premise, we know $I(T_2) \subseteq I(T_2')$, so we can conclude that $t\,t' \in I(T_2')$. But this was what we were trying to prove. $\qquad\square$

Now we can prove the following theorem about STLC extended with subtyping.

Theorem 7.10.2 (Semantic soundness with subtyping). *Suppose $I(b)$ is inverse-reduction closed for all base types b, and whenever $SubBase(b_1, b_2)$, we have $I(b_1) \subseteq I(b_2)$. Suppose further that $\sigma \in [\![\Gamma]\!]\, I$. If $\Gamma \vdash t : T$ in STLC with subtyping (the rules of Figure 7.1 plus subsumption), then we have $\sigma\, t \in [\![T]\!]\, I$.*

Proof. The proof is by induction on the structure of the assumed typing derivation. All cases go through exactly as for Theorem 7.4.1, except for the new case of the subsumption rule:

Case:

$$\frac{\Gamma \vdash t : T_1 \quad T_1 <: T_2}{\Gamma \vdash t : T_2}$$

By the induction hypothesis, we have $\sigma\, t \in [\![T_1]\!]\, I$. By Lemma 7.10.1, we have $I(T_1) \subseteq I(T_2)$. This is sufficient to deduce $\sigma\, t \in [\![T_2]\!]\, I$, as needed for the conclusion of the rule. $\qquad\square$

Corollary 7.10.3 (Normalization with subtyping). *If $\cdot \vdash t : T$ is derivable in STLC with subtyping, then t is normalizing.*

Proof. Let I be the assignment mapping every base type to *Norm*. I clearly satisfying the requirements on the assignment induced by *SubBase*. Theorem 7.10.2 then gives us $t \in [\![T]\!]\, I$. Our interpretation of types is unchanged from Section 7.5, so we may apply Lemma 7.5.2 to conclude that $[\![T]\!]\, I \subseteq Norm$. $\qquad\square$

Corollary 7.10.3 may not seem terribly surprising, since the proof is entirely straightforward. But the result is more remarkable than it might first appear, for small changes to the system lead to the loss of normalization. For example, suppose we were to give a bit more freedom in our rule using *SubBase* (from Figure 7.5), so that the system could be parametrized by a primitive subtyping relation on any types, not just base types. The resulting subtyping rule would be:

$$\frac{SubBase(T_1, T_2)}{T_1 <: T_2}$$

Suppose we have $SubBase(b, b \rightarrow b)$ and $SubBase(b \rightarrow b, b)$. This may seem a bit suspicious, since it looks like we are saying that b is equivalent to $b \rightarrow b$. Indeed, that is the effect of these primitive subtypings, and they are sufficient to type the (non-normalizing) term $(\lambda x.x\ x)\ (\lambda x.x\ x)$. Here is a derivation, written in linear form (where we list out judgments and state which follow from which using the rules):

1.	$\cdot, x : b \vdash x : b$	axiom
2.	$b <: b \rightarrow b$	axiom
3.	$\cdot, x : b \vdash x : b \rightarrow b$	from 1, 2
4.	$\cdot, x : b \vdash x\ x : b$	from 3, 1
5.	$\cdot \vdash \lambda x.x\ x : b \rightarrow b$	from 4
6.	$b \rightarrow b <: b$	axiom
7.	$\cdot \vdash \lambda x.x\ x : b$	from 5, 6
8.	$\cdot \vdash (\lambda x.x\ x)\ (\lambda x.x\ x) : b$	from 5, 7

Indeed, we see that semantically, $[\![b]\!]\ I$ is not a subset, in general, of $[\![b \rightarrow b]\!]\ I$. For example, if I maps every base type to *Norm*, then $\lambda x.x\ x$ is in $[\![b]\!]\ I$, but not in $[\![b \rightarrow b]\!]\ I$. This is because applying it to itself – an argument which we have just noted is in $[\![b]\!]\ I$ – is diverging, and hence not in $[\![b]\!]\ I = Norm$.

7.10.4   Reflexivity and transitivity of subtyping

Since we have just seen that adding a more flexible version of the axiom for primitive subtypings would destroy normalization for the typable terms, we have reason to be nervous about making other changes to the subtyping rules. For example, would it be sound to add a general reflexivity rule?

$$\overline{T <: T}$$

Or what about a transitivity rule?

$$\frac{T_1 <: T_2 \quad T_2 <: T_3}{T_1 <: T_3}$$

The following theorems clarify the situation for these rules (recall from Section 3.3.5 that a rule is admissible iff whenever the premises are derivable, so is the conclusion):

Theorem 7.10.4 (Admissibility of reflexivity). *The general reflexivity rule above is admissible.*

Proof. The proof is by induction on the type T mentioned in the conclusion of the rule.

<u>Case:</u> $T = b$ for some base type b. Then we can use the first rule of Figure 7.5 to derive $b <: b$.

Case: $T = T_1 \to T_2$ for some types T_1 and T_2. We can use this derivation:

$$\frac{\overline{T_1 <: T_1}\ \ IH \quad \overline{T_2 <: T_2}\ \ IH}{T_1 \to T_2 <: T_1 \to T_2}$$

□

Theorem 7.10.5 (Admissibility of transitivity). *Suppose that SubBase is transitive. Then the rule of transitivity shown above is admissible.*

Proof. The proof is by induction on the assumed derivation of $T_1 <: T_2$.

Case:

$$\overline{b <: b}$$

So $T_1 = T_2 = b$. Then the second assumed derivation, of $T_2 <: T_3$, is already a derivation of $T_1 <: T_3$.

Case:

$$\frac{SubBase(b_1, b_2)}{b_1 <: b_2}$$

So $T_1 = b_1$ and $T_2 = b_2$. Let us now case split on the form of the second assumed derivation, of $T_2 <: T_3$. It cannot end in an inference using the function-subtyping rule, since that rule would require T_2 to be a function type, but $T_2 = b_2$. If it ends in an inference using the reflexivity rule for base types, then $T_3 = b_2$, and the first assumed derivation is already a derivation of $T_1 <: T_3$. If it ends in an inference using the primitive-subtyping rule, then $T_3 = b_3$ for some b_3 with $SubBase(b_2, b_3)$. Since $SubBase$ is transitive by assumption, we have $SubBase(b_1, b_3)$, and we can apply the primitive-subtyping rule to get $b_1 <: b_3$.

Case:

$$\frac{T_a' <: T_a \quad T_b <: T_b'}{T_a \to T_b <: T_a' \to T_b'}$$

So $T_1 = T_a \to T_b$ and $T_2 = T_a' \to T_b'$. Let us case split now on the form of the second assumed derivation, of $T_2 <: T_3$. Since $T_2 = T_a' \to T_b'$, the only possibility is that this derivation also ends in an inference by the function-subtyping rule:

$$\frac{T_a'' <: T_a' \quad T_b' <: T_b''}{T_a' \to T_b' <: T_a'' \to T_b''}$$

We may use the following derivation:

$$\frac{\dfrac{T_a'' <: T_a' \quad T_a' <: T_a}{T_a'' <: T_a}\ IH \quad \dfrac{T_b <: T_b' \quad T_b' <: T_b''}{T_b <: T_b''}\ IH}{T_a \to T_b <: T_a'' \to T_b''}$$

□

7.10.5   Algorithmic typing with subtyping

The subtyping relation itself is algorithmic because the rules given in Figure 7.5 are syntax directed. If we are asked to test $T_1 \rightarrow T_2 <: T_3$, the only possible inference that could be used to derive that judgment is with the function-subtyping rule, where T_3 must be $T_1' \rightarrow T_2'$ for some T_1' and T_2'. If we have $b <: T$, then either $T = b$ and the reflexivity rule for base type applies, or else $T = b'$ and we have $SubBase(b, b')$. Furthermore, the rules structurally decrease the types in question as we pass from conclusion to premises. So the rules are both algorithmic and terminating, and we can effectively test (for this particular type system) whether or not $T_1 <: T_2$.

The type-assignment rules for STLC with subtyping are certainly not algorithmic, since just for pure STLC we already observed type assignment is not algorithmic. But there is a new source of nondeterminism we must account for somehow: the subsumption rule can be applied at any point in searching for a type-assignment derivation. This is because the conclusion of the subsumption rule matches every typing judgment. So unlike the other typing rules, it is not **subject directed**: the form of the term we are trying to type does not limit the application of this rule at all. In contrast, the other typing rules are all limited by the form of the term in their conclusions. We now consider several options that can be used to obtain an algorithmic version of STLC with subtyping:

Annotating with cast terms

We can extend one of the annotation schemes for STLC (see Section 7.8) with a new annotation for uses of subsumption. The programmer will have to insert these annotations to tell the type checker when to try to change the type of a term. For algorithmic type computation with annotations on the λ-bound variables, we can add a new term construct *cast t to T*, with the following typing rule:

$$\frac{\Gamma \vdash t : T_1 \quad T_1 <: T_2}{\Gamma \vdash cast\ t\ to\ T_2 : T_2}$$

This rule can be used algorithmically for type computation, since assuming we have computed T_1 from the first premise, we have all the data we need to check $T_1 <: T_2$ (since T_2 is given in the term). Many practical programming languages include explicit typecast or coercion constructs like this, so this option is not so strange in practice.

If we want to extend algorithmic type checking with annotations on applications, we add a new term construct *cast t from T* and this typing rule:

$$\frac{\Gamma \vdash t : T_1 \quad T_1 <: T_2}{\Gamma \vdash cast\ t\ from\ T_1 : T_2}$$

Assuming that the context, term, and type in the conclusion are all inputs to the algorithm, all the meta-variables in the premises will have values when applying the rule algorithmically.

$$\frac{\Gamma(x) = T}{\Gamma \vdash x :: T} \quad \frac{\Gamma, x : T_1 \vdash t : T_2}{\Gamma \vdash \lambda x.t :: T_1 \to T_2} \quad \frac{\Gamma \vdash t_1 : T_2 \to T_1 \quad \Gamma \vdash t_2 : T_2'}{\Gamma \vdash t_1 \ t_2 :: T_1}$$

$$\frac{\Gamma \vdash t :: T_1 \quad T_1 <: T_2}{\Gamma \vdash t : T_2}$$

Figure 7.6: Type-assignment rules alternating STLC rules with subsumption

Working subtyping into the other rules

There is a different way to approach the problem of supporting a rule like subsumption which is not subject directed. The basic idea is to capture the effect that cumulative applications of this new rule could have, and incorporate those effects directly into all the other typing rules. In the case of subtyping, this is actually rather easy to do because there is nothing that multiple applications of subtyping can do that a single application could not. This is because, as we saw in Section 7.10.4), subtyping is both reflexive and transitive. Reflexivity means that 0 applications of subsumption can be imitated by one application of subsumption, and transitivity that many applications of subsumption can be imitated by just one. For other type systems, the issue of summarizing the effect of multiple applications of rules which fail to be subject directed can be significantly trickier: see the treatment of Curry-style System F in Section 4.2 of Barendregt's "Lambda Calculi with Types", for an important example [6].

So the first step to handling rules which are not subject directed, on this approach, is to define a new judgment which captures the effect of multiple applications of those rules. For subtyping, this is easy as we noted: $T_1 <: T_2$ is already such a judgment. The next step is to define a set of rules which strictly interleave applications of the rules which are subject directed with those which are not. For subtyping, such a system is shown in Figure 7.6. Notice that we use two different typing judgments: derivations of $\Gamma \vdash t : T$ must end in a subsumption inference, while derivations of $\Gamma \vdash t :: T$ must end in an inference with one of the three rules for STLC. The premises of the STLC rules (the first line of rules in the figure) use :, while the conclusions use ::. For the subsumption rule (on the second line of the figure), the situation is reversed: the (typing) premise uses :: and the conclusion uses :. This enforces a strict interleaving of the rules, where along any path in a typing derivation, we are alternating between subsumption and STLC rules.

What is the benefit of this approach? We can now rework the system one last time to combine the two layers into one. Since we know that every premise of an STLC rule (in Figure 7.6) must be derived using subsumption, we can think about what role subsumption plays in allowing the STLC inference, which derives a judgment of the form $\Gamma \vdash t :: T$, to proceed. Let us consider the three STLC typing rules in turn:

Variable rule. Any derivation of $\Gamma \vdash x :: T$ must end in the STLC variable rule. There is no application of subsumption.

Lambda rule. Any derivation of $\Gamma \vdash \lambda x.t :: T_1 \to T_2$ must end this way:

$$\frac{\dfrac{\Gamma, x : T_1 \vdash t :: T_2' \quad T_2' <: T_2}{\Gamma, x : T_1 \vdash t : T_2}}{\Gamma \vdash \lambda x.t :: T_1 \to T_2}$$

We see that subsumption is not essential to allowing this inference to take place. If we applied a trivial subsumption instead, where we use reflexivity to change the type of t from T_2' to T_2', the inference could still proceed, though the type assigned would be different:

$$\frac{\dfrac{\Gamma, x : T_1 \vdash t :: T_2' \quad T_2' <: T_2'}{\Gamma, x : T_1 \vdash t : T_2}}{\Gamma \vdash \lambda x.t :: T_1 \to T_2'}$$

More specifically, the type we have derived is a subtype of the one we would have derived using subsumption.

Application rule. Any derivation of $\Gamma \vdash t_1\, t_2 :: T_b$ must end this way:

$$\frac{\dfrac{\Gamma \vdash t :: T' \quad T' <: T_a \to T_b}{\Gamma \vdash t : T_a \to T_b} \quad \dfrac{\Gamma \vdash t :: T'' \quad T'' <: T_a}{\Gamma \vdash t' : T_a}}{\Gamma \vdash t\, t' :: T_b}$$

We know by inversion on the subtyping relation that $T' <: T_a \to T_b$ can only hold if $T' = T_a' \to T_b'$ for some T_a' and T_b', with $T_a <: T_a'$ and $T_b' <: T_b$. So the derivation must actually look like this:

$$\frac{\dfrac{\Gamma \vdash t :: T_a' \to T_b' \quad \dfrac{T_a <: T_a' \quad T_b' <: T_b}{T_a' \to T_b' <: T_a \to T_b}}{\Gamma \vdash t : T_a \to T_b} \quad \dfrac{\Gamma \vdash t :: T'' \quad T'' <: T_a}{\Gamma \vdash t' : T_a}}{\Gamma \vdash t\, t' :: T_b}$$

By transitivity of subtyping (Theorem 7.10.5), we have $T'' <: T_a'$. This is the only constraint essentially needed here to allow an inference with the application typing rule. Except for this, we could just as well use trivial subsumptions, at the cost of assigning a different type to $t\, t'$ (namely, a subtype of T_b):

$$\frac{\dfrac{\Gamma \vdash t :: T_a' \to T_b' \quad \dfrac{T_a' <: T_a' \quad T_b' <: T_b'}{T_a' \to T_b' <: T_a' \to T_b'}}{\Gamma \vdash t : T_a' \to T_b'} \quad \dfrac{\Gamma \vdash t :: T'' \quad \dfrac{T'' <: T_a \quad T_a <: T_a'}{T'' <: T_a'}\,{\scriptstyle 7.10.5}}{\Gamma \vdash t' : T_a'}}{\Gamma \vdash t\, t' :: T_b'}$$

Based on these considerations, we can drop the subsumption rule completely from the system, with the one drawback that the final type we assign might be a

$$\frac{\Gamma(x) = T}{\Gamma \vdash x : T} \quad \frac{\Gamma, x : T_1 \vdash t : T_2}{\Gamma \vdash \lambda x.t : T_1 \to T_2} \quad \frac{\Gamma \vdash t_1 : T_2 \to T_1 \quad \Gamma \vdash t_2 : T_2' \quad T_2' <: T_2}{\Gamma \vdash t_1\, t_2 : T_1}$$

Figure 7.7: Type-assignment rules for STLC directly incorporating subtyping

subtype of the type we would have assigned previously. This results in the system shown in Figure 7.7. The preceding discussion is the essence of a proof of the following theorem (further details omitted):

Theorem 7.10.6. *Suppose that $\Gamma \vdash t : T$ is derivable using the rules of Figure 7.6. Then for some T' with $T' <: T$, the rules of Figure 7.7 allow us to derive $\Gamma \vdash t : T'$.*

What is the import of all this for algorithmic typing? If we consider the (subject-directed) rules of Figure 7.7, we see that the same annotation scheme we used for STLC without subtyping is sufficient here. We annotate λ-bound variables with their types in order to resolve the non-determinism in the typing rule for λ-abstractions. The only change we have to make is then to check that for the types T_2' and $T_2 \to T_1$ which we compute in the rule for applications, the subtyping judgment $T_2' <: T_2$ holds. As we have already observed, the subtyping rules are algorithmic and terminating, so this leads to an effective test for typability in STLC with subtyping.

Yet another alternative would be to develop constraint-generating versions of the type-assignment rules of Figure 7.7, as we did for the STLC type-assignment rules in Section 7.9. The only difference is that we need to add a subtyping constraint in the constraint-generating rule for typing applications. We would then need to extend our unification algorithm of Section 7.9.2 to decompose subtyping constraints between function types: if we have a constraint of the form $T_1 \to T_2 <: T_1' \to T_2'$, we can rewrite this to a pair of constraints $T_1' <: T_1$ and $T_2 <: T_2'$, taking into account the contravariance and covariance of the domain and range parts, respectively, of the function types. Further exploration of this approach is left as an exercise.

7.11   Conclusion

We considered several different type systems for lambda calculus, based on simple types consisting of base types and function types. Type-assignment rules are not algorithmic, but provide a solid foundation for theoretical study, including proofs of two important theorems: Semantic Soundness and Type Preservation. We also saw the Curry–Howard correspondence between proofs in minimal implicational logic and terms typable in simply typed lambda calculus. For algorithmic typing, we can add type annotations to certain subterms (either arguments in applications or λ-bound variables), or we can use constraint-generating rules to produce a set of constraints which, if solvable by unification, determine a substitution that can be applied to determine the most general type for the term. While we have studied these techniques in the setting of the simply typed lambda calculus (STLC), they are also very useful for extensions of STLC, some of which we will consider in subsequent chapters. We concluded with a look at how to extend these ideas to accommodate subtyping for simple types.

7.12   Basic Exercises

7.12.1   For Section 7.1, syntax of simple types

1. Fully parenthesize the following types:

   - $b_1 \to b_2 \to b_1$
   - $b_1 \to (b_1 \to b_2 \to b_3) \to b_4$

2. Drop as many parentheses as possible from these types:

   - $(b_1 \to b_2) \to (b_1 \to b_2)$
   - $(b_1 \to ((b_1 \to b_2) \to b_3))$

7.12.2   For Section 7.3, type-assignment rules

1. For each of the following terms, write out a typing derivation showing that the term can be assigned some particular type in the empty context, using the type-assignment rules of Figure 7.1:

   - $\lambda x.\lambda y.y$
   - $\lambda x.x \; \lambda y.y$
   - $\lambda x.\lambda y.x(xy)$

2. For each of the following, fill in the ? with a typing context which makes the typing judgment derivable (you do not need to write out the derivation):

   - $? \vdash x \, \lambda y.z : A$
   - $? \vdash y \, (z \, x) : A \to A$
   - $? \vdash \lambda z.x \, y \, y : A \to B$

7.12.3   For Section 7.7, the Curry-Howard isomorphism

1. Write derivations using the rules of Figure 7.2 for minimal implicational logic, for the following formulas (recall that $\to$ associates to the right, just as for simple types):

   - $b_1 \to b_2 \to b_1$

- $(b_1 \to b_2 \to b_3) \to (b_1 \to b_2) \to b_1 \to b_3$
- $b_1 \to (b_1 \to b_2) \to b_2$

2. Write down typing derivations for λ-terms which correspond, under the Curry-Howard isomorphism, to the derivations you wrote in the previous problem.

3. Write two more derivations of $b_1 \to (b_1 \to b_2) \to b_2$ (using the rules of Figure 7.2), and then show the corresponding λ-terms. You do not need to write out the typing derivations for those λ-terms.

7.12.4 For Section 7.8, algorithmic typing

1. Write a typing derivation in the empty context for an annotated version of each term below (same as one of the problems above), using the algorithmic type-checking rules with annotated applications:

   - $\lambda x.\lambda y.y$
   - $\lambda x.x \; \lambda y.y$
   - $\lambda x.\lambda y.x(xy)$

2. Repeat the previous exercise except with annotated λ-abstractions, using the algorithmic type computation rules.

7.12.5 For Section 7.9, algorithmic typing via constraint generation

1. Write a typing derivation in the empty context using the constraint-generating rules for the following (unannotated) terms (same as several problems above):

   - $\lambda x.\lambda y.y$
   - $\lambda x.x \; \lambda y.y$
   - $\lambda x.\lambda y.x(xy)$

2. For each of the following pairs of substitutions, state which of the following mutually exclusive possibilities holds: the first is strictly more general than the second, the second is strictly more general than the first, the two are equivalently general, or the two are incomparable.

   - $\{X \mapsto Y \to Z\}$ and $\{X \mapsto Y \to (b \to b)\}$
   - $\{X \mapsto Y \to Z\}$ and $\{X \mapsto Z \to Y\}$

7.12.6 For Section 7.10, subtyping

1. Draw a graph where the nodes are the following types, and there is an edge from T_1 to T_2 iff $T_1 <: T_2$, assuming $SubBase(bool, nat)$ (do not forget to include edges from every type to itself).

$$nat \to bool \qquad\qquad nat \to char$$

$$(bool \to bool) \to bool \qquad bool \to nat$$

$$bool \to nat \to bool \qquad bool \to char$$

$$nat \qquad\qquad nat \to nat \to bool$$

2. Some of the following terms are typable using the type-assignment rules for STLC plus subsumption in the context $\cdot, x : (bool \to nat) \to bool, y : nat$. For those terms which are typable, write out a typing derivation:

(a) $x\, y$

(b) $x\, \lambda z.y$

(c) $x\, (\lambda y.x\, \lambda y.y)$

(d) $\lambda f.\lambda g.g\, (x\, f)\, (f\, y)$

7.13 Intermediate Exercises

7.13.1 For Section 7.3, type assignment

1. Prove by induction on the structure of the derivation that if $\cdot \vdash t : T$ with the type-assignment system, then t must contain at least one λ-abstraction (this statement includes the case where t is itself a λ-abstraction).

7.13.2 For Section 7.4, semantic soundness

1. For this problem, let assignment I be defined as follows:

$$I(b_1) = \{\, t \mid \exists t'.\, t \leadsto^* t' \leadsto t' \,\}$$
$$\forall b \neq b_1.\, I(b) = Norm, \text{ the set of normalizing terms.}$$

Also, define the term $\hat{t}$ as follows:

$$\hat{t} = (\lambda x.\lambda y.y)\, ((\lambda x.x\, x)\, (\lambda x.x\, x))$$

(a) Is $\hat{t}$ in $[\![b_1]\!]\, I$?

(b) Is $\hat{t}$ in $[\![b_2]\!]\, I$, where $b_1 \neq b_2$?

(c) Give an example of a term which is in $[\![b_1 \to b_2]\!]\, I$, where $b_1 \neq b_2$, and argue using the definition above that this term is in that interpretation.

7.13.3   For Section 7.10, subtyping

1. The goal of this problem is to develop constraint-based typing for STLC with subtyping. This is done in several steps:

   (a) Write out constraint-generating versions of the type-assignment rules in Figure 7.7.

   (b) Extend the unification algorithm with new rules for subtyping constraints. How can you extend the termination metric of Section 7.9.5 to show termination of the processing of subtyping constraints?

   (c) Suppose that a set of constraints is in normal form with respect to your unification rules. Characterize when those constraints can be considered solved, and when they should be viewed as unsolvable. For one example, if we have a subtype constraint of the form $b <: T_1 \to T_2$ or $T_1 \to T_2 <: b$, we should consider the constraint set as unsolvable, since our subtyping rules do not permit such constraints.

   (d) Test your algorithm by generating and solving constraints with typing context $\cdot, y : nat \to bool$ and term

$$\lambda x.(\lambda z.(y\ (y\ z)))\ x$$

   This term is indeed typable in that context using the rules of Figure 7.7. What is the final set of solved constraints you compute? How should this be interpreted as describing the set of concrete types which can be assigned to the term in the given context?

Part II
Extra Topics

Chapter 8

Nondeterminism and Concurrency

Execution of WHILE programs is deterministic, as we proved in Chapter 4 (Theorem 4.2.1): there is exactly one possible final state that can result from any given starting state when running a particular command. That is, we cannot have $c, \sigma \Downarrow \sigma_1$ and $c, \sigma \Downarrow \sigma_2$, unless we have $\sigma_1 = \sigma_2$. In this chapter, we will consider three languages for which reduction is not deterministic. The first is a language of so-called *guarded commands*, due to Edsger Dijkstra [11]. In this language, programs contain groups of commands, each of which is guarded by some condition $t \, pred \, t'$. Execution proceeds by selecting a command from that group, when the command's guard is true (in the current state σ). Execution is nondeterministic because multiple guards may be enabled in the same state, and the operational semantics will then allow any one of the corresponding commands to be executed.

We will then consider an extension of WHILE with support for concurrent computation, where multiple commands may execute in an arbitrary interleaved fashion. Execution of such commands exhibits nondeterminism in the choice of interleaving. Concurrently executing commands may exchange information simply by assigning to variables, which are shared across commands; or else by waiting for a condition to become true, and then executing a command atomically.

Our final example of nondeterministic computation will be a language of concurrent interacting processes called simple CCS (Calculus of Communicating Systems), due to Robin Milner, and adapted from Chapter 4 of his book on the Π-calculus [28]. That book is concerned with the operational semantics of a formalism called the Π-calculus, in which concurrent processes can communicate with each other over named channels. A particular innovation in the Π-calculus is the ability of processes to transmit not just regular data over channels, but also the names of channels themselves, thus providing a model of a dynamically changing interconnection network between processes. A formalism very similar to CCS was independently developed by C. A. R. Hoare at around the time of Milner's original work on CCS [20].

More historical notes: Dijkstra won the Turing Award in 1972, Hoare (as we had occasion to note already in Chapter 3) in 1980, and Milner in 1991.

8.1 Guarded commands

The language of guarded commands has the following syntax, slightly adapted from [11].

$$
\begin{array}{lll}
\textit{guarded commands } g & ::= & t \textit{ pred } t' \rightarrow S \\
\textit{statement lists } S & ::= & s \mid S ; S' \\
\textit{statements } s & ::= & \text{if } G \text{ fi} \mid \text{do } G \text{ od} \mid x := t \mid \text{skip} \\
\textit{guarded command sets } G & ::= & g \mid G \ \square \ G'
\end{array}
$$

We will sometimes use E as a meta-variable ranging over any of the above expressions (that is, from any of our four syntactic categories s, S, g, or G). We will take the operators for forming statement lists (the comma operator) and guarded command sets (the box operator) as associating to the right. Let us say that the BNF definition of a syntactic category C_1 **depends on** the BNF definition of another category C_2 if the definition of C_1 mentions C_2. We can see that the definition of g above depends on the definition of S. In fact, we have a cyclic dependency chain:

$$g \text{ depends on } S \text{ depends on } s \text{ depends on } G \text{ depends on } g$$

This explains why the syntax is somewhat more difficult to grasp than the syntax of WHILE.

8.2   Operational semantics of guarded commands

To explain what the unfamiliar constructs of Dijkstra's guarded command language mean, we will use a small-step operational semantics, defined by the rules of Figure 8.2. The rules use the forms of judgments listed in Figure 8.1. First, let us consider the forms of judgments, and then the rules. The first four forms listed in Figure 8.1 are for evaluating statements s and statement lists S. For each of those two syntactic categories (s and S), small-step execution can either produce an S and a possibly new state σ', or else finish with a possibly new state σ'. The second four forms are for evaluating guarded commands g and guarded command sets G. For these syntactic categories, small-step execution either produces a new statement list S to execute, or else there is no execution possible (so execution of the guarded command or guarded command set is "done"). But in either case, the state does not change, and so we have the same σ on the right of the $\rightsquigarrow$-sign as on the left.

Now let us consider the rules themselves. The first three rules of Figure 8.2 are very similar to the small-step rules for assignment and sequencing from Chapter 4, Figure 4.2. The next three rules are for evaluating statements built with the if- and do-constructs. To understand what they are saying, it is helpful to know that the intended meaning of $G \rightsquigarrow S$ is that the guarded command set G can nondeterministically execute in one small step to S, without changing the state. Also, "G done" means that G cannot take a small step (for reasons we will consider shortly). So the if-statement will nondeterministically evaluate to S if G can take a step to S. There is no rule for evaluating an if-statement where G is done. This means that the if-statement does not execute at all in that case. This is an instance of **finite failure** : the statement cannot take a small step, and so does not converge

$$\frac{s,\sigma \rightsquigarrow S,\sigma'}{s,\sigma \rightsquigarrow \sigma'} \qquad \frac{S,\sigma \rightsquigarrow S,\sigma'}{S,\sigma \rightsquigarrow \sigma'}$$

$$\frac{g,\sigma \rightsquigarrow S,\sigma}{g,\sigma \text{ done}} \qquad \frac{G,\sigma \rightsquigarrow S,\sigma}{G,\sigma \text{ done}}$$

Figure 8.1: The forms of judgments used in the small-step rules of Figure 8.2

$$\frac{}{x := t,\sigma \rightsquigarrow \sigma[x \mapsto [\![t]\!]\sigma]} \qquad \frac{S_1,\sigma \rightsquigarrow S_1',\sigma'}{S_1;S_2,\sigma \rightsquigarrow S_1';S_2,\sigma'} \qquad \frac{S_1,\sigma \rightsquigarrow \sigma'}{S_1;S_2,\sigma \rightsquigarrow S_2,\sigma'}$$

$$\frac{G,\sigma \rightsquigarrow S,\sigma}{\texttt{if } G \texttt{ fi},\sigma \rightsquigarrow S,\sigma} \qquad \frac{G,\sigma \rightsquigarrow S,\sigma}{\texttt{do } G \texttt{ od},\sigma \rightsquigarrow S;\texttt{do } G \texttt{ od},\sigma} \qquad \frac{G,\sigma \text{ done}}{\texttt{do } G \texttt{ od},\sigma \rightsquigarrow \sigma}$$

$$\frac{G,\sigma \rightsquigarrow S,\sigma}{G \,\square\, G',\sigma \rightsquigarrow S,\sigma} \qquad \frac{G',\sigma \rightsquigarrow S,\sigma}{G \,\square\, G',\sigma \rightsquigarrow S,\sigma} \qquad \frac{G,\sigma \text{ done} \quad G',\sigma \text{ done}}{G \,\square\, G',\sigma \text{ done}}$$

$$\frac{[\![t \text{ pred } t']\!]\sigma = \text{True}}{t \text{ pred } t' \;\rightarrow\; S,\sigma \rightsquigarrow S,\sigma} \qquad \frac{[\![t \text{ pred } t']\!]\sigma = \text{False}}{t \text{ pred } t' \;\rightarrow\; S,\sigma \text{ done}}$$

Figure 8.2: Small-step rules for guarded commands

to a final state. In this sense, finite failure resembles divergence: neither result in convergence to a final state.

Finally, we have the guarded command sets G and the guarded commands $t \text{ pred } t' \;\rightarrow\; S$. A guarded command transitions to S if the guard $t \text{ pred } t'$ is true in the current state, and is done otherwise. A guarded command set transitions to S iff one of its guarded commands can transition to S, and is done otherwise. The nondeterminism of the language arises because more than one guard can be true in the same state, thus allowing transitions from one guarded command set to distinct statement lists S and S'.

8.2.1 A simple example

Let us first make the following abbreviating definitions:

$$
\begin{aligned}
g_1 &= (x > 0 \;\rightarrow\; x := 1)\\
g_2 &= (x = 0 \;\rightarrow\; x := 2)\\
g_3 &= (x \leq 0 \;\rightarrow\; x := 3)
\end{aligned}
$$

So g_1 abbreviates the guarded command $x > 0 \;\rightarrow\; x := 1$. Then using the rules of Figure 8.2, we have the following derivation of a small-step reduction for the command $g_1 \mathbin{\square} g_2 \mathbin{\square} g_3$:

$$\frac{\dfrac{x = 0 \;\rightarrow\; x := 2, \{x \mapsto 0\} \rightsquigarrow x := 2, \{x \mapsto 0\}}{g_2 \mathbin{\square} g_3, \{x \mapsto 0\} \rightsquigarrow x := 2, \{x \mapsto 0\}}}{g_1 \mathbin{\square} g_2 \mathbin{\square} g_3, \{x \mapsto 0\} \rightsquigarrow x := 2, \{x \mapsto 0\}}$$

But in the starting state $\{x \mapsto 0\}$ which we are using here, command g_3 is also enabled. So we have an alternative reduction from this same starting configuration, as shown by the following derivation:

$$\frac{\dfrac{x \le 0 \;\rightarrow\; x := 3, \{x \mapsto 0\} \rightsquigarrow x := 3, \{x \mapsto 0\}}{g_2 \mathbin{\square} g_3, \{x \mapsto 0\} \rightsquigarrow x := 3, \{x \mapsto 0\}}}{g_1 \mathbin{\square} g_2 \mathbin{\square} g_3, \{x \mapsto 0\} \rightsquigarrow x := 3, \{x \mapsto 0\}}$$

Of course, from each of the configurations we have reached in these two derivations, we can take an additional small step. In the first case, we have:

$$\frac{}{x := 2, \{x \mapsto 0\} \rightsquigarrow \{x \mapsto 2\}}$$

In the second, we have

$$\frac{}{x := 3, \{x \mapsto 0\} \rightsquigarrow \{x \mapsto 3\}}$$

So we have sequences of steps from $g_1 \square g_2 \square g_3, \{x \mapsto 0\}$ which result in different final states. This demonstrates that reduction of guarded commands can nondeterministically lead to different final results.

8.2.2 Multi-step reduction

We saw in Section 4.2.2 how to define multi-step reduction for WHILE from single-step reduction. As we have defined it so far, the semantics for the language of guarded has a rather large number of judgments: the eight of Figure 8.1. We would need quite a few rules if we wanted to describe multi-step reduction as we did in Figure 4.3, by showing how two judgments with matching ending and starting configurations can be concatenated. A more concise approach is to change our view of what the small-step judgments are for guarded commands. Rather than viewing the semantics as based on eight forms of judgment, let us instead view it as based on two judgments, "$C \rightsquigarrow C'$" and "C done" about configurations:

$$configurations\ C \;::=\; s, \sigma \mid S, \sigma \mid g, \sigma \mid G, \sigma \mid \sigma$$

That is, we think of the semantics as showing how to transition from one configuration C to another C', or else as showing that a configuration C is done. The rules of Figure 8.2 do not need to be changed with this change of perspective on the forms of judgment of the system. They are simply reinterpreted as deriving instances of one of the two forms of judgment about configurations, rather than as deriving instances of the eight forms of judgment of Figure 8.1. (Note that we include σ as a form of configuration so that small steps ending in a final state are included as transitions from configuration to configuration.) This change of perspective allows us to describe multi-step reduction as simply the reflexive-transitive closure, defined using the rules of Figure 4.4 in Section 4.2.3, of small-step reduction on configurations.

8.2.3   Determinism

The example in Section 8.2.1 showed that different reduction sequences can lead to different final results. Not all commands exhibit this behavior. Some commands will execute deterministically, even though reduction in the language is in general nondeterministic. Whenever the guards of all the guarded commands in a guarded command set G are mutually exclusive for a particular state, then G will execute deterministically from that state. For example, suppose $n \neq 0$ and suppose we use $\{x \mapsto n\}$ as the starting state for the command $g_1 \square g_2 \square g_3$ considered in Section 8.2.1. In this case, exactly one of the three guards will be enabled:

- $x > 0$ if $n > 0$.

- $x \leq 0$ if $n < 0$.

So there will be only one small-step reduction possible from that guarded command set in state $\{x \mapsto n\}$ with $n \neq 0$. Thus, this command executes deterministically. If an expression executes deterministically from starting state σ, we call that expression **deterministic** from that starting state.

8.2.4   Reduction graphs

Sometimes it is helpful to depict the possible reductions from a configuration graphically. A **reduction graph** does this, using the small-step operational semantics. The nodes of the graph are configurations, and there is an edge between one configuration and another if the corresponding $\leadsto$-judgment is provable using the rules of Figure 8.2. The nodes are usually specified by giving a starting configuration. The rest of the nodes are the ones reachable in one or more small steps from that starting configuration. An example is in Figure 8.3, for starting state $\{x \mapsto 1\}$ and the statement s defined as

$$\text{do } 0 = 0 \ \rightarrow \ x := -x \text{ od}$$

We can see from the graph that this statement is deterministic from starting state $\{x \mapsto 1\}$. Determinism shows up very clearly in a reduction graph, since it is equivalent to the property that each configuration has at most one outgoing edge. In this example, because the reduction graph is cyclic, we have exactly one outgoing edge for each node.

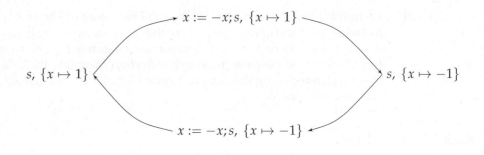

Figure 8.3: An example reduction graph

8.2.5   Confluence

We have just seen that guarded commands can execute nondeterministically lead-ing to different final results, and they can also execute deterministically, if their guards are always mutually exclusive in the states encountered during execution. Let us consider one further possibility (not the only one left). An expression E (from any of our four syntactic categories) is called **confluent** from state σ iff when-ever $E, \sigma \leadsto^* C_1$ and $E, \sigma \leadsto^* C_2$ for any configurations C_1 and C_2, then there exists some third configuration C_3 such that $C_1 \leadsto^* C_3$ and $C_2 \leadsto^* C_3$. A graphical depic-tion of this situation is shown in Figure 8.4. Notice that the property just requires that there is some configuration C_3 where the diverging reduction sequences that lead to C_1 and C_2 can be joined back up. Not every configuration reachable from C_1 or C_2 will play that role in general, nor is it the case that the reduction sequences leading to C_3 are the only ones possible from C_1 and C_2. Those commands might themselves have different reductions paths leading from them, which we might wish to join up at yet some other configurations.

Confluent reduction, which we will consider again in Chapter 9, is a well-behaved form of nondeterminism. A configuration may have multiple distinct reduction sequences leading from it, but such sequences always can be extended to join at a common configuration (C_3 in Figure 8.4). This implies in particular that a command which is confluent from state σ cannot reach distinct final states. For suppose we have $E, \sigma \leadsto^* \sigma_1$ and $E, \sigma \leadsto^* \sigma_2$. Then by confluence, there must be some configuration C_3 such that $\sigma_1 \leadsto^* C_3$ and $\sigma_2 \leadsto^* C_3$. But there are no single-step reductions possible from a configuration consisting of just a state, like configurations σ_1 and σ_2 in this case. So if we have $\sigma_1 \leadsto^* C_3$, this can only be by a 0-step reduction sequence. So $\sigma_1 = C_3$. Similar reasoning applies to $\sigma_2 \leadsto^* C_3$. So we have $\sigma_1 = C_3 = \sigma_2$, and we find that our final results σ_1 and σ_2 are not distinct.

If an expression is deterministic from starting state σ, it is also confluent from that starting state. Intuitively, the reason is that for deterministic expressions E, whenever we have $E \leadsto^* C_1$ and $E \leadsto^* C_2$, we must have either $C_1 \leadsto^* C_2$ or $C_2 \leadsto^* C_1$. This is because a deterministic expression only has a single reduction sequence, and so if we can reach configurations C_1 and C_2 from the starting con-figuration, that can only be because C_1 occurs earlier or at the same point in this

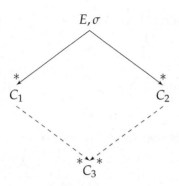

Figure 8.4: Graphical depiction of the property that expression E of the guarded command language is confluent from state σ. Whenever the multi-step reductions shown with solid lines are possible, there must exists a configuration C_3 such that the multi-step reductions shown with dashed lines are possible.

sequence as C_2, or vice versa. One of the exercises in Section 8.9.1 below asks you to make this argument more detailed.

As an example of confluence, consider the following statement, which we will abbreviate $\hat{s}$ below:

$$\text{do } (0 = 0 \to x := x + 1) \;\square\; (0 = 0 \to x := x - 1) \text{ od}$$

This command is confluent from any state σ, which we can prove as follows. First, we can prove that any configuration C reachable from starting configuration $\hat{s}, \sigma$ must be of one of the following three forms, for some state σ' with the same domain as σ:

- $x := x + 1; \hat{s}, \sigma'$

- $x := x - 1; \hat{s}, \sigma'$

- $\hat{s}, \sigma'$

To prove this, we prove by induction on the structure of the derivation of $C_1 \leadsto^* C_2$ that if C_1 is of one of those 3 forms shown (for some σ'), then so is C_2 (for a possibly different σ'). One base case is for when we have a 0-step reduction, using the third rule of Figure 4.4 (for the reflexive-transitive closure). In this case, $C_1 = C_2$, so C_2 is certainly of one of the three required forms if C_1 is. Another base case is for a one-step reduction, using the first rule of Figure 4.4. We just have to confirm that a single step from a configuration of one of the above forms leads to another configuration of such a form. If $C_1 = \hat{s}, \sigma'$, then the reduction to C_2 could be either the one derived this way:

$$\frac{\dfrac{[\![0 = 0]\!]\sigma' = \textit{True}}{0 = 0 \to x := x + 1, \sigma' \rightsquigarrow x := x + 1, \sigma'}}{\dfrac{(0 = 0 \to x := x + 1) \,\square\, (0 = 0 \to x := x - 1), \sigma' \rightsquigarrow x := x + 1, \sigma'}{\hat{s}, \sigma' \rightsquigarrow x := x + 1; \hat{s}, \sigma'}}$$

Or else the one derived this way:

$$\frac{\dfrac{[\![0 = 0]\!]\sigma' = \textit{True}}{0 = 0 \to x := x - 1, \sigma' \rightsquigarrow x := x - 1, \sigma'}}{\dfrac{(0 = 0 \to x := x + 1) \,\square\, (0 = 0 \to x := x - 1), \sigma' \rightsquigarrow x := x - 1, \sigma'}{\hat{s}, \sigma' \rightsquigarrow x := x - 1; \hat{s}, \sigma'}}$$

These are the only two possibilities, and they both result in a configuration C_2 of the appropriate form. If $C_1 = x := x + 1; \hat{s}, \sigma'$, then the only possible reduction is $x := x + 1; \hat{s}, \sigma' \rightsquigarrow \hat{s}, \sigma'[x \mapsto \sigma'(x) + 1]$. Similarly, if $C_1 = x := x - 1; \hat{s}, \sigma'$, then the only reduction is $x := x - 1; \hat{s}, \sigma' \rightsquigarrow \hat{s}, \sigma'[x \mapsto \sigma'(x) - 1]$.

That concludes our consideration of one-step reductions. The only step case of our inductive proof is for when we have an inference of this form:

$$\frac{C_1 \rightsquigarrow^* C' \qquad C' \rightsquigarrow^* C_2}{C_1 \rightsquigarrow^* C_2}$$

But here, by applying our induction hypothesis to the first premise, we know that C' is of one of the three required forms. We can then apply the induction hypothesis to the second premise to conclude that C_2 is, too, as required.

Now that we have established that reduction from $\hat{s}, \sigma$ can only lead to configurations of one of the three forms above, we can show confluence. Suppose we have $\hat{s}, \sigma \rightsquigarrow^* C_1$ and $\hat{s}, \sigma \rightsquigarrow^* C_2$. We will show that $C_1 \rightsquigarrow^* \hat{s}, \hat{\sigma}$ and $C_2 \rightsquigarrow^* \hat{s}, \hat{\sigma}$, where $\hat{\sigma} = \{x \mapsto 0\}$. For this, however, we would like to assume that C_1 and C_2 are both of the form $\hat{s}, \sigma'$ for some σ'. That is, we want to rule out the first two forms of our three listed above. That is easily done because if a configuration C is of one of those two first forms, it reduces (deterministically, though that is not essential to the argument) in one step to a configuration of the third form. So let us assume $C_1 = \hat{s}, \sigma_1$ and $C_2 = \hat{s}, \sigma_2$. We can now prove that for any σ', we have $\hat{s}, \sigma' \rightsquigarrow^* \hat{s}, \hat{\sigma}$. The proof is by induction on n, which we define to be $|\sigma'(x)|$, the absolute value of the integer value of x in state σ'. If $\sigma'(x) = 0$, then we already have $\sigma' = \hat{\sigma}$ and we are done. So suppose $\sigma'(x) \neq 0$. We now consider cases based on whether or not $\sigma'(x)$ is negative. If $\sigma'(x)$ is negative, then we have the following reduction steps:

$$\hat{s}, \sigma' \rightsquigarrow x := x + 1; \hat{s}, \sigma' \rightsquigarrow \hat{s}, \sigma'[x \mapsto n + 1]$$

The induction hypothesis applies since if $n < 0$, we know $|n + 1| < |n|$. So using the induction hypothesis, we get a derivation of $\hat{s}, \sigma'[x \mapsto n + 1] \rightsquigarrow^* \hat{s}, \hat{\sigma}$, which we can connect using the appropriate rule of Figure 4.4 (for reflexive-transitive closure) with the steps displayed above. This gives us the desired reduction sequence. If $\sigma'(x)$ is positive, then we start with the following steps instead:

$$\hat{s}, \sigma' \leadsto x := x - 1; \hat{s}, \sigma' \leadsto \hat{s}\sigma'[x \mapsto n - 1]$$

We again apply the induction hypothesis to conclude $\hat{s}\sigma'[x \mapsto n - 1] \leadsto^* \hat{s}, \hat{\sigma}$, which we can connect with the displayed steps to get the desired reduction sequence.

We have now proved that whenever $\hat{s}, \sigma \leadsto^* C_1$ and $\hat{s}, \sigma \leadsto^* C_2$, then $C_1 \leadsto^* \hat{s}, \hat{\sigma}$ and $C_2 \leadsto^* \hat{s}, \hat{\sigma}$. This shows that $\hat{s}$ is confluent from any starting state σ, as we set out to prove.

8.3 Concurrent WHILE

In this section, we consider an extension of the WHILE language with support for running commands concurrently. Communication between concurrently executing commands $c_1 \parallel c_2$ is supported using variables shared between the two commands, and by a form of guarded atomic action `await` t *pred* t' `then` c. This command will execute c atomically – that is, without allowing any interleaving of execution of any other commands – when the guard becomes true. We call this language concurrent WHILE, and distinguish it from the WHILE language of previous chapters by referring here to that language as *sequential* WHILE. The language we use is essentially the same as the one studied by Owicki and Gries [32]. They present their language via an axiomatic semantics for deriving partial correctness assertions (see Section 3.2), while here we use an operational semantics adapted from [7]. The two works just cited impose different restrictions on the form of command which may be used in the body of an `await`-command. Here, we restrict such commands so that they cannot use concurrent constructs or loops; only conditionals, assignments, and `skip` are allowed.

The abstract syntax of concurrent WHILE is:

$$
\begin{array}{lll}
\textit{simple commands } d & := & \texttt{skip} \mid x := t \mid d_1 \, ; \, d_2 \mid \texttt{if } t \textit{ pred } t' \texttt{ then } d_1 \texttt{ else } d_2 \\
\textit{commands } c & ::= & \texttt{skip} \mid x := t \mid c_1 \, ; \, c_2 \mid \texttt{if } t \textit{ pred } t' \texttt{ then } c_1 \texttt{ else } c_2 \mid \\
& & \texttt{while } t \textit{ pred } t' \texttt{ do } c \mid c_1 \parallel c_2 \mid \texttt{await } t \textit{ pred } t' \texttt{ then } d
\end{array}
$$

The new constructs here are the concurrent command $c_1 \parallel c_2$ and the guarded atomic command `await` t *pred* t' `then` d, where d does not contain concurrent executions, guarded atomic commands, or while loops. These restrictions are imposed on simple commands d to make them more appropriate for executing in an exclusive manner, where no other command can be executing concurrently. If such a command d could run for a long time or even diverge, it would not be suitable for atomic execution, as it would block all other concurrent commands for that whole time.

$$\frac{c_1,\sigma \rightsquigarrow \sigma'}{c_1 \,\|\, c_2, \sigma \rightsquigarrow c_2, \sigma'} \qquad \frac{c_2,\sigma \rightsquigarrow \sigma'}{c_1 \,\|\, c_2, \sigma \rightsquigarrow c_1, \sigma'} \qquad \frac{c_1,\sigma \rightsquigarrow c_1',\sigma'}{c_1 \,\|\, c_2, \sigma \rightsquigarrow c_1' \,\|\, c_2, \sigma'}$$

$$\frac{c_2,\sigma \rightsquigarrow c_2',\sigma'}{c_1 \,\|\, c_2, \sigma \rightsquigarrow c_1 \,\|\, c_2', \sigma'} \qquad \frac{[\![t \ pred \ t']\!]\sigma = \mathit{True} \qquad d,\sigma \rightsquigarrow^* \sigma'}{\texttt{await } t \ pred \ t' \texttt{ then } d, \sigma \rightsquigarrow \sigma'}$$

Figure 8.5: Small-step rules for the concurrent command $c_1 \,\|\, c_2$ and the guarded atomic command $\texttt{await } t \ pred \ t' \texttt{ then } d$.

8.4   Operational semantics of concurrent WHILE

The small-step operational semantics for concurrent WHILE is the same as for sequential WHILE (see Figure 4.2), except for the addition of the nondeterministic rules of Figure 8.5. Since every simple command d is also a command c, we do not give separate rules for execution of simple commands. Reduction of each form of simple command d should be understood to be defined by the rules for the corresponding form of command (so a sequencing simple command $d_1; d_2$ is reduced according to the rule for sequencing commands $c_1; c_2$).

The small-step formalism makes it easy to express atomic execution. The rule for `await`-commands makes use of the multi-step reduction for concurrent WHILE, to state that a single small step of an `await`-command is determined by a completion evaluation of the body d of the command, to a final state. Multi-step reduction is defined exactly as it was for sequential WHILE, using the rules of Figure 4.3 (in Chapter 4).

The model of concurrent execution we are using here is significantly simpler than what one finds in practice, because our rules treat evaluation of assignments and evaluation of guards as atomic actions. In real systems, however, they will not usually be atomic: other commands could be concurrently executed in the middle of evaluation of a guard, for example. We are using the simpler model here so that we can avoid having to define an operational semantics for terms and guards. It would not be difficult to do so, but the central issues with semantics of concurrent execution are already demonstrated without this feature, and adding it would clutter the presentation. We will get a better feel for how the semantics works as we turn now to some examples of concurrent WHILE commands.

8.4.1   Example: interleaved execution of assignments

Many different reduction sequences are possible for concurrently executing commands, due to the large number of interleavings between them. For example, suppose we have the following two commands:

$$\begin{aligned} c_1 &= (x := -1; y := -1) \\ c_2 &= (x := 1; y := 1) \end{aligned}$$

Let us think about the execution of the concurrent command $c_1 \| c_2$ from starting state $\{x \mapsto 0, y \mapsto 0\}$. One reduction sequence is the following, where we execute the first command until it is complete, and then the second one:

$$
\begin{array}{lll}
(x := -1; y := -1) & \| & (x := 1; y := 1), \quad \{x \mapsto 0, y \mapsto 0\} \\
\rightsquigarrow \quad y := -1 & \| & (x := 1; y := 1), \quad \{x \mapsto -1, y \mapsto 0\} \\
\rightsquigarrow & & (x := 1; y := 1), \quad \{x \mapsto -1, y \mapsto -1\} \\
\rightsquigarrow & & y := 1, \quad \{x \mapsto 1, y \mapsto -1\} \\
\rightsquigarrow & & \{x \mapsto 1, y \mapsto 1\}
\end{array}
$$

But there are several other sequences possible. For example, we could have the sequence which executes c_1 for one step, then c_2 for two, and then c_1 again for its last step:

$$
\begin{array}{lll}
(x := -1; y := -1) & \| & (x := 1; y := 1), \quad \{x \mapsto 0, y \mapsto 0\} \\
\rightsquigarrow \quad y := -1 & \| & (x := 1; y := 1), \quad \{x \mapsto -1, y \mapsto 0\} \\
\rightsquigarrow \quad y := -1 & \| & y := 1, \quad \{x \mapsto 1, y \mapsto 0\} \\
\rightsquigarrow \quad y := -1 & & , \quad \{x \mapsto 1, y \mapsto 1\} \\
\rightsquigarrow & & \{x \mapsto 1, y \mapsto -1\}
\end{array}
$$

We can interleave the execution of these assignments in order to get any final state σ' mapping x to either 1 or -1 and similarly for y.

The number of possible interleavings of two sequences of N assignments can be determined combinatorially as follows. An interleaving of two such commands can be thought of as a sequence of length $2 * N$ of the assignments from the two commands, in the order they are executed in that interleaving. For example, the interleavings corresponding to the two reduction sequences for our example are:

$$
\begin{array}{lcl}
\begin{aligned}
x &:= -1; \\
y &:= -1; \\
x &:= 1; \\
y &:= 1;
\end{aligned}
& \quad \text{and} \quad &
\begin{aligned}
x &:= -1; \\
x &:= 1; \\
y &:= 1; \\
y &:= -1;
\end{aligned}
\end{array}
$$

Since the order of commands within each sequence is fixed (in the above example, we cannot execute $y := 1$ before executing $x := 1$, since they are in sequence within the same command), it suffices to count how many different ways we can select N of the total $2 * N$ positions in the interleaving, for the assignments from the first command. The assignments from the second command will then go in the remaining N positions, but there is no choice there: they must be placed in the positions that are left. For the left interleaving displayed above, once we have chosen positions (1) and (2) for the assignments from c_1, then the assignments from c_2 are going to have to go in positions (3) and (4).

There are $\binom{2*N}{N}$ choices of N positions out of the total $2 * N$, so this gives us the number of interleavings:

$$
\binom{2*N}{N} = \frac{(2*N)!}{N! * (2*N - N)!} = \frac{(2*N)!}{N! * N!}
$$

This quantity is exponential in N. For the case of our simple example above, $N = 2$ and $\binom{2*N}{N} = 6$. Since there are only four possible final states for execution of $c_1 \parallel c_2$ in this case, we can conclude that some of the interleavings result in the same final state. *A priori*, it is not obvious whether we have two pairs of two interleavings each that yield the same final state, or three interleavings with the same final state. It turns out that in this case, it is the former situation. The first two interleavings are:

$$
\begin{array}{lll}
\begin{aligned}
x &:= 1; \\
y &:= 1; \\
x &:= -1; \\
y &:= -1;
\end{aligned}
& \text{and} &
\begin{aligned}
x &:= 1; \\
x &:= -1; \\
y &:= 1; \\
y &:= -1;
\end{aligned}
\end{array}
$$

These both result in the state $\{x \mapsto -1, y \mapsto -1\}$. The second two interleavings are then similar, but resulting in state $\{x \mapsto 1, y \mapsto 1\}$:

$$
\begin{array}{lll}
\begin{aligned}
x &:= -1; \\
y &:= -1; \\
x &:= 1; \\
y &:= 1;
\end{aligned}
& \text{and} &
\begin{aligned}
x &:= -1; \\
x &:= 1; \\
y &:= -1; \\
y &:= 1;
\end{aligned}
\end{array}
$$

8.4.2 Example using `await`

Here is an example of using `await` and concurrent commands to implement what is sometimes known as the fork/join concurrent-programming design pattern: a problem is divided into subproblems (the "fork" part of fork/join); these subproblems are given to multiple concurrent commands to solve; and when those commands have all completed their work, the results are recombined (the "join" part). For a simple example, let us consider the problem of computing $2^x + 3^x$ for nonnegative integer x by computing each of the quantities 2^x and 3^x concurrently, and then summing the results. Let us use the abbreviation $exp_{z,y,n}$ for the sequential WHILE command which computes n^y and stores that result in variable z, modifying variable y as it computes:

$$
exp_{z,y,n} = (z := 1; \texttt{while } y > 0 \texttt{ do } y := y - 1; z := z * n)
$$

Now the command to compute $2^x + 3^x$ and store the result in variable z can be written as follows:

$$
y := x; y' := x; (\texttt{exp}_{z,y,2} \parallel \texttt{exp}_{z',y',3} \parallel \texttt{await } y * y' = 0 \texttt{ then } z := z + z')
$$

The command first initializes the temporary variables y and y' to x, and then initiates a concurrent computation. This computation uses $\texttt{exp}_{z,y,2}$ to compute 2^y and store the result in z, and $\texttt{exp}_{z',y',3}$ to compute $3^{y'}$ and store the result in z'. The third concurrently executing command is waiting for both y and y' to become 0, signaling that both loops have finished. When this occurs, that third command sets z to the sum of the two computed quantities.

A note on concurrency and parallelism. Our operational semantics for a command of the form $c_1 \parallel c_2$ says that it executes by some arbitrary interleaving of the executions of c_1 and c_2. This does not appear to be quite the same as a parallel execution of c_1 and c_2, where certain events might truly happen at the same time, or at least at times which we do not distinguish. Indeed, there is a substantial literature in the theory of concurrency concerned with what is sometimes called **true concurrency**, where certain actions taken by concurrently executing commands are judged to have occurred simultaneously, or at least without any ordering between their times of occurrence. Here, we have adopted the simpler route of modeling parallel execution by interleaving, an approach to which a substantial literature is also devoted.

8.5   Milner's Calculus of Communicating Systems

In this section, we consider a fragment of Milner's Calculus of Communicating Systems (CCS), as presented in the first part of [28] (and adapting or building on a number of his definitions and examples). This is a language for concurrently executing processes, which can explicitly synchronize via named synchronization points. I am leaving out one feature from the languaged as defined in [28], just for a slightly simpler presentation: parametrized process names $A\langle a_1, \ldots, a_n \rangle$, which allow a recursively defined process A to be parametrized by values $a_1, \ldots, a_n$. We will also make some other minor modifications to Milner's formalization, for more explicit notation at a few points (in particular, for summations).

Figure 8.6 presents the syntax for unparametrized CCS, adapted from Chapter 4 of [28], omitting parametrized processes, as already mentioned. Note that in the syntax for actions, τ is a special constant (not a meta-variable), representing synchronization between two processes. Synchronization happens when one execution of one process produces label ℓ, and execution of another produces the complementary label $\bar{\ell}$. We will see precisely how this is defined when we consider the operational semantics below. We implicitly identify $\bar{\bar{\ell}}$ with just ℓ. For parsing, the "." operation in $\alpha.P$ binds more tightly than the other operators, and we will treat $+$ and $\mid$ as right-associative constructs of equal precedence.

For an informal introduction to the syntax for processes: A is the name for a recursively defined process; summations $\alpha_1.P_1 + \cdots + \alpha_n.P_n$ are processes which can perform one of the actions α_i and then continue with process P_i (discarding the other possible actions and processes in the summation); $P \mid P'$ is the concurrent process executing P and P' concurrently; new a P introduces a new name a with local scope P; and 0 is an empty process which does nothing. Milner uses notation $\Sigma_{i \in I} \alpha_i.P_i$ with finite index set I to subsume 0 (empty summation) and the summations S as we have defined them. Here we define a syntactic category of summations separately, rather than have the syntax for expressions use finite sets of subexpressions for the summands in Σ-expressions.

$$
\begin{array}{lll}
\textit{process identifiers } A & & \\
\textit{names } a & & \\
\textit{labels } \ell & ::= & a \mid \bar{\ell} \\
\textit{actions } \alpha & ::= & \ell \mid \tau \\
\textit{summations } S & ::= & \alpha.P \mid \alpha.P + S \\
\textit{processes } P & ::= & A \mid S \mid P|P' \mid \texttt{new } a\ P \mid 0
\end{array}
$$

Figure 8.6: Syntax of CCS (with unparametrized process identifiers only)

8.6 Operational semantics of CCS

The operational semantics for CCS is defined as follows. Execution is stateless, but we need to keep track of actions α performed by processes. Furthermore, unlike the presentation in Chapter 5 of [28], we will be explicit about the recursive equations $A = P$ (where A is a process identifier and P is the process it is recursively defined to equal). For this, we use a function Δ from process identifiers to processes. This is a convenient way of modeling of a set of recursive equations: to model $A_1 = P_1, \ldots, A_n = P_n$, we will use the function Δ with domain $\{A_1, \ldots, A_n\}$ which maps A_i to P_i for all $i \in \{1, \ldots, n\}$. We have no need to consider infinite sets of such equations, so we will restrict our attention to functions with finite domain.

Based on these ideas, our judgments for small-step reduction take the form $P \xrightarrow{\alpha}_{\Delta} P'$. Intuitively, this means that process P transitions (in one small step) to process P', executing action α, and possibly making use of recursive equations defined by Δ. The rules defining this small-step operational semantics are given in Figure 8.7. The first row of the figure gives rules for summations, which allow us to transition $\alpha_1.P_1 + \cdots + \alpha_n.P_n$ to P_i with action α_i, for any $i \in \{1, \ldots, n\}$. The second row gives rules for concurrent commands $P|Q$. The first two rules allow a concurrent command to step by allowing one of the concurrently executing commands to step. The third rule allows $P|Q$ to step with action τ if P and Q step with complementary labels ℓ and $\bar{\ell}$. This represents a synchronization of the two processes P and Q on label ℓ. Other processes executing concurrently with P and Q (in some larger process expression) can then no longer observe that an ℓ and a $\bar{\ell}$ action have been performed. They can only observe a τ transition, representing a synchronization action, which is internal to the concurrent process $P|Q$. The third row of Figure 8.7 gives the rule for transitioning from a process identifier A to the process it is defined by Δ to equal; and for process $\texttt{new } a\ P$. The latter transition on any action α as long as that action is not a or $\bar{a}$. The "new a" prefix is retained by the transition, since the resulting process may still make use of a.

8.6.1 Examples

A very simple example of a process is a message buffer. The buffer can receive a signal from its environment (whatever other processes there are with which it is executing concurrently), and then relay that message on. It receives the signal

$$\frac{}{\alpha.P \xrightarrow{\alpha}_\Delta P} \qquad \frac{}{\alpha.P + S \xrightarrow{\alpha}_\Delta P} \qquad \frac{S \xrightarrow{\alpha'}_\Delta P'}{\alpha.P + S \xrightarrow{\alpha'}_\Delta P'}$$

$$\frac{P \xrightarrow{\alpha}_\Delta P'}{P \,|\, Q \xrightarrow{\alpha}_\Delta P' \,|\, Q} \qquad \frac{Q \xrightarrow{\alpha}_\Delta Q'}{P \,|\, Q \xrightarrow{\alpha}_\Delta P \,|\, Q'} \qquad \frac{P \xrightarrow{\ell}_\Delta P' \quad Q \xrightarrow{\bar{\ell}}_\Delta Q'}{P \,|\, Q \xrightarrow{\tau}_\Delta P' \,|\, Q'}$$

$$\frac{\Delta(A) = P \quad P \xrightarrow{\alpha}_\Delta P'}{A \xrightarrow{\alpha}_\Delta P'} \qquad \frac{P \xrightarrow{\alpha}_\Delta P' \quad \alpha \neq a \quad \alpha \neq \bar{a}}{\text{new } a \; P \xrightarrow{\alpha}_\Delta \text{new } a \; P'}$$

Figure 8.7: Small-step reduction rules for CCS

$$\frac{}{P \xrightarrow{\;\;*}_\Delta P} \qquad \frac{P \xrightarrow{\alpha}_\Delta P'}{P \xrightarrow{\alpha\;*}_\Delta P'} \qquad \frac{P \xrightarrow{\gamma}_\Delta P'' \quad P'' \xrightarrow{\gamma'}_\Delta P'}{P \xrightarrow{\gamma\gamma'}_\Delta P'}$$

Figure 8.8: Rules for multi-step reduction for CCS

by synchronizing on one label, and then relays the messages by synchronizing on another. If we adopt the convention that senders use names a while receivers use complementary names $\bar{a}$, then the message buffer can be defined recursively this way, using a process identifier B:

$$B = \bar{a}.b.B$$

To see how this works, suppose we have processes P and Q that are waiting to send and receive using labels a and $\bar{b}$, respectively, and then to continue as P' and Q'. Now consider the concurrent command $P|B|Q$. It can reduce as follows:

$$P|B|Q \xrightarrow{\tau}_\Delta P'|b.B|Q \xrightarrow{\tau}_\Delta P'|B|Q'$$

The derivation for the first of these transitions is the following:

$$\frac{P \xrightarrow{a}_\Delta P' \qquad \dfrac{\dfrac{\Delta(B) = \bar{a}.b.B \quad \overline{\bar{a}.b.B \xrightarrow{\bar{a}}_\Delta b.B}}{B \xrightarrow{\bar{a}}_\Delta b.B}}{B|Q \xrightarrow{\bar{a}}_\Delta b.B|Q}}{P|(B|Q) \xrightarrow{\tau}_\Delta P'|(b.B|Q)}$$

If we wanted to buffer more than one a-signal, either because process P has temporarily gotten ahead of process Q or because we have other processes wanting to communicate by sending a-signals, then we could put use additional copies of B. For example, to allow buffering of two a-signals from P, we could use the process

$P|B|B|Q$, with two buffers B. Note that the order of the processes in the concurrent command does not matter. In fact, we have the following (whose proof is left as an exercise):

Lemma 8.6.1. *Whenever $P|Q \xrightarrow{\alpha}_\Delta P'|Q'$, then we also have $Q|P \xrightarrow{\alpha}_\Delta Q'|P'$.*

For another example, suppose we have a process P which can receive an a-signal and then continue as P'. Suppose further that we want to be able to enable or disable that behavior using a signal b as a toggle. Then we can use a recursively defined process A (represented by a function Δ as above):

$$A = \bar{b}.(\bar{b}.A + P)$$

The idea here is that when A receives a b-signal, then it proceeds as $\bar{b}.A + P$. This process can respond to either a b-signal, in which case it will proceed as A (thus waiting for another b-signal before it will allow communication with P), or else to an a-signal, which will be handled by P. So we have reduction sequences like:

$$A \xrightarrow{\bar{b}}_\Delta (\bar{b}.A + P) \xrightarrow{a}_\Delta P'$$

But we also have sequences like this:

$$A \xrightarrow{\bar{b}}_\Delta (\bar{b}.A + P) \xrightarrow{\bar{b}}_\Delta A$$

So when A interacts with the environment, it may allow an a-signal to reach P or else, if its b-signal is toggled first, it may not.

For an example using new, consider this process:

$$\text{new } a \ (\bar{b}.a.P | \bar{c}.\bar{a}.Q)$$

This process uses a new name "a" as an internal synchronization point: the process does not allow P and Q to continue until both the signals b and c have been received. But unlike the process $\bar{b}.\bar{c}.(P|Q)$, this process allows b and c to be received in either order. One of its possible reduction sequences is this:

$$\text{new } a \ (\bar{b}.a.P | \bar{c}.\bar{a}.Q) \xrightarrow{\bar{b}}_\Delta \text{new } a \ (a.P | \bar{c}.\bar{a}.Q) \xrightarrow{\bar{c}}_\Delta \text{new } a \ (a.P | \bar{a}.Q) \xrightarrow{\tau}_\Delta \text{new } a \ (P|Q)$$

8.6.2   Multi-step reduction for CCS

To define a suitable notion of multi-step reduction, we first define what it means for one process to transition to another generating a sequence of actions $\alpha_1 \ldots \alpha_n$. We will use γ as a meta-variable for sequences of actions, and write $\cdot$ for the empty such sequence, and $\gamma\gamma'$ for concatenation of sequences. The rules of Figure 8.8 derive judgments of the form $P \xrightarrow{\gamma}{}^*_\Delta P'$, with the intended meaning that P transitions in 0 or more small steps to P', generating the sequence of actions γ. For example, recall the following sequence of reductions from our example in Section 8.6.1

above (where we have B recursively defined by Δ to be $a.\bar{b}.B$, and we assume $P \xrightarrow{\bar{a}}_\Delta P'$ and $Q \xrightarrow{b}_\Delta Q'$):

$$P|B|Q \xrightarrow{\tau}_\Delta P'|\bar{b}.B|Q \xrightarrow{\tau}_\Delta P'|B|Q'$$

Connecting these two steps using the rules of Figure 8.8, we get the following multi-step reduction:

$$P|B|Q \xrightarrow{\tau\tau}_\Delta P'|B|Q'$$

Because τ actions are not observable by concurrently executing processes, we may wish to define a version of multi-step reduction which abstracts those steps away (cf. Chapter 6 of [28]). Let us first define the erasure $|\gamma|$ of γ, so that it drops τ actions:

$$\begin{aligned}
|\cdot| &= \cdot \\
|\ell\gamma| &= \ell|\gamma| \\
|\tau\gamma| &= |\gamma|
\end{aligned}$$

Now we define $P \xRightarrow{\gamma}_\Delta P'$ iff there exists γ' such that $|\gamma'| = \gamma$ and $P \xrightarrow{\gamma'}_\Delta P'$. We will call this observational reduction. From the example multi-step reduction above, we get the following observational reduction, because erasure drops both τ actions:

$$P|B|Q \xRightarrow{\cdot}_\Delta P'|B|Q'$$

On the other hand, consider this reduction sequence, for a slightly different starting process (using the same facts about P, B, Q, and Δ as above):

$$P|P|B|Q \xrightarrow{\tau}_\Delta P|P'|\bar{b}.B|Q \xrightarrow{\bar{b}}_\Delta P|P'|B|Q \xrightarrow{\tau}_\Delta P'|P'|\bar{b}.B|Q$$

From this, we can obtain the following multi-step reduction:

$$P|P|B|Q \xrightarrow{\tau\bar{b}\tau}_\Delta P'|P'|\bar{b}.B|Q$$

And from that multi-step reduction, we get this observational reduction:

$$P|P|B|Q \xRightarrow{\bar{b}}_\Delta P'|P'|\bar{b}.B|Q$$

8.6.3 Process algebra based on bisimulation

The small-step operational semantics of CCS provides us with a calculus for reasoning about the execution of processes written in the CCS language. The simplest form of reasoning about execution is simply to prove judgments about processes: single-step, multi-step, or observational reductions. We can also prove lemmas like Lemma 8.6.1 above, that express patterns of reduction.

Going further, the inventors of process calculi like CCS and CSP were interested in deriving algebraic laws equating different processes. It seems reasonable that there should be some notion of equality $\approx$ such that $P|Q \approx Q|P$, for example; or that $P|0 \approx P$ (since 0 cannot perform any actions, running it concurrently with P is the same as just running P). A **process algebra** is an algebraic theory of processes, concerned mostly with notions of equality justifying intuitive equivalences between processes like those just mentioned. The notion of bisimulation is central to process algebras like that for CCS. To define this concept, we first need the notion of a simulation.

Definition 8.6.2 (Simulation). *A simulation of process P by process Q with respect to Δ is a binary relation $\sqsubseteq$ on processes such that whenever $P \xrightarrow{\alpha}_\Delta P'$ and $P \sqsubseteq Q$, then there exists a process Q' such that $Q \xrightarrow{\alpha}_\Delta Q'$ and $P' \sqsubseteq Q'$.*

Process Q simulates P with respect to Δ if there exists a simulation of P by Q with respect to Δ.

If $\sqsubseteq$ is a simulation of P by Q, then intuitively Q can match all the transitions of P (but may have more transitions it can perform). For a well-known simple example, let P be the process $a.b.0 + a.c.0$, and let Q be $a.(b.0 + c.0)$. Since we are not using any recursive equations, the simulation results we are about to discuss hold for any Δ. Given these definitions of P and Q, Q simulates P (with respect to any Δ) but not vice versa. A simulation $\sqsubseteq$ of P by Q can be defined as follows:

$$
\begin{aligned}
a.b.0 + a.c.0 &\sqsubseteq a.(b.0 + c.0)\\
b.0 &\sqsubseteq b.0 + c.0\\
c.0 &\sqsubseteq b.0 + c.0\\
0 &\sqsubseteq 0
\end{aligned}
$$

Let us confirm that this is indeed a simulation of P by Q. For each relational fact $X \sqsubseteq Y$ included in the definition above of $\sqsubseteq$, we must confirm that whenever we have $X \xrightarrow{\alpha}_\Delta X'$, then there is some Y' with $Y \xrightarrow{\alpha}_\Delta Y'$ and $X' \sqsubseteq Y'$.

- For $a.b.0 + a.c.0 \sqsubseteq a.(b.0 + c.0)$: the only transition of the left-hand side (lhs) process is a, but it can lead to two resulting processes, either $b.0$ or $c.0$. The rhs process can only transition via a to one process, namely $b.0 + c.0$. Considering the first transition of the lhs: if we have $a.b.0 + a.c.0 \xrightarrow{a}_\Delta b.0$, then we indeed have $a.(b.0 + c.0) \xrightarrow{a}_\Delta (b.0 + c.0)$ with $b.0 \sqsubseteq b.0 + c.0$. Considering the second: if we have $a.b.0 + a.c.0 \xrightarrow{a}_\Delta c.0$, then we indeed have $a.(b.0 + c.0) \xrightarrow{a}_\Delta (b.0 + c.0)$ with $c.0 \sqsubseteq b.0 + c.0$.

- For $b.0 \sqsubseteq b.0 + c.0$: the lhs process transitions on b to 0. The rhs can also transition to 0 on b, and we have $0 \sqsubseteq 0$. Note that the rhs can also transition to 0 on c, but that is not relevant for showing that the rhs process can match the behavior of the lhs process.

- For $c.0 \sqsubseteq b.0 + c.0$: this case is just like the previous one.

- For $0 \sqsubseteq 0$: the lhs does not transition at all, so the required property is vacuously true.

Let us now show that there does not exist any simulation of Q (that is, $a.(b.0 + c.0)$) by P (that is, $a.b.0 + a.c.0$). It suffices to consider all the possible binary relations holding between processes reachable from Q and those reachable from P, and show that all these relations fail to be simulations. For any such relation $\sqsubseteq$, we must have the following relationship, or else we already can conclude that $\sqsubseteq$ is not a simulation of Q by P:

$$a.(b.0 + c.0) \sqsubseteq a.b.0 + a.c.0$$

Now there is only one transition from the lhs process, namely $a.(b.0 + c.0) \xrightarrow{a}_\Delta b.0 + c.0$. There are two transitions from the rhs process on a, either to $b.0$ or to $c.0$. So for $\sqsubseteq$ to be a simulation, we must have either

$$b.0 + c.0 \sqsubseteq b.0$$

or else

$$b.0 + c.0 \sqsubseteq c.0$$

But in either case, $\sqsubseteq$ fails to be a simulation, since in either case, the lhs process has a transition that the rhs process cannot match. In the first case, we have $b.0 + c.0 \xrightarrow{c}_\Delta 0$, but the rhs process has no c transition; and in the second, we have $b.0 + c.0 \xrightarrow{b}_\Delta 0$, but the rhs process has no b transition. So no $\sqsubseteq$ can be a simulation of Q by P, and hence by definition, P does not simulate Q.

Recall from basic set theory that if R is a binary relation on a set A, then its inverse R^{-1} is the relation defined by:

$$\{(y, x) \in A \times A \mid (x, y) \in R\}$$

Definition 8.6.3. *A bisimulation between processes P and Q with respect to Δ is a binary relation $\sqsubseteq$ on processes such that $\sqsubseteq$ is a simulation of P by Q and $\sqsubseteq^{-1}$ is a simulation of Q by P.*

Process P and Q are bisimilar with respect to Δ if there exists a bisimulation between P and Q with respect to Δ.

If the relation in question is an equivalence relation $\approx$, then $\approx^{-1} = \approx$ (since the relation is symmetric), and we must just check that whenever $P \approx Q$ and $P \xrightarrow{\alpha}_\Delta P'$, there exists $Q' \approx P'$ such that $Q \xrightarrow{\alpha}_\Delta Q'$.

Let us consider an example of bisimilar processes, where we use abbreviations X and Y:

$$\begin{aligned} X &= \text{new } a\ (b.a.P | c.\bar{a}.Q) \\ Y &= b.c.\tau.(P|Q) + c.b.\tau.(P|Q) \end{aligned}$$

Let $\approx$ be the symmetric closure of the relation defined by the following facts:

$$\begin{aligned} X &\approx Y \\ \text{new } a\ (a.P | c.\bar{a}.Q) &\approx c.\tau.(P|Q) \\ \text{new } a\ (b.a.P | \bar{a}.Q) &\approx b.\tau.(P|Q) \\ \text{new } a\ (a.P | \bar{a}.Q) &\approx \tau.(P|Q) \\ \text{new } a\ (P|Q) &\approx (P|Q) \end{aligned}$$

Confirming that this is indeed a bisimulation is left as an exercise.

There is much more one can study about process algebra. I recommend Milner's book [28] as a starting point for further topics, including notions of bisimulation based on observational reduction (where different numbers of τ-actions need not prevent processes from being bisimilar), and communication of data rather than just synchronization.

8.7   Conclusion

In this chapter, we have explored operational semantics for three different languages featuring nondeterministic computation. The language of guarded commands has a nondeterministic operational semantics, because multiple guards can be enabled in the same state, resulting in a nondeterministic choice of which of the commands which are being guarded should be executed. The concurrent WHILE language allows multiple WHILE commands to be executed concurrently, and also has a language feature `await` for guarded atomic commands: when the guard of the `await`-command is true, the body of the command is executed in a single atomic step. Finally, Milner's Calculus of Communicating Systems (CCS) is based on a stateless model of concurrent computation, where processes synchronize via named signals. All three of these languages have been important historically in the theoretical study of concurrency, and considering them all from the standpoint of operational semantics provides a common foundation for comparison. For example, of these languages, only concurrent WHILE explicitly includes a notion of atomic action. Efficient implementation of atomic regions using a method called software transactional memory (STM) has been, at the time of writing, a subject of significant recent research interest [35]. Another notable difference is CCS's focus on synchronization between concurrently executing processes, which is not explicitly supported in the other two languages. There is certainly much more to the theory and practice of concurrent computation than we have surveyed in this chapter, but the formalisms we have considered are foundational for much of the research literature on this topic. Furthermore, studying them has provided a good testbed for operational semantics, which has given us a clear and notationally light way to define their semantics.

8.8   Basic exercises

8.8.1   For Section 8.1, syntax of guarded commands

1. Identify the syntactic category or categories to which the following expressions, which are all syntactically well-formed, belong. Note that certain expressions are both statements s and statement lists S, for example, so there might be two categories for some expressions (you should indicate both in such cases).

(a) $x > 0 \rightarrow x := x - 1$

(b) `if` $x > 0 \rightarrow$ `do` $0 = 0 \rightarrow$ `skip od fi`

(c) $x := 1;$ `skip`

(d) $(x > 0 \rightarrow x := x - 1) \,\square\, (y > 0 \rightarrow y := y - 1)$

8.8.2 For Section 8.2, operational semantics of guarded commands

1. Write down a derivation using the rules of Figure 8.1 for each of the following small-step reductions, where s is the statement `if` $x \geq y \rightarrow z := x \,\square\, x \leq y \rightarrow z := y$ `fi`, σ_1 is $\{x \mapsto 4, y \mapsto 3, z \mapsto 0\}$, and σ_2 is $\{x \mapsto 3, y \mapsto 3, z \mapsto 0\}$:

   (a) $s, \sigma_1 \rightsquigarrow z := x, \sigma_1$

   (b) $s, \sigma_2 \rightsquigarrow z := x, \sigma_2$

   (c) $s, \sigma_2 \rightsquigarrow z := y, \sigma_2$

2. For each of the expressions E in Problem 1 of Section 8.8.1, write down a reduction sequence from $E, \{x \mapsto 1, y \mapsto -1\}$ to some final state σ. You do not need to write down derivations for the steps in this sequence.

3. Draw the reduction graph for the expression below, from starting state $\{x \mapsto 6\}$:

$$\text{do } x > 0 \rightarrow x := x - 3 \,\square\, x \geq 0 \rightarrow x := x - 5$$

8.8.3 For Section 8.4, operational semantics of concurrent WHILE

1. Write down a derivation of the following judgment:

$$x := 2 \,\|\, y := x, \{x \mapsto 0, y \mapsto 1\} \rightsquigarrow \{x \mapsto 2, y \mapsto 2\}$$

2. Are any other final states reachable by executing $x := 2 \,\|\, y := x$ from starting state $\{x \mapsto 0, y \mapsto 1\}$ (besides the one in the previous problem)?

8.8.4 For Section 8.6, operational semantics of CCS

1. Write down derivations, using the rules of Figure 8.7, for the following judgments:

   (a) $(a.0 + b.0)|\bar{b}.0 \xrightarrow{a}_{\Delta} 0|\bar{b}.0$

   (b) $(a.0 + b.0)|\bar{b}.0 \xrightarrow{\tau}_{\Delta} 0|0$

   (c) $0|\tau.a.0 \xrightarrow{\tau}_{\Delta} 0|a.0$

2. Write down one reduction sequence starting with the given process and ending in a process for which no further reduction is possible. There may be more than one reduction sequence possible, in which case you should just pick one and show that. If Δ is specified, then use it for your sequence.n

(a) $b.(a.0 + \bar{a}.0)$

(b) new a $(a.b.0|\bar{a}.c.0)$

(c) new a $(a.a.A|\bar{a}.b.a.B)$, where $\Delta(A) = b.A$ and $\Delta(B) = \bar{b}.B$.

(d) $(a.b.0 + \bar{a}.\bar{b}.0)|a.0|b.0$

(e) $A + B$, where $\Delta(A) =$ new c $a.c.A$ and $\Delta(B) = b.A$

8.9 Intermediate exercises

8.9.1 For Section 8.2, operational semantics of guarded commands

1. For each of the following configurations, draw the reduction graph starting at the configuration, and state whether the given expression is deterministic, confluent but not deterministic, or nonconfluent from the given starting state.

   (a) do $x \leq 1 \rightarrow x := x + 1 \square x \geq -1 \rightarrow x := x - 1$ od, $\{x \mapsto 0\}$

   (b) if $x = y \rightarrow x := x + 1 \square x \leq y \rightarrow x := x - 1; y := y + 1$ fi, $\{x \mapsto 0, y \mapsto 1\}$

2. Give an example of an expression E which is deterministic for a state σ_1, confluent but not deterministic for a state σ_2, and not confluent for a state σ_3. Show the expression, the three states, and the reduction graphs demonstrating the relevant properties (deterministic, confluent but not deterministic, and non-confluent) for each state.

3. Give a detailed proof of the fact that if expression E is deterministic from state σ, then whenever we have $E, \sigma \leadsto^* C_1$ and $E, \sigma \leadsto^* C_2$, we must have $C_1 \leadsto^* C_2$ or $C_2 \leadsto^* C_1$. Hint: reason by induction on the derivation of $E, \sigma \leadsto^* C_1$, with a case analysis of the derivation of $E, \sigma \leadsto^* C_2$. Your proof will essentially construct a derivation of $C_1 \leadsto^* C_2$ or else $C_2 \leadsto^* C_1$, by taking apart the derivations of $E, \sigma \leadsto^* C_1$ and $E, \sigma \leadsto^* C_2$.

8.9.2 For Section 8.4, operational semantics of concurrent WHILE

1. Show all possible reduction sequences of the concurrent command $x := 1 \mathbin{||} y := x \mathbin{||} x := 2$ from starting state $\{x \mapsto 5, y \mapsto 10\}$. You do not need to write out formal derivations for the reductions in the sequence.

2. Give an example of a concurrent command which has both a terminating and a diverging reduction sequence.

8.9.3 For Section 8.6, operational semantics of simple CCS

1. Find a process P with the following characteristics:

- it does not explicitly use τ (in any summation), and

- it has exactly one reduction sequence, which is infinite and produces only τ actions.

2. Give a detailed proof of Lemma 8.6.1. Hint: proceed by induction on the structure of the assumed derivation of $P|Q \xrightarrow{\alpha}_\Delta P'|Q'$.

3. Prove that the following relation (from Section 8.6.3) is indeed a bisimulation between the first two processes listed:

$$
\begin{array}{rcl}
\text{new } a\ (b.a.P|c.\bar{a}.Q) & \approx & b.c.\tau.(P|Q) + c.b.\tau.(P|Q) \\
\text{new } a\ (a.P|c.\bar{a}.Q) & \approx & c.\tau.(P|Q) \\
\text{new } a\ (b.a.P|\bar{a}.Q) & \approx & b.\tau.(P|Q) \\
\text{new } a\ (a.P|\bar{a}.Q) & \approx & \tau.(P|Q) \\
\text{new } a\ (P|Q) & \approx & (P|Q)
\end{array}
$$

4. For each of the following pairs of processes, state whether or not the first simulates the second. Justify your answers by exhibiting the simulation relation in question and arguing that it is indeed a simulation, or else by arguing that no simulation is possible (as we did in Section 8.6.3).

   (a) $(\text{new } a\ (a.0|\bar{a}.0))$ and $\tau.\tau.0$.

   (b) $a.(b.0|c.0)$ and $a.(b.0 + c.0)$.

   (c) $\tau.\tau.0$ and $a.b.0|\bar{a}.0|\bar{b}.0$.

Chapter 9

More on Untyped Lambda Calculus

In this chapter, we consider several results and ideas related to untyped lambda calculus, as presented in Chapter 5. The first is *confluence* of full β-reduction (see Section 5.2) for untyped lambda calculus. Confluence says that if we can reduce a starting term t to terms s_1 and s_2 in multiple steps, then there must exist some term $\hat{s}$ to which we can reduce both s_1 and s_2 (again, in multiple steps). We considered confluence already in this book, when we were studying nondeterministic reduction of guarded commands (Section 8.2.5). Our study here will begin with an abstract consideration of confluence, not tied to a particular reduction relation. We will then present a proof of confluence due to Tait and Martin-Löf, and simplified by Takahashi [37].[1] The proof is short and elegant, and will give us an occasion to see a number of useful generic concepts about reduction relations.

Second, we will consider an even more minimalistic programming language than lambda calculus, known as a combinator language. The language uses two primitive constants S and K, which manipulate their arguments in certain ways when applied. It has no notion of variable at all, making it more primitive, in that sense, than lambda calculus. We will define a small-step operational semantics for these combinators, and show the remarkable result that terms of lambda calculus can be faithfully translated into combinators, at least under call-by-value semantics.

Finally, we will study an alternative syntax for untyped lambda calculus, based on so-called de Bruijn indices. In this notation, λ-abstraction has the syntax $\lambda.t$. The λ-abstractor does not actually introduce a named variable. Rather, whenever one wishes to refer in t to the variable introduced by that abstractor, one uses a number n equal to the number of other λ-abstractors which intervene between the use of the variable and the abstractor which introduced it. This notation avoids many of the difficulties of working with named variables and α-equivalence, at the cost of a more complex notion of substitution.

9.1   Confluence of untyped lambda calculus

We will work in this section with full β-reduction for untyped lambda calculus. As we noted in Section 5.2.4, lambda calculus is nondeterministic. We can have terms which reduce in multiple different ways, depending on the order in which we contract their β-redexes. For example, consider this term, where I abbreviates

---

[1]According to Takahashi, neither of the original proofs by Tait and Martin-Löf were ever published by them [37]. Section 3.2 of Barendregt's contains a version of their proof [5].

$\lambda y.y$:

$$(\lambda x.x\ x)\ \lambda x.I\ (x\ x)$$

If we reduce the outermost redex consisting of the whole term, we will get:

$$(\lambda x.I\ (x\ x))\ \lambda x.I\ (x\ x)$$

If we again reduce the outermost redex, we have:

$$I\ ((\lambda x.I\ (x\ x))\ \lambda x.I\ (x\ x))$$

We can continue this reduction sequence to get this:

$$I\ (I\ ((\lambda x.I\ (x\ x))\ \lambda x.I\ (x\ x)))$$

We can get any number of applications of the identity function I at the beginning of this term:

$$I\ \cdots\ (I\ ((\lambda x.I\ (x\ x))\ \lambda x.I\ (x\ x)))$$

But remarkably, all of these terms can be reduced to a common term. For we could reduce the innermost β-redex of the original term $(\lambda x.x\ x)\ \lambda x.I\ (x\ x)$, namely $I\ (x\ x)$, to obtain the familiar looping term:

$$(\lambda x.x\ x)\ \lambda x.x\ x$$

And all the above terms can be reduced to this. For example, we have:

$$
\begin{aligned}
&I\ (I\ ((\lambda x.I\ (x\ x))\ \lambda x.I\ (x\ x)))\\
\leadsto\ &(I\ ((\lambda x.I\ (x\ x))\ \lambda x.I\ (x\ x)))\\
\leadsto\ &(\lambda x.I\ (x\ x))\ \lambda x.I\ (x\ x)\\
\leadsto\ &(\lambda x.x\ x)\ \lambda x.I\ (x\ x)\\
\leadsto\ &(\lambda x.x\ x)\ \lambda x.x\ x
\end{aligned}
$$

While it may have seemed intuitive that this would work out, since we always have $I\ t \leadsto t$, it is not obvious that all reductions from a starting term can always be extended to some common term, or how to prove this. The fact that we do have this property – that lambda calculus is **confluent** – will be proved in the rest of this section. The proof itself is remarkably short, though somewhat tricky. First, though, we will consider a generic notion of confluence, and study some of its properties. Confluence is important in programming languages theory generally, and so it is worthwhile to stop and look into it more deeply.

9.1.1   Abstract reduction systems and their properties

A generic notion of confluence can be elegantly developed in the context of *abstract reduction systems* (ARSs) (cf. Chapter 1 of [38], or Chapter 2 of [3]). See the "Mathematical Background" section at the end of this book for a refresher on some of the concepts we will now use to define ARSs and related notions. This section builds up enough of this theory to prove the correctness of one particular approach, embodied in Theorem 9.1.8 below, to showing confluence. There are many more important results in the theory of confluence than we will be able to cover here. The interested reader can consult the two books cited above for much more on this topic.

An abstract reduction system $(A, \rightarrow)$ consists of a set A of some objects, and a binary relation $\rightarrow$ on A (so $\rightarrow \subseteq A \times A$). We will write $a_1 \rightarrow a_2$ to mean $(a_1, a_2) \in \rightarrow$ (that is, a_1 and a_2 are related by relation $\rightarrow$). Any directed graph can be viewed as an abstract reduction system, since a graph consists of a set V of vertices and a set E of directed edges. This exactly matches the form of an ARS: V is the set of objects, and E is the relation on it. We will now define several important concepts related to ARSs.

Composition

If we have ARSs $(A, \rightarrow_1)$ and $(A, \rightarrow_2)$, then we can compose their relations to get an ARS $(A, \rightarrow_1 \cdot \rightarrow_2)$, where $\rightarrow_1 \cdot \rightarrow_2$ denotes the composition of the relations:

$$\rightarrow_1 \cdot \rightarrow_2 = \{(x, z) \in A \times A \mid \exists y.\, x \rightarrow_1 y \wedge y \rightarrow_2 z\}$$

Composition of a relation with itself can be iterated, using this recursive definition, which implicitly depends on A (that is, the relation $\rightarrow^0$ will be different if the underlying set A of the ARS is different, even if the relational part of the ARS is the same):

$$\begin{aligned} \rightarrow^0 &= \{(a, a) \mid a \in A\} \\ \rightarrow^{n+1} &= \rightarrow \cdot \rightarrow^n \end{aligned}$$

The relation $\rightarrow^0$ (with A implicitly specified) is also called the identity relation on A, and sometimes denoted Id_A.

For an example, suppose that ARS $(A, \rightarrow)$ is presented graphically as:

Then the ARS $(A, \rightarrow^0)$ (the identity relation on A) can be depicted as:

The ARS $(A, \rightarrow^1)$ is just the original relation, since composing $\rightarrow$ with the identity relation on A just results in $\rightarrow$. The relation $(A, \rightarrow^2)$ is the following. For every 2 edges consecutive edges in the original graph, we get a single edge here for $\rightarrow^2$:

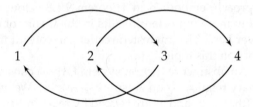

The ARS $(A, \rightarrow^3)$ is:

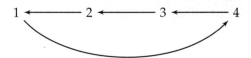

And the ARS $(A, \rightarrow^4)$ is again just the identity relation:

Iterating $\rightarrow$ further times will repeat the above graphs.

Closures

For the following definitions, we are considering an ARS $(A, \rightarrow)$.

- $\rightarrow^*$ denotes the reflexive transitive closure of $\rightarrow$. It can be defined using the rules of Figure 4.4 presented in Chapter 4. Equivalently, we can define it as follows (the proof of equivalence is left as an exercise below):

$$\xrightarrow{*} = \bigcup_{n \in \mathbb{N}} \rightarrow^n$$

So $x \rightarrow^* y$ iff there exists $n \in \mathbb{N}$ such that $x \rightarrow^n y$.

- The transitive closure of $\rightarrow$ is denoted $\rightarrow^+$, and can be defined this way:

$$\xrightarrow{+} = \bigcup_{n \in (\mathbb{N} - \{0\})} \rightarrow^n$$

So it is just like the reflexive transitive closure, except that we do not include $\rightarrow^0$ (the identity relation on A).

- $\leftarrow$ denotes the inverse of $\rightarrow$:

$$\leftarrow = \{(y, x) \mid x \rightarrow y\}$$

- $\leftrightarrow$ denotes the symmetric closure of $\rightarrow$:

$$\leftrightarrow \; = \; (\leftarrow \cup \rightarrow)$$

- The reflexive closure is denoted $\overset{=}{\rightarrow}$:

$$\overset{=}{\rightarrow} \; = \; (\rightarrow \cup \rightarrow^0)$$

Some important properties of the reflexive-transitive closure, which we will use below, are proved next:

Lemma 9.1.1 (Monotonicity of reflexive-transitive closure). *Suppose R_1 and R_2 are binary relations on a set A. Then if $R_1 \subseteq R_2$, we have $R_1^* \subseteq R_2^*$.*

Proof. Assume an arbitrary pair $(x, y) \in R_1^*$. It suffices to prove $(x, y) \in R_2^*$. By the definition of reflexive-transitive closure, from our assumption $(x, y) \in R_1^*$ we know that there must exist $n \in \mathbb{N}$ such that $(x, y) \in R_1^n$. We will proceed by induction on this n. If $n = 0$, then $x = y$ by the definition of iterated composition, and we therefore also have $(x, y) \in R_2^0 \subseteq R_2^*$. So suppose $n = n' + 1$ for some $n' \in \mathbb{N}$. Then by the definition of iterated composition, $(x, y) \in R_1^n$ is equivalent to

$$(x, y) \in (R_1 \cdot R_1^{n'})$$

By the definition of composition, this implies that there exists q such that:

- $(x, q) \in R_1$, and

- $(q, y) \in R_1^{n'}$.

Now we can apply our assumption that $R_1 \subseteq R_2$, to deduce $(x, q) \in R_2$ from the first of the above displayed facts. The induction hypothesis applies to the second of those facts, to give us $(q, y) \in R_2^*$. From these deduced facts we can easily obtain the required $(x, y) \in R_2^*$, using the definitions of reflexive transitive closure and iterated composition. $\qquad \square$

Lemma 9.1.2 (Idempotence of reflexive-transitive closure). *If R is a binary relation on A, then $(R^*)^* = R^*$.*

Proof. We always have $R \subseteq R^*$, for any relation R, since R^* is defined to be the union, for all $n \in \mathbb{N}$, of R^n. This union therefore includes $R^1 = R \cdot R^0$, which is easily seen to equal just R. So if we take R to be R^*, this reasoning shows that $R^* \subseteq (R^*)^*$. So the interesting direction is to show $(R^*)^* \subseteq R^*$ (and showing these two inclusions is sufficient, by basic set theory).

So assume an arbitrary $(x, y) \in (R^*)^*$. We must prove that $(x, y) \in R^*$. By the definition of reflexive-transitive closure, there exists $n \in \mathbb{N}$ with $(x, y) \in (R^*)^n$. Let us proceed by induction on this n. If $n = 0$, then $x = y$, and $(x, y) \in R^0 \subseteq R^*$. So assume $n = n' + 1$ for some $n' \in \mathbb{N}$. Then from our assumption that $(x, y) \in (R^*)^{n'}$, we deduce (as in the proof of Lemma 9.1.1) that there exists some q such that $(x, q) \in R^*$ and $(q, y) \in (R^*)^{n'}$. By the induction hypothesis applied to this latter fact, we have $(q, y) \in R^*$. Since R^* is indeed transitive (since it can be formulated equivalently using the rules of Figure 4.4, see the exercise in Section 9.5.1 below), we obtain the required $(x, y) \in R^*$ from $(x, q) \in R^*$ and $(q, y) \in R^*$.

□

Normality

Suppose $(A, \rightarrow)$ is an ARS. Then an element $x \in A$ is called normal (or a normal form) with respect to that ARS iff it is not the case that $x \rightarrow y$ for any y. That is, there is no y such that $(x, y) \in \rightarrow$. We write $x \nrightarrow$ to indicate that x is normal.

Normalizing

An element x of ARS $(A, \rightarrow)$ is called normalizing iff there exists some y such that

$$x \rightarrow^* y \nrightarrow$$

That is, x can reach a **normal form** y in 0 or more steps using $\rightarrow$. If every element of A is normalizing with respect to $(A, \rightarrow)$, then $(A, \rightarrow)$ is called normalizing.

Terminating

An element x of ARS $(A, \rightarrow)$ is called terminating with respect to that ARS iff intuitively, one cannot follow some path of $\rightarrow$ steps forever starting from x. One can define this more formally using the following rule, interpreted as giving an inductive definition of a *Terminating* relation:

$$\frac{\forall y. \ (x \rightarrow y) \implies Terminating \ y}{Terminating \ x}$$

This states that x is terminating iff every element reachable from y is terminating. The case where x is normal is covered, since in that situation there are no elements y such that $x \rightarrow y$, so the premise is vacuously true. Since this is an inductive definition, we cannot prove x terminating using it if there is an infinite path starting from x: the derivation we would try to write down in that case would be infinitely deep.

If every element of A is terminating with respect to $(A, \rightarrow)$, then $(A, \rightarrow)$ is said to be terminating. A simple alternative characterization of this is that $\rightarrow$ is terminating iff there exists some $n \in \mathbb{N}$ such that $\rightarrow^n = \emptyset$.[2]

---

[2]This characterization was suggested to me by Ryan McCleeary. Interestingly, one does not find it in standard sources on ARS theory, like [38] or [3]. One does see definitions stating that x is strongly normalizing iff the reduction tree rooted at x is bounded (e.g., Definition 2.8 of [4]). This is certainly the same idea, but it is very succinct to phrase strong normalization of $\rightarrow$ as existence of $n \in \mathbb{N}$ with $\rightarrow^n = \emptyset$.

Uniqueness of normal forms

An element $x \in A$ has the property of uniqueness of normal forms with respect to ARS $(A, \rightarrow)$ iff whenever $x \rightarrow^* y$ and $x \rightarrow^* z$ for normal elements y and z of A, then $y = z$ (that is, y and z are the same element of A). Notice that according to this definition, an element which has no normal forms at all has the property of uniqueness of normal forms. The property just insists that if an element x does have a normal form, then it has only one normal form. An ARS has this property iff all its elements do.

The diamond property

An element x of ARS $(A, \rightarrow)$ is said to have the diamond property with respect to that ARS if for all $y, z \in A$, whenever we have

- $x \rightarrow y$, and

- $x \rightarrow z$;

then there exists some $q \in A$ such that

- $y \rightarrow q$, and

- $z \rightarrow q$.

Graphically, this is often depicted as follows, where the custom is that whenever the solid lines and the elements they are connecting exist, then the dotted lines and elements they are connecting must also exist:

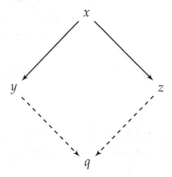

If every element of A has the diamond property with respect to $(A, \rightarrow)$, then $(A, \rightarrow)$ is said to have the diamond property. One can write a very compact set-theoretic statement expressing that $(A, \rightarrow)$ has the diamond property:

$$(\leftarrow \cdot \rightarrow) \subseteq (\rightarrow \cdot \leftarrow)$$

To see why this concise definition matches the graphical one, let us walk through the meanings of its various operators. We have a subset relationship ($\subseteq$), so we are stating that any element of the first set is also an element of the second set. Since the sets in question are relations, their elements are pairs. So this is stating that any time we have

$$(y, z) \in (\leftarrow \cdot \rightarrow)$$

then we also have

$$(y, z) \in (\rightarrow \cdot \leftarrow)$$

By the definition of composition ($\cdot$), the first condition holds when there is some x such that $(y, x) \in \leftarrow$ and $(x, z) \in \rightarrow$. But this is just the same as saying:

- $y \leftarrow x$, which is equivalent to $x \rightarrow y$; and

- $x \rightarrow z$.

Those are the antecedent conditions considered in the first definition given above for x to have the diamond property. And the consequent conditions can then also be derived from $(y, z) \in (\rightarrow \cdot \leftarrow)$. For this holds if there is some q such that:

- $y \rightarrow q$, and

- $q \leftarrow z$, which is equivalent to $z \rightarrow q$.

Here is an example of an ARS, shown graphically, which has the diamond property:

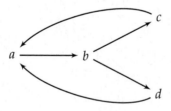

Every time we have $x \rightarrow y$ and $x \rightarrow z$, even in the special case where $y = z$, we can find some node q with $y \rightarrow q$ and $z \rightarrow q$. For a degenerate example (with $y = z$): suppose the x, y, and z in question are a, b, and b. Then we can take q to be c:

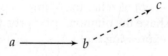

For a nondegenerate example, if x, y, and z are b, c, and d, then we can take a to be q:

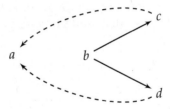

The relaxed diamond property

The diamond property has the somewhat irritating property that it only applies to ARS's $(A, \rightarrow)$ where we never have $x \rightarrow y \not\rightarrow$ for any x and y in A. The reason is that if we have $x \rightarrow y$, then we are required, by the definition of the diamond property, to have $y \rightarrow q$ for some $q \in A$. But since by assumption y is normal, there is no such q, and the relation lacks the diamond property.

The way to work around this annoyance in practice is to prove what I propose we call the *relaxed* diamond property. Terese, Chapter 1, uses the terminology "subcommutative" for this, and some rewriting literature calls this property itself the "diamond property". I propose the terminology relaxed diamond property, as relating the property more closely with the diamond property, yet distinguishing the two concepts.

For the definition: an element x of A has the relaxed diamond property with respect to $(A, \rightarrow)$ iff whenever $x \rightarrow y$ and $x \rightarrow z$, there exists some q such that $y \stackrel{=}{\rightarrow} q$ and $z \stackrel{=}{\rightarrow} q$. An ARS $(A, \rightarrow)$ has the relaxed diamond property iff every element of A does with respect to $(A, \rightarrow)$. Similarly to the case for the diamond property, we can also write a concise set-theoretic statement to express that $(A, \rightarrow)$ has the relaxed diamond property:

$$(\leftarrow \cdot \rightarrow) \subseteq (\stackrel{=}{\rightarrow} \cdot \stackrel{=}{\leftarrow})$$

The definitions of the relaxed diamond property for elements and ARSs are very to the definitions for the diamond property, except that we are using reflexive closures (see above) on the right of the subset statement and the conditions on q.

If we are trying to show an element x satisfies the relaxed diamond property, we must show that whenever $x \rightarrow y$ and $x \rightarrow z$, then there exists a q such that $y \stackrel{=}{\rightarrow} q$ and $z \stackrel{=}{\rightarrow} q$. This allows any of the following possibilities:

- $y \neq q$ and $z \neq q$
- $y = q$ and $z \neq q$
- $y \neq q$ and $z = q$
- $y = q$ and $z = q$

So to show the relaxed diamond property, we may show either the usual condition (that there exists q such that $y \rightarrow q$ and $z \rightarrow q$, corresponding to the first possibility listed), or else $y \leftrightarrow z$ (corresponding to the second and third possibilities), or else just $y = z$ (corresponding to the last possibility). These three relations, for example, lack the diamond property but do have the relaxed diamond property:

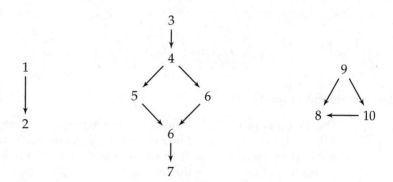

The connection between the relaxed diamond property and the diamond property is made by the following lemma:

Lemma 9.1.3. *If x has the relaxed diamond property with respect to $(A, \rightarrow)$, then x has the diamond property with respect to $(A, \overset{=}{\rightarrow})$.*

Proof. To show that x has the diamond property with respect to $(A, \overset{=}{\rightarrow})$, it suffices to assume we have arbitrary elements y and z of A satisfying:

- $x \overset{=}{\rightarrow} y$, and

- $x \overset{=}{\rightarrow} z$;

And exhibit some q such that

- $y \overset{=}{\rightarrow} q$, and

- $z \overset{=}{\rightarrow} q$.

Let us consider several cases related to our assumptions about x, y, and z. First suppose we have $x \overset{=}{\rightarrow} y$ because in fact we have $x = y$. Then the assumption $x \overset{=}{\rightarrow} z$ is equivalent to $y \overset{=}{\rightarrow} z$. So take the required q to be z. We can observe that we have the two required facts about q:

- $y \overset{=}{\rightarrow} q$ holds, because this is equivalent to $y \overset{=}{\rightarrow} z$, to which we already observed one of our assumptions is equivalent; and

- $z \overset{=}{\rightarrow} q$ holds, because this is equivalent to $z \overset{=}{\rightarrow} z$, which holds by the definition of $\overset{=}{\rightarrow}$.

So now suppose that we have $x \overset{=}{\rightarrow} y$ because we in fact have $x \rightarrow y$. We will now case split on whether $x \overset{=}{\rightarrow} z$ because $x = z$ or because $x \rightarrow z$. In the first case ($x = z$), we can reason as just above to show that taking q to be y, we get the required conditions on q. So suppose $x \to z$. Now we have $x \to y$ and $x \to z$. We are assuming that $(A, \to)$ satisfies the relaxed diamond property, so this implies that there is a q such that $y \overset{=}{\to} q$ and $z \overset{=}{\to} q$. That is just what is needed to complete this case of the proof.

□

It is also easy to observe the following:

Lemma 9.1.4. *If x has the diamond property with respect to $(A, \to)$, then it also has the relaxed diamond property with respect to $(A, \to)$.*

Proof. To prove that x has the relaxed diamond property with respect to $(A, \to)$, it suffices to assume arbitrary y and z with $x \to y$ and $x \to z$, and then exhibit an element $q \in A$ with $y \overset{=}{\to} q$ and $z \overset{=}{\to} q$. But since x has the diamond property, we know that there exists $q \in A$ satisfying $y \to q$ and $z \to q$. Those latter two facts are sufficient to show that q satisfies $y \overset{=}{\to} q$ and $z \overset{=}{\to} q$, by the definition of the reflexive closure $\overset{=}{\to}$ of $\to$.

□

Confluence and semi-confluence

An element x of an ARS $(A, \to)$ is called confluent with respect to $(A, \to)$ iff it has the diamond property with respect to the ARS $(A, \to^*)$. If all elements of A are confluent with respect to $(A, \to)$, then $(A, \to)$ is said to be confluent. Graphically, confluence of x can be depicted as follows:

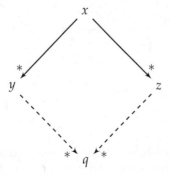

The relaxed diamond property implies confluence, but not the other way around. We will show both these facts.

Lemma 9.1.5. *An ARS can be confluent without satisfying the relaxed diamond property.*

Proof. Here is an example:

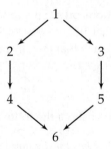

This relation is confluent: whatever three points we choose for x, y, and z with $x \to^* y$ and $x \to^* z$, there is indeed some point q with $y \to^* q$ and $z \to^* q$. For example:

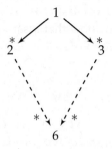

But we do not have:

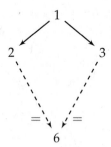

So the relation, which can be observed to be confluent, does not satisfy the relaxed diamond property (and hence also it does not satisfy the diamond property, by Lemma 9.1.4).

□

To show that the relaxed diamond property (and hence also the diamond property, again by Lemma 9.1.4) implies confluence, we make use of an intermediate concept called **semi-confluence**. An element $x \in A$ is semi-confluent with respect to ARS $(A, \to)$ iff whenever $x \to y$ and $x \to^* z$, then there exists a $q \in A$ such that $y \to^* q$ and $z \to^* q$. As usual, an ARS is said to be semi-confluent iff all its elements are. Graphically, the picture is similar to that for confluence, but one star in the upper part of the diagram is missing:

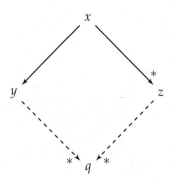

It is straightforward to observe that confluence implies semi-confluence. We will now see that the relaxed diamond property implies semi-confluence, which in turn implies confluence.

Lemma 9.1.6. *If $(A, \to)$ has the relaxed diamond property, then it is also semi-confluent.*

Proof. It suffices to show that an arbitrary $x \in A$ is semi-confluent with respect to $(A, \to)$. So assume $y, z \in A$ with $x \to y$ and $x \to^* z$, and show there is some $q \in A$ with $y \to^* q$ and $z \to^* q$. By the definition of $\to^*$, our assumption $x \to^* z$ implies that there exists some $n \in \mathbb{N}$ such that $x \to^n z$. Let us do induction on this natural number n. If $n = 0$ (the base case), then $x = z$. In this case, we can take q to be y. This satisfies the required properties:

- $y \to^* q$: since $y = q$, this is equivalent to $y \to^* y$, which holds by the definition of $\to^*$.

- $z \to^* q$: since $x = z$ and $y = q$, this is equivalent to $x \to^* y$, which follows from our assumption $x \to y$ by the definition of $\to^*$.

For the step case of the induction on n, we assume $n = n' + 1$ for some n'. So we have $x \to^{n'+1} z$. Because the relation $\to^{n'+1}$ is defined to equal $\to \cdot \to^{n'}$, this statement is equivalent to $x(\to \cdot \to^{n'})z$. By the definition of relational composition, this implies that there is some x' such that $x \to x' \to^{n'} z$. Applying the assumption that $\to$ has the relaxed diamond property to the facts $x \to x'$ and $x \to y$, we deduce that there exists a q' such that $x' \overset{=}{\to} q'$ and $y \overset{=}{\to} q'$. Graphically, the situation looks like this:

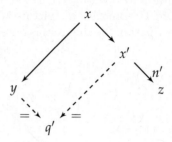

Now let us case split on whether or not $q' = x'$. If it does, then we can take z for q. This satisfies the required conditions:

- $y \to^* q$: since $q = z$, this is equivalent to $y \to^* z$, which holds because we have $y \to q' = x' \to^* z$.

- $z \to^* q$: since $q = z$, this is equivalent to $z \to^* z$.

Graphically, this case looks like this:

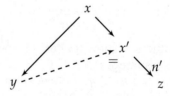

Now consider the case where $q \neq x'$. So we have this situation:

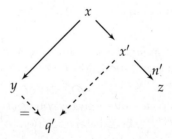

We can now apply our induction hypothesis to the facts $x' \to q'$ and $x' \to^{n'} z$. This tells us that there exists some q'' with $q' \to^* q''$ and $z \to^* q''$. The picture looks like this:

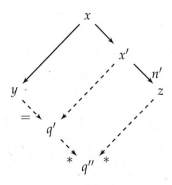

Now it is clear that we can take q'' for q, and the desired properties hold.

$\square$

Lemma 9.1.7. *If* $(A, \to)$ *is semi-confluent, then it is also confluent.*

Proof. This proof is similar to that for Lemma 9.1.6. Assume arbitrary $x, y, z \in A$ with $x \to^* y$ and $x \to^* z$. We must exhibit q satisfying $y \to^* q$ and $z \to^* q$. By the definition of $\to^*$, there exists some n such that $x \to^n z$. We will proceed by induction on this number n. If $n = 0$ (the base case), then $x = z$, and we can take q to be y. This satisfies the requirements on q:

- $y \to^* q$: since $q = y$, this is equivalent to $y \to^* y$.

- $z \to^* q$: since $x = z$ and $q = y$, this is equivalent to our assumption $x \to^* y$.

For the step case, $n = n' + 1$ for some n', and we have $x \to x' \to^{n'} z$ for some $x' \in A$. We can now apply our assumption that x is semi-confluent (with respect to $(A, \to)$) to the facts $x \to x'$ and $x \to^* y$. So there exists some q' such that $x' \to^* q'$ and $y \to^* q'$. The situation looks like this:

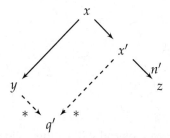

Now we can apply the induction hypothesis to the facts $x' \to^* q'$ and $x' \to^{n'} z$ (because the induction hypothesis allows us to assume what we are trying to prove, when the number of steps along the right side of our diagram is n'). So there is some q'' such that $q' \to^* q''$ and $z \to^* q''$. The picture looks like this:

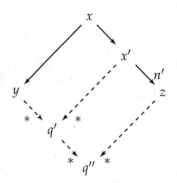

Now it is clear that we can take q'' for q, to conclude.

□

Theorem 9.1.8. *If $(A, \to)$ has the (relaxed) diamond property, then it is also confluent.*

Proof. This follows from Lemmas 9.1.6 and 9.1.7.

□

Local confluence

For proving confluence of lambda calculus, we are going to use Theorem 9.1.8. But there is another result which is so elegant and useful that we cannot avoid mentioning it here. This is based around the concept of **local confluence**.

An element $x \in A$ is locally confluent with respect to $(A, \to)$ iff for all $y, z \in A$, if $x \to y$ and $x \to z$, then there exists a q such that $y \to^* q$ and $z \to^* q$. Graphically, this situation is depicted like this:

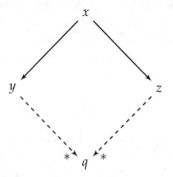

This diagram looks a lot like others we have seen above. The differences between them are all in which edges in the diagram have stars. Here, every time we can take exactly one step (with $\to$) from x to y and from x to z, we must be able to take 0 or more steps (with $\to^*$) from y to some q, and also from z to that q. As usual, we call an ARS $(A, \to)$ locally confluent iff all elements of A are locally confluent with respect to $(A, \to)$.

Local confluence is so similar to the properties above, one wonders how it is related, in particular to the most important property, confluence. Certainly confluence implies local confluence, because confluence says that no matter how many steps one takes from x to reach y and to reach z, then there is a common point reachable in 0 or more steps from y and similarly from z. So this covers the case where y and z are reachable in exactly one step from x. On the other hand, we have this result:

Lemma 9.1.9. *Local confluence does not imply confluence.*

Proof. The following is a famous counterexample, attributed to Kleene:[3]

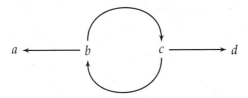

This ARS is clearly not confluent, because if we start from b, say, and go to a and d, we cannot find any common element at which to join up a and d (since they are normal). On the other hand, it is locally confluent. For example, from b we can reach a and c in exactly one step, and those can be joined up at a. Similarly, from c we can reach b and d in exactly one step, and they can be joined at d.

□

We can observe that the ARS for the Kleene counterexample, while normalizing (see definition earlier in this section) is not terminating: there is an infinite path which forever cycles from b to c and back again. It turns out that this nontermination is indeed the source of the failure for local confluence to imply confluence. The result is due to Newman and bears his name. The paper in which Newman proves this, however, is not formulated in terms of ARSs, and is difficult to follow [30]. Fortunately, Huét developed an amazingly clear and simple proof of the result, which is now the standard way of proving it [21].

Theorem 9.1.10 (Newman's Lemma). *If $(A, \rightarrow)$ is terminating and locally confluent, then it is confluent.*

Proof (Huet). Since $(A, \rightarrow)$ is terminating we may proceed by induction on $\rightarrow$: to prove some property $P(x)$, we are allowed to assume $P(y)$ for any y such that $x \rightarrow y$. As $\rightarrow$ is terminating, we will eventually reach a normal form x, for which we

---

[3]The attributional situation here is a little complicated. The example can be found in a paper of Hindley [18], but it is not attributed there to Kleene. It is commonly called Kleene's counterexample, however, and on page 14 of [38], it is described as "attributed by Hindley to Kleene" (though which work of Hindley's attributes it to Kleene is not specified).

will have no assumptions $P(y)$ to help us. That is the base case for the induction. The property we wish to prove in this case is confluence (of an element $x \in A$).

To show that $x \in A$ is confluent, assume we have y and z in A with $x \rightarrow^* y$ and $x \rightarrow^* z$. We now consider cases for $x \rightarrow^* y$ and $x \rightarrow^* z$. From these two facts, based on the definition of $\rightarrow^*$, we have either $x = z$ or $x \rightarrow^+ z$, and either $x = y$ or $x \rightarrow^+ y$. If $x = z$, then we can take y to be q, and satisfy the requirements on q:

- $z \rightarrow^* q$: since $x = z$ and $q = y$, this is equivalent to $x \rightarrow^* y$ which we have.

- $y \rightarrow^* q$: this is equivalent to $y \rightarrow^* y$.

The case where $x = y$ is symmetric to the case we just considered, so we omit the details. So finally we are left with the situation where $x \rightarrow^+ y$ and $x \rightarrow^+ z$. By the definition of $\rightarrow^+$, we must have x' and x'' with $x \rightarrow x' \rightarrow^* z$ and $x \rightarrow x'' \rightarrow^* z$. The diagram for the situation thus looks like this:

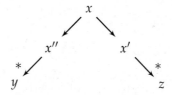

Now we can apply our assumption of local confluence to the facts $x \rightarrow x'$ and $x \rightarrow x''$, to obtain some q' with $x' \rightarrow^* q'$ and $x'' \rightarrow^* q'$:

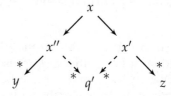

Now since $x \rightarrow x''$, we are entitled to apply our induction hypothesis to it x'' with the facts $x'' \rightarrow^* q'$ and $x'' \rightarrow^* y$. This gives us some q_1 with $q' \rightarrow^* q_1$ and $x'' \rightarrow^* q_1$:

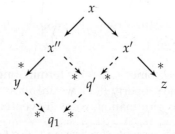

Now since $x \rightarrow x'$, we can again apply our induction hypothesis, with the facts $x' \rightarrow^* q_1$ and $x' \rightarrow^* z$, to obtain some q_2 satisfying $q_1 \rightarrow^* q_2$ and $z \rightarrow^* q_2$:

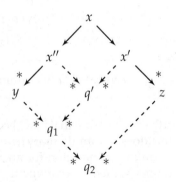

Now it is clear we can take q_2 for our q, and satisfy the required properties that $y \to^* q$ and $z \to^* q$. ☐

9.1.2 Lambda calculus lacks the diamond property

Having developed these tools from the theory of abstract reduction systems, we are going to apply Theorem 9.1.8 to prove confluence of full β-reduction for untyped lambda calculus. But first, we should observe that the theorem does not apply directly. Let us write *terms* for the set of untyped lambda-calculus terms, and $\rightsquigarrow$ for the full β-reduction relation, defined in Section 5.2.

Lemma 9.1.11. *(terms, $\rightsquigarrow$) does not have the relaxed diamond property.*

Proof. Here is a counterexample:

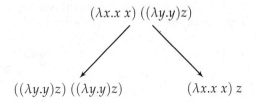

There is no common term to which we can reduce both the left and the right terms in this peak in 0 or 1 steps. The terms we can obtain by one step of full β-reduction from the left term are:

- $z\,((\lambda y.y)z)$

- $((\lambda y.y)z)\,z$

And the only term we can obtain by one step of β-reduction from the right term is

- $z\,z$

So the set consisting of the left term and those reachable in 1 step from it does not overlap with the set consisting of the right term and those reachable in 1 step from it. Hence, $(\lambda x.x\ x)\,((\lambda y.y)z)$ lacks the relaxed diamond property.

☐

$$\frac{}{x \Rightarrow x} \qquad \frac{t \Rightarrow t'}{\lambda x.t \Rightarrow \lambda x.t'} \qquad \frac{t_1 \Rightarrow t_1' \quad t_2 \Rightarrow t_2'}{t_1\, t_2 \Rightarrow t_1'\, t_2'} \qquad \frac{t_1 \Rightarrow t_1' \quad t_2 \Rightarrow t_2'}{(\lambda x.t_1)\, t_2 \Rightarrow [t_2'/x]t_1'}$$

Figure 9.1: The definition of parallel reduction

It is worth emphasizing that just because $(terms, \rightsquigarrow)$ lacks the relaxed diamond property, this does not imply that $(terms, \rightsquigarrow)$ is not confluent. For Theorem 9.1.8 just gives a sufficient condition for an ARS to be confluent: if it has the relaxed diamond property, then it is confluent. But if the ARS lacks the relaxed diamond property, then Theorem 9.1.8 gives us no information about $(terms, \rightsquigarrow)$. Indeed, we already observed in Lemma 9.1.5 that an ARS can be confluent and lack the relaxed diamond property.

9.1.3   Parallel reduction

So how can we make use of Theorem 9.1.8 to show that $(terms, \rightsquigarrow)$ is confluent, given that $(terms, \rightsquigarrow)$ lacks the (relaxed) diamond property? The ingenious solution, proposed by Tait and Martin-Löf (see the note at the start of this chapter), is to define another relation $\Rightarrow$, where $(terms, \Rightarrow)$ does have the diamond property, and where $\Rightarrow^* = \rightsquigarrow^*$. Since by definition, $(A, \rightarrow)$ is confluent iff $(A, \rightarrow^*)$ has the diamond property, showing confluence of $(terms, \Rightarrow)$ will be sufficient to show confluence of $(terms, \rightsquigarrow)$, if indeed $\Rightarrow^* = \rightsquigarrow^*$. This relation $\Rightarrow$, called **parallel reduction** (or by some authors, *simultaneous reduction*), is defined in Figure 9.1.

Parallel reduction allows several redexes in a term to be contracted in a single $\Rightarrow$ step. For example, we have this derivation for a $\Rightarrow$ reduction of $(\lambda x.x\, x)\, ((\lambda y.y\, y)\, z)$:

$$\frac{\dfrac{\dfrac{}{x \Rightarrow x} \quad \dfrac{}{x \Rightarrow x}}{\dfrac{x\, x \Rightarrow x\, x}{\lambda x.x\, x \Rightarrow \lambda x.x\, x}} \qquad \dfrac{\dfrac{\dfrac{}{y \Rightarrow y} \quad \dfrac{}{y \Rightarrow y}}{\dfrac{y\, y \Rightarrow y\, y}{\lambda y.y\, y \Rightarrow \lambda y.y\, y}} \quad \dfrac{}{z \Rightarrow z}}{(\lambda y.y\, y)\, z \Rightarrow z\, z}}{(\lambda x.x\, x)\, ((\lambda y.y\, y)\, z) \Rightarrow (z\, z)\, (z\, z)}$$

This example might suggest that parallel reduction can always reduce normalizing terms to their normal forms. Here is a simple example showing that this is not the case:

$$\frac{\dfrac{\dfrac{}{x \Rightarrow x}}{\lambda x.x \Rightarrow \lambda x.x} \quad \dfrac{\dfrac{}{y \Rightarrow y}}{\lambda y.y \Rightarrow \lambda y.y}}{\dfrac{(\lambda x.x)\, (\lambda y.y) \Rightarrow \lambda y.y \qquad \dfrac{}{z \Rightarrow z}}{(\lambda x.x)\, (\lambda y.y)\, z \Rightarrow (\lambda y.y)\, z}}$$

Redexes that are created during a single step of parallel reduction cannot be reduced by that step of reduction. Only redexes which exist in the starting term for that step can get reduced.

9.1.4   Some properties of parallel reduction

Parallel reduction has several properties which play a role in showing confluence of full β-reduction. The starting point for using parallel reduction for confluence is the property mentioned already in Section 9.1.3: $\Rightarrow^* = \leadsto^*$. We prove this as Theorem 9.1.14 below. Before we can prove this, though, we must prove a number of subsidiary lemmas.

Lemma 9.1.12 (Reflexivity of parallel reduction). *For all terms t, we have $t \Rightarrow t$.*

Proof. The proof is by induction on the structure of t. If t is a variable x, then we use this derivation:

$$\overline{x \Rightarrow x}$$

If $t = t_1\, t_2$, then by the induction hypothesis we have $t_1 \Rightarrow t_1$ and $t_2 \Rightarrow t_2$, and so can use this derivation:

$$\frac{t_1 \Rightarrow t_1 \quad t_2 \Rightarrow t_2}{t_1\, t_2 \Rightarrow t_1\, t_2}$$

Finally, if $t = \lambda x.t_1$, then by the induction hypothesis we have $t_1 \Rightarrow t_1$, and can use this derivation:

$$\frac{t_1 \Rightarrow t_1}{\lambda x.t_1 \Rightarrow \lambda x.t_1}$$

$\square$

Lemma 9.1.13. $\leadsto\, \subseteq\, \Rightarrow\, \subseteq\, \leadsto^*$.

Proof. To prove $\leadsto\, \subseteq\, \Rightarrow$, we proceed by induction on the structure of a derivation (with the rules of Figure 5.2 from Chapter 5) of $t \leadsto t'$.

Case:

$$\frac{}{(\lambda x.\, t)\, t' \leadsto [t'/x]t}\ \beta$$

We can use the following derivation:

$$\frac{\dfrac{}{\lambda x.t \Rightarrow \lambda x.t}\ Lemma\ 9.1.12 \quad \dfrac{}{t' \Rightarrow t'}\ Lemma\ 9.1.12}{(\lambda x.t)\, t' \Rightarrow [t'/x]t}$$

Case:

$$\frac{t \leadsto t'}{\lambda x.\, t \leadsto \lambda x.\, t'}\ lam$$

By the induction hypothesis (IH), we have $t \Rightarrow t'$, and we can apply the lambda rule for parallel reduction:

$$\frac{t \Rightarrow t'}{\lambda x.t \Rightarrow \lambda x.t'}$$

Case:

$$\frac{t_1 \leadsto t_1'}{(t_1\, t_2) \leadsto (t_1'\, t_2)}\ app1$$

By the IH, we have $t_1 \Rightarrow t_1'$, and we can use this derivation:

$$\frac{t_1 \Rightarrow t_1' \quad t_2 \Rightarrow t_2}{(t_1\ t_2) \Rightarrow (t_1'\ t_2)}\ Lemma\ 9.1.12$$

Case:

$$\frac{t_2 \rightsquigarrow t_2'}{(t_1\ t_2) \rightsquigarrow (t_1\ t_2')}\ app2$$

By the IH, we have $t_2 \Rightarrow t_2'$, and we can use this derivation:

$$\frac{\overline{t_1 \Rightarrow t_1}\ Lemma\ 9.1.12 \quad t_2 \Rightarrow t_2'}{(t_1\ t_2) \Rightarrow (t_1\ t_2')}$$

Now we will prove $\Rightarrow\ \subseteq\ \rightsquigarrow^*$ by induction on the structure of a derivation of $t \Rightarrow t'$:

Case:

$$\overline{x \Rightarrow x}$$

We have $x \rightsquigarrow^* x$ by the definition of reflexive-transitive closure.

Case:

$$\frac{t \Rightarrow t'}{\lambda x.t \Rightarrow \lambda x.t'}$$

By the induction hypothesis, we have $t \rightsquigarrow^* t'$. Now we use Lemma 5.2.1 (from Chapter 5) to conclude $\lambda x.t \rightsquigarrow^* \lambda x.t'$.

Case:

$$\frac{t_1 \Rightarrow t_1' \quad t_2 \Rightarrow t_2'}{t_1\ t_2 \Rightarrow t_1'\ t_2'}$$

By the induction hypothesis applied separately to each of the premises, we have $t_1 \rightsquigarrow^* t_1'$ and $t_2 \rightsquigarrow^* t_2'$. Applying Lemma 5.2.2 to the first of these facts, and Lemma 5.2.3 to the second, we obtain:

$$t_1\ t_2 \rightsquigarrow^* t_1'\ t_2 \rightsquigarrow^* t_1'\ t_2'$$

Transitivity of $\rightsquigarrow^*$ then gives us the desired $t_1\ t_2 \rightsquigarrow^* t_1'\ t_2'$.

Case:

$$\frac{t_1 \Rightarrow t_1' \quad t_2 \Rightarrow t_2'}{(\lambda x.t_1)\ t_2 \Rightarrow [t_2'/x]t_1'}$$

By the induction hypothesis applied to the premises, we have $t_1 \rightsquigarrow^* t_1'$ and $t_2 \rightsquigarrow^* t_2'$. We can apply Lemma 5.2.1 to the first of these facts to obtain $\lambda x.t_1 \rightsquigarrow^* \lambda x.t_1'$.

Then, similarly to the previous case of this proof, we can use Lemmas 5.2.2 and 5.2.3 to obtain:

$$(\lambda x.t_1)\, t_2 \rightsquigarrow^* (\lambda x.t_1')\, t_2 \rightsquigarrow^* (\lambda x.t_1')\, t_2'$$

We can complete the reduction sequence by applying the β rule (of Figure 5.2), and then injecting into the reflexive-transitive closure. This adds one more step, to complete the reduction sequence as follows:

$$(\lambda x.t_1)\, t_2 \rightsquigarrow^* (\lambda x.t_1')\, t_2 \rightsquigarrow^* (\lambda x.t_1')\, t_2' \rightsquigarrow^* [t_2'/x]t_1'$$

So we have the desired result of $(\lambda x.t_1)\, t_2 \rightsquigarrow^* [t_2'/x]t_1'$.

$\square$

Theorem 9.1.14. $\Rightarrow^* = \rightsquigarrow^*$.

Proof. Since $\rightsquigarrow\, \subseteq\, \Rightarrow$ by Lemma 9.1.13, we have $\rightsquigarrow^* \subseteq\, \Rightarrow^*$ by Lemma 9.1.1. Similarly, using the same lemmas: since $\Rightarrow\, \subseteq\, \rightsquigarrow^*$, we also have $\Rightarrow^* \subseteq (\rightsquigarrow^*)^*$. So we have:

1. $\rightsquigarrow^* \subseteq\, \Rightarrow^*$.

2. $\Rightarrow^* \subseteq (\rightsquigarrow^*)^*$.

Now Lemma 9.1.2 tells us that $(\rightsquigarrow^*)^* = \rightsquigarrow^*$, so these two facts are really equivalent to:

1. $\rightsquigarrow^* \subseteq\, \Rightarrow^*$.

2'. $\Rightarrow^* \subseteq\, \rightsquigarrow^*$.

And these together imply the desired result by basic set theory, since they are saying that the two relations we are trying to prove equal (namely $\rightsquigarrow^*$ and $\Rightarrow^*$) are subsets of each other.

$\square$

Lemma 9.1.15 (Substitution and parallel reduction). *If $t_a \Rightarrow t_a'$ and $t_b \Rightarrow t_b'$, then $[t_b/y]t_a \Rightarrow [t_b'/y]t_a'$.*

Proof. The proof is by induction on the structure of the derivation of $t_a \Rightarrow t_a'$.

Case:

$$\frac{}{x \Rightarrow x}$$

Here we must case split on whether or not $x = y$. If $x = y$, then what we need to prove is equivalent to:

$$[t_b/x]x \Rightarrow [t_b'/x]x$$

This, in turn, is equivalent to just $t_b \Rightarrow t_b'$, which we have by assumption. On the other hand, if $x \neq y$, then what we need to prove is equivalent to just $y \Rightarrow y$, which is derivable.

Case:

$$\frac{t \Rightarrow t'}{\lambda x.t \Rightarrow \lambda x.t'}$$

We will make the following assumptions about the bound variable x:

- $x \neq y$
- $x \notin FV(t_b)$
- $x \notin FV(t'_b)$

These assumptions are justified, since we can always safely rename the variable bound by the λ-abstraction to be something different from y, and all the free variables in t_b and t'_b. So what we must prove is equivalent to:

$$\lambda x.[t_b/x]t \Rightarrow \lambda x.[t'_b/x]t'$$

This can be derived by applying the induction hypothesis (IH) to $t \Rightarrow t'$ and $t_b \Rightarrow t'_b$, with this final derivation:

$$\frac{\dfrac{t \Rightarrow t' \quad t_b \Rightarrow t'_b}{[t_b/x]t \Rightarrow [t'_b/x]t'} \; IH}{\lambda x.[t_b/x]t \Rightarrow \lambda x.[t'_b/x]t'}$$

Case:

$$\frac{t_1 \Rightarrow t'_1 \quad t_2 \Rightarrow t'_2}{t_1 \, t_2 \Rightarrow t'_1 \, t'_2}$$

Applying the IH to the premises, we obtain this derivation:

$$\frac{\dfrac{t_1 \Rightarrow t'_1}{[t_b/x]t_1 \Rightarrow [t'_b/x]t'_1} \; IH \quad \dfrac{t_2 \Rightarrow t'_2}{[t_b/x]t_2 \Rightarrow [t'_b/x]t'_2} \; IH}{([t_b/x]t_1)\,([t_b/x]t_2) \Rightarrow ([t'_b/x]t'_1)\,([t'_b/x]t'_2)}$$

Since for any t_1 and t_2, the definition of substitution tells us that $([t_b/x]t_1)\,([t_b/x]t_2) = [t_b/x](t_1 \, t_2)$, what we have just derived is equivalent to the desired statement of parallel reduction.

Case:

$$\frac{t_1 \Rightarrow t'_1 \quad t_2 \Rightarrow t'_2}{(\lambda y.t_1) \, t_2 \Rightarrow [t'_2/y]t'_1}$$

Applying the IH to the premises, we obtain:

$$\frac{\dfrac{t_1 \Rightarrow t'_1}{[t_b/x]t_1 \Rightarrow [t'_b/x]t'_1} \; IH \quad \dfrac{t_2 \Rightarrow t'_2}{[t_b/x]t_2 \Rightarrow [t'_b/x]t'_2} \; IH}{(\lambda y.[t_b/x]t_1)\,[t_b/x]t_2 \Rightarrow [[t'_b/x]t'_2/y]([t'_b/x]t'_1)}$$

To complete this derivation, we need to show this equality:

$$[[t'_b/x]t'_2/y]([t'_b/x]t'_1) = [t'_b/x]([t'_2/y]t'_1)$$

The following lemma can be used to show this, since we may assume $y \notin FV(t'_b)$ (because y is a λ-bound variable, we can always choose it to lie outside the set $FV(t'_b)$). The proof of this lemma is by induction on the structure of t''; we omit the details.

Lemma 9.1.16. *If $y \notin FV(t)$, then we have $[t/x]([t'/y]t'') = [[t/x]t'/y]([t/x]t'')$.*

$\square$

9.1.5 The complete-development term of a term

Recall from Section 9.1.3 that our plan (following Tait and Martin-Löf) is to prove confluence of $\rightsquigarrow$ by proving that the parallel reduction relation $\Rightarrow$ has the diamond property. So we need to show that whenever we have terms $t, t_1,$ and t_2 with $t \Rightarrow t_1$ and $t \Rightarrow t_2$, then there exists a $\hat{t}$ such that $t_1 \Rightarrow \hat{t}$ and $t_2 \Rightarrow \hat{t}$. As a diagram, this condition can be depicted this way:

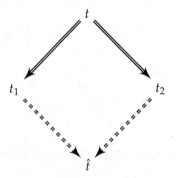

The original method of Tait and Martin-Löf (as given in Section 3.2 of Barendregt's book [5]) gives a constructive proof that $\Rightarrow$ has the diamond property. The constructive nature of the proof shows, in effect, how to compute $\hat{t}$ from $t, t_1,$ and t_2. In Section 11.2 of his book, Barendregt proves that in fact, $\hat{t}$ can be computed directly from t, independently of t_1 and t_2, using the idea of *complete developments* (see also the exercise on complete developments in Section 5.10, and Section 11.2 of [5]). A complete development reduces all the redexes in t, in some order. Barendregt proves that this process is guaranteed to result in a unique term, which turns out to be suitable for playing the role of $\hat{t}$ above. I propose we call this term the **complete-development term** of t (or just the **complete development** of t). This terminology risks some ambiguity, since a reduction sequence from t to this unique term is standardly called a complete development of t.

Instead of proving that the complete-development term of t always exists and is unique, Takahashi gives a direct recursive definition of the complete development t^* of t [37]. This is a very simple and direct way to show that $\Rightarrow$ has the diamond property, so we will follow her approach here. The definition of the complete development t^* of t is given in Figure 9.2 (note that Takahashi's formulation is equivalent but slightly different [37]).

The essential idea of Takahashi's definition (Figure 9.2) is to recursively reduce all redexes occurring in t. Of course, we could not reduce all redexes created by doing such reductions, or else we would not be able to compute a final result (since

$$
\begin{array}{rcl}
x^* & = & x \\
(\lambda x.t)^* & = & \lambda x.(t^*) \\
(x\ t_2)^* & = & x\ t_2^* \\
((t_a\ t_b)\ t_2)^* & = & (t_a\ t_b)^*\ t_2^* \\
((\lambda x.t_1)t_2)^* & = & [t_2^*/x]t_1^*
\end{array}
$$

Figure 9.2: The definition of the complete development (term) of t

we could reduce redexes forever). Here is an example of computing a complete-development term:

$$
\begin{array}{rcl}
((\lambda x.x\ x)\ ((\lambda y.y)\ \lambda z.z))^* & = & [((\lambda y.y)\ \lambda z.z)^*/x](x\ x)^* \\
& = & [((\lambda y.y)\ \lambda z.z)^*/x](x\ x^*) \\
& = & [((\lambda y.y)\ \lambda z.z)^*/x](x\ x) \\
& = & [([(\lambda z.z)^*/y]y^*)/x](x\ x) \\
& = & [([(\lambda z.z)^*/y]y)/x](x\ x) \\
& = & [([\lambda z.z^*/y]y)/x](x\ x) \\
& = & [([\lambda z.z/y]y)/x](x\ x) \\
& = & [\lambda z.z/x](x\ x) \\
& = & (\lambda z.z)\ \lambda z.z
\end{array}
$$

Here, we are just applying the equations from Figure 9.2 one at a time, anywhere inside a meta-expression for a term. The order of applying the equations is not important: since Figure 9.2 is a well-founded recursive definition with a single equation matching (on its left hand side) every possibility for the input term t, it is computing a unique result t^*, no matter what order we apply its defining equations. Notice that in this case, we ended up with a term which is not normal. But that term does not contain any *residual* of a redex from the original. Intuitively, a residual redex would be one which is not created by substitution, but rather can be traced to a redex which is already present in the starting term t. More formally, a residual could be identified by inserting labels onto every subterm of t, and then seeing which labels were still left after computing t^* (see the exercise on complete developments in Section 5.10, or Section 11.2 of [5]).

To warrant calling t^* the complete-development term of t, we should really prove that it indeed is the unique normal form for all complete-development reduction sequences of t. We will not do exactly this here, but we will see in Lemma 9.1.17 a related fact, which is sufficient for proving the diamond property of parallel reduction $\Rightarrow$.

9.1.6 Parallel reduction has the diamond property

In this section, we prove that parallel reduction indeed has the diamond property, using complete-development terms. We need the following critical lemma first. If we identify a parallel reduction $t \Rightarrow t'$ with a development (that is, with reducing some subset of the redexes that occur in t), then Lemma 9.1.17 shows one sense in which "complete-development term" is an appropriate name for t^*:

Lemma 9.1.17 (The complete-development term does complete developments). *If* $t_a \Rightarrow t'_a$, *then* $t'_a \Rightarrow t^*_a$.

Proof. The proof is by induction on the structure of the derivation of $t_a \Rightarrow t'_a$.

Case:

$$\overline{x \Rightarrow x}$$

In this case, we have

$$t'_a = x \Rightarrow x = x^* = t^*_a$$

Case:

$$\frac{t \Rightarrow t'}{\lambda x.t \Rightarrow \lambda x.t'}$$

We can apply the IH to get this derivation:

$$\frac{\dfrac{t \Rightarrow t'}{t' \Rightarrow t^*} \; IH}{\lambda x.t' \Rightarrow \lambda x.t^*}$$

We just have to observe that $\lambda x.t^* = (\lambda x.t)^*$ by the definition of complete-development term, to see that this derivation suffices.

Case:

$$\frac{t_1 \Rightarrow t'_1 \quad t_2 \Rightarrow t'_2}{t_1 \, t_2 \Rightarrow t'_1 \, t'_2}$$

Here we must consider two subcases, for whether t_1 is a λ-abstraction or not. If t_1 is not a λ-abstraction, then it must be either a variable or an application. Either way, $(t_1 \, t_2)^* = t^*_1 \, t^*_2$, and thus the following derivation is sufficient:

$$\frac{\dfrac{t_1 \Rightarrow t'_1}{t'_1 \Rightarrow t^*_1} \; IH \quad \dfrac{t_2 \Rightarrow t'_2}{t'_2 \Rightarrow t^*_2} \; IH}{t'_1 \, t'_2 \Rightarrow t^*_1 \, t^*_2}$$

Now suppose that t_1 is a λ-abstraction, say $\lambda x.\hat{t}$. The assumed judgment $t_1 \Rightarrow t'_1$ is thus equivalent to $\lambda x.\hat{t} \Rightarrow t'_1$. By inversion on the derivation of this judgment, we see that it must end in this inference, for some $\hat{t}'$:

$$\frac{\hat{t} \Rightarrow \hat{t}'}{\lambda x.\hat{t} \Rightarrow \lambda x.\hat{t}'}$$

Now we can complete the derivation this way:

$$\frac{\dfrac{\hat{t} \Rightarrow \hat{t}'}{\hat{t}' \Rightarrow \hat{t}^*} \; IH \quad \dfrac{t_2 \Rightarrow t'_2}{t'_2 \Rightarrow t^*_2} \; IH}{(\lambda x.\hat{t}) \, t'_2 \Rightarrow [t^*_2/x]\hat{t}^*}$$

This derivation suffices, because the derivation we are considering (in this particular case and subcase of our proof) proves:

$$(\lambda x.\hat{t})\, t_2 \Rightarrow (\lambda x.\hat{t}')\, t_2'$$

Hence, what we should derive is

$$(\lambda x.\hat{t}')\, t_2' \Rightarrow ((\lambda x.\hat{t})\, t_2)^*$$

And by the definition of complete-development term, we have

$$((\lambda x.\hat{t})\, t_2)^* = [t_2^*/x]\hat{t}^*$$

So the derivation we constructed above does prove the right judgment, since it proves:

$$(\lambda x.\hat{t}')\, t_2' \Rightarrow [t_2^*/x]\hat{t}^*$$

Case:

$$\frac{t_1 \Rightarrow t_1' \quad t_2 \Rightarrow t_2'}{(\lambda x.t_1)\, t_2 \Rightarrow [t_2'/x]t_1'}$$

We can construct this derivation:

$$\frac{\dfrac{t_1 \Rightarrow t_1'}{t_1' \Rightarrow t_1^*}\; IH \quad \dfrac{t_2 \Rightarrow t_2'}{t_2' \Rightarrow t_2^*}\; IH}{[t_2'/x]t_1' \Rightarrow [t_2^*/x]t_1^*}\; Lemma\ 9.1.15$$

□

Theorem 9.1.18. *Parallel reduction has the diamond property.*

Proof. Suppose that $t \Rightarrow t_1$ and $t \Rightarrow t_2$. By Lemma 9.1.17, we have $t_1 \Rightarrow t^*$ and $t_2 \Rightarrow t^*$. Take t^* as the completing term q that is required by the diamond property, and we have the desired result.

□

9.1.7   Concluding confluence

To conclude this section, we can derive our main result:

Theorem 9.1.19 (Confluence of full β-reduction). *Full β-reduction for untyped lambda calculus is confluent.*

Proof. By Theorem 9.1.14, it suffices to prove confluence of $\Rightarrow$, since $\Rightarrow^* = \leadsto^*$. By Theorem 9.1.8, to prove confluence of $\Rightarrow$, it suffices to prove the diamond property for $\Rightarrow$. And Theorem 9.1.18 proves this.

□

Let us summarize the work we have done in this section: we developed concepts related to confluence in the general context of abstract reduction systems (ARSs) $(A, \rightarrow)$, where A is a set of objects and $\rightarrow$ is a binary relation on A. The main result we take from ARS theory is that the diamond property implies confluence (Theorem 9.1.8). We applied this result in the form of the Tait/Martin-Löf method for showing confluence of λ-calculus. With this method, we must find an intermediate relation $\Rightarrow$ which has the diamond property and which satisfies:

$$\leadsto \; \subseteq \; \Rightarrow \; \subseteq \; \leadsto^*$$

We showed in Theorem 9.1.14 that this condition implies that $\Rightarrow^* = \leadsto^*$, thus reducing the problem of confluence of $\leadsto$ to confluence of $\Rightarrow$. The Tait/Martin-Löf method not only proposes this general approach to showing confluence; it proposes the relation of parallel reduction for $\Rightarrow$, which turns out to satisfy the inclusion constraints above and also have the diamond property. Barendregt shows how the diamond property of $\Rightarrow$ can be proved using complete developments, which are reduction sequences reducing all the redexes contained in a starting term t, in some order. Takahashi's addition to this approach is to give an explicit recursive definition of the canonical (i.e., unique normal) term t^*, which we can call the complete-development term, resulting from any complete development of t. This approach leads to a relatively succinct proof of confluence of full β-reduction for untyped lambda calculus.

These central ideas of parallel reduction, complete-development terms, and the diamond property for showing confluence can be adapted and applied to extensions of lambda calculus, or other reduction semantics of other languages. They are thus worth knowing for any aspiring programming-language designer or theorist.

9.2 Combinators

The λ-calculus as studied in Chapters 5 and 6 may already seem to represent a strange way to program: all data are encoded as functions, including numbers, and there is no notion of state. The value of a variable can hardly be said to be assigned by substituting a term for it during β-reduction. The assignment is completely transitory, and certainly cannot be changed the way we can change the value of a variable in WHILE by assignment.

As strange as λ-calculus might have seemed, we can go one step further in striving for a minimalistic programming language. Where λ-calculus dispenses with mutable variables, combinators provide a way to program without any variables at all. As shocking as this might sound, we will see in this chapter how to translate λ-calculus into combinators in a way that is sound for call-by-value reduction.

9.2.1 Syntax and operational semantics of combinators

$$combinators\ c\ ::=\ S \mid K \mid c\ c'$$

We will write a, b, and c for combinators below. The small step operational semantics is defined by these rules:

$$\overline{\mathcal{C}[S\ a\ b\ c] \rightsquigarrow \mathcal{C}[(a\ c)\ (b\ c)]} \qquad \overline{\mathcal{C}[K\ a\ b] \rightsquigarrow \mathcal{C}[a]}$$

$$combinator\ contexts\ \mathcal{C}\ ::=\ * \mid \mathcal{C}\ c \mid c\ \mathcal{C}$$

The rule for K makes $K\ a$ a constant-valued function: it always returns a no matter what argument b it is applied to. The rule for S is more complex, but we can see something like self-application here, since we have a term containing c applied to another term containing c (hence, this suggests the potential for applying c to itself). We saw in Chapters 5 and 6 that self-application gives us computational power, and indeed, the language of combinators is Turing-complete, as we will show below by showing how to translate lambda-terms to combinators.

9.2.2 Examples

One straightforward example is the combinator $S\ K\ K$. This function behaves exactly like the identity function, and indeed is often called I. Given an argument a, the identity function is just supposed to return a, after some number of steps. So we are supposed to have:

$$I\ a \rightsquigarrow^* a$$

Let's see how this works with I defined to be $S\ K\ K$. So we start with $(S\ K\ K)\ a$. Are there any redexes here? Indeed, there is an S redex, because despite the possibly confusing parenthesization, S here is applied to three arguments. This is clearer if we write the term with the minimal parenthesization: $S\ K\ K\ a$. Now we can do an S-reduction:

$$S\ K\ K\ a \rightsquigarrow (K\ a)\ (K\ a)$$

Again, it takes some practice to be able to find the next redex (which must be a K-redex, since S is not present). And again, it is easier if we use the minimal parenthesization, which in this case is $K\ a\ (K\ a)$. Now we can see the K-redex:

$$K\ a\ (K\ a) \rightsquigarrow a$$

This is just what we were looking for to see that $S\ K\ K$ behaves like the identity function.

9.2.3 Translating lambda calculus to combinators

In this section, we will see how to translate lambda-terms to combinators. To describe this translation, we need a language for expressions which are like combinators, but can contain free variables:

$$\begin{aligned} &\textit{variables } x \\ &\textit{var-combinators } d \quad ::= \quad x \mid S \mid K \mid d\, d' \end{aligned}$$

We define small-step reduction for var-combinators exactly as for combinators (we just use exactly the same rules and contexts, except that we have var-combinators everywhere those rules have combinators). The formal definition is omitted, since it is the same as for combinators, except with meta-variable root d everywhere instead of c. We now define an operation λ^*, which takes a variable x and a var-combinator d, and returns another var-combinator d', where d' contains exactly the same free variables as d, except not x. The intention is that $\lambda^* \, x \, d$ should be a var-combinator which behaves just like the lambda-term $\lambda x.\,d$. The definition is by recursion on the structure of the var-combinator d. In the second clause we make use of a meta-level function $\textit{Vars}$, for computing the set of variables occurring in a var-combinator d.

$$\begin{aligned} \lambda^* \, x \, x \quad &= \quad S\,K\,K \\ \lambda^* \, x \, d \quad &= \quad K\,d,\ \text{if } x \notin \textit{Vars}(d) \\ \lambda^* \, x \, (d_1\, d_2) \quad &= \quad S\,(\lambda^* \, x \, d_1)\,(\lambda^* \, x \, d_2),\ \text{if } x \in \textit{Vars}(d_1\, d_2) \end{aligned}$$

Examples

We compute the value of $\lambda^* \, x \, (x\, x)$ as follows:

$$\lambda^* \, x \, (x\, x) = S\,(\lambda^* \, x \, x)\,(\lambda^* \, x \, x) = S\,I\,I$$

where $I = S\,K\,K$ as in Section 9.2.2 above. Since $(\lambda x.\, x\, x)\,(\lambda x.\, x\, x)$ evaluates to itself, we might expect something similar for the combinator $(\lambda^* \, x \, (x\, x))\,(\lambda^* \, x \, (x\, x))$. Indeed, we have:

$$\begin{aligned} (\lambda^* \, x \, (x\, x))\,(\lambda^* \, x \, (x\, x)) \quad &= \quad (S\,I\,I)\,(S\,I\,I) \\ &= \quad S\,I\,I\,(S\,I\,I) \\ &\rightsquigarrow \quad (I\,(S\,I\,I))\,(I\,(S\,I\,I)) \\ &\rightsquigarrow^* \quad (S\,I\,I)\,(S\,I\,I) \\ &= \quad (\lambda^* \, x \, (x\, x))\,(\lambda^* \, x \, (x\, x)) \end{aligned}$$

In the second step, I am just dropping parentheses to emphasize that the whole expression is indeed an S-redex: the three arguments to S are I, I, and $S\,I\,I$. Notice that it takes several steps for $(\lambda^* \, x \, (x\, x))\,(\lambda^* \, x \, (x\, x))$ to reduce to itself, while for $(\lambda x.\, x\, x)\,(\lambda x.\, x\, x)$, it takes just one step. We will see in the next section that while the translations of λ-terms to combinators evaluate just like those λ-terms, they may require more steps to do so.

Basic property of $\lambda^* \, x \, d$

We can confirm that $\lambda^* \, x \, d$ behaves just like $\lambda x.\, d$, with the following lemma.

Lemma 9.2.1 (Basic property of λ^*). $(\lambda^* \, x \, d)\, d' \rightsquigarrow^* [d'/x]d$

Proof. The proof is by induction on the structure of d.

Case: $d = x$. We must show:

$$(\lambda^* \, x \, x) \, d' \rightsquigarrow^* [d'/x]x$$

We have:

$$(\lambda^* \, x \, x) \, d' = S \, K \, K \, d' \rightsquigarrow^* d' = [d'/x]x$$

The reduction here holds, as we already showed in Section 9.2.2.

Case: $x \notin Vars(d)$. We have

$$(\lambda^* \, x \, d) \, d' = K \, d \, d' \rightsquigarrow d = [d'/x]d$$

The fact that $d = [d'/x]d$ follows from the assumption that $x \notin Vars(d)$.

Case: $d = d_1 \, d_2$. This is the most interesting case. By the definition of λ^*, we have:

$$(\lambda^* \, x \, (d_1 \, d_2)) \, d' = S \, (\lambda^* \, x \, d_1) \, (\lambda^* \, x \, d_2) \, d'$$

We can now use the S rule:

$$S \, (\lambda^* \, x \, d_1) \, (\lambda^* \, x \, d_2) \, d' \rightsquigarrow ((\lambda^* \, x \, d_1) \, d') \, ((\lambda^* \, x \, d_2) \, d')$$

By the induction hypothesis, we know:

$$1.\ ((\lambda^* \, x \, d_1) \, d') \rightsquigarrow^* [d'/x]d_1$$
$$2.\ ((\lambda^* \, x \, d_2) \, d') \rightsquigarrow^* [d'/x]d_2$$

So we can reduce the term we got just above as follows:

$$((\lambda^* \, x \, d_1) \, d') \, ((\lambda^* \, x \, d_2) \, d') \rightsquigarrow^* ([d'/x]d_1) \, ([d'/x]d_2)$$

This latter term equals $[d'/x](d_1 \, d_2)$ (by the definition of substitution), as required.
$\square$

It is worth mentioning that more space-efficient translations to combinators do exist, though they use additional primitive combinators beyond just S and K [24].

9.2.4   The translation and its verification

Now we can define the translation from lambda terms to combinators, using the function λ^* and var-combinators as intermediate results. The translation is defined as follows. Given a lambda-term t, possibly with some free variables, we define *lam-to-comb*$[\![t]\!]$ to be a var-combinator term:

$$\begin{aligned}
[\![x]\!] &= x \\
[\![t \, t']\!] &= [\![t]\!] \, [\![t']\!] \\
[\![\lambda x. t]\!] &= \lambda^* \, x \, [\![t]\!]
\end{aligned}$$

The idea here is that we translate terms recursively, using λ^* to help translate λ-abstractions.

Theorem 9.2.2 (Soundness of translation for call-by-value). *Whenever we have $t \rightsquigarrow$ t' with left-to-right call-by-value reduction (see Section 5.4.1), we also have $[\![t]\!] \rightsquigarrow^* [\![t']\!]$.*

To prove this theorem, we need some additional definitions and lemmas, given next.

9.2.5 Lemmas for Theorem 9.2.2

The main lemmas developed in this section are Lemmas 9.2.4 and 9.2.6. Building up to the proof of the latter in particular is unfortunately rather involved.

Definition 9.2.3 (Context interpretation). *For C a left-to-right call-by-value context (see Section 5.4.1), we define $[\![C]\!]$ as follows:*

$$
\begin{aligned}
[\![*]\!] &= * \\
[\![C\ t]\!] &= [\![C]\!]\ [\![t]\!] \\
[\![v\ C]\!] &= [\![v]\!]\ [\![C]\!]
\end{aligned}
$$

Note that the resulting context is a combinator context (see Section 9.2).

Lemma 9.2.4 (Context interpretation commutes with grafting). *For C a left-to-right call-by-value context, we have the following:*

$$[\![C[t]]\!] = [\![C]\!][[\![t]\!]]$$

This states that if we first graft term t into C and then interpret the resulting term, we get the same result as if we first interpreted C and t separately, and grafted the resulting term into the resulting combinator context.

Proof. The proof is by induction on C. If $C = *$, then we have

$$[\![C[t]]\!] = [\![*[t]]\!] = [\![t]\!] = *[[\![t]\!]] = [\![C]\!][[\![t]\!]]$$

If C equals $C'\ t'$ or $v\ C'$, then we have (for example):

$$
\begin{aligned}
[\![C[t]]\!] &= [\![(C'\ t')[t]]\!] \\
&= [\![C'[t]\ t']\!] \\
&= [\![C'[t]]\!]\ [\![t']\!] \\
&= [\![C']\!][[\![t]\!]]\ [\![t']\!] \\
&= [\![C'\ t']\!][[\![t]\!]] \\
&= [\![C]\!][[\![t]\!]]
\end{aligned}
$$

The fourth step uses the induction hypothesis, and the others use the definition of the interpretation of contexts (or the assumption that $C = C'\ t$). These are all the cases for left-to-right call-by-value contexts.

$\square$

Lemma 9.2.5. *If $y \notin Vars(t')$ and $x \neq y$, then*

$$[[\![t']\!]/x](\lambda^*\ y\ d) = \lambda^*\ y\ [[\![t']\!]/x]d$$

Proof. The proof is by induction on d. If $d = y$, then we have:

$$
\begin{aligned}
[\![t']\!]/x](\lambda^* \, y \, d) &= [\![t']\!]/x](\lambda^* \, y \, y) \\
&= [\![t']\!]/x] S \, K \, K \\
&= S \, K \, K \\
&= (\lambda^* \, y \, y) \\
&= \lambda^* \, y \, [\![t']\!]/x] y \\
&= \lambda^* \, y \, [\![t']\!]/x] t
\end{aligned}
$$

These steps are justified by the definition of $[\![t]\!]$ and of substitution, and the assumption $t = y$. For the other base case, assume $y \notin Vars(d)$. Then we have:

$$
\begin{aligned}
[\![t']\!]/x](\lambda^* \, y \, d) &= [\![t']\!]/x](K \, d) \\
&= K \, [\![t']\!]/x] d \\
&= \lambda^* \, y \, [\![t']\!]/x] d
\end{aligned}
$$

For the third step, we are using the facts that $y \notin Vars(d)$ and $y \notin Vars([\![t']\!])$ to conclude that $y \notin Vars([\![t'/x]d]\!])$. Finally, for the inductive step, we have:

$$
\begin{aligned}
[\![t']\!]/x](\lambda^* \, y \, ([\![t_1]\!] \, [\![t_2]\!])) &= [\![t']\!]/x](S \, (\lambda^* \, y \, [\![t_1]\!]) \, (\lambda^* \, y \, [\![t_2]\!])) \\
&= (S \, [\![t']\!]/x](\lambda^* \, y \, [\![t_1]\!]) \, [\![t']\!]/x](\lambda^* \, y \, [\![t_2]\!])) \\
&= (S \, (\lambda^* \, y \, [\![t']\!]/x] t_1) \, (\lambda^* \, y \, [\![t']\!]/x] t_2)) \\
&= \lambda^* \, y \, ([\![t']\!]/x] t_1 \, [\![t']\!]/x] t_2) \\
&= \lambda^* \, y \, [\![t']\!]/x](t_1 \, t_2)
\end{aligned}
$$

We are using the induction hypothesis (twice) for the third step, and pushing substitutions and $[\![\cdot]\!]$ into and out of applications by the definition of those operations. $\square$

Lemma 9.2.6 (Interpretation commutes with substitution).

$$
[\![t]\!]/x][\![t']\!] = [\![[t/x]t']\!]
$$

Proof. The proof is by induction on the structure of t'. If t' is a variable x' (possibly equal to x), then we have

$$
[\![t]\!]/x][\![t']\!] = [\![t]\!]/x][\![x']\!] = [\![[t/x]x']\!] = [\![[t/x]t']\!]
$$

If $t' = t'_1 \, t'_2$, then we have

$$
\begin{aligned}
&[\![t]\!]/x][\![t']\!] \\
&= [\![t]\!]/x][\![t'_1 \, t'_2]\!] \\
&= [\![t]\!]/x][\![t'_1]\!] \, [\![t]\!]/x][\![t'_2]\!] \\
&= [\![[t/x]t'_1]\!] \, [\![[t/x]t'_2]\!] \\
&= [\![[t/x](t'_1 \, t'_2)]\!]
\end{aligned}
$$

Here, we are using our induction hypothesis (twice) in the third step, and pushing substitutions and $[\![\cdot]\!]$ into and out of applications by the definition of those operations. Finally, if $t' = \lambda y.\, t'_1$, then we have

$$
\begin{aligned}
& [\![t]\!]/x]\,[\![t']\!] \\
=\ & [\![t]\!]/x]\,[\![\lambda y.\, t'_1]\!] \\
=\ & [\![t]\!]/x]\lambda^* y\, [\![t'_1]\!] \\
=\ & \lambda^* y\, [\![t]\!]/x]\,[\![t'_1]\!] \\
=\ & \lambda^* y\, [\![t/x]t'_1]\!] \\
=\ & [\![\lambda y.\, [t/x]t'_1]\!]
\end{aligned}
$$

Here, we use Lemma 9.2.5 to push the substitution into the body of the λ^* meta-expression.

$\square$

9.2.6 Proof of Theorem 9.2.2

We can now return to give the proof of Theorem 9.2.2:

Whenever we have $t \rightsquigarrow t'$ with left-to-right call-by-value reduction, we also have $[\![t]\!] \rightsquigarrow^*$ $[\![t']\!]$.

Proof. Suppose we have $\mathcal{C}[(\lambda x.t)\, v] \rightsquigarrow \mathcal{C}[[v/x]t]$ with left-to-right call-by-value reduction, where $\mathcal{C}$ is as defined in Section 5.4.1. Then by Lemma 9.2.4 we have

$$
[\![\mathcal{C}[(\lambda x.t)\, v]]\!] = [\![\mathcal{C}]\!]\,[\![[(\lambda x.t)\, v]\!]]
$$

By the definition of $[\![t]\!]$, we then have

$$
[\![\mathcal{C}]\!]\,[\![[(\lambda x.t)\, v]\!]] = [\![\mathcal{C}]\!]\,[(\lambda^* x\, [\![t]\!])\, [\![v]\!]]
$$

Now by Lemma 9.2.1, we have

$$
(\lambda^* x\, [\![t]\!])\, [\![v]\!] \rightsquigarrow^* [\![[v]\!]/x]\,[\![t]\!]
$$

It is easy to prove that $d \rightsquigarrow^* d'$ implies $\mathcal{C}'[d] \rightsquigarrow^* \mathcal{C}'[d']$, for any combinator context $\mathcal{C}'$, by induction on the derivation of $d \rightsquigarrow^* d'$ (I omit that proof). So using also the fact that $[\![\mathcal{C}]\!]$ is a combinator context, we can derive

$$
[\![\mathcal{C}]\!]\,[(\lambda^* x\, [\![t]\!])\, [\![v]\!]] \rightsquigarrow^* [\![\mathcal{C}]\!]\,[[\![v]\!]/x]\,[\![t]\!]]
$$

Finally, by Lemma 9.2.6, we have

$$
[\![\mathcal{C}]\!]\,[[\![v]\!]/x]\,[\![t]\!]] = [\![\mathcal{C}]\!]\,[\![[v/x]t]\!]]
$$

$\square$

9.2.7   A note on other reduction orders

Translation to combinators is best suited as a semantics for λ-calculus when the reduction order used for the operational semantics does not reduce inside λ-abstractions. So call-by-name reduction, for example, can be handled this way, but normal-order reduction (Section 5.4.3 above) cannot. For an example of the difficulty, we have the following reduction in normal order:

$$\lambda x.(\lambda y.y)\, x \rightsquigarrow \lambda x.x$$

Let us compute the interpretation of the first term:

$$
\begin{aligned}
[\![\lambda x.(\lambda y.y)\, x]\!] &= \lambda^* x\, ((\lambda^* y\, y)\, x) \\
&= \lambda^* x\, (I\, x) \\
&= S\, (\lambda^* x\, I)\, (\lambda^* x\, x) \\
&= S\, (K\, I)\, I
\end{aligned}
$$

This combinator is in normal form. So it cannot match the reduction which the original λ-term has in normal order.

9.3   Conclusion

We have proved confluence of untyped lambda calculus using Takahashi's variant of the Tait-Martin-Löf proof. The essential idea of the Tait-Martin-Löf proof is to define a notion of parallel reduction which can be proven to have the diamond property, from which confluence easily follows. Takahashi's variant of the proof is to show the diamond property by recursively defining the complete-development term t^* of term t, and showing that whenever t parallel-reduces to t', then t' parallel-reduces to t^*. This yields the diamond property for parallel reduction in a particularly succinct and elegant way.

We also have seen how the language of SK combinators supports programming without any variables. The language is Turing-complete, since we can translate (Turing-complete) λ-calculus to combinators, in a way that preserves reduction (Theorem 9.2.2).

9.4   Basic exercises

9.4.1   For Section 9.1 on confluence of untyped lambda calculus

1. This problem is about the material on abstract reduction systems (ARSs) in Section 9.1.1. Let $A = \{1, 2, 3, 4, 5, 6\}$ and let $\rightarrow_1$ and $\rightarrow_2$ be defined as follows:

$$
\begin{aligned}
\rightarrow_1 &= \{(2,1),(2,3),(4,3)\} \\
\rightarrow_2 &= \{(3,2),(3,4),(4,5)\}
\end{aligned}
$$

(a) Draw $(A, \rightarrow_1)$ and $(A, \rightarrow_2)$ as graphs (you should include the node 6 in your graphs even though it is not connected to any other node).

(b) Draw $(A, \rightarrow_1 \cdot \rightarrow_2)$ and $(A, \rightarrow_2 \cdot \rightarrow_1)$.

(c) Draw $(A, \rightarrow_1 \cup \rightarrow_2)$ and $(A, (\rightarrow_1 \cup \rightarrow_2)^+)$ (the latter has quite a few edges).

(d) Which elements of $(A, \rightarrow_1 \cup \rightarrow_2)$ are normal?

(e) Is $(A, \rightarrow_1 \cup \rightarrow_2)$ normalizing? Is it terminating?

(f) List all the elements of $(A, \rightarrow_1 \cup \rightarrow_2)$ which lack the diamond property.

(g) Define a relation $\rightarrow_3$ which includes $\rightarrow_1 \cup \rightarrow_2$ (that is, we should have $(\rightarrow_1 \cup \rightarrow_2) \subseteq \rightarrow_3$) and which is confluent. Try to add as few edges to $\rightarrow_1 \cup \rightarrow_2$ as possible. To show your answer, just draw $(A, \rightarrow_3)$.

2. Which of the following terms have the relaxed diamond property with respect to the ARS $(terms, \leadsto)$, where $\leadsto$ is full β-reduction?

- $\lambda x.x\ x$
- $(\lambda x.x)\ \lambda y.y$
- $(\lambda x.(\lambda y.y)\ x)\ \lambda x.x$
- $(\lambda x.\lambda y.y\ x)\ ((\lambda x.x)\ \lambda z.z)$

3. Write out a derivation for each of the following judgments of parallel reduction, using the rules of Figure 9.1:

(a) $(\lambda x.x)\ ((\lambda y.y)\ \lambda z.z) \Rightarrow \lambda z.z$

(b) $(\lambda w.w)\ (\lambda x.x\ x)\ ((\lambda y.y)\ z) \Rightarrow (\lambda x.x\ x)\ z$

(c) $(\lambda x.(\lambda y.y)\ x)\ \lambda z.z \Rightarrow (\lambda x.x)\ \lambda z.z$

(d) $(\lambda x.x\ ((\lambda x.x)\ x))\ \lambda y.(\lambda z.z)\ y\ y\ y \Rightarrow (\lambda y.(\lambda z.z)\ y\ y\ y)\ ((\lambda x.x)\ \lambda y.(\lambda z.z)\ y\ y\ y)$

9.4.2 For Section 9.2 on the syntax and semantics of combinators

1. Reduce the following terms to normal form:

(a) $K\ K\ K\ K\ K$

(b) $S\ S\ S\ S\ S$

(c) $S\ (K\ (S\ I))\ (S\ (K\ K)\ I)\ a\ b$, assuming a and b are some unknown combinators in normal form.

2. Compute the following applications of the λ^* function:

(a) $\lambda^*\ x\ (x\ \lambda y.y)$

(b) $\lambda^*\ x\ (\lambda^*\ y\ y)$

(c) $\lambda^*\ x\ (\lambda^*\ y\ (x\ y))$

9.5   Intermediate exercises

9.5.1   For Section 9.1 on confluence of untyped lambda calculus

1. In Section 9.1.1, an alternative characterization of the reflexive-transitive closure of a binary relation R on a set A was stated:

$$R^* = \bigcup_{n \in \mathbb{N}} R^n$$

Prove that this way of defining R^* is equivalent to defining it using rules as in Figure 4.4 of Chapter 4. Hint: prove that $(x, y) \in R^*$ as defined by the rules of Figure 4.4 implies that there exists $n \in \mathbb{N}$ such that $(x, y) \in R^n$. This can be done by induction on the structure of the derivation (with the rules of Figure 4.4). Then to prove the reverse implication, prove that if $(x, y) \in R^n$, then $(x, y) \in R^*$ (as defined by Figure 4.4). This latter proof can be done by induction on n.

2. Argue that for any ARS $(A, \rightarrow)$, if $x \in A$ is normal, then x has the diamond property.

3. This problem is related to Section 9.1.2.

   (a) Give an example of a non-normal lambda term which has the diamond property.

   (b) Give an example of a non-normal lambda term which has the relaxed diamond property but not the diamond property.

4. Prove, either directly or using lemmas and theorems from Section 9.1, that for every term t, we have $t \Rightarrow t^*$ (see Section 9.1.3 for the definition of $\Rightarrow$, and Section 9.1.5 for t^*).

9.5.2   For Section 9.2 on the syntax and semantics of combinators

1. Let us temporarily define K^n as follows:

$$\begin{aligned} K^0 &= K \\ K^{n+1} &= K\,K^n \end{aligned}$$

   (a) Compute the normal forms of K^3, K^4, and K^5.

   (b) Characterize the normal form of K^n as $K^{f(n)}$, for some function f of n. You should give an exact definition of this function f.

   (c) Prove by induction on n that your characterization is correct.

Chapter 10
Polymorphic Type Theory

In this chapter, we consider extending simply typed (pure) lambda calculus with support for **parametric polymorphism**, which is the ability of a term to operate on data of different types. We begin with System F, a powerful polymorphic type theory based on universal types $\forall X.\ T$. System F can be viewed as an extension of Simply Typed Lambda Calculus (STLC, see Chapter 7), which assigns many more lambda terms a type than STLC did. We will see how System F allows us to type Church-encoded data (discussed in Chapter 6) and operations on such data. STLC is not powerful enough to allow much typing of lambda-encoded data and operations on them, so this is a significant advance. We first look at a type-assignment version of System F, and then consider a system with annotated terms.

Next, we will consider System F_ω, which extends System F with λ-abstraction at the type level. That is, we obtain the ability to compute types from other types. For example, we might want to compute the type $X * X$ from X, for pairs of elements where both elements have type X. In System F_ω, we can do that with the type-level λ-abstraction $\lambda X.X * X$. The resulting system is quite expressive, but suffers from some duplications: λ-abstraction and application exist at two different levels in the language, leading to duplication of typing rules. Such duplication can be eliminated using so-called Pure Type Systems; see Barendregt's "Lambda Calculi with Types" [6].

10.1   Type-assignment version of System F

For the type-assignment formulation of System F, the terms are just the usual unannotated lambda terms from Chapter 5:

$$terms\ t\ ::=\ x\ |\ t\ t'\ |\ \lambda x.\,t$$

The notions of reduction we may consider are those of untyped lambda calculus. Let us suppose we are working here with full β-reduction (Section 5.2). The new features of System F all are concerned with typing. The syntax of polymorphic types T is given by

$$T\ ::=\ X\ |\ T_1 \to T_2\ |\ \forall X.T$$

where X is from an infinite set of **type variables**. We could also include base types b as types, as we did for STLC, but this is not really needed, since we can simulate them with free type variables X. The type-form $\forall X.T$ is for **universal** types. We will use universal types to classify polymorphic functions. We have two parsing conventions. First, we again treat $\rightarrow$ as right associative, so that $X \rightarrow Y \rightarrow Z$ is fully parenthesized as $(X \rightarrow (Y \rightarrow Z))$. Second, the scope of the universal quantifier extends as far to the right as possible. So $\forall X.X \rightarrow X$ is fully parenthesized as $(\forall X.(X \rightarrow X))$.

10.1.1   Type-assignment rules

Our type-assignment system for System F extends that of STLC with new rules for universal types. Because universal types bind a type variable X, we need to extend our notion of typing contexts to include declarations for type variables. We do this by writing $X : \star$. The use of $\star$ as the classifier for a type variable will be consistent with the notation we will introduce for System F_ω below.

$$typing\ contexts\ \Gamma \quad ::= \quad \cdot \mid \Gamma, x : T \mid \Gamma, X : \star$$

The typing rules are given in Figure 10.1. As for simple typing, we are writing $\Gamma(x) = T$ to mean that the result of looking up the type for term variable x in context Γ is T (i.e., the function Γ returns type T for x). We will assume that λ- and $\forall$-bound variables are tacitly renamed to ensure that the typing context always has at most one declaration for any variable (either term variable x or type variable X), and that in $\Gamma, X : \star$, the type variable X does not occur anywhere in Γ. This will ensure we do not confuse scopes of term or type variables with the same names. It also ensures that we are not able to universally quantify a type variable in such a way to separate it from its use in $\Gamma(x)$. That is, we are not allowed to perform the last inference in this derivation:

$$\frac{\cdot, x : X, X : \star \vdash x : X}{\cdot, x : X \vdash x : \forall X.X}$$

This would certainly be unsounded with respect to our intended semantics: it would say that if you know x has some unknown type X, you can conclude that it has the universal type $\forall X.X$. In effect, an x that has some fixed but unknown type would become an x that can take on any type at all (through universal instantiation). This is not sound.

In the elimination rule for universal types, we use substitution $[T/X]T'$ to replace all free occurrences of X in T' with T. Similarly to the case for term-level substitution $[t/x]t'$, this substitution at the level of types must respect the binding structure of the types involved. So we will tacitly rename variables which are bound in T', to avoid capturing variables free in T.

The type-assignment formulation of System F is not algorithmic, and differently from STLC, we cannot devise a constraint-based typing algorithm that works in general. The problem is that the constraints we generate end being second-order unification constraints, and that problem is provably unsolvable [16]. Indeed, it is in general undecidable whether or not an unannotated term can be assigned a type in System F. So we will turn to annotated terms for an algorithmic type system for System F.

$$\frac{\Gamma(x) = T}{\Gamma \vdash x : T} \qquad \frac{\Gamma \vdash t_1 : T_2 \to T_1 \quad \Gamma \vdash t_2 : T_2}{\Gamma \vdash t_1\, t_2 : T_1} \qquad \frac{\Gamma, x : T_1 \vdash t : T_2}{\Gamma \vdash \lambda x.t : T_1 \to T_2}$$

$$\frac{\Gamma, X : \star \vdash t : T}{\Gamma \vdash t : \forall X.T} \qquad \frac{\Gamma \vdash t : \forall X.T'}{\Gamma \vdash t : [T/X]T'}$$

Figure 10.1: Type-assignment rules for System F

10.1.2 Metatheory

The following metatheoretic results can be proved for System F. The first is a straightforward extension of the proof of Type Preservation for STLC (see Theorem 7.6.1 of Chapter 7). We now need two substitution theorems: one for substituting a term into a term, and another for substituting a type into a term. The proof of strong normalization is based on reducibility, as for simple types, but requires a major innovation, due to Jean-Yves Girard, to define reducibility for universal types $\forall X.t$. For this, see "Proofs and Types" [15].

Theorem 10.1.1 (Type Preservation). *If $\Gamma \vdash t : T$ (in System F) and $t \rightsquigarrow t'$, then $\Gamma \vdash t' : T$.*

Theorem 10.1.2 (Strong Normalization). *If $\Gamma \vdash t : T$ (in System F), then $t \in SN$.*

An important idea related to strong normalization is **parametricity**, which is based on a relational semantics for types, and intuitively shows that inhabitants of universal types $\forall X.T$ must work parametrically for any type that could be substituted for X. Parametricity is a deep concept which we will not be able to explore further here; see [41]. Parametricity has intriguing consequences for proving properties of programs [40].

10.2 Annotated terms for System F

Just as we did for STLC, we can devise a language of annotated terms, to obtain an algorithmic type system for System F. The standard approach to annotating these terms uses the following syntax:

$$t \quad ::= \quad x \mid (t_1\, t_2) \mid \lambda x : T.t \mid t[T] \mid \lambda X.t$$

The first three term constructs are as for simply typed or untyped lambda calculus. The constructs $t[T]$ and $\lambda X.t$ are annotations for **type instantiation** and **type abstraction**, respectively.

10.2.1   Examples

Polymorphic identity

We can compute a single type, rather than a type scheme, for a System F term implementing the polymorphic identity function. The typing is:

$$\lambda X.\lambda x : X.x \ : \ \forall X.X \to X$$

The idea in System F is that our annotated terms can abstract over types (with $\lambda X.t$) and then instantiate a type abstraction (with $t[T]$). The type for a type abstraction $\lambda X.t$ is $\forall X.T$, where t has type T in a context where X is declared.

$\lambda x.(x\ x)$

The term $\lambda x.(x\ x)$ is not simply typable, but we can give an annotated System F term corresponding to it which is typable. This example demonstrates also the use of instantiation. The typing is

$$\lambda x : \forall X.X. \, (x[(\forall X.X) \ \to \ (\forall X.X)] \, x) \ : \ (\forall X.X) \to (\forall X.X)$$

Let us consider this example in more detail. The term in question first takes in x of type $\forall X.X$. Such an x is a very powerful term, since for any type T, we have $x[T] : T$. So this term can, via its instantiations, take on any type T we wish. So the term in question instantiates x at the type $(\forall X.X) \ \to \ (\forall X.X)$. The instantiated x now has the type of a function taking an input of type $\forall X.X$ and returning an output of the same type. So we can apply the instantiated x to x itself. The type of the application is then $\forall X.X$, which completes the explanation of the typing of this term. Note that typing prevents us from applying the term

$$\lambda x : \forall X.X. \, (x[(\forall X.X) \ \to \ (\forall X.X)] \, x)$$

to itself. This is good, since we know that applying $\lambda x.(x\ x)$ to itself diverges.

10.3   Semantics of annotated System F

We can now define type computation for annotated System F. We can also define reduction directly on annotated terms, in case we wish to preserve annotations while reducing.

10.3.1   Type-computation rules

Figure 10.2 inductively defines a relation of type computation for System F. (Contexts Γ are as defined above for the type-assignment system.) In the judgments $\Gamma \vdash t : T$, the context Γ and subject term t are inputs, and the type T is the output. In the typing rule for instantiation, we must substitute the type T into the body of

$$\frac{\Gamma(x) = T}{\Gamma \vdash x : T} \qquad \frac{\Gamma \vdash t_1 : T_2 \to T_1 \quad \Gamma \vdash t_2 : T_2}{\Gamma \vdash t_1\, t_2 : T_1} \qquad \frac{\Gamma, x : T_1 \vdash t : T_2}{\Gamma \vdash \lambda x : T_1.t : T_1 \to T_2}$$

$$\frac{\Gamma, X : \star \vdash t : T}{\Gamma \vdash \lambda X.t : \forall X.T} \qquad \frac{\Gamma \vdash t : \forall X.T'}{\Gamma \vdash t[T] : [T/X]T'}$$

Figure 10.2: Type computation rules for System F

the $\forall$-type. This is what allows us, for example, to give $x[(\forall X.X) \to (\forall X.X)]$ the type $(\forall X.X) \to (\forall X.X)$ if x has type $\forall X.X$. (The body T' in this case is just X.)

Of course, we should prove the following theorem (details omitted):

Theorem 10.3.1. *If t is an annotated term and $\Gamma \vdash t : T$ (using the rules for annotated terms), then we also have $\Gamma \vdash |t| : T$ using the rules for unannotated terms, where $|t|$ is the erasure of t, which drops all annotations.*

10.3.2 Reduction semantics

Annotations are added to a language of terms in order to enable algorithmic typing. The type-assignment rules are usually non-algorithmic, and the annotations provide just the right information to resolve the nondeterminism about which rules to apply, with which instantiations of meta-variable. From this point of view, there is no need to define a reduction relation directly on annotated terms. We can prove properties like Type Preservation on unannotated terms using our type-assignment rules (see Section 7.6). The annotations on terms do not contribute anything to this, since they have no computational relevance.

In some situations, however, it is desirable to define reduction directly on annotated terms. For example, we might like to be able to reduce a term t and still be able to type check it. This requires us to preserve annotations as we reduce, and hence using the reduction relation for untyped lambda terms on the erasure (dropping annotations) of t will not be sufficient.

So let us define a reduction semantics for System F that works directly on our annotated terms:

$$\mathcal{C}[(\lambda x : T.t)\, t'] \rightsquigarrow \mathcal{C}[[t'/x]t]$$
$$\mathcal{C}[(\lambda X.t)[T]] \rightsquigarrow \mathcal{C}[[T/X]t]$$

Here, the contexts $\mathcal{C}$ allow reduction anywhere:

$$\mathcal{C} ::= * \mid (\mathcal{C}\, t) \mid (t\, \mathcal{C}) \mid \lambda x : T.\mathcal{C} \mid \lambda X.\mathcal{C} \mid \mathcal{C}[T]$$

The theorem of interest is then (proof omitted):

Theorem 10.3.2 (Preservation of annotated typing). *If t is an annotated term with $\Gamma \vdash t : T$ and $t \rightsquigarrow t'$ with the reduction relation for annotated terms, then $\Gamma \vdash t' : T$.*

10.4   Programming with Church-encoded data

One of the amazing things about System F is that we can express quite interesting algorithms (for example, sorting of lists) as typable System F terms. Since every typable term in System F is strongly normalizing, this means that we can prove totality of functions, for example, just by encoding them in System F. From recursion theory, we know that not all total functions can be encoded in System F, since there is no recursive language consisting of all and only the total functions. But still, System F is remarkably expressive, as we will now see. To emphasize: all the functions we write below are guaranteed to terminate on all inputs, just in virtue of the fact that they type check in System F.

Recall from Chapter 6 that in the Scott encoding, data are encoded by their own case-statements; while in the Church encoding, data are encoded by their own iterators. Operations on Scott-encoded data are not typable, in general, in System F. But operations on Church-encoded data are. So we will use Church encodings below. Also, for algorithmic typing, we will use annotated System F terms.

10.4.1   Unary numbers

The typed Church encodings for 0 and the successor function in System F, and the type of natural numbers, are definable like this:

$$
\begin{aligned}
nat &:= & \forall X.(X \to X) \to X \to X \\
0 &:= & \lambda X.\, \lambda s : X \to X.\, \lambda z : X.z \\
S &:= & \lambda n : nat.\, \lambda X.\, \lambda s : X \to X.\, \lambda z : X.(s\,(n[X]\,s\,z))
\end{aligned}
$$

Recall from Chapter 6 that the idea is that a natural number n is something which takes a function f of type $X \to X$, and a starting point a, and returns $f^n(a)$ (in the sense of Definition 2.6.5, from Chapter 2); and this works for any type X. In the type for natural numbers,

$$
\forall X.\, (X \to X) \to X \to X
$$

we are universally quantifying over the type X. The rest of the type expresses that the number takes in a function of type $X \to X$ and a starting point of type X, and returns something of type X. You can confirm that we then have these typings:

$$
\begin{aligned}
0 &: & nat \\
S &: & nat \to nat
\end{aligned}
$$

Addition. The System F term for addition is:

$$
plus \quad := \quad \lambda n : nat.\, \lambda m : nat.\, (n[nat]\, S\, m)
$$

This term will iterate the successor function n times, starting from m. This will indeed produce $(S\,(S\,\cdots\,m))$, with n calls to successor.

Multiplication. We have already seen that multiplication can be viewed as iterated addition. This can be expressed in System F as follows:

$$mult \quad := \quad \lambda n : nat.\, \lambda m : nat.\, (n[nat]\, (plus\ m)\, 0)$$

The body here says to iterate the *plus m* function n times, starting from 0. This will indeed compute $n * m$, as desired.

10.4.2 Booleans

The System F terms for Church-encoded booleans are:

$$
\begin{aligned}
bool &= \forall X.X \to X \to X \\
true &= \lambda X.\, \lambda t : X.\, \lambda f : X.\, t \\
false &= \lambda X.\, \lambda t : X.\, \lambda f : X.\, f
\end{aligned}
$$

The type $\forall X.X \to X \to X$, which *bool* is defined to be, says that for any type X, if you give a boolean two values of type X (one for if the boolean is *true*, and another for if it is *false*), it will return a value of type X.

10.4.3 Polymorphic lists

For container types like lists, the situation in System F is not quite as nice as for natural numbers and booleans. If A is some System F type, for the elements of the lists, then we can make the following definitions:

$$
\begin{aligned}
\langle list\ A \rangle &:= \quad \forall X.(A \to X \to X) \to X \to X \\
nil &:= \quad \lambda A.\, \lambda X.\, \lambda c : A \to X \to X.\, \lambda n : X.n \\
cons &:= \quad \lambda A.\, \lambda a : A.\, \lambda l : \langle list\ A \rangle. \\
& \qquad \lambda X.\, \lambda c : A \to X \to X.\, \lambda n : X.(c\ a\ (l[X]\ c\ n))
\end{aligned}
$$

You can confirm that we then have these typings:

$$
\begin{aligned}
nil &: \quad \forall A.\ \langle list\ A \rangle \\
cons &: \quad \forall A.\ A \to \langle list\ A \rangle \to \langle list\ A \rangle
\end{aligned}
$$

What is somewhat unsatisfactory here is that we could only define the type $\langle list\ A \rangle$, not the type constructor *list*. Defining *list* itself requires the ability to define a function at the type level which can take in the type A, and return the type $\forall X.(A \to X \to X) \to X \to X$ which we defined to be $\langle list\ A \rangle$. Type-level functions are supported by System F_ω, which we consider next.

$$\begin{aligned}
kinds\ K\quad &::=\quad \star \mid K_1 \to K_2 \\
types\ T\quad &::=\quad X \mid T_1 \to T_2 \mid \forall X : K.T \mid (T_1\ T_2) \mid \lambda x : K.T \\
terms\ t\quad &::=\quad x \mid (t_1\ t_2) \mid \lambda x : T.t \mid t[T] \mid \lambda X : K.t
\end{aligned}$$

Figure 10.3: Syntax for terms, types, and kinds of F_ω

10.5 Higher-kind polymorphism and System F_ω

We consider the annotated version of System F_ω, as this is typically what is studied in the literature. The main innovation of F_ω over System F is to add functions at the type level. Once we do this, we naturally require a type system for those type-level functions, to prevent writing diverging type-level expressions. Types which classify expressions at the type level are standardly called **kinds**. So the type of a type-level expression is a kind. F_ω adopts the simplest (known) kind system for type-level functions, namely simple typing, with a single base kind, standardly denoted $\star$. Universal types $\forall X.T$ are extended so that they can quantify over types of any kind. In F_ω, in summary, we have terms classified by polymorphic types, which in turn are classified by simple kinds.

The syntax of F_ω is given in Figure 10.3. We have three syntactic categories: kinds K, types T, and terms t. Types can have kinds inside them as subexpressions; for example, $\forall X : \star.X$ is a type, and it contains the kind $\star$. Terms can contain types and kinds; for example, $\lambda X : \star.\lambda x : X.x$ is the polymorphic identity function, and it contains both a kind $\star$ and a type X. So we have a somewhat richer syntactic structure than we saw for STLC or System F.

10.5.1 Typing, kinding, and reduction

As in previous systems, we will now give rules for deriving certain classification judgments, involving contexts Γ of the following variety:

$$typing\ contexts\ \Gamma ::= \cdot \mid \Gamma, x : T \mid \Gamma, X : K$$

We assume that the context does not declare the same variable twice, and we write $\Gamma(X) = K$ and $\Gamma(x) = T$ to indicate the unique classifier associated with the given variable, if there is one.

In F_ω we have two classification judgments. The typing judgment $\Gamma \vdash t : T$ expresses that term t has type T in typing context Γ, while the kinding judgment $\Gamma \vdash T : K$ expresses that type T has kind K in context Γ. The kinding rules for F_ω are given in Figure 10.4, and the typing rules in Figure 10.5. The typing rules include a rule (the last one in the figure) for changing the type T of a term to some other type T', when $T = T'$. This typing rule is usually called a **conversion** rule. We need such a rule so that type-level computation can be incorporated into the

$$\frac{\Gamma(X) = K}{\Gamma \vdash X : K} \qquad \frac{\Gamma \vdash T_1 : \star \quad \Gamma \vdash T_2 : \star}{\Gamma \vdash T_1 \to T_2 : \star}$$

$$\frac{\Gamma, X : K \vdash T : \star}{\Gamma \vdash \forall X : K.T : \star} \qquad \frac{\Gamma \vdash T_1 : K \to K' \quad \Gamma \vdash T_2 : K}{\Gamma \vdash T_1 \, T_2 : K'}$$

$$\frac{\Gamma, X : K \vdash T : K'}{\Gamma \vdash \lambda X : K.T : K \to K'}$$

Figure 10.4: Kinding rules for F_ω

$$\frac{\Gamma(x) = T}{\Gamma \vdash x : T} \qquad \frac{\Gamma \vdash t_1 : T \to T' \quad \Gamma \vdash t_2 : T}{\Gamma \vdash t_1 \, t_2 : T'}$$

$$\frac{\Gamma \vdash T : \star \quad \Gamma, x : T \vdash t : T'}{\Gamma \vdash \lambda x : T.t : T \to T'} \qquad \frac{\Gamma \vdash t : \forall X : K.T' \quad \Gamma \vdash T : K}{\Gamma \vdash \lambda t[T] : [T/X]T'}$$

$$\frac{\Gamma, X : K \vdash t : T}{\Gamma \vdash \lambda X : K.t : \forall X : K.T} \qquad \frac{\Gamma \vdash t : T \quad T = T'}{\Gamma \vdash t : T'}$$

Figure 10.5: Typing rules for F_ω

system. If T can be simplified to T', for example, by type-level computation, the conversion rule allows us to change the type of a term t from T to T'. The rules defining the conversion relation on types are given in Figure 10.6; the type-level β-reduction rule (first in the figure) is the central one.

It is desirable to ensure that all the types being used in the context Γ are actually kindable. This is expressed using the judgment $\Gamma \vdash$, defined in Figure 10.7. In all the typing and kinding rules, it can be easily confirmed that if the typing context is well-formed ($\Gamma \vdash$) in the conclusion, it still will be in the premises. This requires one extra check, in the rule for typing λ-abstractions whose bound variable ranges over terms: we enforce that the classifier of the variable is kindable. Alternatively, we could have included $\Gamma \vdash$ as an extra premise of the axioms of the rules, to make sure that Γ is well-formed. Subsequent to these definitions, we will require $\Gamma \vdash$ whenever we form a judgment $\Gamma \vdash t : T$ or $\Gamma \vdash T : K$.

Figure 10.8 defines a reduction relation for F_ω, similar to the definition for annotated System F in Section 10.3.2.

10.5.2 Typed Church-encoded containers

Thanks to type-level computation, we can now return to the problem we encountered in Section 10.4.3, and give an unparametrized definition of the type constructor for lists:

$$(\lambda X : K.T')\ T = [T/X]T'$$

$$\frac{T_1 = T_1'}{T_1\ T_2 = T_1'\ T_2} \qquad\qquad \frac{T_2 = T_2'}{T_1\ T_2 = T_1\ T_2'}$$

$$\frac{T = T'}{\lambda X : K.T = \lambda X : K.T'} \qquad\qquad \frac{T = T'}{\forall X : K.T = \forall X : K.T'}$$

$$\frac{T_1 = T_1'}{T_1 \to T_2 = T_1' \to T_2} \qquad\qquad \frac{T_2 = T_2'}{T_1 \to T_2 = T_1 \to T_2'}$$

$$\frac{T_2 = T_1}{T_1 = T_2} \qquad\qquad \frac{T_1 = T_2 \quad T_2 = T_3}{T_1 = T_3}$$

Figure 10.6: Rules for type conversion in F_ω

$$\frac{}{\cdot \vdash} \qquad \frac{\Gamma \vdash T : \star}{\Gamma, x : T \vdash} \qquad \frac{\Gamma \vdash}{\Gamma, X : K \vdash}$$

Figure 10.7: Rules ensuring that the context is well-formed for F_ω

$$(\lambda x : T.t')\ t \leadsto [t/x]t' \qquad (\lambda X : K.t')[T] \leadsto [T/X]t'$$

$$\frac{t_1 \leadsto t_1'}{t_1\ t_2 \leadsto t_1'\ t_2} \qquad\qquad \frac{t_2 \leadsto t_2'}{t_1\ t_2 \leadsto t_1\ t_2'}$$

$$\frac{t_1 \leadsto t_1'}{t_1\ t_2 \leadsto t_1'\ t_2} \qquad\qquad \frac{t_2 \leadsto t_2'}{t_1\ t_2 \leadsto t_1\ t_2'}$$

$$\frac{t \leadsto t'}{\lambda x : T.t \leadsto \lambda x : T.t'} \qquad\qquad \frac{t \leadsto t'}{\lambda X : K.t \leadsto \lambda X : K.t'}$$

Figure 10.8: Reduction rules for F_ω

$$list \quad := \quad \lambda A : \star. \forall X : \star. (A \to X \to X) \to X \to X$$

We are using a type-level λ-abstraction of A to allow us to express that *list* takes in a type (A) as input and produces a type ($\forall X : \star. (A \to X \to X) \to X \to X$) as output. So *list* is defined to be a type-level function in F_ω. With this definition, we can type the constructors for lists, as well as other operations.

$$nil \quad := \quad \lambda A : \star. \lambda X : \star. \lambda c : A \to X \to X. \lambda n : X.n$$
$$cons \quad := \quad \lambda A : \star. \lambda a : A. \lambda l : list\ A.$$
$$\lambda X : \star. \lambda c : A \to X \to X. \lambda n : X.(c\ a\ (l[X]\ c\ n))$$

We then have these typings and kindings:

$$list \quad : \quad \star \to \star$$
$$nil \quad : \quad \forall A : \star. list\ A$$
$$cons \quad : \quad \forall A : \star.\ A \to list\ A \to list\ A$$

10.5.3 Metatheory and algorithmic typing

Type-level computation complicates several metatheoretic results. The proof of strong normalization is complicated by the need to interpret λ-abstractions at the type level. Standard approaches solve this problem by interpreting type-level functions as meta-level functions; an example, for a system called the Calculus of Constructions which contains F_ω as a subsystem, can be found in [14]. We will not consider normalization for F_ω further here. Instead, let us focus our attention on issues raised by the need for an algorithmic version of typing in F_ω.

The typing rules of Figure 10.5 are not algorithmic, due to the presence of the conversion rule. First, it is not immediately obvious that the type conversion relation (Figure 10.6) that is referenced in the premise of the conversion rule is decidable. To prove that it is, the standard approach is to define a reduction relation $\leadsto$ on types as in Figure 10.9. We then show that $\leadsto$ on types is strongly normalizing and confluent (cf. Section 9.1), and that the conversion relation is the reflexive, symmetric, transitive closure of $\leadsto$. These results imply that every type expression has a unique computable normal form, and testing $T_1 = T_2$ reduces to computing the normal forms of T_1 and T_2, and comparing those for syntactic identity (modulo safe renaming of bound variables). We will not prove these results, but just record this summary:

Theorem 10.5.1. $T = T'$ *iff there exists a normal form T'' such that $T \leadsto^* T''$ and $T' \leadsto^* T''$.*

The other issue with the conversion rule is that it can be applied at any point in a typing derivation, thus rendering the search for a typing derivation nondeterministic. It is curious that the usual way of defining the typing rules for F_ω (as

$$\overline{(\lambda X : K.T')\ T \rightsquigarrow [T/X]T'}$$

$$\frac{T_1 \rightsquigarrow T_1'}{T_1\ T_2 \rightsquigarrow T_1'\ T_2} \qquad\qquad \frac{T_2 \rightsquigarrow T_2'}{T_1\ T_2 \rightsquigarrow T_1\ T_2'}$$

$$\frac{T \rightsquigarrow T'}{\lambda X : K.T \rightsquigarrow \lambda X : K.T'} \qquad\qquad \frac{T \rightsquigarrow T'}{\forall X : K.T \rightsquigarrow \forall X : K.T'}$$

$$\frac{T_1 \rightsquigarrow T_1'}{T_1 \rightarrow T_2 \rightsquigarrow T_1' \rightarrow T_2} \qquad\qquad \frac{T_2 \rightsquigarrow T_2'}{T_1 \rightarrow T_2 \rightsquigarrow T_1 \rightarrow T_2'}$$

Figure 10.9: Rules for type-level reduction

in [6]), which we followed above, is this mixture of algorithmic (all the rules except conversion) and non-algorithmic rules. It is not too common to see the details of a completely algorithmic version of F_ω or similar systems worked out in the literature. Recall that we considered two approaches to handling typing rules like conversion which are not subject-directed, when we considered the subsumption rule for subtyping in Section 7.10.5. Here we will consider one of these approaches, applied to conversion: using a further annotation in the term syntax.

To define an algorithmic type-computation relation, we include an explicit cast-term as part of the annotated syntax, and replace the conversion rule with this rule:

$$\frac{\Gamma \vdash t : T \quad T = T'}{\Gamma \vdash cast\ t\ to\ T'\ :\ T'}$$

Now all our rules are subject-directed, and we have an algorithmic type-computation system. One important difference between our situation here and the one we considered for STLC with subtyping is that if we wish to define reduction on (annotated) terms of F_ω, as we are currently doing, we are going to need reduction rules to shift these casts off of λ-abstractions that would otherwise take part in β-reductions. For we could have a term like this:

$$(cast\ \lambda x : T.t'\ to\ T_1 \rightarrow T_2)\ t$$

which would reduce if the cast were not on the $\lambda x : T.t'$ term which is being applied. To shift the cast in this case and in the case of instantiating a universal type, we can add these rules to our reduction relation:

$$(cast\ (\lambda x : T.t')\ to\ T_1 \rightarrow T_2)\ t' \rightsquigarrow cast\ [(cast\ t'\ to\ T)/x]t'\ to\ T_2$$

$$(cast\ (\lambda X : K.t')\ to\ \forall X : K.T)[T'] \rightsquigarrow cast\ [T'/X]t'\ to\ [T'/X]T$$

This is not quite enough, since we could have multiple casts on the term being applied. But only the outermost cast matters, so we can resolve the difficulty with a cast-smashing reduction rule:

$$cast\ (cast\ t\ to\ T') \ to\ T \ \rightsquigarrow \ cast\ t\ to\ T$$

We also need a rule which allows reduction to take place beneath *cast* terms:

$$\frac{t \ \rightsquigarrow \ t'}{cast\ t\ to\ T \ \rightsquigarrow \ cast\ t'\ to\ T}$$

With these modifications to the reduction relation, we can prove Type Preservation and Progress theorems, relying on a substitution lemma similar to Lemma 7.6.2 for STLC, and a substitution lemma for substituting a type into a term (proofs omitted). Note that we have to substitute into the type part of the typing judgment in the second of these substitution lemmas:

Lemma 10.5.2 (Substitution of a term). *If* $\Gamma, x : T \vdash t' : T'$ *and* $\Gamma \vdash t : T$ *then* $\Gamma \vdash [t/x]t' : T'$.

Lemma 10.5.3 (Substitution of a type). *If* $\Gamma, X : K \vdash t' : T'$ *and* $\Gamma \vdash T : K$ *then* $\Gamma \vdash [T/X]t' : [T/X]T'$.

Theorem 10.5.4 (Type Preservation). *If* $\Gamma \vdash t : T$ *and* $t \rightsquigarrow t'$ *then* $\Gamma \vdash t' : T$.

Proof. The proof is by induction on the structure of the second assumed derivation. Most cases proceed as for STLC. We just consider a couple of the cases with casts:

Case:
$$(cast\ (\lambda x : T.t')\ to\ T_1 \to T_2)\ t' \ \rightsquigarrow \ cast\ [(cast\ t'\ to\ T)/x]t'\ to\ T_2$$

By inversion, the assumed typing derivation must look like:

$$\frac{\dfrac{\dfrac{\Gamma, x : T \vdash t' : T'}{\Gamma \vdash \lambda x : T.t' : T \to T' \quad T \to T' = T_1 \to T_2}}{\Gamma \vdash cast\ (\lambda x : T.t')\ to\ T_1 \to T_2 : T_1 \to T_2 \quad \Gamma \vdash t' : T_1}}{\Gamma \vdash (cast\ (\lambda x : T.t')\ to\ T_1 \to T_2)\ t' : T_2}$$

By Theorem 10.5.1, we know that $T \to T'$ and $T_1 \to T_2$ must be joinable using the reduction relation $\rightsquigarrow$ defined on types (Figure 10.9). This implies that T and T_1 are joinable, and T' and T_2 are joinable, since only reductions inside the subexpressions of an arrow type are possible (an arrow type itself cannot be a redex). By Theorem 10.5.1 again, this implies that $T = T_1$ and $T' = T_2$. So we can construct this typing derivation:

$$\dfrac{\dfrac{\Gamma, x : T \vdash t' : T' \quad \dfrac{\Gamma \vdash t' : T_1 \quad T_1 = T}{\Gamma \vdash cast\ t'\ to\ T : T}}{\Gamma \vdash [(cast\ t'\ to\ T)/x]t' : T'} \ Subst \quad T' = T_2}{\Gamma \vdash cast\ [(cast\ t'\ to\ T)/x]t'\ to\ T_2 : T_2}$$

Case:

$$(cast\ (\lambda X : K.t')\ to\ \forall X : K.T)[T'] \leadsto cast\ [T'/X]t'\ to\ [T'/X]T$$

By inversion, the assumed typing derivation must look like:

$$\frac{\dfrac{\Gamma, X : K \vdash t' : T_1}{\dfrac{\Gamma \vdash \lambda X : K.t' : \forall X : K.T_1 \quad \forall X : K.T_1 = \forall X : K.T}{\Gamma \vdash cast\ (\lambda X : K.t')\ to\ \forall X : K.T : \forall X : K.T} \quad \Gamma \vdash T' : K}}{\Gamma \vdash (cast\ (\lambda X : K.t')\ to\ \forall X : K.T)[T'] : [T'/X]T}$$

By applying Theorem 10.5.1 similarly to the previous case, we obtain $T_1 = T$. It is easy to prove that type-level equality is closed under substitution, so this implies $[T'/X]T_1 = [T'/X]T$. We can then construct this derivation:

$$\frac{\dfrac{\Gamma, X : K \vdash t' : T_1 \quad \Gamma \vdash T' : K}{\Gamma \vdash [T'/X]t' : [T'/X]T_1}\ Subst \quad [T'/X]T_1 = [T'/X]T}{\Gamma \vdash cast\ [T'/X]t'\ to\ [T'/X]T : [T'/X]T}$$

Case:

$$cast\ (cast\ t\ to\ T')\ to\ T \leadsto cast\ t\ to\ T$$

By inversion, the assumed typing derivation must look like:

$$\frac{\dfrac{\Gamma \vdash t : T'' \quad T'' = T'}{\Gamma \vdash cast\ t\ to\ T' : T' \quad T' = T}}{\Gamma \vdash cast\ (cast\ t\ to\ T')\ to\ T : T}$$

We can construct this derivation:

$$\frac{\Gamma \vdash t : T'' \quad \dfrac{T'' = T' \quad T' = T}{T'' = T}}{\Gamma \vdash cast\ t\ to\ T : T}$$

$\square$

We must also prove that the cast-shifting rules we have added are sufficient to prevent stuck redexes. For this, let us define the following notion of basic values and values:

$$\begin{array}{lcl} basic\ values\ w & ::= & \lambda x : T.t \mid \lambda X : K.t \\ values\ v & ::= & cast\ w\ to\ T \mid w \end{array}$$

Values are casts of basic values. We can now prove:

Theorem 10.5.5 (Progress). *If* $\cdot \vdash t : T$ *then either t is a value, or $t \leadsto t'$ for some t'.*

Proof. The proof is by induction on the assumed typing derivation. The variable case cannot arise, since the context is empty.

Case:

$$\frac{\cdot \vdash t_1 : T \to T' \quad \Gamma \vdash t_2 : T}{\cdot \vdash t_1\ t_2 : T'}$$

The IH applies to the premises. If either t_1 or t_2 reduces, then $t_1\ t_2$ reduces. So suppose both are values. If t_1 is of the form $\lambda x : T_1.t_1'$, then the application reduces. We cannot have t_1 of the form $\lambda X : K.t_1'$, by inversion: no typing rule can derive $\Gamma \vdash \lambda X : K.t_1' : T \to T'$. Finally, t_1 might be of the form $cast\ (\lambda x : T_1.t_1')\ to\ T \to T'$, but then the application reduces. By inversion, t_1 cannot be of the form $cast\ (\lambda X : K.t_1')\ to\ T \to T'$.

Case:

$$\frac{\cdot \vdash t : \forall X : K.T \quad \cdot \vdash T' : K}{\cdot \vdash t[T'] : [T'/X]T}$$

We proceed as in the previous case. The IH applies to the premise. If t steps, then so does $t[T']$. So suppose t is a value. Similar reasoning by inversion as in the above case shows that either we have t of the form $\lambda X : K.t$, or else $cast\ \lambda X : K.t\ to\ \forall X : K.T$. In either case, the term $t[T']$ reduces.

Case:

$$\frac{\cdot \vdash t : T \quad T = T'}{\cdot \vdash cast\ t\ to\ T' : T'}$$

If t steps then so does the cast-term. If t is a basic value, then the cast term is a value. Finally, if t is a cast-term itself, then the term in the conclusion steps, using the cast-smashing rule. □

10.6 Conclusion

In this chapter, we have considered parametric polymorphism in System F, and its extension to higher kinds, F_ω. We have seen how data which have been Church-encoded as pure lambda terms can be typed in System F. Container types like lists require the type-level computation available in F_ω, in order to give definitions for type constructors. We also took a look at some of the technical issues which the addition of type-level computation in F_ω raises.

10.7 Exercises

10.7.1 Basic exercises

1. For each of the following terms of System F, indicate whether it is an encoding of a boolean value, a unary natural number, or a list. Then, write the corresponding constructor term which would compute that value. To make the problem somewhat more interesting, I am not using suggestive names for the bound variables.

(a) $\lambda X.\, \lambda x : X.\, \lambda y : X.\, x$

(b) $\lambda X.\, \lambda x : X \to X.\, \lambda y : X.\, x\, y$

(c) $\lambda X.\, \lambda x : A \to X \to X.\, \lambda y : X.\, x\, (\lambda X.\, \lambda x : X.\, \lambda y : X.\, y)\, y$

2. Write out the typing derivation in System F to show that the Church-encoding of the numeral 1 has type *nat* (see Section 10.4.1).

3. Write out the typing derivation in F_ω that shows that *nil* has type

$$\forall A : \star.\mathit{list}\ A$$

Make sure to note where the conversion rule (of Figure 10.5) is used.

10.7.2   Intermediate exercises

1. Define (in System F) the type $\langle pair\ A\ B \rangle$ for pairs of elements, where the first component of each pair has type A, and the second type B. Also, define a constructor *mkpair* which takes two types, then two elements of those types, respectively, and creates a pair out of them. Use this constructor to compute the normal form of the expression *mkpair* [*bool*] [*nat*] *true* 0. Write out the resulting term in full detail, without using any of the definitions above (so, fully expand the definitions for *true* and 0).

2. Write out a term in F_ω extended with explicit cast-term (Section 10.5.3) corresponding to *cons* from Section 10.5.2. Show the reduction sequence you get, using the cast-shifting reduction rules of Section 10.5.3, when you reduce the term

$$cons\,[nat]\ 1\ nil$$

3. This problem asks you to carry out the second approach in Section 7.10.5 to work conversion into the type-computation rules, thus obtaining a type-computation system for F_ω without using *cast*-annotations. Define a set of rules which strictly interleaves applications of the conversion rule with the subject-directed rules (all the other rules of Figure 10.5). Then rework the system to combine the two layers into one. Confirm that your set of rules is algorithmic, and explain informally the relationship to the system of Figure 10.5.

Chapter 11

Functional Programming

This chapter is about programming languages based on typed lambda calculus, extended with various primitives operations. Such languages are usually called *functional programming* (FP) languages, since the central abstraction of the language is the possibly anonymous function, defined using lambda abstraction. We could call any language based on anonymous functions a functional language. Many languages include a feature like anonymous functions, but are not based on that abstraction as the central organizing idea. Such languages probably do not warrant the name "functional".

One can distinguish a stronger sense in which a language can be functional: all programs defined within the language behave like mathematical functions, which deterministically compute the same output whenever given the same inputs. Not many implemented programming languages are functional in this stronger sense. Of mainstream contemporary languages, Haskell is the only one I know which is strongly functional. For most mainstream languages have library functions like `gettimeofday()`, which are intended to return different answers every time they are called. These functions consult some implicit state (like time information maintained by the hardware and operating system of the computer) in order to compute their answers. In Haskell, there is no implicit state: a function like `gettimeofday()` must, in effect, take an extra argument representing the state of the computer. Haskell uses an abstraction known as *monads* and an inference algorithm based on what are called *type classes* in order to thread such extra arguments through code, without requiring the programmer to keep track of them explicitly.

There is a long and rich history of the use of lambda calculus in practical programming languages (ones which have been implemented and seen at least some widespread use). The first programming language, it seems, which made explicit use of ideas from the lambda calculus, including lambda abstractions, was LISP, developed by John McCarthy [27]. Many functional languages, or languages borrowing ideas from lambda calculus, have followed. In this chapter, we consider functional programming with call-by-value semantics (Section 11.1), and then with call-by-name semantics (Section 11.3). As a representative of eager FP, we consider OCaml (Section 11.2), and of lazy FP, Haskell (Section 11.4). A full treatment of either language is beyond the scope of this book. The interested reader can find many more resources about these and other functional programming languages online.

11.1   Call-by-value functional programming

In this section, we explore programming in extensions of the simply typed lambda calculus, with small-step left-to-right, call-by-value operational semantics. Call-by-value semantics is sometimes also called an **eager** semantics, in contrast to lazy semantics, which we will see in Section 11.3. We will add direct support for familiar programming constructs and features, including arithmetic, booleans and *if-then-else*, tuples, lists, and recursion. We have already seen, of course, that these features can be encoded directly in untyped lambda calculus, using the Scott encoding (Chapter 6). For efficient code, however, direct implementations are preferable over encodings into pure lambda calculus, as they can employ optimizations or take advantage of the underlying hardware (for arithmetic, for example). Also, even if we were to use Scott encodings for these features, we still have to see how to design types for them, as our Scott encoding is untyped. One can devise typed Scott encodings, but they are more involved than the typed Church encodings we considered in Chapter 10. Finally, we connect up with programming practice with a short introduction to functional programming in the OCaml functional programming language.

11.1.1   Extending the language

We begin by extending our simple types and simple type assignment rules to other constructs we added previously to lambda calculus. We design type computation rules for annotated lambda terms, though one could also design type assignment rules, or use one of the other approaches in Chapter 7.

Arithmetic

We assume we have base types *int* for integers and *bool* for booleans. We extend the syntax for terms from untyped lambda calculus as follows:

$$
\begin{array}{ll}
\text{integer literals } n & \\
\text{terms } t & ::= \quad \cdots \mid + \mid * \mid - \mid n \mid true \mid false \mid < \mid = \mid >
\end{array}
$$

And of course, we can include other operations as well. One simple convention used in both OCaml and Haskell is that arithmetic terms are parsed in infix notation using standard parsing conventions, but arithmetic operators may be used as any other functional term if written in parentheses. This approach allows us to write $((+)\, 3)$ for the function of type $int \to bool$ that adds 3 to its argument.

The operational semantics of these operations is defined by first extending our notion of values from the left-to-right call-by-value semantics for untyped lambda calculus, which we saw in Section 5.4.1). All the new operations we have introduced are themselves values, so we are just duplicating our new syntax for terms here:

$$
\text{values } v \quad ::= \quad \cdots \mid + \mid * \mid - \mid n \mid true \mid false \mid < \mid = \mid >
$$

Now we can write special reduction rules for these operations. A representative example is the following, where the occurrence of "+" in the premise of the rule denotes the real mathematical (meta-level) addition function:

$$\frac{n_3 = n_1 + n_2}{C[n_1 + n_2] \rightsquigarrow C[n_3]}$$

Finally, we can add new base types *int* and *bool*, and special typing rules for all the new constructs. A representative such rule is:

$$\overline{\Gamma \vdash + : int \rightarrow int \rightarrow int}$$

If-Then-Else

We again extend our syntax for terms:

$$terms \; t \; ::= \; \cdots \; | \; if \; t_1 \; then \; t_2 \; else \; t_3$$

We now need to extend our notion of evaluation contexts from the one we had for left-to-right CBV evaluation:

$$contexts \; C \; ::= \; \cdots \; | \; if \; C \; then \; t \; else \; t'$$

Notice that we do not allow reduction in the *then*- or *else*-branch of an *if-then-else* term, since the desired semantics is that we only reduce one of these, depending on the value of the guard (i.e., the term right after the "*if*"). We have two new reduction rules:

$$\overline{C[if \; true \; then \; t \; else \; t'] \rightsquigarrow C[t]}$$

$$\overline{C[if \; false \; then \; t \; else \; t'] \rightsquigarrow C[t']}$$

Finally, we have a new typing rule:

$$\frac{\Gamma \vdash t_1 : bool \quad \Gamma \vdash t_2 : T \quad \Gamma \vdash t_3 : T}{\Gamma \vdash if \; t_1 \; then \; t_2 \; else \; t_3 : T}$$

Notice that the rule requires the types of the two terms t_2 and t_3 to be the same (they are both T). This reflects the fact that statically, we do not know which of the two terms will be executed, and so we abstract their results to a single common type. An alternative could be to include an *if-then-else* operator at the type-level, but this is beyond what is done in practice in languages like OCaml and Haskell, and would require substantial complication of the type system.

Tuples

We can again extend our syntax of terms with notation for tuples, where $i \in \{1, 2, \ldots\}$ (the set of non-zero natural numbers):

$$terms \; t \; ::= \; \cdots \; | \; (t_1, \ldots, t_n) \; | \; t.i$$

We need to extend our notation for values and evaluation contexts:

$$
\begin{aligned}
\text{values } v & \quad ::= \quad \cdots \mid (v_1, \ldots, v_n) \\
\text{evaluation contexts } C & \quad ::= \quad \cdots \mid (v_1, \ldots, v_k, C, t_1, \ldots, t_l) \mid C.i
\end{aligned}
$$

The first new clause for contexts here just says that reduction may take place at a component of a tuple as long as all components to the left of that component (i.e., $v_1, \ldots, v_k$) are values; all the components to the right (i.e., $t_1, \ldots, t_l$) may be arbitrary terms. We then add this reduction rule:

$$
\frac{i \in \{1, \ldots, n\}}{C[(v_1, \ldots, v_n).i] \rightsquigarrow C[v_i]}
$$

Note that we could just as well start our component indices at 0 instead of 1. We now need to extend the syntax of simple types with a type for tuples:

$$
\text{types } T \quad ::= \quad \ldots \mid T_1 * \cdots * T_n
$$

We then add these typing rules:

$$
\frac{\Gamma \vdash t_1 : T_1 \quad \cdots \quad \Gamma \vdash t_n : T_n}{\Gamma \vdash (t_1, \ldots, t_n) : T_1 * \cdots * T_n} \qquad \frac{\Gamma \vdash t : \langle t_1, \ldots, t_n \rangle : T_1 * \cdots * T_n \quad i \in \{1, \ldots, n\}}{\Gamma \vdash t.i : T_i}
$$

Of course, these n-**ary** products (that is products that work for any arity, or any number n of subsidiary types) could be implemented using just binary products. So $bool * bool * bool$ could be implemented by $bool * (bool * bool)$. While this approach may be adequate in many situations, n-ary products can be implemented somewhat more space-efficiently in a compiler for such a language. All the components of the tuple can be stored in the same record (contiguous region) in memory. In contrast, with binary products, a tuple of n components will generally need to be stored in a structure that ends up being a linked list. Each cell in that list holds two pointers, one to the first component of the pair, and the other to the second component. Tuples implemented as nested pairs will require individual records in memory for each pair, where for all but the last of these pairs, one of the pointers from the region will be to the next pair in the nested structure. This is less space-efficient (and also less time-efficient, as one must traverse the linked-list structure to reach more deeply nested elements) than contiguously storing all components of the tuple in one record.

Lists

Languages like OCaml and Haskell allow programmers to declare their own inductive datatypes. Rather than describe general machinery for declaring new inductive datatypes, we will here just consider the example of the list datatype, which is a central data structure in all functional programming languages. We extend the syntax for terms as follows:

$$
\text{terms } t \quad ::= \quad \cdots \mid nil_T \mid cons\ t\ t' \mid match\ t\ with\ nil \Rightarrow t_1, cons\ x\ x' \Rightarrow t_2
$$

We are annotating *nil* with a type in order to have algorithmic type-computation rules below. Since OCaml and Haskell both implement type inference, such annotations are not necessary in those languages. Next, we extend our syntax for values and evaluation contexts:

$$
\begin{aligned}
\text{values } v &\quad ::= \quad \cdots \mid nil_T \mid cons\ v\ v' \\
\text{evaluation contexts } C &\quad ::= \quad \cdots \mid cons\ C\ t \mid cons\ v\ C \mid \\
&\qquad\qquad match\ C\ with\ ni\ \Rightarrow\ t_1\ ,\ cons\ x\ x'\ \Rightarrow\ t_2
\end{aligned}
$$

Like an *if-then-else* term, *match*-terms do not evaluate in the case branches t_1 and t_2, until we know whether the **scrutinee** t (the term immediately after "*match*") is a *nil*- or *cons*-term. This explains the form of the third new clause for contexts above. We have these new reduction rules:

$$
\overline{C[match\ nil_T\ with\ nil\ \Rightarrow\ t_1,\ cons\ x\ x'\ \Rightarrow\ t_2] \rightsquigarrow C[t_1]}
$$

$$
\overline{C[match\ (cons\ v\ v')\ with\ nil\ \Rightarrow\ t_1,\ cons\ x\ x'\ \Rightarrow\ t_2] \rightsquigarrow C[[v/x, v'/x']t_2]}
$$

Finally, we extend our typing relation. Each of our lists will hold data of a single type (they are *homogeneous*), but different lists can hold data of different types (so lists are *polymorphic*; cf. Chapter 10). We extend the syntax of types:

$$
\text{types } T\ ::=\ list\ T
$$

And we add these new typing rules:

$$
\overline{\Gamma \vdash nil_T : list\ T}
$$

$$
\frac{\Gamma \vdash t : T \quad \Gamma \vdash t' : list\ T}{\Gamma \vdash cons\ t\ t' : list\ T}
$$

$$
\frac{\Gamma \vdash t : list\ T \quad \Gamma \vdash t_1 : T' \quad \Gamma, x : T, x' : list\ T \vdash t_2 : T'}{\Gamma \vdash match\ t\ with\ nil\ \Rightarrow\ t_1,\ cons\ x\ x'\ \Rightarrow\ t_2 : T'}
$$

Recursion

Since simply typed lambda calculus is normalizing (see Section 7.5), we need to add something to the language in order to have a Turing-complete programming language. It can be shown that just the additions we have made so far are not enough. So we will add a fixed-point construct, which is like the *fix* operator we defined in Section 6.5, except that here we take it as a primitive construct (and do not give a complicated definition for it, as we did there). We also add special reduction and typing rules for this new construct. The syntax is

$$
\text{terms } t\ ::=\ \cdots \mid rec\ f : T.t
$$

We do not need to modify our definitions of values or reduction contexts. The new operational rule is

$$
\overline{C[rec\ f : T.t] \rightsquigarrow C[[rec\ f : T.t/f]t]}
$$

So we will substitute the whole term for f in t. This means that wherever t is using f to make a recursive call, it will actually have the whole term again. The typing rule is then:

$$\frac{\Gamma, f : T \vdash t : T}{\Gamma \vdash rec\ f : T.t : T}$$

This says that if t has type T, assuming that all uses (e.g., for recursive calls) of f do, then so does the entire *rec*-term.

11.1.2   Type safety

Our type system, as defined by extension from the one for simply typed lambda calculus, prevents certain errors from happening, such as trying to call $(+\ true\ \lambda x.x)$. We can prove it is working correctly by proving two theorems.

Theorem 11.1.1 (Type Preservation). *If $\Gamma \vdash t : T$ and $t \rightsquigarrow t'$, then $\Gamma \vdash t' : T$.*

Theorem 11.1.2 (Progress). *If $\cdot \vdash t : T$, then either $t \rightsquigarrow t'$ or else t is a value.*

Together, these theorems imply that "well-typed programs don't go wrong" (this is a famous slogan due to Turing award winner Robin Milner). Let us define a program (i.e., a term) to be *safe* if it is either a value or reduces to a *safe* term. So safe programs can never reduce to *stuck* terms like $(+\ \lambda x.x)$. Then all well-typed programs are safe.

The proof of Type Preservation just extends the proof we saw in Section 7.6 of Type Preservation for simply typed lambda calculus (STLC). We will not go through the details here. We did not prove Progress for STLC, because it is trivially true in that case: no closed terms are stuck. Here, however, proof is required. We will consider just the cases for simply typed lambda calculus extended with booleans and *if-then-else*.

Proof of Progress for STLC with booleans and if-then-else. The proof is by induction on the structure of the assumed typing derivation.

Case:

$$\frac{}{\cdot \vdash x : T}$$

This case cannot arise, since the context is empty.

Case:

$$\frac{}{\cdot \vdash true : bool}$$

The term is a value in this case, so the required result holds. The case for *false* is exactly similar.

Case:

$$\frac{\cdot \vdash t_1 : bool \quad \cdot \vdash t_2 : T \quad \cdot \vdash t_3 : T}{\cdot \vdash if\ t_1\ then\ t_2\ else\ t_3 : T}$$

By the induction hypothesis, t_1 either steps to some t_1', in which case the whole *if-then-else* term steps to *if t_1' then t_2 else t_3*; or else t_1 is a value. If it is a value, then by inversion on the assumed derivation of $\cdot \vdash t_1 : bool$, it must either be *true* or *false*. In either case, the whole *if-then-else* term steps.

Case:

$$\frac{\cdot, x : T \vdash t : T'}{\cdot \vdash \lambda x : T.t : T \to T'}$$

The term in question is already a value, as required.

Case:

$$\frac{\cdot \vdash t_1 : T \to T' \qquad \cdot \vdash t_2 : T}{\cdot \vdash t_1 t_2 : T'}$$

By the induction hypothesis, either t_1 steps, in which case the whole application steps, also; or else t_1 is a value. By inversion on the assumed typing derivation for t_1, this value must be a λ-abstraction, in which case the whole application β-reduces, as required. $\square$

11.2 Connection to practice: eager FP in OCaml

The OCaml programming language supports ideas similar to those discussed above in an eminently usable and performant implementation, with excellent documentation, freely available online. This section gives a quick tutorial to central features of OCaml. For more information, see various resources, including an excellent reference manual with thorough documentation of standard library functions, linked from `http://caml.inria.fr` (the OCaml compiler can also be downloaded from that site).

11.2.1 Compiling and running OCaml programs

File structure

An OCaml file contains non-recursive definitions of the form

```
let a x1 ... xn = t ;;
```

where x_1 through x_n are input variables to a (or omitted, if a is not a function or is just defined to be an explicit functional term), and t is the body of the function. There are also recursive definitions of the form

```
let rec a x1 ... xn = t ;;
```

These are similar, but a may be used in t to make recursive calls. OCaml files can also just contain terms by themselves:

```
t;;
```

which will be evaluated when the program is executed (note that their values will not be printed from output compiled as described next). For example, to write a hello-world program, it is sufficient to put the following in a file called `test.ml` and compile it as described below.

```
print_string "Hello, world.\n";;
```

This calls the standard-library function `print_string`. OCaml files can also contain several other kinds of top-level commands, including type declarations, discussed below.

Compiling to bytecode

OCaml can be easily compiled to OCaml bytecode format, which is then efficiently executed by an OCaml virtual machine, on many platforms, including Linux, Windows, and Mac (I have personally tried the former two with OCaml version 3.11.1). Native-code compilation is also supported on some platforms, but in my experience can be harder to get working on Windows (though it is easy on Linux). To compile a single OCaml source file to a bytecode executable, run

```
ocamlc -o file file.ml
```

To compile multiple sources files `a.ml`, `b.ml`, and `c.ml`, use the following commands:

```
ocamlc -c a.ml
ocamlc -c b.ml
ocamlc -c c.ml
```

This will generate files ending in `.cmo` (also ones ending in `.cmi`). To link these together into an executable called `test`, use this command:

```
ocamlc -o test a.cmo b.cmo c.cmo
```

Note that the order of these `.cmo` files matters: if file `b.ml` depends on file `a.ml`, then one must list `a.cmo` earlier than `b.cmo`, as shown.

Running online

At the time of this writing, you can also run OCaml programs at the `http://codepad.org` web site. You just enter your program text into a provided input pane, select "OCaml" from the list of supported programming languages, and submit the code for compilation and execution.

Using the `ocaml` interpreter

To evaluate expressions directly, just start the OCaml interpreter `ocaml`. On Linux, this can be done from the shell like this (on Windows, one can start OCaml from the `cmd` program, or by launching the OCaml interpreter that is included with the distribution):

```
ephesus:~/papers/plf-book$ ocaml
        Objective Caml version 3.11.2

#
```

Now one can enter expressions to evaluate, after the # sign:

```
ephesus:~/papers/plf-book$ ocaml
        Objective Caml version 3.11.2

# 3+4+5;;
- : int = 12
#
```

The interpreter prints out the type int and the value 12 to which this expression evaluates.

11.2.2 Language basics

Basic top-level functions

We can define non-recursive top-level functions in OCaml like this:

```
let square x = x * x;;
```

This defines the function square to take in an input x. The value returned by the function is then x * x. The names of defined functions must begin with lower-case letters. So the following is not allowed and will trigger an error:

```
let Square x = x * x;;
```

In keeping with its connection to mathematics, functional languages do not explicitly use return to state that something is the ordinary return-value for a function (Haskell does use return, but only for a more advanced functional-programming design pattern called a *monad*). Notice that it is not necessary to state any type information for an OCaml program like this. Type information is inferred automatically by the OCaml type checker, and is thus purely optional. If we want to include type information, we can include it like this for function definitions:

```
let square (x:int) : int = x * x;;
```

This states that the type of the input x is int. Also, the second ": int" indicates that the return type of the function is also int. Note that OCaml supports basic arithmetic operations like the multiplication used here. It has operations for 32-bit integers and also floating point numbers. The type int is for 32-bit integers. See the OCaml Reference Manual for complete details [26].

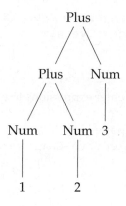

Figure 11.1: Example abstract syntax tree

Inductive datatypes

OCaml allows programmers to define their own datatypes, called inductive because each piece of data is uniquely and incrementally built by applying constructors to other data – central characteristics of inductive definitions. Members of these datatypes can be thought of as trees, storing different kinds of data. For example, we might wish to define a datatype for abstract syntax trees for a language with addition and integers. An example of the kind of abstract syntax tree we want to support for this language is in Figure 11.1. The tree shown might be the one a parser generates for the string "1+2+3". To declare the type for abstract syntax trees like this one, we can use the following OCaml code:

```
type expr = Plus of expr * expr | Num of int;;
```

This declares a new OCaml type called `expr`, with constructors `Plus` and `Num` for building nodes of the abstract syntax tree. The code "`of int`" following `Num` expresses that the `Num` constructor holds an `int`. Similarly, the `of expr * expr` code expresses that `Plus` holds a pair of two `expr`'s.

Pattern matching

OCaml supports pattern matching on members of datatypes like the `expr` datatype shown above. For example, the following top-level non-recursive function uses pattern matching to check whether or not an `expr` has `Plus` at its root (we call such an `expr` a `Plus`-expr), or not:

```
let isPlus e =
  match e with
    Plus(_,_) -> true
  | _ -> false;;
```

This code defines a function called `isPlus` which accepts an input e. The function pattern-matches on e. If e matches the pattern `Plus(_,_)`, then the value returned by the function is `true`, which is declared in OCaml's standard library as a `bool`. The underscores tell OCaml that we do not care about the left and right parts of the tree while matching against this pattern. If the tree e does not have `Plus` at its root, then OCaml will consider the next case. Here, we have just an underscore, indicating that we do not care what the tree looks like in this case. The boolean value `false` is then the return value for this case.

For another simple example, the following function returns the left subtree of a `Plus`-expr. It uses pattern variables `l` and `r` to refer to the left and right subtrees, respectively, of any matching `Plus`-expr. We could also have used an underscore instead of `r`, since the code for that case does not use `r`, but only `l` (for which we then could not have used an underscore, since we wish to refer to the matching value in that case).

```
let getLeft e =
  match e with
    Plus(l,r) -> l;;
```

Because the `getLeft` function does not have a case for Num-values, OCaml will issue a warning that not all cases are covered. And evaluating `getLeft (Num(3))` will trigger an error.

Pairs and tuples

To put two pieces of data x and y together into a pair, we just use the standard ordered pair notation `(x,y)`. To take apart a pair p into its first and second components x and y, we can use pattern matching. For example, the following code defines a function `addComponents` which takes a pair of two `int`'s and returns their sum:

```
let addComponents (p : int * int) : int =
  match p with
    (x,y) -> x + y;;
```

Here we see that the type of the input (i.e., the ordered pair) is `int * int`, which demonstrates the OCaml syntax for types of pairs. Note that the type `int * (int * int)` is not considered the same, in OCaml, as the type of triples `int * int * int`. We can write the same thing more concisely by using a pattern right in the argument list for `addComponents`, in place of the input p:

```
let addComponents (x,y) : int = x + y;;
```

Lists

Lists are used frequently in functional programming as a basic data structure, and both OCaml and Haskell (which we will discuss in Section 11.3) have special syntax for common operations on lists. OCaml provides some special syntax for lists. The empty list is denoted `[]`, and adding (or "consing") a new element a to the start of a list L is denoted `a::L`. This notation can be used in pattern-matching terms as well. For example, a recursive function to compute the length of a list can be written like this:

```
let rec length l =
  match l with
    [] -> 0
  | x::l' -> 1 + (length l')
;;
```

Here, as noted above, "let rec" introduces a top-level recursive function. The name of the function is length, and the input argument is named l. The function does pattern matching on l, with two cases. In the first case, l is [], the empty list. In that case, the returned value is 0. In the second case, the list l matches the pattern x::l'. This means that its first element is x, and the rest of it is the list l'. We return one plus the result of recursively computing the length of the list l'.

OCaml has some other notation related to lists. First, if we wish to write down the list of the first four numbers starting from 0, we could write 0::1::2::3::[]. That is the list we get by putting three onto the front of the empty list, then two onto the front of that, then 1, and finally 0. Alternative, slightly more readable notation in OCaml for this same list is [0 ; 1 ; 2 ; 3]. The general form of this alternative notation is to list elements in between square brackets, separated by semi-colons. The empty list [] can then be seen as a special case of that notation. Similarly, a *singleton* list containing exactly one element is also: we can write [2] for the list containing the single element 2. Finally, the operation which appends two lists can be written using infix @. So [1 ; 2] @ [3 ; 4 ; 5] is notation for calling the append function on the two given lists. This will result, of course, in the list [1 ; 2 ; 3 ; 4 ; 5].

OCaml supports a form of polymorphism (cf. Chapter 10) so lists are allowed with any (single) type of element. A list of integers has type int list in OCaml, and a list of booleans bool list. In general, a list of elements of type 'a (OCaml uses names beginning with a single quotation mark for type variables) has type 'a list. So list is a type constructor. OCaml generally writes type constructors in postfix notation. So we have the following typings:

```
1::2::3::4::[] : int list
true::true::false::[] : bool list
(fun x -> x)::(fun y -> y + y)::[] : (int -> int) list
```

True to its nature as a functional language, OCaml allows functions to be manipulated much like any other data, as demonstrated in the third example just above.

Unit type and side effects

The convention is that computations that are performed only for their side effects have type unit. The sole value of this type is denoted () in OCaml. This has the pleasant consequence that one can use the unit type when there is no other input to a function f, and then write f() to call that function. This results in syntax identical to what is used in other languages like C or Java for calling a function with no arguments. An example of code executed only for side effects is printing code, as in

```
print_string "Hello, world.\n";;
```

This has type unit, and returns () as its output, in addition to printing the given string on the standard output channel of the program.

If expression e_1 has type unit and e_2 has any other type T, then one can write $e_1; e_2$ for the computation which first evaluates e_1 (for its side effects), and then returns the value of e_2. This whole expression has type T, since this is the type of the value returned (if any).

Let-terms

To give a name for the value computed by some expression, OCaml provides let-notation. For example:

```
let x = 10 * 10 in
  x * x
```

This makes x refer to the value of 10 * 10 in its *body*, which is the subexpression following the in-keyword. So this whole expression has value 10,000. The type of the let-term is the type of its body. Functions, both non-recursive and recursive, can be defined using let-terms. For example, here is some code which uses a let-term to abstract out some code for logging from a bigger function foo:

```
let foo (log:out_channel) arg1 ... argn =
  let write_log (msg:string) =
    output_string log msg in
  ...
  write_log "some message";
  write_log "another";
  ...
;;
```

The let-term defining the function write_log uses a similar syntax as for top-level functions (see above). Notice how the definition of write_log refers to a variable in the surrounding context, namely log, without requiring it as an extra input. This helps keep calls to write_log more concise.

Mutually inductive datatypes, mutually recursive functions

In addition to the inductive datatypes and recursive functions explained above, OCaml also supports the definition of mutually inductive datatypes, and mutually recursive functions. Two or more types (respectively, two or more functions) are defined, and the definition of each can refer to the other. The keyword and is used to separate the definitions, for both types and recursive functions. Here is a simple example:

```
let rec plusee (e1:even) (e2:even) : even =
  match e1 with
    Z -> e2
  | Se(o1) -> Se(plusoe o1 e2)
and plusoe (o:odd) (e:even) : odd =
  match o with
    So(e1) -> So(plusee e1 e)
and pluseo (e:even) (o:odd) : odd =
  match e with
    Z -> o
  | Se o1 -> So(plusoo o1 o)
and plusoo (o1:odd) (o2:odd) : even =
  match o1 with
    So e -> Se(pluseo e o2)
;;
```

Figure 11.2: Addition on the types for even and odd natural numbers, in OCaml

```
type even = Z | Se of odd
  and odd = So of even;;
```

This declares two mutually inductive types, of even and odd numbers in unary notation (see Section 6.2.1). OCaml reports the following typings for some example terms built using the constructors for these types:

```
Z : even
(So Z) : odd
(Se (So Z)) : even
(So (Se (So Z))) : odd
(Se (So (Se (So Z)))) : even
```

The odd numbers indeed have type odd, and the even numbers even. The definitions in Figure 11.2 define addition functions for all possible combinations of even and odd inputs. Note how the return types correctly capture the behavior of the usual definition of unary addition: for example, adding two odd numbers produces an even number.

11.2.3 Higher-Order Functions

As essential aspect of functional programming, well supported by OCaml, is the use of higher-order functions. These are functions that accept other functions as inputs, or produce them as outputs. Anonymous functions are also commonly used, and can be nested inside other functions. The notation for an anonymous function in OCaml is

```
fun x -> t
```

So the squaring function we defined in the previous section as a top-level function can be written as an anonymous function like this:

```
fun x -> x * x
```

Functions as inputs

Here is a top-level function called `applyTwice`, which accepts a function `f` and argument `x` as inputs, and applies `f` twice: first to `x`, and then to the result of the first application:

```
let applyTwice f x = f (f x)
```

Note, in passing, the notation for a nested function call: parentheses are placed around the call of `f` on `x`; `f` is then applied again to that parenthesized expression.

We can call `applyTwice` with our anonymous squaring function and the argument 3 to raise 3 to the fourth power:

```
applyTwice (fun x -> x * x) 3
```

If we were using our top-level definition of the squaring function, we could just as well write

```
applyTwice square 3
```

Partial applications

In OCaml, functions defined with N input variables can be called with fewer than N arguments. An application of a function to fewer than the number of input variables stated in its definition is called a partial application. For example, the `applyTwice` function we just defined has two input variables, `f` and `x`. But we are allowed to call it with just the first one; for example,

```
applyTwice (fun x -> x * x)
```

What value is it that we get back from a partial application like this one? We get back a new function, which is waiting for the remaining arguments. In this case, we get back a function which, when given the remaining needed argument `x`, will return the square of the square of `x`. Suppose we write a top-level definition like this:

```
let pow4 = applyTwice (fun x -> x * x);;
```

If we can call `pow4` on an argument like 3, we will get 81. If we call it on 4, we will likewise get the expected result (256). So by using a partial application, we have abstracted out an interesting piece of functionality, namely raising to the fourth power by applying squaring twice. This abstracted value, `pow4`, can now be used repeatedly with different arguments; for example:

```
pow4 3;;
pow4 4;;
```

This is more concise than writing the following, for example, to process several numbers:

```
applyTwice (fun x -> x * x) 3;;
applyTwice (fun x -> x * x) 4;;
```

One quirk in OCaml is that constructors that take arguments, like the Se constructor for the even datatype above, must be fully applied.

List combinators

OCaml has a module List in its standard library for operations on lists. In addition to first-order operations on lists that you might expect (such as the append operation mentioned in Section 11.2.2), the List module defines several higher-order functions on lists that are commonly used. Here are a few examples:

- List.iter f l applies function f to every element of list l, where f returns unit. This is a type which has exactly one element, denoted (), and is used when computations are not intended to return results, but solely to be executed for their side effects (such as printing out a string).

- List.map f l applies function f to every element of list l, collecting the results in a new list.

- List.filter p l returns the list of those elements of list l which satisfy predicate p. This p must have type 'a -> bool, where 'a is the type for elements of l.

11.3   Lazy programming with call-by-name evaluation

In this section, we consider how call-by-name evaluation (first considered in Section 5.4.4) can be used for practical programming. The main benefit of call-by-name evaluation is that terms do not have to be evaluated to be passed as arguments to functions. This opens up the possibility of **lazy evaluation**, where computation is deferred until it absolutely must be performed in order to satisfy an immediate need for a value, such as to print it or communicate it over a network channel. For better performance, implementations of lazy programming use an optimized form of call-by-name evaluation, known as **call-by-need**. The basic idea of this optimization is as follows. When doing call-by-name evaluation, unevaluated terms can be duplicated by β-reduction. While lazy evaluation will try to avoid evaluating any of those copies of the term, it could happen that several of them do need to be evaluated. In that case, it is wasteful to evaluate each of the duplicate copies of the term separately, since the computation is exactly the same in each case. Call-by-need evaluation caches the result the first time that term is evaluated. If subsequent computation requires evaluating a copy of the term, call-by-need evaluation just uses the cached result, instead of re-evaluating the term. Languages like Haskell are typically implemented using call-by-need evaluation.

We will consider lazy programming using just call-by-name evaluation, since except for possibly (much) slower execution, this gives the same results as call-by-need. We will consider Haskell (Section 11.4) as an example lazy programming language.

11.3.1 Syntax and typing for lazy programming

Here, we develop a small lazy programming language based on call-by-name evaluation. The language has basic arithmetic, λ-abstractions, list constructs, and a recursion operator, and is thus quite similar to the eager (call-by-value) language we studied in Section 11.1. The typing rules for these constructs are just as they were for our eager language. The difference between the lazy and the eager languages will come with the operational semantics. We collect here the complete syntax we will use for terms and types:

$$
\begin{aligned}
\textit{types } T \quad ::= \quad & int \mid bool \mid list\ T \mid T_1 \rightarrow T_2 \\
\textit{terms } t \quad ::= \quad & x \mid t_1\ t_2 \mid \lambda x : T.t \mid rec\ x : T.t \mid +\mid *\mid -f \mid n \mid <\mid =\mid >\mid \\
& true \mid false \mid if\ t_1\ then\ t_2\ else\ t_3 \mid nil_T \mid cons\ t\ t' \mid \\
& match\ t\ with\ nil\ \Rightarrow\ t_1\ ,\ cons\ x\ x'\ \Rightarrow\ t_2
\end{aligned}
$$

The typing rules are exactly the same as those from Section 11.1 for the corresponding constructs of the eager language. For example, we have this typing rule for the recursion operator:

$$
\frac{\Gamma, f : T \vdash t : T}{\Gamma \vdash rec\ f : T.t : T}
$$

Consult Section 11.1 for the rest of the rules.

11.3.2 Operational semantics of call-by-name

The operational semantics for our lazy language does differ from that of the eager language of Section 11.1, but not by as much as one might expect. The main differences are that we do not require arguments to be evaluated to values before doing a β-reduction, and we consider list-terms to be values even if their subdata are not. To achieve this latter property, we use the following definitions for contexts and values:

$$
\begin{aligned}
\textit{values } v \quad ::= \quad & \lambda x : T.t \mid +\mid *\mid -\mid n \mid true \mid false \mid <\mid =\mid >\mid \\
& nil_T \mid cons\ t\ t'
\end{aligned}
$$

$$
\begin{aligned}
\textit{contexts } \mathcal{C} \quad ::= \quad & * \mid \mathcal{C}\ t \mid if\ \mathcal{C}\ then\ t\ else\ t' \mid \mathcal{C} + t \mid v + \mathcal{C} \mid \\
& match\ \mathcal{C}\ with\ nil\ \Rightarrow\ t_1\ ,\ cons\ x\ x'\ \Rightarrow\ t_2
\end{aligned}
$$

Crucially, there is no clause allowing evaluation in the argument position of a term. Also, there is no clause for *cons*-contexts (unlike for the eager language), and a *cons*-term can be a value even if the subdata are just terms t and t'. The corresponding clause for values for the eager language has *cons* $v\ v'$ instead. The

$$\overline{\mathcal{C}[(\lambda x : T.\, t)\ t'] \rightsquigarrow \mathcal{C}[[t'/x]t]}$$

$$\frac{n_3 = n_1 + n_2}{\mathcal{C}[n_1 + n_2] \rightsquigarrow \mathcal{C}[n_3]}$$

$$\overline{\mathcal{C}[\textit{if true then } t \textit{ else } t'] \rightsquigarrow \mathcal{C}[t]}$$

$$\overline{\mathcal{C}[\textit{if false then } t \textit{ else } t'] \rightsquigarrow \mathcal{C}[t']}$$

$$\overline{\mathcal{C}[\textit{match nil}_T \textit{ with nil} \Rightarrow t_1, \textit{ cons } x\ x' \Rightarrow t_2] \rightsquigarrow \mathcal{C}[t_1]}$$

$$\overline{\mathcal{C}[\textit{match cons } t\ t' \textit{ with nil} \Rightarrow t_1, \textit{ cons } x\ x' \Rightarrow t_2] \rightsquigarrow \mathcal{C}[[t/x, t'/x']t_2]}$$

$$\overline{\mathcal{C}[\textit{rec } f : T.\, t] \rightsquigarrow \mathcal{C}[[\textit{rec } f : T.\, t/f]t]}$$

Figure 11.3: Left-to-right call-by-name small-step operational semantics for our lazy language

only point at which we have to choose between left-to-right and right-to-left evaluation is in evaluating the arguments to binary arithmetic operators. We actually must give special clauses for contexts built with such operators. This was not necessary in the eager language, because there all arguments must be evaluated to values before an application (including an application of an arithmetic operator) can be reduced. But here, since arguments are not reduced by default, we must specify that they are explicitly. Since this is done in the same way for every binary operator, we just show one clause for the definition of contexts built with such.

Figure 11.3 then gives the left-to-right call-by-name small-step operational semantics for the language. We just give one example of a rule for evaluating arithmetic terms. Notice that the β-rule (the first one in the figure) has t' for the argument. In the eager language, our call-by-value β-rule has v for the argument.

11.3.3 Programming with lazy infinite data structures

Since cons-terms are values even if their subterms are not, our call-by-name language supports a style of programming based on lazy infinite data structures. Here is a simple example:

$$\textit{threes} = \textit{rec } f : \textit{list int. cons } 3\ f$$

This expression behaves just like an infinitely long list of 3's, under our lazy semantics. First, let us see how this term evaluates. Here and below, I am underlining redexes. Also, some steps are reduction steps ($\rightsquigarrow$), and some are equational steps, just to show in more detail how a substitution is computed or a definition unfolded.

$$
\begin{array}{rl}
& \textit{threes} \\
= & \textit{rec } f : \textit{list int. cons } 3 \ f \\
\rightsquigarrow & \overline{\textit{cons } 3 \ (\textit{rec } f : \textit{list int. cons } 3 \ f)} \\
= & \textit{cons } 3 \ \textit{threes}
\end{array}
$$

This last *cons*-term is now a value, despite the fact that its tail (*rec f : list int. cons 3 f*) is not. If we want to see more of the list, we have to inspect it using our *match*-construct. For example, let us add the first two elements of the list:

$$
\begin{array}{rl}
& \textit{match threes with} \\
& \quad \textit{nil} \Rightarrow 0, \ \textit{cons } x \ x' \Rightarrow x + (\textit{match } x' \textit{ with nil} \Rightarrow 0, \ \textit{cons } x \ x' \Rightarrow x) \\[2mm]
= & \textit{match rec } f : \textit{list int. cons } 3 \ f \textit{ with} \\
& \quad \overline{\textit{nil} \Rightarrow 0}, \ \textit{cons } x \ x' \Rightarrow x + (\textit{match } x' \textit{ with nil} \Rightarrow 0, \ \textit{cons } x \ x' \Rightarrow x) \\[2mm]
\rightsquigarrow & \textit{match cons } 3 \ \textit{rec } f : \textit{list int. cons } 3 \ f \textit{ with} \\
& \quad \underline{\textit{nil} \Rightarrow 0, \ \textit{cons } x \ x' \Rightarrow x + (\textit{match } x' \textit{ with nil} \Rightarrow 0, \ \textit{cons } x \ x' \Rightarrow x)} \\[2mm]
\rightsquigarrow & [3/x, \textit{rec } f : \textit{list int. cons } 3 \ f/x'](x + (\textit{match } x' \textit{ with nil} \Rightarrow 0, \ \textit{cons } x \ x' \Rightarrow x)) \\[2mm]
= & (3 + (\textit{match } \underline{\textit{rec } f : \textit{list int. cons } 3 \ f} \textit{ with nil} \Rightarrow 0, \ \textit{cons } x \ x' \Rightarrow x)) \\[2mm]
\rightsquigarrow & (3 + (\textit{match } \underline{\textit{cons } 3 \ \textit{rec } f : \textit{list int. cons } 3 \ f} \textit{ with nil} \Rightarrow 0, \ \textit{cons } x \ x' \Rightarrow x)) \\[2mm]
\rightsquigarrow & (3 + [3/x, \textit{rec } f : \textit{list int. cons } 3 \ f/x']x) \\[2mm]
= & \underline{(3 + 3)} \\[2mm]
\rightsquigarrow & 6
\end{array}
$$

This example shows how lazy infinite data structures are computed only as much as needed to perform some desired computation.

11.3.4   The lazy infinite list of all natural numbers

One way to define the lazy infinite list of all natural numbers is to write a function *nums* which given starting value n, computes the lazy infinite list of all natural numbers greater than or equal to n. This setup makes it possible to compute the lazy infinite tail of the list by making a recursive call to *nums*:

$$
\textit{nums} \ = \ \textit{rec nums} : \textit{int} \rightarrow \textit{list nat. } \lambda \ n : \textit{int. cons } n \ (\textit{nums}(n + 1))
$$

Now we can define the lazy infinite list of all natural numbers as just

$$
\textit{nats} \ = \ \textit{nums } 0
$$

Let us use observational equivalence to help see how *nats* behaves. We will show some lists which are observationally equivalent to *nats*, which help give insight into how *nats* will behave if inspected using *match*. Let us temporarily denote observational equivalence with $\approx$. For readability, I will expand and contract the definition of *nums* implicitly, in several places:

$$
\begin{aligned}
nats & = \\
nums\ 0 & = \\
(rec\ nums : int & \to list\ nat.\ \lambda\ n : int.\ cons\ n\ (nums\ (n+1)))\ 0 \rightsquigarrow \\
(\lambda\ n : int.\ cons\ n\ (nums\ (n+1)))\ 0 & \rightsquigarrow \\
cons\ 0\ (nums\ (0+1)) & \approx \\
cons\ 0\ (nums\ 1) & \approx \\
cons\ 0\ ((\lambda\ n : int.\ cons\ n\ (nums\ (n+1)))\ 1) & \approx \\
cons\ 0\ (cons\ 1\ (nums\ (1+1))) & \approx \\
cons\ 0\ (cons\ 1\ (nums\ 2)) & \cdots
\end{aligned}
$$

Using observational equivalence, we can unfold the lazy infinite list, without actually computing it. The normal form of *nats* is just $cons\ 0\ (nums\ (0+1))$, so to see more of the structure of the list, we cannot write further terms to which $cons\ 0\ (nums\ (0+1))$ reduces. Instead, we are writing further terms to which it is observationally equivalent. I am using the property that in our call-by-name language, two terms are equivalent if one reduces to the other using full β-reduction.

11.4   Connection to practice: lazy FP in Haskell

As remarked at the start of this chapter, Haskell is a functional programming language in the strong sense: every expression defined in Haskell computes the same result. Haskell is based on a call-by-need operation semantics, which as noted in Section 11.3, produces the same results as call-by-name, though possibly more quickly. As for OCaml, there are many excellent materials online for learning Haskell. A good place to start is http://www.haskell.org, where you can also download the GHC Haskell compiler for use on your computer. In this section, we will restrict our attention to lazy computation. There are many interesting other innovations in Haskell; for example, monads provide a pure functional implementation of impure operations like input/output. Also, Haskell supports higher-kind polymorphism, as in F_ω (Chapter 10). But these features are mostly beyond the scope of the present chapter, which is focused on how call-by-need operational semantics enables lazy programming. See [22] for an in-depth look at how Haskell uses monads for effectful computations. We will start with a few basic matters.

11.4.1   Running Haskell

There are several ways to run a Haskell program. One simple way is to invoke the GHC interpreter `ghci` with a Haskell source file (say `main.hs`):

```
ghci main.hs
```

GHC will compile the given file, and then drop you into a command shell where you can interact with your compiled Haskell code:

```
*Main>
```

Typing in a Haskell expression will evaluate it and print the result. The command :t takes an expression and tells you its type. So we have this interaction:

```
*Main> :t "hi"
"hi" :: [Char]
```

The Haskell Prelude elegantly defines String to be [Char] (lists of characters) – in contrast, OCaml does not define string to be char list – and so we see [Char] as the type for the string "hi".

The command :k shows you the kind (see Section 10.5) for a type. For example:

```
*Main> :k Int
Int :: *
*Main> :k ([])
([]) :: * -> *
```

The type Int has kind *, while the type construct [], for lists types, has kind * -> *, indicating that it takes a type (a type a of elements) and produces a type (the type of lists with elements of type a).

The :r command reloads the module you are currently processing (so you can edit a file like main.hs, and then just enter :r in ghci to reload it without quitting ghci). To quit, use :q. The :? command will list other commands available from this ghci command shell. You can also just invoke ghci with no arguments, to enter expressions at the command prompt.

Functions can be defined directly from the ghci prompt using some slightly different syntax, but the preferred method is to put function definitions and definitions of datatypes in a source file, and then invoke ghci on that source file. So in the code examples below, unless you see the ghci prompt listed explicitly, please assume the code is in a source file (like main.hs).

At the time of this writing, http://codepad.org also supports Haskell, but uses the compiler rather than the interpreter. This requires a little bit of additional code. Where you could have just typed an expression e into ghci to see its value (assuming the value can be converted to a String, as described below), with compiled Haskell (as on codepad), you would write:

```
main =
  do putStrLn $ show e
```

This defines a main result which just prints out (putStrLn) the string version (show) of the result of the expression *e*. The dollar sign is a low-precedence application operator. So putStrLn $ show e is equivalent to putStrLn (show e).

11.4.2   Lists in Haskell

Lists in Haskell are defined by `[]` (for nil) and `:` (for cons). So the list consisting of the first three natural numbers can be written `0:1:2:[]`. If you enter this at the `ghci`'s command prompt, `ghci` will reply with the list in another notation: `[0,1,2]`. This is analogous to OCaml's `[0;1;2]` notation. To append two lists, the infix operator is `++`. The type for a list of elements of type `a` is `[a]`. For more operations on lists, see the `Prelude` module of Haskell's standard library. This module is already opened when `ghci` starts.

11.4.3   Defining functions with equations

Functions in Haskell are usually defined with equations. For example, suppose we want to define an append function on two lists. This can be done quite elegantly in Haskell using these equations:

```
append [] ys = ys
append (x:xs) ys = x:append xs ys
```

The idea is to write equations whose right-hand sides define the behavior of the function when presented with data which matches the patterns in the left-hand sides. The notation is quite similar to the standard mathematical notation of recursive equations which we have used throughout this book (e.g., Section 1.6).

11.4.4   Defining datatypes

The basic syntax for defining a datatype in Haskell is similar to that of OCaml. For example, if we want to define the mutually recursive types of even and odd natural numbers as we did above for OCaml, we use this code in Haskell:

```
data Even = Z | Se Odd
data Odd = So Even
```

Types and functions in a Haskell module are allowed to be mutually recursive, and the order in which they are given does not matter. So these two separate declarations of types `Even` and `Odd` are allowed to refer to each other, without any additional syntax. Recall from above that in the OCaml version of this example, special syntax is needed to define these as mutually recursive types.

Note that similarly to OCaml, Haskell requires the names of data constructors like `Z`, `Se`, and `So` to be capitalized. Opposite to OCaml, though, Haskell also requires the names of types (and type constructors) like `Even` and `Odd` to be capitalized.

11.4.5   Type classes

Suppose we have added the code in the previous subsection to `main.hs` to define the types `Even` and `Odd`. From `ghci`, we would expect we can then evaluate some terms of those types, like (So Z), and see that they have the expected type. But when we try this in ghci, we get this error:

```
*Main> (Se (So Z))

<interactive>:1:1:
    No instance for (Show Even)
      arising from a use of `print'
    Possible fix: add an instance declaration for (Show Even)
    In a stmt of an interactive GHCi command: print it
```

The issue here is that ghci will print out values of expressions only if they can be converted to type String, the type of strings.

If we look more closely at the error message from ghci, we see it is telling us that there is "no instance for (Show Even)", and suggesting that we should "add an instance declaration for (Show Even)". What are instances and instance declarations? They are part of a subsystem of Haskell for operator overloading. The basic idea is to group together types which all support a common set of operations. The group of types is called a *type class*. For example, there is a type class called Show (defined in the Haskell Prelude) for types a which have a show operation of type a -> String. If our Even type were a member of this class, we would not get the error message we saw above when we evaluate (Se (So Z)).

Instance declarations

To tell Haskell that our types Even and Odd are members of the type class Show, we first need to define functions which convert elements of these types to strings:

```
pr_even Z = "Z"
pr_even (Se o) = "(Se " ++ pr_odd o ++ ")"
pr_odd (So e) = "(So " ++ pr_even e ++ ")"
```

Then we can use these *instance declarations* to tell Haskell that the show function of the type class Show is instantiated by pr_even in the case of Even, and pr_odd in the case of Odd:

```
instance Show Even where
  show = pr_even

instance Show Odd where
  show = pr_odd
```

Now if we repeat our earlier attempt to have Haskell print back the value of the constructor term (Se (So Z)), we indeed get back the expected result:

```
*Main> (Se (So Z))
(Se (So Z))
*Main>
```

Deriving clauses

Making a datatype an instance of the `Show` type class is so common, and basic code for converting to strings is so similar, that Haskell provides a very easy way to do this, using `deriving` clauses. These instruct Haskell to derive a basic `show` function and add the datatype to the type class, fully automatically. One just adds `deriving Show` to the datatype definition:

```
data Even = Z | Se Odd deriving Show
data Odd = So Even deriving Show
```

Haskell declares `Show Even` and `Show Odd`, using a function for `show` in each case, which Haskell automatically generates to conform to a specification in the Haskell 98 Report (see Section 10 of `http://www.haskell.org/onlinereport/index.html`). The function behaves very similarly to the one we wrote above, although the specification requires it to omit parentheses where they are not needed. So we get:

```
*Main> (Se (So Z))
Se (So Z)
*Main>
```

11.4.6   Another example of equational definitions

Here is the definition of the addition functions on even and odd numbers in Haskell:

```
plusee Z e2 = e2
plusee (Se o1) e2 = Se(plusoe o1 e2)

plusoe (So e1) e2 = So(plusee e1 e2)

pluseo Z o2 = o2
pluseo (Se o1) o2 = So(plusoo o1 o2)

plusoo (So e) o = Se(pluseo e o)
```

While this is still a bit convoluted, the equational definitions seem easier to read than the version in OCaml (Figure 11.2 above).

11.4.7   Lazy infinite data structures in Haskell

Although there are many important differences, what most centrally distinguishes Haskell from OCaml is Haskell's lazy (call-by-need) operational semantics. This enables elegant programming idioms based on lazy infinite data structures (as introduced in Section 11.3.3 above), which are evaluated only as much as needed to produce some observable result. A paradigmatic example is programming with lazy infinite lists. For example, here is Haskell code to define the lazy infinite list of all the natural numbers:

```
natsup n = n : (natsup (n+1))
nats = natsup 0
```

The idea in this short piece of code is to define a function called natsup which produces the lazy infinite list of all the natural numbers starting at a given number n, the input to natsup. Then nats is defined as the list of all natural numbers starting with 0. If you define nats as above (in main.hs, say), and then ask ghci to evaluate nats, it will run forever printing out all the natural numbers. Printing a list is an example of an observation, and so it makes sense that ghci will be forced to evaluate the lazy data structure in this case. But there is a slightly subtle phenomenon going on even with this diverging behavior: ghci does not attempt to evaluate nats first, and then print it. It begins printing it, and as it needs to observe more and more of it, additional parts of nats are actually computed. So laziness is at work even in this case. To see just the first few elements of nats, use the take function from the Prelude:

```
*Main> take 7 nats
[0,1,2,3,4,5,6]
```

Another classic example in Haskell is the Fibonacci sequence (which starts with $0, 1$ and continues by adding the two previous numbers):

$$0, 1, 1, 2, 3, 5, 8, 13, 21, 34, \cdots$$

The Fibonacci sequence can be defined as a lazy infinite list in many different ways in Haskell. The following is a particularly concise and cute way to do it:

```
fibs = 0 : 1 : zipWith (+) fibs (tail fibs)
```

Let us first confirm this works, and then try to understand what the code is saying. Requesting the first 10 elements of fibs using the take function produces:

```
*Main> take 10 fibs
[0,1,1,2,3,5,8,13,21,34]
```

The definition of fibs starts out in a way we can easily understand, with the first two values of the sequence, cons'ed together using the (:) operator:

```
fibs = 0 : 1 :
```

Now let us look at the next bit of code, which is defining fibs after the first two elements:

```
zipWith (+) fibs (tail fibs)
```

Here we have a call to the Prelude function zipWith. We can ask ghci what its type is:

```
*Main> :t zipWith
zipWith :: (a -> b -> c) -> [a] -> [b] -> [c]
```

So in a call `zipWith f x y`, the argument `f` is a function of type `a -> b -> c`, the argument `x` is a list of elements of type `a`, and `y` is a list of elements of type `b`. Suppose `x` is `[x_1, x_2, ... ]` and `y` is `[y_1, y_2, ...]`. Then the result of such a call to `zipWith` will be the list of the results of calling `f` on corresponding elements of `x` and `y` (if the lists are of different lengths, the results are computed only up to the shorter length):

$$[f \ x_1 \ y_1, f \ x_2 \ y_2, ...]$$

The `zipWith` function is a generalization of the `map` function, which is present in the Haskell Prelude and corresponds to the `List.map` function of OCaml. Here in the code for `fibs`, we are zipping together the list `fibs` itself, which we are in the middle of defining, and the tail of `fibs`. So to get the third element of `fibs`, we need to know what the head (first element) of `fibs` is, and also the head of `tail fibs` (the second element). But the definition of `fibs` has specified these values, so `zipWith` can compute the third element. And then to get the fourth element we must know the second and third, which we do; and so forth.

11.5   Conclusion

In this chapter, we have considered some of the theory and practice of strongly typed functional programming. On the theory side, we considered extensions to simply typed lambda calculus to support realistic programming, using either call-by-value or call-by-name semantics. We extended STLC with features like primitive arithmetic operations and structured data. We saw a little of how these ideas are worked out further in OCaml and Haskell. Books have been written on each of these languages, and indeed on other function programming languages like Standard ML (a relative of OCaml), Scheme, and LISP. Other languages like Scala also incorporate functional programming features. This chapter has of necessity been a quick peek at the rich paradigm and practice of functional programming. Readers are encouraged to explore it further through other books and online resources – and by writing some code in these languages yourself!

11.6   Basic Exercises

11.6.1   For Section 11.2, OCaml programming

1. Using the OCaml interpreter (`ocaml`), determine the types of each of the following expressions:

   - `(3,4+5)`
   - `((3,4),5)`
   - `(3,4,5)`
   - `fun x -> [x]`

- `fun f x -> f x`
- `fun f x -> f (f x)`
- `[(fun x -> x); fun y -> y + 1]`

2. The goal of this problem is to implement a recursive function `addlist` to add up all the numbers in a list. If the list is empty, `addlist` should return 0.

   (a) What type should `addlist` have?

   (b) Give your OCaml code for `addlist`.

3. Implement a function `nth` of type `'a list -> int -> 'a` in OCaml, which takes in a list l and an integer n, and returns the n'th element in the list, where 0 is considered the first element. Your code can just assume the list has at least $n + 1$ elements.

11.6.2   For Section 11.3, lazy programming

Solve the following problems using the lazy language defined at the start of this chapter (not Haskell).

1. Write a term to compute the lazy infinite list of odd numbers.

2. Write a term (in the lazy language described in this chapter) representing the lazy infinite list of powers of two.

3. Write a term to compute the Fibonacci sequence as a lazy infinite list.

11.6.3   For Section 11.4, programming in Haskell

1. Using the Haskell interpreter (`ghci`), determine the types of the following functions from the Prelude, and explain intuitively what the types express about those functions' behavior:

   - `map`
   - `filter`
   - `concat`

2. Using recursive equations, define a function which takes in a base b, and computes the infinite sequence of powers of b:

$$b^0, b^1, b^2, \cdots$$

3. The following Haskell code declares a polymorphic datatype of possibly infinite binary trees with data at the nodes (deriving the `Show` type class, as described in Section 11.4.4):

```
data Tree a = Leaf
            | Node a (Tree a) (Tree a) deriving Show
```

Define a function called ttake of type Int -> Tree a -> Tree a, where ttake n t will return a Tree which is just like the Tree t, except that it stops after level n. This means that if n is greater than the depth of the tree, the whole tree is returned, and if n is less than the depth of the tree, we are going to discard the lower (further from the root) parts of the tree. As an example of the latter, you should see:

```
*Main> ttake 1 (Node 'a' (Node 'b' Leaf Leaf) Leaf)
Node 'a' Leaf Leaf
```

11.7   Intermediate exercises

11.7.1   For Section 11.2, OCaml programming

1. Implement a function mergesort of type int list -> int list, for sorting a list of integers. One way to do this is to write the following three functions:

   - split, to split a list into two sublists of roughly equal length. The type you might want to use for this function is int list -> int list * int list. That is, your function will return a pair of lists, one for each half of the input list. Note that you can inspect a pair using pattern matching:

     ```
     match p with
         (p1,p2) -> ...
     ```

   - merge, to combine two sorted lists into a new sorted list. What type would you expect this to have?

   - mergesort, which handles the trivial cases of an empty list or list of length 1 specially, and otherwise splits the input list using split, then recursively calls mergesort on each one, and finally combines the results again with merge.

11.7.2   For Section 11.3, lazy programming

Solve the following problems using the lazy language defined at the start of this chapter (not Haskell).

1. Write a function *map* (this is the traditional name for this function) that takes in a list *L* and a function *f*, and returns a new list that is just like *L* except that each element *a* of *L* is replaced by (*f a*). You should include a suitable base case for when *L* is *nil*, thus handling both finite and infinite lists. Use

your function to compute the list of even numbers from the list of natural numbers by multiplying every element of the list by 2.

2. Write a function that takes in a list L of natural numbers, and returns a list of all the lists which are prefixes of L. Here, by a prefix of L I mean a list L' such that L equals L' appended with some other list L''. Your code should include a base case for when L is *nil*, so that again, it works for both infinite and finite lists.

11.7.3   For Section 11.4, programming in Haskell

1. The following definition (used in a problem above) defines a polymorphic datatype of possibly infinite binary trees with data at the nodes:

```
data Tree a = Leaf
            | Node a (Tree a) (Tree a) deriving Show
```

Define a function `bfs` of type `Tree a -> [a]` that collects the values stored in the `Node`s of the tree in breadth-first order. So calling `bfs` on the following expression should return `[1,2,3,4]`:

```
Node 1 (Node 2 (Node 4 Leaf Leaf) Leaf) (Node 3 Leaf Leaf)
```

Mathematical Background

Formalism

Formalism is the practice of introducing and manipulating notation – linguistic abstractions – to describe objects or concepts, and their properties. The basic process of abstraction we use in formal development can be illustrated by an example. Suppose we have four circles:

$$\bigcirc \qquad \bigcirc \qquad \bigcirc \qquad \bigcirc$$

Or four rectangles:

$$\square \qquad \square \qquad \square \qquad \square$$

Or else four triangles:

$$\triangle \qquad \triangle \qquad \triangle \qquad \triangle$$

We seem to have some ability to abstract from all these examples to just some abstract, bare indication of four objects of some kind:

$$| \qquad | \qquad | \qquad |$$

This kind of abstraction gives rise to the simplest kind of numeric notation system, unary notation (discussed also in Chapter 6):

|	one
||	two
|||	three
||||	four
|||||	five
. . .	

Because this notation system requires very large expressions to denote large numbers, people devised other notation systems – for example, decimal notation or scientific notation – in order to compress the size of the expression needed to denote a large number. But the basic point is seen with unary numbers: we devise notations as abstractions.

Trees instead of strings

One of the advances in formalism which took place in the 20th century was to shift from strings of characters or symbols to trees as the basic linguistic basis for notation. To explain: one can think of an arithmetic expression like "(1 + 2) * 3" in two ways. It can be viewed as a sequence of characters and symbols: we have the character '(', then '1', then a space, then '+', etc. We could describe this sequence more explicitly like this (or horizontally, which is even less readable):

$$'('$$
$$'1'$$
$$'\ '$$
$$'+'$$
$$'\ '$$
$$'2'$$
$$')'$$
$$'\ '$$
$$'*'$$
$$'\ '$$
$$'3'$$

This is rather unwieldy, and does not reflect at all the syntactic structure of the expression. That structure is best represented as a tree (where parentheses, which are simply used to show structure in linear text, have been dropped):

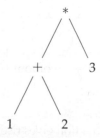

Indeed, so natural and useful are trees for structuring expressions that most formalists have dispensed with strings as the basis for their notations, and work directly with trees (often called abstract syntax trees in the Computer Science literature). Of course, in practice, one can, and sometimes must, parse strings of characters into such trees. But for theoretical works, this is unnecessary, and we can work with trees directly. In this book we will limit ourselves to finite trees unless stated otherwise.

Grammars to describe sets of trees

When describing languages, we invariably wish to describe certain sets of finite trees that we will consider at least preliminarily syntactically well-formed. The custom is to do this with context-free grammars written in a compact style called Backus-Naur Form (BNF). We will use a common variant of BNF, in which meta-variables are used to range over syntactic categories, both in grammars and in subsequent expressions (in contrast, nonterminals in BNF grammars are supposed to be enclosed in angle brackets like $\langle expr \rangle$). For example, suppose we want to specify that the allowed trees in a syntactic category called *expr* are either numerals N or else trees of the following form, where e_1 and e_2 are any trees in syntactic category *expr*:

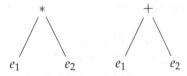

Then we can do so with this grammar:

$$
\begin{array}{lll}
\textit{numerals } N & ::= & 0 \mid 1 \mid \ldots \\
\textit{exprs } e & ::= & N \mid +(e_1, e_2) \mid *(e_1, e_2)
\end{array}
$$

We call e_1 and e_2 meta-variables because they are variables in our meta-language in which we are describing the language of expressions e. A tree like the example one shown above can be written as "$*(+(1,2),3)$". This is prefix notation for the finite trees in the syntactic category of *expr*. Often we will allow ourselves to introduce more common mathematical notation in grammars, for better readability. So we could use this grammar instead, which uses infix notation for the operators:

$$
\begin{array}{lll}
\textit{numerals } N & ::= & 0 \mid 1 \mid \ldots \\
\textit{exprs } e & ::= & N \mid e_1 + e_2 \mid e_1 * e_2
\end{array}
$$

Once we start using infix notations like $e_1 + e_2$, however, we must be prepared to allow parentheses in our textual representations of trees, in order to be able to disambiguate expressions like "1*2+3", which could be viewed as either "$(1*2) + 3$" or "$1 * (2+3)$".

Introducing meta-variables in our grammars has the added benefit that it is now very convenient to describe sets of trees with a certain form. For example, suppose we want to describe the set of all *exprs* e where the root of e is labeled with $*$, then the right child is 3 and the left child has root labeled with $+$. This set can be described by the pattern $(e_1 + e_2) * 3$. Some example trees in this set are:

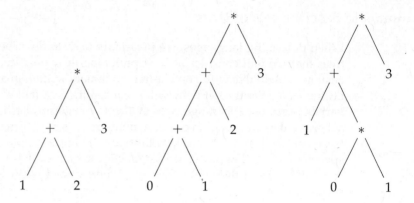

Sets and related concepts

We will often need to use basic concepts from set theory, such as found, for example, in Halmos's introductory book [17]. A set is just a collection of elements of some kind. Two sets are considered equal if and only if they contain exactly the same elements. We can write finite sets explicitly using curly brackets this way:

$$\{0, 1, 2\}$$

Since the identity of sets is determined by which objects are their elements, the number of times an element is listed in an explicit description of a set, and the order of elements, is irrelevant. So we have equalities like this:

$$
\begin{aligned}
\{0, 0, 1, 2, 2, 2\} &= \{0, 1, 2\} \\
\{100, 10, 20\} &= \{10, 20, 100\} \\
\{0, 0, 0, 0\} &= \{0\}
\end{aligned}
$$

We often extend the notation of explicit description to infinite sets. This relies on our intuitive understanding of what the set is intended to be, and is thus not fully precise. For example, the set of natural numbers, denoted $\mathbb{N}$, can be indicated (but not formally defined) as follows:

$$\mathbb{N} = \{0, 1, 2, \ldots\}$$

This already relies on our idea of how that sequence "$0, 1, 2, \ldots$" continues. Giving a fully precise definition of the set of natural numbers is rather involved, and we will take it for granted that we understand what the set $\mathbb{N}$ is.

Set comprehensions are descriptions of sets based on a property. This property can be expressed in our informal mathematical meta-language, or in a more precise formal language. If A is a set and $\phi(x)$ is a formula (again, from some mathematical language) which might mention x, then the set of all elements x of A which satisfy the property described by $\phi(x)$ is denoted this way:

$$\{x \in A \mid \phi(x)\}$$

For example, the set of even numbers can be defined like this:

$$\{x \in \mathbb{N} \mid x \text{ is a multiple of } 2\}$$

Or if we were using a language like $FO(\mathbb{Z})$ (see Chapter 1) for the formula used in the set comprehension, we could express this more formally, by saying that there exists a number y such that x equals 2 times y:

$$\{x \in \mathbb{N} \mid \exists y.\ x = 2 * y\}$$

The union $S_1 \cup S_2$ of two sets S_1 and S_2 is the set consisting of those objects which are elements of either S_1 or S_2. For example, the set of natural numbers can be viewed as the union of the set of all odd numbers with the set of all even numbers:

$$\{0, 2, 4, 8, \ldots\} \cup \{1, 3, 5, 7, \ldots\}$$

The intersection $S_1 \cap S_2$ of two sets S_1 and S_2 is the set consisting of all the elements of S_1 which are also elements of S_2. For example, let *Pres* be the set of current or past presidents of the United States, and let *VP* be the set of current or past vice presidents. Then the intersection of these two sets is the set of all people who have served as both president and vice president, and includes people like Lyndon Johnson and George H. W. Bush, for example.

The difference $S_1 - S_2$ (also written $S_1 \setminus S_2$) of two sets S_1 and S_2 is the set consisting of those elements of S_1 which are not elements of S_2. For example, if we wanted the set of all presidents of the United States who were not members of the Democratic party, we could define that as *Pres − Democrats* (assuming *Democrats* is the set of all Democratic-party politicians, for example).

Ordered pairs (x, y) are mathematical structures containing x and y in order. The first component of the ordered pair is x, and y is the second component. Any mathematical objects x and y can be used in an ordered pair (x, y). Sometimes we make use of ordered triples (x, y, z) or ordered **tuples** $(x_1, \ldots, x_n)$ with more components. As long as there are only finitely many components, though, these tuples can be considered to be nested pairs. For example, (x, y, z) can be viewed as $((x, y), z)$.

The empty set $\emptyset$ is the unique set which does not contain any elements at all.

Subset property: A set S_1 is a subset of a set S_2 iff every element of S_1 is an element of S_2. This property is denoted $S_1 \subseteq S_2$ (some authors also just write $S_1 \subset S_2$). For example, the set of even natural numbers is a subset of the set of all natural numbers. Also, $\emptyset \subseteq S$ for any set S, because the requirement that all elements of the empty set $\emptyset$ must be elements of S is vacuously true: there are no elements of $\emptyset$, and so the requirement to be in S is not imposed on any elements.

Relations and functions

A relation is just a set of tuples. If we wish to emphasize that those are pairs, we call it a **binary** relation. Each ordered pair (x, y) can be thought of as expressing the idea that x is related to y. For example, if we wish to relate U.S. capitol cities to their states, we might have an ordered pair like $(Des\ Moines, Iowa)$. The set of all such ordered pairs is then considered to be the relation:

$$\{(Des\ Moines, Iowa), (Albany, New\ York), (Sacramento, California), \dots\}$$

Functions are binary relations which do not contain (x, y) and (x, z) with $y \neq z$. So every time we have an ordered pair (x, y) in the relation, y is the only element to which x is related (by the relation). In this case, the first component of each ordered pair in the relation is called an **input** to the function, and the second component is the corresponding **output**. The state-capitol relation we were just considering is a function, since no city is the capitol of two different states: if we have an ordered pair (C, S) where C is a city and S is a state, then there cannot be any other pair (C, S') with $S \neq S'$, expressing that C is also the capitol of S'. This relation is a function, because it associates a unique output state with each input capitol.

References

[1] S. Abramsky, D. Gabbay, and T. Maibaum, editors. *Handbook of Logic in Computer Science*. Oxford University Press, 1992.

[2] Z. Ariola and H. Herbelin. Minimal classical logic and control operators. In *Proceedings of the 30th International Conference on Automata, Languages and Programming (ICALP)*, pages 871–885. Springer Verlag, 2003.

[3] F. Baader and T. Nipkow. *Term Rewriting and All That*. Cambridge University Press, 1998.

[4] F. Barbanera and S. Berardi. A symmetric lambda calculus for classical program extraction. *Information and Computation*, 125(2):103 – 117, 1996.

[5] H. Barendregt. *The Lambda Calculus, Its Syntax and Semantics*. North-Holland, 1984.

[6] H. Barendregt. *Lambda Calculi with Types*, pages 117–309, Volume 2 of Abramsky et al. [1], 1992.

[7] S. Brookes. Full abstraction for a shared variable parallel language. In *In Proceedings, 8th Annual IEEE Symposium on Logic in Computer Science (LICS)*, pages 98–109. IEEE Computer Society Press, 1993.

[8] S. Chaudhuri and A. Solar-Lezama. Smooth interpretation. *SIGPLAN Notices*, 45:279–291, June 2010.

[9] A. Church. *The Calculi of Lambda Conversion*. Princeton University Press, 1941.

[10] P. Cousot and R. Cousot. Abstract interpretation: a unified lattice model for static analysis of programs by construction or approximation of fixpoints. In *Proceedings of the 4th ACM SIGACT-SIGPLAN Symposium on Principles of Programming Languages (POPL)*, pages 238–252. ACM, 1977.

[11] E. Dijkstra. Guarded commands, nondeterminacy and formal derivation of programs. *Communications of the ACM*, 18(8):453–457, 1975.

[12] M. Felleisen, R. Findler, and M. Flatt. *Semantics Engineering with PLT Redex*. The MIT Press, 1st edition, 2009.

[13] R. W. Floyd. Assigning meanings to programs. In *Proceedings of the American Mathematical Society Symposium in Applied Mathematics*, pages 19–31. American Mathematical Society, 1967.

[14] H. Geuvers. A short and flexible proof of strong normalization for the calculus of constructions. In Peter Dybjer, Bengt Nordström, and Jan M. Smith, editors, *Types for Proofs and Programs, International Workshop TYPES'94, Båstad, Sweden, June 6-10, 1994, Selected Papers*, volume 996 of *Lecture Notes in Computer Science*, pages 14–38. Springer, 1995.

[15] J.-Y. Girard, Y. Lafont, and P. Taylor. *Proofs and Types*. Cambridge University Press, 1990.

[16] W. Goldfarb. The undecidability of the second-order unification problem. *Theoretical Computer Science*, 13(2):225 – 230, 1981.

[17] P. Halmos. *Naive Set Theory*. Springer Verlag, 1974. [Reprinted from original 1960 edition.]

[18] R. Hindley. An abstract Church-Rosser theorem. II: applications. *The Journal of Symbolic Logic*, 39(1): 1–21, 1974.

[19] C. A. R. Hoare. An axiomatic basis for computer programming. *Communications of the ACM*, 12(10):576–580, 1969.

[20] C. A. R. Hoare. *Communicating Sequential Processes*. Prentice-Hall, 1985.

[21] G. Huet. Confluent Reductions: Abstract Properties and Applications to Term Rewriting Systems. *Journal of the ACM*, 27(4):797–821, 1980.

[22] S. P. Jones. Tackling the awkward squad: monadic input/output, concurrency, exceptions, and foreign-language calls in Haskell. In C. A. R. Hoare, M. Broy, and R. Steinbrüggen, editors, *NATO Advanced Study Institute on Engineering Theories of Software Construction (2000: Marktoberdorf)*, pages 47–96. IOS Press, 2002.

[23] S. Jost, K. Hammond, H.-W. Loidl, and M. Hofmann. Static determination of quantitative resource usage for higher-order programs. In *Proceedings of the 37th Annual ACM SIGPLAN-SIGACT symposium on Principles of programming languages*, pages 223–236. ACM, 2010.

[24] M. S. Joy, V. J. Rayward-Smith, and F. W. Burton. Efficient combinator code. *Computer Languages*, 10(3–4):211–224, 1985.

[25] J. Lambek. The Mathematics of Sentence Structure. *The American Mathematical Monthly*, 65(3): 154–170, 1958.

[26] X. Leroy, D. Doligez, A. Frisch, J. Garrigue, D. Rmy, and J. Vouillon. *The Objective Caml System: Documentation and Users Manual*. Available at http://caml.inria.fr/pub/docs/manual-ocaml/, 2010, accessed July 1, 2013.

[27] J. McCarthy. Recursive functions of symbolic expressions and their computation by machine, Part I. *Communications of the ACM*, 3(4):184–195, 1960.

[28] R. Milner. *Communicating and Mobile Systems: The π-Calculus*. Cambridge University Press, 1999.

[29] N. Nagappan and T. Ball. Static analysis tools as early indicators of pre-release defect density. In *Proceedings of the 27th International Conference on Software Engineering (ICSE)*, pages 580–586. ACM, 2005.

[30] M. H. A. Newman. On theories with a combinatorial definition of "equivalence". *The Annals of Mathematics*, 43(2): 223–243, 1942.

[31] F. Nielson, H. Nielson, and C. Hankin. *Principles of Program Analysis*. Springer Verlag New York, Inc., 1999.

[32] S. Owicki and D. Gries. An axiomatic proof technique for parallel programs I. *Acta Informatica*, 6:319–340, 1976.

[33] B. Pierce. *Types and Programming Languages*. The MIT Press, 2002.

[34] G. Plotkin. The origins of structural operational semantics. *Journal of Logic and Algebraic Programming*, 60–61:3 – 15, 2004.

[35] N. Shavit and D. Touitou. Software transactional memory. *Distributed Computing, Special Issue*, 10:99–116, 1997.

[36] M. Sørensen and P. Urzyczyn. *Lectures on the Curry-Howard Isomorphism, Volume 149 (Studies in Logic and the Foundations of Mathematics)*. Elsevier Science Inc., New York, NY, USA, 2006.

[37] M. Takahashi. Parallel reductions in -calculus. *Information and Computation*, 118(1):120 – 127, 1995.

[38] Terese, editor. *Term Rewriting Systems*, volume 55 of *Cambridge Tracts in Theoretical Computer Science*. Cambridge University Press, 2003.

[39] A. Troelstra and H. Schwichtenberg. *Basic Proof Theory*. Cambridge University Press, 2nd edition, 2000.

[40] P. Wadler. Theorems for free! In *Fourth International Conference on Functional Programming and Computer Architecture (FPCA)*, pages 347–359. ACM, 1989.

[41] P. Wadler. The Girard-Reynolds isomorphism (second edition). *Theoretical Computer Science*, 375(1-3):201–226, 2007.

[42] G. Winskel. *The Formal Semantics of Programming Languages: An Introduction*. MIT Press, 1993.

Index